New Essa the Philosophy
of L guage and Mind

New Essays in the Philosophy of Language and Mind

Edited by
Maite Ezcurdia,
Robert J. Stainton,
and Christopher Viger

University of Calgary Press
Calgary, Alberta, Canada

ISSN 0229-7051   ISBN 0-919491-30-8

P
37
N43
2004

#61476305

1-11-06

c.1

University of Calgary Press
2500 University Drive NW
Calgary, Alberta
Canada T2N 1N4
www.uofcpress.com

Library and Archives Canada Cataloguing in Publication

New essays in the philosophy of language and mind / edited by
Maite Ezcurdia, Robert J. Stainton, and Christopher Viger.

(Canadian journal of philosophy. Supplementary volume,
ISSN 0229-7951 ; 30) *cat. sup.*

Includes bibliographical references and index.

ISBN 0-919491-30-8

1. Psycholinguistics. 2. Language and languages--Philosophy.
I. Viger, Christopher David, 1963- II. Stainton, Robert J., 1964-
III. Ezcurdia, Maite IV. Title. V. Series.

P37.N43 2005   401'.9   C2005-905562-6

We acknowledge the financial support of the Government of Canada
through the Book Publishing Industry Development Program
(BPIDP), the Alberta Foundation for the Arts and the Alberta Lottery
Fund—Community Initiatives Program for our publishing activities.

Printed and bound in Canada.

∞ This book is printed on acid-free paper.

Cover design by Mieka West. Typesetting by Eileen Eckert.

Canada

Canada Council   Conseil des Arts
for the Arts   du Canada

Table of Contents

Introduction

MAITE EZCURDIA
ROBERT J. STAINTON
CHRISTOPHER VIGER

Although philosophical interest in natural language and the mind has been prevalent since Plato, the Twentieth Century produced some of the more significant contributions in their philosophical study. This was due to new working methodologies for each area of study, some of which were crucially influenced by the advent of cognitive science, including theoretical linguistics.

Some saw theorizing about language as dependent on theorizing about the mind, and vice versa. Donald Davidson, for example, considered that theorizing about a language depended on having an interpretation of the user of that language, that is, an interpretation of her linguistic and non-linguistic actions based on a belief–desire schema. But he also considered that one could not theorize about the mind of an individual, without interpreting a speaker's language. Noam Chomsky, on the other hand, considered the study of language as the study of a human cognitive capacity, but believed that one could study the linguistic capacity without needing to study the belief–desire systems of speakers. Whilst it is right to think that there are deep connections between the study of language and that of the mind, there are issues about the study of mind which are largely independent of the study of language, and there are issues in the study of language which are largely independent of what one thinks about the connection between language and mind.

In this volume, we include recent essays on the philosophy of language, the philosophy of mind, and their intersection, which show

judgements about speakers' utterances, is a tacitly known theory of the relevant language. This (supposed) theory is taken to be part of our general folk-psychological theory, a theory by means of which we interpret, predict, and explain our own and other people's behaviour, including linguistic behaviour; it is also meant to determine the conditions for a phrase to be meaningful. Her objection depends on the claim that, as with any theory, this theory would be subject not only to the possibility that it might be wrong but that a better theory may replace it, a theory that does not posit meanings. One avoids such semantic eliminativism, according to Bar-On, if one rejects that our linguistic ability is grounded on tacit knowledge of a theory at all.

Diana Pérez's contribution defends the view that the concepts expressed by mental terms such as "pain", "belief", "fear", etc, are concepts of a particular theory, our folk psychology, and argues in favour of their being natural-kind concepts. Unlike Bar-On, however, she argues in favour of the usefulness of taking folk psychology to be a theory, and gives reasons for why ultimately it will not be eliminated.

Although the question of whether there is any *a priori* knowledge is essentially an epistemological question, the answer that is given may depend on certain views about our minds. According to Georges Rey, many of the answers given to this question (whether negative or positive) depend on the mistaken view that the nature or structure of our minds should be more or less readily available through introspection or behavioural tests. However, as much of the work in the cognitive sciences has taught us, this is just not so. The nature or structure of our minds is itself something on which empirical sciences have a say. According to Rey, even the question of whether there is any *a priori* knowledge of analytic truths based on the existence of semantic rules, will depend on theorizing about the structure of our minds in the sort of way in which Chomskian linguistics has theorized about the structure of our language faculty.

Section C includes six papers on topics in the philosophy of mind that do not touch directly on issues about language. They have more to do with metaphysical and epistemological issues about the mind and mental states.

Irwin Goldstein's article is concerned with the mind–body problem, and more particularly, with the claim that a mental event or property is a neural event or a neural event's orthodox material property, i.e., a defining property that provides a necessary condition for something being physical. Goldstein's aim is to show that there are some properties of mental states or events that are not orthodox material properties of neural events.

Mark Lance and Alessandra Tanesini's paper focuses on the role of certain types of mental states, *viz.*, emotions, in rationality. Although it is widely recognized that rationality depends on the beliefs had, and that agents' actions depend (at least partly) on their emotions, little is said of how the rationality of an epistemic agent depends on her emotional states. This is perhaps because emotions are not typically thought of having an epistemic role. In contrast, in their contribution Lance and Tanesini defend the claim that emotions not only have an epistemic role, but further, that they have a crucial and essential role in characterizing a rational epistemic agent.

Concerning the issue of our epistemic access to our own mental states which was touched upon by Rey's paper, and continuing with connections to cognitive science, Shaun Nichols and Stephen Stich explore an account of what is involved in being aware of our own mental states. They consider and reject the account according to which individuals might use a theory in becoming aware of their own states, a theory that is also used in coming to know, explain and predict others' behaviour. This is the Theory Theory of Mind.[1] In their paper, Nichols and Stich present their own theory of self-awareness, the Monitoring Mechanism Theory, and argue that evidence from developmental psychology favours their view and counts against the Theory Theory, contrary to what their defenders usually hold.

One of the more recently discussed arguments in favour of an intentionalist account of experience, be it a sensation or a perceptual state, and against the existence of *qualia*, is one which appeals to what we are aware of in our experience. Harman (1989) and Tye (1992 and 2000) have suggested (as Strawson (1979) did previously) that what we are aware of upon seeing a scene are not certain qualities that are intrinsic to our experience of seeing, but rather the objects seen: the door, the ocean, etc. This argument is sometimes called "the argument

---

1 See Pérez's and Bar-On's contributions.

from the transparency of experience", or as Daniel Stoljar calls it, "the argument from diaphanousness." In his paper, Stoljar identifies various versions of this argument, including its use in favour of the claim that the phenomenal aspects of our experience are intentional, and argues against all of them.

The mental state of doubting a proposition is usually taken to be a state of epistemic uncertainty, of neither believing nor not believing a proposition. Paul Thagard construes doubt not only as a cognitive state but also as an emotional state – specifically, as a form of emotional incoherence, on the basis of which he provides a framework for determining when it is reasonable or unreasonable to doubt in certain contexts.[2]

Our volume ends with Rob Wilson's discussion of a recently held view by Fodor (2000), according to which the mind is only modular where the perceptual systems are concerned, and some forms of cognitive processing are global. These two claims pose a threat to computation models of the mind that claim that the mind is to a great extent, if not wholly, modular, and that all cognitive processing is computational processing, hence local processing. Wilson examines not only the development of Fodor's ideas since his initial work on modularity, but also the arguments given by Fodor against extending the modularity hypothesis to central cognition. Fodor's arguments are, according to Wilson, essentially *a priori*, rather than empirical, yet the sorts of considerations that might settle the question whether all cognitive processes could be understood computationally or whether the mind is mostly or fully modular come from the empirical sciences. Wilson points to work in developmental neuroscience and artificial intelligence that seems relevant to answering this question.

We would like to thank Julie Walsh for her help with copy-editing this volume, and the contributors to this volume for allowing us to include their papers and for their extraordinary patience.

---

2 See Lance and Tanesini's contribution.

References

Almog, J., Perry, J., and Wettstein, H., eds. 1989. *Themes From Kaplan*. Oxford: Oxford University Press.

Fodor, J.A. 2000. *The Mind Doesn't Work That Way*. Cambridge, MA: MIT Press.

Kaplan, D. 1977. "Demonstratives." In Almog, *et al*. 1989, 481–563.

———. 1989. "Afterthoughts." In Almog, *et al*. 1989, 564–614.

Harman, G. 1989. "The Intrinsic Quality of Experience." In *Philosophical Perspectives 4: Action Theory and Philosophy of Mind*, ed. J. Tomberlin, 31–52. Atascadero, CA: Ridgeview.

Strawson, P.F. 1979. "Perception and its Objects." In *Perception and Identity: Essays Presented to A. J. Ayer*, ed. G.F. Macdonald, 41–60. London: Macmillan.

Tye, M. 1992. "Visual qualia and visual content." In *The Contents of Experience*, ed. T. Crane, 158-176. Cambridge: Cambridge University Press.

———. 2000. *Color, Content and Consciousness*. Cambridge, MA: MIT Press.

PART A

Language

A Tall Tale: In Defense of Semantic Minimalism and Speech Act Pluralism

HERMAN CAPPELEN AND ERNEST LEPORE

In *Insensitive Semantics* (2005), we argue for two theses: Semantic Minimalism and Speech Act Pluralism. In this paper, we outline our defense against two objections often raised against Semantic Minimalism. We begin with five stage-setting sections. These lead to the first objection, *viz.*, that it might follow from our view that comparative adjectives are context *in*sensitive. We defend our view against that objection (not, as you might expect, by denying that implication, but by endorsing it). Having done so, we address a second objection, *viz.*, that Semantic Minimalism makes it difficult to see what role semantic content plays in communicative exchanges. We respond and end with a reversal, i.e., we argue that even though the second objection fails against us, it works against those who raise the objection. In particular, we show that our critics, in particular, Carston (2002) and Recanati (2004), end up with a notion of communicated content that fails various tests for psychological reality.

Stage Setting I: Semantic Minimalism

Three features of Semantic Minimalism are important in the context of this paper (all elaborated on in *Insensitive Semantics*):

(i)   The most salient feature of Semantic Minimalism is that it recognizes few context sensitive expressions, and hence, acknowledges a very limited effect of the context of utterance on the semantic content of an utterance. The only context sensitive expressions are the completely obvious ones ('I', 'here', 'now', 'that', etc.; essentially those Kaplan lists in "Demonstratives" [1989, 489]). These are not only obvious, they also pass certain tests for context sensitivity we spell out below.

(ii) It follows that all semantic context sensitivity is grammatically (i.e., syntactically or morphemically) triggered.

(iii) Beyond fixing the semantic value of these obviously context sensitive expressions, the context of utterance has no effect on the proposition semantically expressed or the semantic truth conditions. In this sense, the semantic content of a sentence S is that proposition that all utterances of S express (when we adjust for or keep stable the semantic values of the obvious context sensitive expressions in S).

Some illustrations: keeping tense fixed,[1] any utterance of (1)

(1) Rudolf is a reindeer.

is true just in case Rudolf is a reindeer, and expresses the proposition that Rudolf is a reindeer.[2]

Any utterance of (2)

(2) Rudolf has a red nose.

is true just in case Rudolf has a red nose, and expresses the proposition that Rudolf has a red nose.

Any utterance of (3)

(3) Rudolf is happy.

is true just in case Rudolf is happy, and expresses the proposition that Rudolf is happy.

---

1 As we will throughout this paper.

2 Semantic Minimalism need not take a stand on whether semantic content is a proposition, or truth conditions, or what have you. Throughout we try to remain neutral by couching the issues both in terms of truth conditions and in terms of propositions.

Any utterance of (4)

> (4)   Rudolf has had breakfast.

is true just in case Rudolf has had breakfast, and expresses the proposition that Rudolf has had breakfast.

Any utterance of (5)

> (5)   Rudolf doesn't know that penguins eat fish.

is true just in case Rudolf doesn't know that penguins eat fish and expresses the proposition that Rudolf doesn't know that penguins eat fish.

If you find it surprising that we are writing a paper or (worse) a book defending conclusions so obvious, we have a great deal of sympathy. The problem is that a wide range of our contemporary colleagues rejects these views. (It's probably no exaggeration to say that our views about (1)–(5) are now held only by a small minority of philosophers, at least among those who have thought about the surrounding issues.)[3] In our book, we rebut these influential objections; here we want to elaborate on some implications of the view defended.

Stage Setting II: Speech Act Pluralism

Here's one way to summarize Speech Act Pluralism:

> No one thing is said (or asserted, or claimed, or ...) by any utterance: rather, indefinitely many propositions are said, asserted, claimed, or stated. What is said (asserted, claimed, etc.) depends on a wide range of factors other than the proposition semantically expressed. It depends on a potential infinitude of features of the context of utterance and of the context of those who report on (or think about) what was said by the utterance.

---

3   See Chapter 2 of Insensitive Semantics for extensive discussion of this point.

It follows from this view that an utterance can assert propositions not even (logically) implied by the proposition semantically expressed. Nothing even prevents an utterance from asserting (saying, claiming, etc.) propositions incompatible with the proposition semantically expressed by that utterance.

From this it further follows that if you want to use intuitions about speech act content to fix semantic content, you must be extremely careful. It can be done, but it's a subtle and an easily corrupted process.[4]

These points are connected to our defense of Semantic Minimalism because one underlying assumption in many anti-minimalist arguments is the idea that semantic content has to be closely connected to speech act content. If Speech Act Pluralism is correct, then no such close connection exists, and so, this requirement is revealed to be a philosophical prejudice. (Another way to see the connection is this: If there really were (or had to be) a close connection between speech act content and semantic content, then all the data we think support Speech Act Pluralism would also serve to undermine Semantic Minimalism.)

At this initial stage, it's worth highlighting one more aspect of Speech Act Pluralism that has both wide-ranging implications and sets our view apart from (all?) other contemporary accounts of context sensitivity. We don't think everything speakers say by uttering a sentence in a context C is determined by features of C. The speaker's intentions, facts about the audience, the place and time of utterance, background knowledge salient in C, previous conversations salient in C, etc., are not even together sufficient to fix what the speaker said. According to Speech Act Pluralism, a theory of speech act content has to take into account the context of those who say or think about what the speaker said, i.e., the context of those who report on what's said by the utterance can, in part, determine what was said by that utterance. (As far as we can tell, we are on our own defending this view; see, Cappelen and Lepore (1997).)

---

4 For some instructions on how to proceed, see Chapter 7 of Insensitive Semantics.

Stage Setting III: Opponents

We have many opponents; indeed, it often feels as if we have only opponents. What our opponents have in common is a commitment to some form of semantic contextualism. Semantic contextualists, as we mark them, posit more semantic context sensitivity than is generally recognized. Sometimes their motives are opportunistic; e.g., they claim they can solve sorites, liar, skeptical, moral and Fregean puzzles/paradoxes by positing that vague, semantic, knowledge, moral and psychological attributions are semantically context sensitive. Sometimes they posit context sensitivity because they believe themselves to have uncovered more of it than linguists/philosophers have so far recognized. Sometimes they conclude that entire semantic programs collapse under the weight of their discoveries; sometimes they are more modest, concluding only that their contributions are to the general project of semantics for natural language – *viz.*, modest extensions to the already recognized indexicals and demonstratives. No matter how ambitious or modest their motivations, we have come to the same conclusion about them: they are all wrong; none of the contextualist candidates are semantically context sensitive.

We have argued against contextualism with a variety of dialectical strategies: One of our favourite argumentative strategies is to present direct and simple tests for context sensitivity, and to show that traditionally recognized context sensitive expressions pass these tests with flying colours, while contextualist candidates all fail them. In order to present the first objection to Semantic Minimalism, we'll briefly rehearse a couple of these tests (both discussed at greater length in Chapter 7 of *Insensitive Semantics*).

Stage Setting IV: Test No. 1 – Context Sensitive Expressions Block Inter-contextual Disquotational Indirect Reports

Take an utterance u of S in C. Let C' be a context relevantly different from C (i.e., different according to the standards significant according to contextualists about S). If there's a true disquotational indirect report of u in C', then that's evidence S is context insensitive. So, take an obviously context sensitive expression, e.g., the first person pronoun 'I' and its utterance in the sentence 'I went to Ottawa' made by Sarah-Jane. If Rich tries to report what Sarah-Jane said with 'Sarah-Jane said that I went to Ottawa', his report is false because the expression 'I' fails to pick out what it picked out in Sarah-Jane's mouth. The presence of 'I' in the disquotational report figures prominently in an explanation of why the report is false.

It's (almost) a matter of definition that context sensitive expressions tend to block inter-contextual disquotational indirect reports. The reason why is obvious: u is context sensitive only if u shifts semantic value between relevantly different contexts of utterance. It's obvious that all the traditionally recognized context sensitive expressions ('he', 'now' 'that', 'you', etc.) block inter-contextual disquotational indirect reports.

Stage Setting V: Test No. 2: Context sensitive Expressions Block Collective Descriptions

Here's another test applied to verbs first: If a verb phrase v is context sensitive (i.e., if it changes its semantic value from one context of use to another), then on the basis of merely knowing that there are two contexts of utterance in which 'A v-s' and 'B v-s' are true, respectively, we *cannot* automatically infer that there is a context in which 'v' can be used to describe what A and B have both done.

In short, from there being contexts of utterance in which 'A v-s' and 'B v-s' are true it doesn't *follow* that there is a true utterance of 'A and B both v.' This is because the semantic value of 'v' in the previous collective sentence is determined in one context, and we have no guarantee that that semantic value, whatever it is, "captures" (whatever that means) the semantic values of 'v' in those contexts of utterance where they were used alone.

On the other hand, *if* for a range of true utterances of the form 'A v-s' and 'B v-s' we obviously *can* describe what they all have in common by *using* 'v' (i.e., by using 'A and B v'), then that's evidence in favour of the view that 'v' in these different utterances has the same semantic content, and hence, is not context sensitive. A parallel point extends to singular terms.

If a (n unambiguous) singular term N is context *in*sensitive and there's a range of true utterances of the form 'N is F' and 'N is G', then we, for example, in *this* context, can truly utter 'N is F and G.' Similarly, if N is context sensitive, we shouldn't be able to do this. As an illustration, consider the context sensitive 'yesterday': Suppose we know of two contexts in which 'Yesterday, John left' and 'Yesterday, Bill left' are true, respectively (though we don't know the days of these contexts). It doesn't follow there is a context in which 'Yesterday John and Bill left' is true.

Again, all traditionally recognized context sensitive expressions pass this test of collectivity.

There are others tests for context sensitivity; one of our favourites we call the Inter-Contextual Disquotational Test (different from Test No. 1 above). In discussing this test, we distinguish between two kinds of context shifting arguments – Real and Impoverished – arguing that only the former identifies context sensitive expressions. (Context shifting arguments involve an appeal to speaker intuitions about distinct utterances of a single, unambiguous sentence shifting in truth-value, or in proposition expressed, or in what's said.)

The Inter-Contextual Disquotation Test was our first, and we feel a sentimental attachment to it. However, audiences tend to find it a bit confusing, so we'll leave it alone for now and direct those interested to our published work (Cappelen and Lepore, 2003). Instead, we'll take our two tests involving indirect reporting and collectivity and turn to what most contextualists take to be a fundamental flaw in our position

First Objection: 'Tall' Is Self-Evidently Context Sensitive

We have argued that the contextualists' candidates fail the various tests for context sensitivity. This applies to 'know', 'good', 'red', quantifier words, and so on. A standard reply is that there must be something wrong with our reasoning, since words self-evidently context sensitive also seem to fail our tests: e.g., comparative adjectives like 'tall'.

So, for example, look at our first test: Suppose A utters in a context C, 'Rudolf is tall'. Suppose that in C the contextually salient comparison class consists of giraffes. According to contextualists, the proposition semantically expressed by A's utterance is *that Rudolf is tall for a giraffe*. This result is rendered possible because 'is tall' is alleged to be context sensitive. But look at our tests: we take it as obvious that anyone reporting *A*'s utterance can accurately utter '*A* said that Rudolf is tall', and this is so regardless of the context the reporter happens to find herself in, i.e., even if the context of the report and the context of the reported utterance are relevantly different, i.e., even if giraffes are not particularly salient in the context of the report. The reporter might not know that Rudolf is a giraffe; she might be unsure what kind of animal Rudolf is, or suspect he is a reindeer. The point is this: if the context of the first utterance and the context of the second utterance are relevantly dissimilar, then this report ought to be impossible – *if* 'tall' really is context sensitive.

Now turn to the second test: Take distinct utterances of 'Mount Everest is tall' and 'Kobe Bryant is tall' and 'The Empire State Building is tall'. Suppose that in the first context, mountains are salient, in the second, NBA players are, and in the third, skyscrapers are. Suppose you are collecting these utterances into a context in which mountains and basketball players and skyscrapers are not (particularly) salient. Then any utterance of 'Mount Everest, Kobe Bryant, and the Empire State Building are all tall' (or 'Mount Everest is tall, and Kobe Bryant and the Empire State Building are, too' – an appeal to a fourth test involving VP deletion; see *Insensitive Semantics*, Chapter 7) should be false, on the assumption that 'tall' is context sensitive. It's our intuition, however, that there are contexts in which such utterances can be true; it's hard to see how that could be so if 'tall' isn't taking as its semantic value something the original utterances have in common.

Contextualists of every flavor have mocked, ridiculed, snickered, flat out laughed, and, even worse, completely ignored our views because of these results. The current attitude seems to be that any argument that leads to the view that 'tall' (or any other comparative adjective) is not semantically context sensitive must be seriously flawed.

There are at least three responses to our arguments:

> (i)   Your tests for semantic context sensitivity are no good.
>
> (ii) Comparative adjectives do pass your tests, but for one reason or another, you can't hear their uses as passing these tests.

(iii) "That's right" (a respondent might say). "These words fail the tests and they are context *in*sensitive – contrary to what we all once thought."

We have considered and replied to the first two options elsewhere (Cappelen and Lepore, 2003). Here, we would like to try something bolder: we'd like to run with option (iii). This requires investigating what others have thought of as the absolute absurdity of Semantic Minimalism, e.g., that comparative adjectives are (semantically) context insensitive.

To this end, we'll tease out our critics' argument, and try to establish it has nothing to do with semantics but rather reflects a metaphysical concern – one we do not think semanticists have to address. We present the objection in three stages, only the third of which will require an extended answer (though it is important to see how that stage is different from the first two).

First Stage of Objection to (iii): Dismissive, Incredulous Stare

The objection to the view that 'tall' is context insensitive typically starts out with the kind of stare David Lewis characterized as incredulous. This stare is typically accompanied by a dismissive utterance of something along the lines of: 'Are you crazy?! Of course, there can be both true and false utterances of (6):

(6) Osama Bin Laden is tall.

If in one context the topic of discussion is the heights of NBA players, your utterance will be (taken to be) false, and if in another, the topic is the heights of Saudi Arabians, your utterance will be (taken to be) true.'

Reply to First Stage

If you followed our brief introduction of Semantic Minimalism and Speech Act Pluralism above, you'll immediately understand that this reply can be pushed only by someone who does not understand our view. It is based on nothing but confusion. It should be obvious that our Speech Act Pluralism can accommodate the same data. In one context, the utterance says something true, and in another, an utterance of the same sentence says something false. But intuitions about the speech act content of these distinct utterances are not reliable guides to the semantic content of (6) or even of its utterances, and so intuitions about the former need not be a good guide for conclusions about the latter.

Second Stage of Objection to (iii): Honest Request for Further Elaboration

Opponents who bypass the deeply confused first stage typically move on to a second stage of confusion. They ask: Well, what is it to be tall *simpliciter*? That is, what is it to satisfy the semantic truth conditions of '*A* is tall'? If it is not to be tall for an *X*, or according to some standard, what then is it?

Reply to Second Stage

Our quick, and we think completely satisfactory, reply is given by (6_{TC}) and (6_P):

(6_{TC}) 'Osama Bin Laden is tall' is true iff Osama Bin Laden is tall.

(6_P) 'Osama Bin Laden is tall' semantically expresses the proposition *that Osama Bin Laden is tall*.

Here is our problem: We think this is a conclusive reply, but our opponents insist on further elaboration. They move on to the third stage of the objection.

Third Stage of Objection to (iii): Confused Demand for Further Elaboration

Faced with (6_{TC}) and (6_P), our opponents tend to react with something like this: (6_{TC}) and (6_P) just aren't enough. I can't take this theory seriously unless you tell me more about what the right hand side of those biconditionals mean (or require, or demand, or ...). You just don't have a semantic theory unless you say more. If you can't tell me what it is to be tall, then you don't have a semantic theory.

Reply to Third Stage

We've presented this third stage of the objection so that it both reflects innumerable conversations we have had about this topic, but (we hope) also reflects how unreasonable the demand is. We really don't think we, *qua* semanticists, are required to respond to this challenge. To demand that semanticists tell you what it is to be tall is to start down a most slippery slope. For example, why not also require that semanticists tell us what it takes, or is, to be tall for a man? Is that something semanticists are supposed to explore? Or take the word 'change'. Are semanticists required to reveal what the property of change is in order to do their job? Or what it is to be funny in order to deal with the semantics of the word 'funny'?

Though we take the answers to these various questions, *qua* semanticists, to be quite obvious, we also realize that sticking to our position is almost impossible (certainly unrewarding), since all the people whom we like to talk to about these issues seem to lose interest if we don't elaborate. So: partially for selfish reasons (we don't want people to ignore us), partly out of the goodness of our hearts (we seek philosophical harmony), we'll engage in a little bit of metaphysics. We do this, however, filled with resentment and, ultimately, with the goal of getting our opponents to realize how absurd it is to require that we respond to her challenge.

Here goes: Think about dancing: Some people dance by stepping, some crawl around the floor (like Martha Graham), some have music, some don't have music, some jump in the air, some wave their arms, some hold on to other people, some are alone, some slide on ice, some fly in the air, etc. What do all these activities have in common in virtue of which they are all dancing? This is certainly not our area of expertise, but suppose metaphysicians inform us that to dance is to move in some way W, where W is what all those different events of dancing have in common. There can be different accounts of W, and as far as we can tell, both Semantic Minimalism and Semantic Contextualism are compatible with each and every one of them.

Or, think about eating: some people eat sandwiches, some soup, some apples, some eat in Norway, some in the East Village of New York City, some eat with a spoon, some with their fingers. More generally, there are many things to eat, many places to do it, and many ways to eat. Any event of eating is of a specific thing, in some way, in some location. What is this property of eating? Well, isn't the simplest answer something along the lines of: to engage in the kind of activity that all these different events have in common, i.e., what eating soup, apples, sandwiches, with finger, spoons, in Norway or New York, etc., have in common? Again, we're not specialists, but whatever they all have in common, that's what the activity of eating is. Notice: Semantic Minimalism and Semantic Contextualism are compatible with any answer to these questions. Neither the former nor the latter need take a stand on what eating is.

Now think about funny things: There are funny people, funny jokes, funny paintings, funny movements, etc. People who are funny can be so by moving around in a funny way, by saying funny things, but writing funny, etc. The expression 'funny' presumably has as its semantic value whatever all these things have in common. Here are some conjectures about this property: It might be dispositional: for an object to be funny is for it to trigger a certain reaction in an audience. Whether or not an act is funny might depend on the context in which it is performed (e.g., the interests, expectations, etc., of the salient audience). Any such account of the semantic value of 'funny' is compatible with Semantic Minimalism and with Semantic Contextualism.[5]

Finally, turn to the property of being tall. We suppose that to figure out what tallness is, you proceed much as in these earlier cases: Engage in a little bit of tallness-metaphysics. Consider, for example, the Empire State Building, Mount Everest, and Kobe Bryant. Ask what, if anything, do they all have in common? Naturally, one answer is that they are all tall. If that's so, and it is, then it triggers the following metaphysical question: What is it in virtue of which these three objects are all tall? Or, what do they all have in common? Tallness? But what's that? What does it take for something to instantiate tallness? Because, as in all matters metaphysical, we are rank amateurs, we don't have much to say, but here are four preliminary options (there are obviously others):

---

5 In all these cases you could attempt to respond that it is a philosophical prejudice that there is something that all these things have in common. That it is a pun to say they are all dancing, eating, funny. We do not address that response here, but see Chapter 11 of *Insensitive Semantics* for further discussion.

1. For something to instantiate tallness there must be *some* comparison class or other with respect to which it's tall. If that's all it takes to instantiate tallness, it's very easy to do so. We take this to be an exceedingly unpromising account of tallness.

2. It might be that to instantiate tallness it's insufficient to be tall with respect to *some* comparison class. For each object there might be one such class that's privileged, say, for natural kinds, the natural kind they belong to, for artifacts the artifact they instantiate. Since objects belong to many kinds, work would have to be done to show one of these is privileged.

3. The circumstances the object is in at a time *t* single out a comparison class that's the one the object has to be tall with respect to in order to be tall at *t*. Again, work would have to be done to figure out how this comparison class is picked out.

4. The property of being tall corresponds to being taller than the average height for all objects that have height. Since we have no idea how many objects have heights we have no idea exactly what has this property.[6]

If you agree that there's a property of tallness – how could you not? – but have a better account of what it is to instantiate it, that's fine with us. Try it out on us. Which one is correct? We are not sure even how to determine an answer to this question. However, the only serious objection we can contemplate is to deny that there's any such thing as the property of being tall. Such cynicism would be to endorse Metaphysical Nihilism about tallness, i.e., it would be to endorse the

---

6 A more elaborate discussion of these options would, in some ways, mirror contemporary debates about knowledge attributions. Both Stanley and Hawthorne propose theories according to which knowledge is some kind of interest relative property, but where this does not necessarily make "know" a context-sensitive expression (See Stanley, unpublished manuscript, and Hawthorne, 2003). We imagine analogous arguments being made in connection with comparative adjectives. For some suggestions along these lines, see Graff 2002, and a reply by Stanley (2003).

view that there's nothing *A* and *B* have in common if *A* is tall for a *G* and *B* is tall for an *F*. That view is, as far as we can tell, a rather bizarre view to hold, because no one, as far as we know, denies there is any such a thing as *being tall with respect to some comparison class*. No one can deny there's such a thing as *being tall with respect to a privileged comparison class* or *being tall with respect to a contextually salient comparison class*; or having the property of *being taller than the average height of all objects that have heights*. If this is so, then everyone agrees with us that at least for these four accounts of what the property of tallness is, each picks out something that exists. Whether it's the "right" account is another topic.

In sum, our response the first objection is this: If you think there is such a thing as tallness, then let that be the semantic value of 'tall' in 'Osama bin Laden is tall', and in answer to the question as to what it takes for that sentence to be true we say that it is whatever it takes for Osama bin Laden to have that property. To keep this answer in perspective, remember:

1. We don't accept that it is a necessary condition on an acceptable semantic theory for English that it tells us what tallness is (even though we have given you some modest pointers for how to proceed).
2. According to Speech Act Pluralism, the semantic content of 'Osama bin Laden is tall' is not all of what the speaker who utters that sentence says; more generally, it does not fully determine the content of speech acts performed by people who utter that sentence.

First (and Only) Digression:
Being Tall For an F *is No Better Than Being Tall*

Suppose you're baffled by the idea that there's such a thing as tallness. We'll now try to show that if you are, you should be equally baffled by the idea that there is such a thing as, for example, being tall for a giraffe, or more generally, by the sort of property expressed by being tall for an *F*. This claim is dialectically significant, because Semantic Contextualists tend to hold that this alleged problem occurs only for those who are Semantic Minimalists (as applied to comparative adjectives in particular). The fix, according to Semantic Contextualists, is supposed to reside in relativizing comparative adjectives to comparison classes, i.e., in a commitment to contextualism for 'tall' and other comparative adjectives.

Adjectives like 'tall' are to treated as relational with, for example, an unpronounced place for a comparison class that gets indexed in a context of use. So, in effect, the sentence '*A* is tall' is equivalent, on this contextualist suggestion, at some level of linguistic analysis, say, at the level of logical form, with the representation '*A* is tall for an *F*', where '*F*' is an indexical that somehow receives its semantic value in context. For a sentence like (6), in one context of utterance the indexed comparison class (or property, or whatever) might be NBA players; and in another it might be Saudi Arabians.

Recall that the alleged problem for *tallness* is that it's mysterious what it is to be tall *simpliciter*: "There can be no such thing as tallness *simpliciter*. To claim Kobe Bryant, Mount Everest, and the Empire State Building all have something in common – *viz.*, *tallness* – is a mistake, and any semantics that presupposes there could be such a thing must be mistaken. Since Semantic Minimalism, as characterized, is committed to this possibility, it should be rejected."

If this objection issues from anyone content with properties like *being tall for an F*, then it is terribly misplaced. Take the property of *being tall for a giraffe* as an example, i.e., we're imagining an opponent who thinks that many things can instantiate the property of *being tall for giraffes*. Before proceeding with our inquiry, consider the following basic giraffe facts: Giraffes have hairy ears. The fleshy part of the ear stops before the hairs on the ears stop. Not every giraffe can stretch his neck all they way up; some are old and arthritic. (With assistance they might be able to stretch their necks further than without help.) Giraffes can stand on their back legs and lift their front legs into the air, and thereby, push themselves further up into the air. That makes them longer. They have hoofs, and these hoofs wear down with usage.

Holding these simple giraffe facts in mind, consider two giraffes, say, *A* and *B*. What would it be for *A* and *B* to both instantiate the property of being tall for giraffes? The problem is this: There are many ways to be tall for a giraffe. For starters, there are indefinitely many ways to measure the tallness of giraffes. Consider these few illustrations. A giraffe's height can be measured:

- From the bottom of his hoof to the fleshy tip of his ear with a self-stretched neck;
- From the bottom of a hoof to the tip of his snout with a self-stretched neck;
- From the bottom of a hoof to the hairy tip of an ear with a self-stretched neck;
- From the bottom of a hoof to the tip of a snout when standing on his back legs with his front legs lifted into the air;
- Any of the above, with an artificially stretched neck, i.e., by a machine or something else that can stretch the neck out further than the giraffe can by herself. (Remember, some giraffes are arthritic, and have very stiff necks.)

Then, of course, there's the question of which comparison class, or property, or whatever, we are to compare any given giraffe to. Here are but a few options:

- All living giraffes;
- A stereotypical giraffe;
- French giraffes;
- All giraffes that have ever lived, are alive, and will ever live;
- All possible giraffes;
- All giraffes in the vicinity of a certain giraffe.

Then, of course, there's the question of the (optimum) conditions under which to measure a particular giraffe (holding the method of measurement and the comparison class fixed). Here are but a few of indefinitely many options:

- Right after a bath (giraffes shrink a bit after having taken a bath);
- Right after a long walk (their hoofs wear down);
- When dead (again, death shrinks us all);
- When hungry (they tend to stretch their necks further);
- When pregnant (their necks are rendered less flexible).

Let's stop here, even though there is much else that has to be settled – but now ask yourself: What is it to *be tall for a giraffe*? What is *giraffe-*

tallness? It all depends on *which giraffes* you compare any given giraffe to, *how* you measure it, the conditions of the giraffe when being measured, and so on. The "and so on" here is vital. There are no obvious or *a priori* limits on the different variations on *giraffe-tallness*.

Just to remind you why this matters: We're imagining a Semantic Contextualist opponent who's completely baffled by the idea that there's such a thing as tallness and that it can be the semantic value of 'tall'. We've just tried to make that seem a little less peculiar, by showing that the kind of worry that triggers befuddlement with respect to being *tall* should also, if legitimate, trigger the same sort of befuddlement with respect to being *tall for a giraffe*. Now, since we expect at least some of opponents to be completely non-befuddled about being *tall for a giraffe*, at least before seeing our examples, this discussion might remove or alleviate some of their resistance to tallness.

Of course, we expect many opponents to say: "Of course, there's no such thing as being tall-for-a-giraffe *simpliciter*. You have to fill it out: you have to add something about the class of giraffes, the condition of the giraffes, the measuring methods, and so on." To these critics we say: Okay, just do it. Let's see how that gets incorporated into semantics and then we'll continue the debate.

Second Objection: Role of Semantic Content in Communication

Remember that according to Speech Act Pluralism, speakers use sentences to make claims, assertions, suggestions, requests, statements, to state hypotheses, raise inquiries, etc., the contents of which can be (and typically are) radically different from the semantic contents of (the propositions semantically expressed by) these utterances. The speech act content (i.e., what was said, asserted, claimed, asked, etc.) depends on a potentially indefinite range of facts about the speaker, his audience, their shared context, the reporter (i.e., the person recounting what was said), the reporter's audience, and their shared context. These facts have no bearing on the semantic content of the utterance.

Here's a potential worry for this position: What communicators actually *care* about in a discourse exchange *is* the speech act content and *only* the speech act content. What they care about is what the speaker said, asserted, claimed, stated, suggested, asked, etc. If this *isn't* the semantic content – if the semantic content is, so to speak, always hidden, if it never surfaces – then what purpose does it serve? Isn't it just an idle wheel? What would be lost if our theory just let it go? So, even if there is tallness, and even if the semantic value of 'is tall' somehow involves it, what role can this peculiar property play in communication? Does it have any kind of psychological reality? Let's call this the Psychological Challenge to Semantic Minimalism.

Reply to Second Objection:
Semantic Content Does Have a Role to Play in Communication

We think the answer is simple and obvious, but we can't over-emphasize its importance. We begin by reminding you of some basic facts about communication. Then we respond directly to this Psychological Challenge. What we are about to say presupposes there being a clear notion of *a shared context*. We doubt there is one, but we'll place our reservations to the side for now. If there are shared contexts, then that will make life even harder for the Semantic Contextualist.

i) Basic Facts About Speakers and Audiences who Share a Context

Speakers are sometimes wrong (or have incomplete information) about their audience, e.g., about:

> What the audience believes and knows;
> What the audience remembers about prior conversations;
> How the audience has interpreted previous conversations;
> How the audience perceives their shared environment; and
> What the audience believes about the speaker.

Audiences are sometimes wrong (or have incomplete information) about speakers, e.g., about:

> What the speaker believes and knows;
> What the speaker remembers about previous conversations;
> How the speaker has interpreted previous conversations;
> How the speaker perceives their shared environment; and
> What the speaker believes about the audience.

Audiences and speakers are both often wrong (or have incomplete information) about the context that they find themselves in, e.g., about:

> What their perceptual environment is; and
> What the contents of preceding conversations were.

Speakers and audiences know that they can be wrong and can have incomplete information about each other in the ways just specified.

ii) Basic Facts about Speakers and Audiences who do not Share a Context

Sometimes, the audience of an utterance doesn't share a context with the speaker. This can happen in any of several ways, the most salient of which being the reproduction of a speech act, as in published articles. Writers often have no idea who their reader is; they know next to nothing about her beliefs, or about her perceptual environment; all they know is that it is not shared. Yet, nonetheless, writers have audiences (no matter how small they might be).

Another typical device through which a speech act can reach an audience in another context is indirect quotation. This is when S says in C to A what another speaker S' said in another context C' to another audience A'. In these cases the sources of confusion are multiplied. The added complications should be obvious; there is not even the illusion of a shared context.

iii) Basic Facts about Inter-Contextual Content Sharing

a. People can and often do say the same thing in different contexts. People in different contexts can say that Napoleon was short.

b. According to Semantic Contextualists, no two contexts (are likely to) share exactly the same content-fixing parameters, e.g., the intentions are not the same, the background knowledge is not the same, previous conversations are not the same, what's normal is not the same, and so on (see, e.g., Sperber and Wilson, 1986, 118, 192–93; Carston 2001, 26–27; Recanati 2004, 149; Bezuidenhout, 1997, 212–13).

c. It is possible to say in a context C that people in a range of contexts C_1–C_n said the same thing, e.g., there are true reports, say, in C, of the form 'They all said that Napoleon was short' about different speakers' utterances in contexts C_1–C_n. (Similarly, distinct utterances can be collected; true utterances of the form 'A is tall', 'B is tall' and 'C is tall' said in contexts C_1, C_2, and C_3 can be collected in a single context C_4 with an utterance of 'A, B and C are tall').

Note that if someone denies (a)–(c), we don't want to talk to her or about her (because she doesn't think she can say what we say, so she can't deny what we say, and (according to her) we can't say what she said, and so we can't say that we disagree with what she said.)

VI: The Cognitive Role of Minimal Semantic Content

What, then, is the cognitive role of minimal semantic content? The answer should be (almost) self-evident by now:

1. Speakers know that their audience can be (and often are) mistaken (or have incomplete information) about the communication-relevant facts about the context of utterance. The proposition semantically expressed is that content the speaker can expect the audience to grasp (and expect the audience to expect the speaker to expect them to grasp) even if they have mistaken or incomplete communication-relevant information.

2. Audiences know that the speaker can be (and often is) mistaken (or has incomplete information) about the communication-relevant facts about the context of utterance. The proposition semantically expressed is that content the audience can expect the speaker to grasp (and expect the audience to grasp) even if she (they) has (have) such mistaken or incomplete information.

3. The proposition semantically expressed is that content which can be grasped and expressed by someone who isn't even a participant in the context of utterance.

4. The proposition semantically expressed is that content which speakers and audiences know can be transmitted

through indirect quotation or reproduction (in the form of audio tapes, video recordings, etc.) to, or collected by, those who find themselves in contexts radically different from the original context of utterance.

In short: the proposition semantically expressed is our minimal defense against confusion/misunderstanding/indifference, and it is that which guarantees communication across contexts of utterance. It's what allows us to collect, report, and reproduce others' utterances.

Possible Counter-reply

We expect this sort of reply: "Hold it – you're saying that the minimal semantic content is a shared, fallback content' and that this content serves to guard against confusion and misunderstandings. But given what you've told us about minimal propositions, how could they serve that purpose? Consider, for example, an utterance of (6). Suppose a speaker utters it to communicate that Osama Bin Laden is tall for a Saudi Arabian (or something like that). That's what the speaker is trying to say. How would it help an audience to know that the minimal proposition, i.e., *that Osama bin Laden is tall*, was expressed? It might not be what the speaker wanted to assert. What help could it be to know that this proposition was expressed?"

Our response is simple: It is a starting point. The audience knows that the speaker is talking about Osama Bin Laden and attributes tallness to him, and not, for example, about Sprite cans, Sweden, Britney Spears, or pig ears. There's lots to talk about in the universe. The proposition semantically expressed pares it down considerably. Knowledge that this proposition was semantically expressed provides the audience with the *best possible* access to the speaker's mind, given the restricted knowledge she has of that speaker. In general, audiences know what to look for in such situations; they know what kind of information would help narrow down more closely what the speaker wanted to communicate.[7]

---

7 There are many theories about how speakers go from semantic content to speech act content, and we do not mean to, nor do we need to, endorse any one of those here.

To sum up our counter-reply: Consider the following charge from Recanati against Semantic Minimalism and our reply. Recanati writes of minimal propositions:

> Let the semanticist use it if he or she wants to, provided he or she agrees that ... the minimal proposition has no psychological reality. It does not correspond to any stage in the process of understanding the utterance, and need not be entertained or represented at any point in that process. (2004, 89)

If there's a difference between having a cognitive function and corresponding to a stage in processing/having psychological reality, we don't know what that difference consists in. If (1)–(4) immediately above are insufficient to "correspond to a stage in the process of understanding the utterance and need not be entertained or represented at any point in that process," then we don't know what is.

In some sense, we're taking a stab in the dark, here, since we're not at all sure what Semantic Contextualists have in mind by the psychological requirement. What we have said is sufficient to render the propositions semantically expressed psychologically real, but we're genuinely confused, since we have no idea how Semantic Contextualists satisfy their own requirement.

Concluding Point: The Second Objection Reversed: (or Why Recanati's Account of What-Is-Said Doesn't Satisfy His Own Availability Principle)

Suppose we focus, as Semantic Contextualists tend to, on the context of the speaker and her audience. The factors that figure in fixing the what-was-said/explicature include, *inter alia*, (i)–(iv):

(i) Information triggered in the speaker and the audience by prior discourse contents;

(ii) Information conversational partners share about each other;

(iii) Information the conversational partners have acquired through observation of their mutual, perceptual environment;

(iv)   Information conversational partners have about each oth-
        er's purposes and abilities (e.g., whether the person is being
        deceitful or sincere, whether the person tends to verbosity, or
        is a person of few words).

These in no way exhaust the facts that are, according to Semantic
Contextualists, content determinants, but what we have to say about
(i)–(iv) generalizes. The problem is this: Suppose (i)–(iv) are factors
that fix the explicature (i.e., the proposition expressed) of an utterance
u of some sentence S. Now (i)–(iv) involve the mental states of several
people (i.e., the speaker and her audience). None of the participants
knows all the relevant facts about all the other participants: Herman
doesn't know all the information triggered in Ernie by their many previous discussions; Ernie doesn't know what information Herman has
about him. (He undoubtedly knows things about him that he doesn't
even know he knows.) He doesn't always know what he will pay
attention to in their sometimes shared, perceptual environment; and
so on.

The point here is obvious: If the explicature is fixed by these sorts
of facts (what else?), then no one of the participants has direct access
to the explicature. It is fixed intra-personally, and so there's no reason
to think the resulting content is "represented" at any stage of that person's processing of the relevant utterance. There is no reason to think
that the resulting proposition is psychologically real.

Recanati discusses a version of this objection, and the utter failure
of his reply illustrates just how hard it is for Semantic Contextualists
to satisfy their own psychological reality requirement. In particular,
it illustrates why Recanati can't satisfy his Availability Principle (his
version of the Psychological Requirement).

Hence my 'Availability Principle' (Recanati, 1993, 48), according
to which 'what is said' must be analysed in conformity to the
intuitions shared by those who fully understand the utterance
– typically the speaker and the hearer, in a normal conversational setting. I take the conversational participants' intuitions
concerning what is said to be revealed by their views concerning the utterance's truth-conditions. I assume that whoever
fully understands a declarative utterance knows which state of

affairs would possibly constitute a truth-maker for that utterance, i.e., knows in what sort of circumstance it would be true. (Recanati, 2004, 20–21)

Recanati's theory, based on his Availability Principle, is supposed to be an alternative to theories according to which the explicature/content/what-is-said is not psychologically accessible. Recanati's idea is that, since his what-is-said corresponds to the speaker's intuitions about what is said, it will figure in the process of understanding (an utterance of) the sentence. He raises this worry:

> Have we not equated what is said with their [i.e., the speaker's and audience's] understanding of what is said? ... We have not. We have equated what is said with what a normal interpreter would understand as being said, in the context at hand. A normal interpreter knows which sentence was uttered, knows the meaning of that sentence, knows the relevant contextual facts (who is being pointed to, etc.) Ordinary users of the language are normal interpreters, in most situations. They know the relevant facts and have the relevant abilities. But there are situations ... where the actual users make mistakes and are not normal interpreters. In such situations their interpretations do not fix what is said. To determine what is said, we need to look at the interpretation that a normal interpreter would give. This is objective enough, yet remains within the confines of the pragmatic construal. (2004, 27)

But what's *normal* is not something speakers have psychological access to. What's normal need not "be in the speaker's mind when the sentence is understood"; it certainly needn't figure into any psychological processes that the speaker goes through when understanding (an utterance of) a sentence. This is so for several obvious reasons; here are perhaps the most obvious ones:

- A speaker can be abnormal, but think that she is normal.
- A speaker might know that she is not normal, but not know what normal is.
- A speaker might think that she is not normal, but not be.

- More generally: Even for speakers who are normal and know that they are normal, they might not know what counts as a normal understanding of some specific feature of a context that they happen to find themselves in.

A lot of situations have no "normal" set of expectations associated with them. Suppose you meet someone in a cafe on a hot, New York City summer day. What "normality" are we looking for? Normal for you when talking to strangers in a cafe in New York City on a hot, summer day? There's no such thing!

In other words: If what's normal, in part, determines what-is-said, and if what is normal is not represented at any stage in the processing of the utterance, then the resulting what-is-said cannot be so represented. Then, we suppose (though, as we have admitted, we're not sure we entirely understand the Semantic Contextualists here), Recanati's what-is-said is not psychologically real.

In sum: the Semantic Minimalist has a response to the Psychological Objection; it is the Semantic Contextualist who, surprisingly, does not.

References

Bezuidenhout, A. 1997. "The Communication of De Re Thoughts." *Noûs* 31 (2): 197–225.

Cappelen, H. and Lepore, E. 1997. "On an Alleged Connection between Indirect Quotation and Semantic Theory." *Mind and Language* (12): 278–296.

———, E. 2003. "Context Shifting Arguments." *Philosophical Perspectives* (17): 25–50.

———Cappelen, H. and, E. 2005. *Insensitive Semantics.* Oxford: Basil Blackwell.

Carston, R. 2001. "Explicature and Semantics." In *Semantics: A Reader*, ed. S. Davis and B. Gillon. Oxford: Oxford University Press.

———. 2002. *Thoughts and Utterances: The Pragmatics of Explicit Communication.* Oxford: Blackwell.

Graff, D. 2002. "Shifting Sands: An Interest Relative Theory of Vagueness." *Philosophical Topics* 28 (1): 45–81.

Hawthorne, J. 2003. *Knowledge and Lotteries.* Oxford: Oxford University Press.

Kaplan, D. "Demonstratives." In *Themes from Kaplan*. ed. J. Almog, J. Perry, and H. Wettstein. Oxford: Oxford University Press, 481–563.

Recanati, F. 1993. *Direct Reference: From Language to Thought*. Oxford: Blackwell.

———. 2004. *Literal Meaning*. Cambridge: Cambridge University Press.

Sperber, D. and D. Wilson. 1986. *Relevance*. Oxford: Blackwell.

Stanley, J. 2003. "Context, Interest-Relativity, and the Sorites." *Analysis* 63 (4): 269–80.

———. Unpublished manuscript. Context, Interest-relativity, and Knowledge.

CANADIAN JOURNAL OF PHILOSOPHY
Supplementary Volume 30

Binding into Character

JOSHUA DEVER

Abstract

Since Kaplan's "Demonstratives," it has become common to distinguish between the character and content of an expression, where the *content* of an expression is what it contributes to "what is said" by sentences containing that expression, and the *character* gives a rule for determining, in a context, the content of an expression. A tacit assumption of theories of character has been that character is autonomous from content – that semantic evaluation starts with character, adds context, and then derives content. One consequence of this autonomy thesis is that the rules for character can contain no variables bound by content-level operators elsewhere in the sentence. Tacit appeal to this consequence features essentially both in Jason Stanley's recent argument, in "Context and Logical Form," that all contextual ambiguity must be linked to "elements in the actual syntactic structure of the sentence uttered", and in my arguments against character-based theories of complex demonstratives in my "Complex Demonstratives." However, I argue here that the autonomy thesis is unmotivated, and show that we can separate Kaplan's notion of character into two independent components: an aspect of meaning which is context-sensitive, and an aspect of meaning that is exempted from scopal interactions with other operators. The resulting semantic framework allows constructions similar to Kaplan's rejected notion of "monsters begat by elegance," but which are both more empirically adequate and more theoretically versatile. Having made the distinction between context-sensitivity and autonomy from scopal interaction, I show how that distinction allows binding into the character of expressions and hence undermines the immediate success of both Stanley's argument and my previous argument against character-based theories of complex demonstratives, and discuss briefly the prospects for reinstating modified versions of those arguments. Finally, I show how that same distinction allows a defusing of Kripke's modal argument against a descriptive theory of names. Once autonomy from semantic interaction is separated from context-sensitivity, the first of those two alone can be used to capture the modal rigidity of proper names. I argue that the resulting semantic account, which bears important resemblances to (but is, I think, a significant generalization on) Recanati's use of the REF feature, captures some of the core intuitions of wide-scope responses to the modal argument without incurring the weaknesses of those responses.

I. Character and the Autonomy Thesis

In his seminal paper "Demonstratives," Kaplan distinguishes between what he calls "two kinds of meaning" (1977, 500). The first type of meaning is content, of which Kaplan says:

> The content of a sentence in a given context is what has tradi-
> tionally been called a proposition.... It is *contents* that are evalu-
> ated in circumstances of evaluation. If the content is a proposi-
> tion (i.e., the content of a sentence taken in some context), the
> result of the evaluation will be a truth-value. The result of evalu-
> ating the content of a singular term at a circumstance will be an
> object. (1977, 500–1)

Content is, roughly, the pre-Kaplanian familiar notion of meaning – the determiner of truth value, the Gricean what-is-said. The innovation in "Demonstratives" is the identification of a second kind of meaning: character. Of character, Kaplan says:

> The character of an expression is set by linguistic conventions
> and, in turn, determines the content of the expression in every
> context. Because character is what is set by linguistic conven-
> tions, it is natural to think of it as *meaning* in the sense of what is
> known by the competent language user. (1977, 505)

To take a familiar example, the *character* of the word 'I' will be given[1] by a rule along the following lines:

"'I' refers to the speaker or writer" (Kaplan 1977, 505)

In any particular context, that rule will then pick out some individual, who will then be the *content* of the (utterance of the) word 'I' in that context.

Given character and content as Kaplan understands them, there is a logical progression between the two types of meaning. Semantic evaluation of an expression begins with character, and then adds context to arrive at content. Content is then combined with a circumstance of evaluation (a time, a world) to derive an extension. As Kaplan schematically puts it:

Character: Contexts ⇒ Contents
Content: Circumstances ⇒ Extensions
(1977, 506)

This picture of the logical relation of character to content encourages a certain autonomy thesis:

(AT) The character of an expression is not affected by the content of that expression.

This thesis is quite vague as it stands, but I want to draw out one particular, precise consequence of it, and discuss that consequence.

Kaplan talks initially as if the character of an expression can be understood as a rule of some sort. Thus, as noted above, he gives the character of 'I' by the (admittedly rough-and-ready) rule "the speaker or writer." This rule picks out, in a given context, an individual to serve as the content of 'I' by virtue of the satisfaction of that individual (in the context) of certain predicates (or, avoiding semantic assent, by virtue of the possession of that individual (in the context) of certain properties). We thus get the following broad semantic picture:

---

1 At least initially – as we'll see below, there's an important shift in the characterization of characters later in Kaplan's discussion.

31

Each expression in the language carries a certain semantic value. Exploiting Kaplan's favoured metaphor of structured propositions, we can think of that semantic value as some sort of entity (an object, a descriptive condition, a property, a truth function, etc), but we needn't be wedded to that particular framework – thinking of the semantic values of some expressions as compositional rules, for example, works just as well. It's tempting to call this semantic value 'the content of the expression', but this creates undue confusion when combined with Kaplan's character/content terminology, so we'll call it somewhat loosely the *meaning* of the expression. Expressions can then contribute their meanings either to character or to content – contextually sensitive expressions, such as 'I,' contribute their meaning to character, while contextually insensitive expressions, such as 'Aristotle', contribute their meaning to content. (We can, if we like, think of all meanings as contributed to character and then some simply passed down unaltered to content. Nothing will hang on the way we phrase it). Meanings contributed to character are then combined with context to yield some new meaning, which is, in turn, passed on to content.

Thus, for example, the meaning of the word 'I' is, as Kaplan suggests, some descriptive condition along the lines of *the speaker or writer*. That meaning is contributed to character, where it combines with context to yield some specific object (me, in this case), which is, in turn, passed on to content (to form part of a singular proposition). The meaning of the word 'Aristotle', on the other hand, is a specific individual, who is contributed directly to content (or contributed to character and passed unaltered to content).

The Autonomy Thesis encapsulates a certain crucial difference between the role of meanings as contributed to character and the role of meanings as contributed to contents. The character-level meaning associated with 'I' is in a important sense *insulated* from the content of expressions containing 'I'. Thus suppose I utter:

(1)   Necessarily, I am the child of George and Cindy Dever.

The modal modification which is induced by the content of the operator 'necessarily' in (1) has an effect on the evaluation of the *contents* of the expressions in (1). Because of the initial modal operator, we are concerned not only with the extension of the child-of relation in the actual world, but also the extension of that relation in other alethically possible worlds.

That same modal modification, however, has no impact on the evaluation of the *characters* of the expressions in (1). The descriptive conditions *speaker* and *writer*, as they appear in the character of 'I,' are not impacted in their evaluation by the modal modification induced by the content of 'necessarily'. We are not concerned with the extensions of 'speaker' and 'writer' in all alethically possible worlds, but only with their extensions in the actual world.

It is this insulation of character from content that makes (1) have the same content as:

> (1′)   Necessarily, Josh Dever is the child of George and Cindy Dever.

and not the same content as:

> (1″)   Necessarily, the speaker or writer is the child of George and Cindy Dever.

Thus the insulation of character from content allows indexical expressions to have a descriptive character (a rule that descriptively determines their content-in-a-context) while maintaining their rigid modal profile. As such, that insulation is crucial for reconciling the two principles regarding demonstratives that Kaplan announces at the beginning of his paper:

Principle 1: The referent of a pure indexical depends on the context, and the referent of a demonstrative depends on the associated demonstration.

Principle 2: Indexicals, pure and demonstrative alike, are directly referential. (1977, 492)

The descriptive aspect of character captures the force of Principle 1, and then the insulation of character from content allows the rigidity demanded by Principle 2.

The same sort of insulation that prevents the modal modification induced by the contents of modal operators from affecting the evaluation of character-rules also prevents the quantificational effects induced by the contents of quantifiers from affecting the evaluation of character-level rules. Without such insulation, we could in principle have indexical expressions whose character-level rules had free variables:

The character of 'schmi' is the man between the speaker and x

which variables could then be semantically affected by quantifiers elsewhere in the sentence:

(2) Every philosopher admires schmi.

This consequence of the insulation of character from content will be of particular interest to us later.

Here, then, is a precise corollary to the rather broad autonomy thesis advanced earlier:

No Binding Principle (NBP): There can be no semantic binding of the character-level rule of an expression φ by the contents of operators elsewhere in an utterance ψ of which φ is a part.

In particular:

- If the character-level rule of φ contains predicates, the evaluation of those predicates is unaffected by intensional operators in ψ.
- If the character-level rule of φ contains variables, the quantificational distribution of those variables is unaffected by quantifiers in ψ.

II. Two Applications of the No Binding Principle

I want next to consider the way that the no binding principle (NBP) has been put to work in two recent papers in the philosophy of language. Both of these papers attempt to argue that certain semantic phenomena cannot receive a character-level explanation, by implicitly assuming the NBP, noting that autonomy is violated by the relevant phenomena, and then applying *modus tollens*.

II.i. *Character and Complex Demonstratives*

The first paper is my own "Complex Demonstratives" (Dever 2001). In that paper, I set out and defend a certain view on the semantics of constructions of the form 'that *F'*. In the process of doing so, I argue that previous accounts of such constructions all fail to satisfy at least one of two desiderata for an acceptable account:

> *Existential Generalization*: The proposition that that *F* is *G* logically implies the proposition that some *F* is *G*.
>
> *Binding Principle*: A pronoun in a complex demonstrative can be anaphoric on a term outside that demonstrative only if the anaphora is of the sort which generally functions cross-clausally rather than intra-clausally.

The second principle (the one which will concern us here) is motivated by observing the following distribution of data:

(3) That friend of every man$_i$ who admires his$_i$ father was fond of dogs.

(4) *Every boy$_i$ read this book he$_i$ liked.

(5) Several eyewitnesses$_i$ described that assailant they$_i$ saw.

(3) demonstrates that the descriptive component of complex demonstratives can contain variables bound within that descriptive component – note that the variable 'his' is bound by the quantifier 'every man', which is also part of the descriptive component of the complex demonstrative.

(4), on the other hand, demonstrates that variables in the descriptive component of a complex demonstrative cannot straightforwardly be bound by quantifiers external to that demonstrative – trying to bind 'he' by 'every boy' results here in an uninterpretable utterance.

Finally, (5) demonstrates that certain kinds of binding in are acceptable. The variable 'they' in 'that assailant they saw' can be bound by the external 'several eyewitnesses' *provided* that the binding is of the cross-clausal *donkey anaphora* type. The clue to this proviso is that 'they' in the above example, like other pronouns externally bound in complex demonstratives, allows an undistributed reading. (5), that is, can be understood as:

(5′) Several eyewitnesses described that assailant the eyewitnesses saw.

where the anaphoric pronoun picks out all of the eyewitness, not just some several-sized group satisfying the quantificational condition. Thus the semantic behaviour of the bound pronoun 'they' is like the semantic behaviour of donkey pronouns, as in:

(6) Every farmer who owned a donkey vaccinated it.

where 'it' picks out all the donkeys owned by a given farmer, rather than just one donkey satisfying the existential 'a'.

In my earlier paper, I then use the Binding Principle to argue against the view – defended by Braun (1994) and Borg (2000) – that in a complex demonstrative 'that φ', the descriptive meaning of φ contributes to the character of the complex demonstrative, thus allowing that demonstrative, in a given context of utterance, to have as content whatever object is both conversationally salient and φ. I then argue that since the descriptive material is "entirely removed from the propositional content," it follows that "all forms of binding" into the complex demonstrative are forbidden (thus falsifying the Binding Principle by disallowing the cross-clausal binding that complex demonstratives do in fact support). What has since become clear to me is that this argument rests tacitly on the NBP – without assuming that principle, there is no reason why removal of the descriptive meaning to the character of the complex demonstrative would make it inaccessible for binding by operators elsewhere in the sentence. This rejection of a character-based analysis of complex demonstratives, then, stands or falls with the correctness of the Autonomy Thesis and its corollary, the NBP.

II.ii. Stanley on Contextual Ambiguity

In his recent paper "Context and Logical Form," Jason Stanley argues for the bold claim that "all truth-conditional effects of extra-linguistic context can be traced to logical form." Thus any time that the content of a claim exhibits a sensitivity to context of utterance, as in

I am a philosopher.   [referent of 'I']
All the beers are warm.   [domain of quantification of 'all beers']

It is three o'clock.   [time zone]
It's raining.   [location of rain]

there must be some syntactic element of the sentence which has the semantic feature of being appropriately sensitive to context. In the case of 'I am a philosopher', of course, the syntactic element is overt, but in the other cases, Stanley will posit covert variables in logical form which provide a domain of quantification, a time zone, and a location respectively.

Among the targets of Stanley's claim are cases of what Perry (1986) calls *unarticulated constitutents*. As Stanley puts it:

> x is an unarticulated constituent of an utterance u iff (1) x is an element supplied by context to the truth-conditions of u, and (2) x is not the semantic value of any constituent of the logical form of the sentence uttered. (2000, 410)

A proponent of unarticulated constituents, then, will hold that the syntactic form of the sentence

(7) It's raining.

in conjunction with the semantic rules for assigning content to that syntactic form, yields too little to assign truth conditions to the sentence. We might say that syntax plus semantics gives us the propositional fragment:

$$\langle \text{RAIN}, \_\_, \_\_ \rangle$$

(where the binary relation of raining (which holds between a time and a place) is provided by the content of the verb 'rains', but the two relata for that relation are missing) and that context then interacts with a syntactic marker for the present tense to enhance this fragment to:

$$\langle \text{RAIN}, t, \_\_ \rangle$$

(where t is the time of utterance), but that even after each syntactic element seeks its interpretation through semantic rules or through contextual supplementation, the argument position for location is still lacking and must be directly supplied by context as an unarticulated constituent to form the complete proposition:

$$\langle \text{RAIN}, t, l \rangle$$

However, use of the structured-proposition idiom is optional; the crucial point is that some information necessary for truth-conditional evaluation is introduced directly by context without overt or covert syntactic trigger.

Unarticulated constituents, were there any genuine such, would be a counter-example to Stanley's claim that contextual sensitivity traces back to logical form, since such constituents would provide an extra-syntactic route for context to make truth-conditional contributions. Stanley, however, argues that analyses based on unarticulated constituents are incorrect. His argument centers around the ability of putative unarticulated constituents to enter into binding relations with operators elsewhere in the sentence.

Thus consider the following example:

(8) Every time John lights a cigarette, it rains.

As Stanley points out, there is a natural reading of (8) on which it means:

(8′) Every time John lights a cigarette, it rains where John lights the cigarette.

Thus the location of the raining – not overtly provided for in (8) and, on the view of fans of unarticulated constituents supplied as an unarticulated constituent by context – is bound by the quantifier 'every time John lights a cigarette'.

Stanley does not phrase the unarticulated constituent position in terms of the character–content distinction. We can, however, easily rework it in those terms. Consider an expression which induces an unarticulated constituent, such as 'rains'. Stanley provides (on behalf of the unarticulated-constituent theorist) the following semantic clause for 'rains':

> Den("rains") relative to a context c = that function f that takes $\langle t,l \rangle$ to True if it is raining at t and l, where l is the contextually salient location in c, takes $\langle t,l \rangle$ to False if it is not raining at t and l, where l is the contextually salient location, and is undefined otherwise. (2000, 415)

Putting this in Kaplanesque terms, we might specify the character of rains as follows:

> 'rains' picks out a function which maps the ordered pair of a time t and the location to True if it is raining at the location at t, and which maps the ordered pair of a time t and the location to False if it is not raining at the location at t, and which is undefined otherwise,

where "the location" serves to pick out the locative element of the context of utterance. Given this reworking, Stanley's objection via (8) is that there are constructions that seem to require that an element of the character (the specification of location) be bound by a content-level operator ('every time John lights a cigarette'). His rejection of such constructions is then driven by implicit acceptance of the NBP.

The implicit acceptance of the NBP can be located in one of two places in Stanley's argument. Stanley distinguishes between *narrow indexicals* and *unarticulated constituents*. About narrow indexicals, Stanley says:

> In the narrow sense of the term "indexical," it applies to words such as 'I,' 'here,' 'you,' and 'now.' The three central features of such words is, first, that they are primitive lexical items, second, that they are not bindable by operators, and, third, that their interpretation shifts from context to context. (2000, 411)

Here Stanley simply builds unbindability into the definition of 'narrow indexicals'. If Stanley intends narrow indexicals to exhaust the contribution of context via character to content, then he here presupposes the truth of the NBP. Unfortunately, Stanley's position on this question is unclear. He does recognize the existence of other types of context dependence:

My own view of the truth-conditional role of context is very conservative. First, there are expressions which are obviously indexicals in the narrow sense of the word, such as 'I,' 'here,' 'you,' 'now' and their brethren. Second, there are expressions which are obviously demonstratives, such as 'this' and 'that.' Third, there are expressions that are obviously pronouns, such as 'he' and 'she.' Overt expressions that are in none of these classes are not context-dependent. (2000, 400)

However, it is unclear whether Stanley thinks that non-narrow indexicals, such as 'she' or 'that', continue to have a context-dependent aspect (that is, make a distinctively character-level semantic contribution) when they occur in bound constructions. It would certainly seem that in sentences like:

(9) Every girl believes she will be president when she grows up.

(10) If a farmer owns a donkey, he vaccinates that donkey.

the expressions 'she' and 'that' are no longer context-dependent, having their referents fixed entirely by the quantificational and anaphoric structure of their linguistic surroundings. If Stanley in fact thinks that narrow indexicality and distinctively character-level semantic contribution go hand in hand, then his views on narrow indexicality amount to an acceptance of the NBP.

If, on the other hand, Stanley thinks that there can be context-dependent, non-narrow indexicals, then his implicit acceptance of the NBP comes via his endorsement of what he calls the 'Binding Assumption':

> *The Binding Assumption* (BA): If α and β are within the same clause, and α semantically binds β, then α is, or introduces, a variable-binding operator which is co-indexed with, and stands in a certain specified structural relation to, a variable which is either identical to, or is a constituent of, β. (2000, 412)

Stanley takes the BA to show that if the location of the rain is anaphoric on the location of John's lighting a cigarette, then there must be a syntactic variable bound by the 'every time John lights a cigarette' quantifier.

On the face of it, it is unclear why a proponent of an unarticulated constituent analysis would accept the BA. Presumably such a proponent, faced with an example like (8), would suggest that in some cases the unarticulated constituent provided by context is a variable – not given by the syntax of the original sentence – which is then bound by a quantifier in the original sentence. In response to a potential such proposal, Stanley says:

> It is easy to see how an object or a property could be provided by pragmatic mechanisms: it need only be made salient in the context either by the speaker's intentions, or contextual cues, depending on one's account of salience. However, denotations of bound variables are odd, theoretically complex entities. It is difficult, if not impossible, to see how, on any account of salience, such an entity could be salient in a context. Certainly neither it, nor instances of it, could be perceptually present in the context. It is equally difficult to see how speaker intentions could determine reference to such an entity. (2000, 414)

But this seems an odd way of construing the proposal of the proponent of unarticulated constituents. Surely the view would be, roughly, that the character of an expression like "rains", which induces an unarticulated constituent has an argument place which elicits a value from context and which, in constructions such as (8), can also have its interpretation governed by an operator elsewhere in the sentence. On this view, there is no need for pragmatic mechanisms to supply the denotation of the bound variable. Those mechanisms supply only the context, which interacts with character where appropriate to yield content; the contributions of the bound variables in character to content are governed by the binding operator elsewhere in the sentence. It seems that Stanley is assuming here that pragmatically provided semantic values must come entirely and autonomously from context, and cannot be guided by binding from the content of the rest of the expression. In making this assumption, he is thereby assuming the truth of the NBP.

In short, Stanley tries to argue for the presence of a syntactic variable contributing directly to the content of utterances by the existence

41

of certain binding phenomena. Those phenomena simply necessitate the existence of a content-level variable in order to have something to bind:

> Operators in a sentence can only interact with variables in the sentence that lie within their scope. But, if the constituent is unarticulated, it is not the value of any variable in the sentence. Thus, its interpretation cannot be controlled by operators in the sentence. (Stanley 2000, 410–11)

> In cases such as [(8)], a variable in the location parameter is bound. But if the location parameter is a contextual parameter, as it is if the narrow indexical analysis is correct, then it is simply not accessible for binding, any more than the speaker coordinate is. (Stanley 2000, 418)

But unless the NBP is true, there is another place to put such bound variables: in the *character* of an expression, as variables not syntactically represented, but making a contribution to content via the influence of context.

III. An Alternative to the Autonomy Thesis

Having seen how the NBP lies behind two recent arguments in the philosophy of language, I now want to show how we can reject that principle, and the Autonomy Thesis with it. My claim is that Kaplan, in "Demonstratives," unnecessarily (and tacitly) connects two distinct semantic notions:[2]

---

2 I presuppose here a form of semantic innocence by supposing that whether an expression exhibits these two features is a simple feature of that expression, independent of the context of occurrence. One could envision systems which abandon that innocence – for example, Braun's (1994) approach to complex demonstratives can be read as involving an abandonment of innocence by allowing that, for example, the expression "dog with a blue collar" exhibits escape from content when it appears in the context of a complex demonstrative:

• It is a necessary truth that that dog with a blue collar is wearing a blue collar.

but not when it appears in the context of a regular quantified noun phrase:

• It is a necessary truth that every dog with a blue collar is wearing a blue collar.

Context Sensitivity: An expression is *context sensitive* if its contribution to content can be evaluated only relative to a context of use.

Autonomy From Content: An expression exhibits autonomy from content if its meaning is evaluated independently from the evaluation of content.

An indexical like 'I' displays both of these features. What 'I' contributes to content can be evaluated only relative to a context of use, and the meaning which allows 'I' to contribute a specific individual relative to a context is unaffected by content (e.g., by the modal modification induced by the content of modal operators elsewhere in the sentence).

But these two features need not come as a pair. We can have expressions which are context-sensitive, but do not exhibit escape from content, and we can have expressions which exhibit escape from content, but are not context-sensitive. While the formal system LD that Kaplan gives in "Demonstratives" is not actually incompatible with making this distinction, it is awkward to see the distinction clearly in his system. Thus I will give here a slightly modified formal semantics for a character-based language designed to separate sharply the issues of context sensitivity and escape from content.

III.i. The Formal System

We begin by defining the syntax for the new formal language. Syntactically, the language is quite similar to Kaplan's LD, with some changes for simplicity.[3] Thus we have the following lexicon:

---

thus allowing the second sentence, unlike the first, to have a reading on which it is true. I will not further pursue such non-innocent paths here.

3 Specifically, the type-distinction between locative and objectual terms has been dropped, as has the category of functors. The logical predicates 'exist' and 'located' have also been dropped, as has the 'dthat' operator (which, for reasons explained below, is superfluous in my system). A category of constants ("proper names") has been added, while the logical constants 'I' and 'here' have been dropped for reasons discussed below.

- Variables: $u, v, w, x, y, z, u_1, v_1, \ldots$
- Constants: $a, b, c, \ldots, t, a_1, b_1, \ldots$
- Predicates: $A^1_1, B^1_1, \ldots, Z^1_1, A^1_2, \ldots$
  $A^2_1, B^2_1, \ldots, Z^2_1, A^2_2, \ldots$
- Connectives: $\neg$, ,& $\lor$, $\to$, $\leftrightarrow$
- Quantifiers: $\forall, \exists$
- Definite Description Operator: the
- Identity: =
- Logical Modal Operators: , $\lozenge$
- Non-Logical Modal Operators: M1, M2, …
- Logical Tense Operators: F, P
- Non-Logical Tense Operators: T1, T2, …
- Grouping: (,)

Syntactic well-formedness is then defined in the usual way:

- If ν is a variable, then ν is a term.
- If κ is a constant, then κ is a term.
- If φ is a formula and ν is a variable, then 'the ν φ' is a term
- If Π is an n-ary predicate and $\tau 1, \ldots \tau n$ are terms, then '$\Pi \tau 1 \ldots \tau n$' is a formula.
- If $\tau 1, \tau 2$ are terms, then '$\tau 1 = \tau 2$' is a formula.
- If φ is a formula, then '$\neg \varphi$' is a formula.
- If φ, ψ are formulae, then '$(\varphi \& \psi),$' '$(\varphi \lor \psi),$' '$(\varphi \to \psi),$' and '$(\varphi \leftrightarrow \psi)$' are formulae.
- If φ is a formula and ν is a variable, then '$\forall \nu \varphi$' and '$\exists \nu \varphi$' are formulae.
- If φ is a formula and Ω is a (logical or non-logical) (modal or tense) operator, then '$\Omega \varphi$' is a formula.

Next the semantics of the formal language needs to be defined. As Braun (1995) observes, Kaplan in LD counter-intuitively takes the character of an expression to be fixed independent of the choice of structure:

> Where Γ is either a term or a formula, the Character of Γ is that function which assigns to each structure U, assignment f, and context c of U, $\{\Gamma\}_{cf}^U$ [that is, the content of Γ as interpreted in U and evaluated relative to c and f] (1995, 548)

thus giving all non-logical expressions (i.e., all expressions whose interpretation is structure-dependent) of the same semantic category the same character up to isomorphism. Since I want the character (or, better, the two independent aspects of what Kaplan calls character) of an expression to be one possible manifestation of the meaning of that expression, I will change the semantic scheme to make the assignment of (my analogues of) character structure-internal.

Following (albeit somewhat imperfectly) Kaplan, a structure will be defined as an ordered 5-tuple $\langle C, W, U, T, I \rangle$ where:

- C is the set of contexts
- W is the set of worlds
- U is the set of objects (the domain of quantification)
- T is the set (structured by a linear "before" ordering) of times
- I is the interpretation function for non-logical expressions.

Unlike Kaplan, I will think of a context as an unstructured particular (it can, if one likes, be equated with a token utterance). This will allow us to make explicit the descriptive meaning of context-sensitive expressions. Note that while Kaplan initially speaks of the character of 'I' as being in the form of a rule ("the speaker or writer") with internal conceptual articulation, when he comes to give the formal implementation of character, this conceptual articulation disappears in favour of a direct assignment of a function from contexts to one particular element of the n-tuple defining contexts. This suppression of the internal structure of character is, for my purposes, a bad thing, since I'm interested in the potential effects of binding operators on the semantic components of character.

It is in the interpretation function that my approach differs most radically from Kaplan's. In Kaplan's semantics, the interpretation function simply assigns intensions, in the form of functions from worlds to extensions, to predicates and functors. My semantics will assign to all non-logical expressions (i) a structured entity to be the meaning of that entity, and (ii) an evaluation-level matrix (to be explained below) for that meaning. The structured entity will be some complex of properties, objects, and logical operations.

True thoroughness would now require specifying another formal language for describing these structured entities, and giving a recursive theory correlating some structured entities with truth values. However, life is short and the details are long and dull, so I will rather sloppily use a mixture of object-language expressions and meta-language, set-theoretic expressions to represent the structured entities in question.[4] Thus, for example, the object-language expression:

(11) F(the x Rxx)

might be assigned the structured complex which contains the logical definite-description operator, the property of F-ness, and the relation of R-ness. Informally, we might represent this complex as:

$$\langle F, \langle \text{the } x \ Rxx \rangle \rangle$$

The process of evaluating an expression relative to a structure will involve transforming one structured entity into another structured entity in a graduated process of extensionalization, culminating in a truth value. Thus, at another stage of evaluation we might need to replace properties with their extensions, and associate with (11) the complex:

$$\langle \{1, 2, 3\}, 2 \rangle$$

which we would then, in the final evaluative stage, evaluate as True on the grounds that

$$2 \in \{1,2,3\}.$$

In addition to a structured complex, the structure assigns to each expression an evaluation-level matrix. The evaluation-level matrix for an expression contains two features: context-dependence (C) and

---

4   Each world w in the set W will then be associated with a standard extensional interpretation function I_w which should be thought of as specifying the distribution of properties in that world. To capture the necessity of identity, we require that for all constants κ and all worlds w_1 and w_2, we have:

$$I_{w1}(\kappa) = I_{w2}(\kappa)$$

autonomy from content (*A*). An expression can thus be marked as any of the following:

[+*C*, +*A*], [+*C*, –*A*], [–*C*, +*A*], [–*C*, –*A*]

Having defined the notion of a structure, it remains only to define the evaluation of an expression relative to a structure. This evaluation will take place relative to a world and a context, and involves the "extensionalization" of the various structured entities assigned to expressions. Roughly, we will:

- Replace the structured entity associated with each term with an object, or a function from worlds and/or times to objects, or a sequence of objects (where the term involves a quantified position), or a sequence of functions from worlds and/or times to objects.
- Replace the structured entity associated with each predicate with a set, or a function from worlds and/or times to sets.
- Replace the structured entity associated with each non-logical, intensional operator with a function from (modal or temporal) intensions to truth values.

However, the way in which this replacement is performed for a particular expression α depends on the evaluation-level matrix assigned to α. Thus:

- If α is assigned the feature +*C*, then among the objects that can appear in the structured entity associated with α is the context *c*, aspects of which (its speaker, its time, its location) can then be descriptively isolated and used in constructing the extension of α.
- If α is assigned the feature –*C*, then the context *c* cannot appear as a component of the structured entity assigned to α.
- If α is assigned the feature +*A*, then the extensionalization of α cannot be influenced by the structured entities assigned to other terms with the feature –*A*. In particular:

(i) Variables in α can be bound only by quantifiers with the feature +*A*.

    (ii)   Predicates in α can be influenced only my modal and temporal operators with the feature +*A*.

If α is assigned the feature −*A*, then the extensionalization of α can be influenced by the meanings of any other expressions in the syntactic environment.

III.ii. Some Examples

Consider a few simple examples to see how this formalism works out in practice. Take the sentence:

    (12)   I meet Ernie.

which we represent in the formal language as:

    (12′)   *Mie*

Suppose that our structure assigns meanings as follows:

    i: 'the *x Scx*', [+C, +*A*]
    M: '*Mxy*', [−C, −*A*]
    e: Ernie [−C, −*A*]

and that we are evaluating (12) relative to a world w in which M is assigned to the set {⟨Josh, Ernie⟩ and S is assigned to the set {⟨*c*, Josh⟩}. (Here M is to be thought of as assigned the meeting relation, and S the relation which holds between a context and the speaker in that context.) Prior to any evaluation, we then have the following structured entity:

    ⟨*Mxy*, ⟨the *x*: *Scx*, Ernie⟩⟩

The expression 'i', with its feature matrix [+C, +*A*], is evaluated without the influence of the rest of the sentence. Evaluation relative to our world w and a context c will then take 'the *x*: *Scx*' to Josh, leaving us with the following structured entity after the first evaluative pass:

    ⟨*Mxy*, ⟨Josh, Ernie⟩⟩

Both 'M' and 'e' have the feature matrix [$-C$, $-A$] and thus can potentially be influenced by the rest of the sentence, but in this example there is no prompt for such influence. Thus evaluation will take 'Mxy' to {<Josh, Ernie>} and 'e' to Ernie, giving us the following structured entity:

$$\langle \{\langle \text{Josh, Ernie}\rangle\}, \langle \text{Josh,Ernie}\rangle\rangle$$

A simple compositional procedure, here shoved into the background, will then map this structured entity to the truth value True.

Next consider:

(13)   Necessarily, I meet Ernie.

which we represent in the formal language as:

(13′)   Mie

Suppose that our structure assigns meanings as above, but that our structure provides two worlds:

$w1$:

(a) M: {⟨Josh, Ernie⟩}
(b) S: {⟨c, Josh⟩}

$w2$:

(a) M: {⟨Herman, Ernie⟩}
(b) S: {⟨c, Herman⟩}

Suppose that we are evaluating (13) with respect to world $w1$ and context c. Evaluation of the [$+C$, $+A$] term 'i' proceeds independently of the necessity operator elsewhere in the sentence, so we simply find the unique object which bears S to c at $w1$, which is Josh. Thus we have:

$$\langle \text{NECESSITY}, \langle Mxy, \langle \text{Josh, Ernie}\rangle\rangle\rangle$$

We then evaluate 'M' and 'e,' which are both [$-C$, $-A$]. 'e' has no predicative meaning, so is unaffected by the modal operator and is simply assigned the value *Ernie*. 'M,' on the other hand, does have predicative meaning, and since that meaning is flagged $-A$, it interacts with the modal operator to yield:

⟨NECESSITY, ⟨{⟨$w1$, ⟨Josh, Ernie⟩⟩, ⟨$w2$, ⟨Herman, Ernie⟩⟩}, ⟨Josh, Ernie⟩⟩

This complex is then assigned False, because ⟨Josh, Ernie⟩ does not fall in the extension of M at each world given by the structure.

(13) thus behaves exactly as we would expect – 'I', despite its descriptive meaning, continues to pick out the same object even when appearing within the scope of the modal operator. However, if we consider the same sentence but change the feature matrix for 'I' from $[+C, +A]$ to $[+C, -A]$, then its interpretation will be influenced by the modal operator, and we will end up with:

⟨NECESSITY, ⟨{⟨$w1$, ⟨Josh, Ernie⟩⟩, ⟨$w2$, ⟨Herman, Ernie⟩⟩}, ⟨{⟨$w1$, Josh⟩, ⟨$w2$, Herman⟩}, Ernie⟩⟩

which will yield True. 'I' with a feature matrix of $[+C, -A]$ is thus a ductile context-dependent term, acting much like the definite description "the speaker."

Finally, consider a case in which an expression has descriptive meaning with a free variable. Thus recall the earlier proposed indexical 'schmi' meaning *the man between me and x*, and consider:

(2)   Every philosopher admires schmi.

which we represent formally as:

(2') $\forall x (Px \rightarrow Axs)$

Suppose our structure assigns meanings as follows:

P: 'Px', $[-C, -A]$
A: 'Axy', $[-C, -A]$
s: 'the y $B(y,$ the z: Scz, $x)$', $[+C, -A]$

and that we are evaluating (2') relative to context c and a world w assigning extensions as follows:

P: {Herman, Ernie}
S: {$\langle c$, Josh$\rangle$}
B: {$\langle$Saul, Josh, Ernie$\rangle$, $\langle$David, Josh, Herman$\rangle$}
A: {$\langle$Ernie, Saul$>$, $\langle$Herman, David$\rangle$}

Prior to evaluation, we start with the following complex built out of the meanings of the terms:

$$\langle \text{EVERY}x, \langle \text{IF}, \langle\langle Px, \langle Axy, \langle \text{the } y \ B(y, \text{the } z \ Scz, x)\rangle\rangle\rangle\rangle\rangle\rangle$$

Evaluation of the two $[-C, -A]$ predicates P and A simply takes them to their extensions, yielding:

$$\langle \text{EVERY}x, \langle \text{IF}, \langle\langle\{\text{Herman, Ernie}\}, x>, \langle\langle\langle\text{Ernie, Saul}>, \langle\text{Herman, David}>\}, \langle x, \langle \text{the } y \ B(y, \text{the } z \ Scz, x)\rangle\rangle\rangle\rangle\rangle\rangle$$

Evaluation of the $[+C, -A]$ term 's' allows the influence both of context and of the universal quantifier at the beginning of the sentence, to yield a sequence of functions mapping a choice of x to the person who (in w) bears the B relation to the pair of x and the person who bears the S relation to the context c. Thus, we end up with a claim equivalent to the following:

$$\forall x \in \{\text{Herman, Ernie}\} \ \langle x, f(x) \rangle \in \{\langle\text{Ernie, Saul}\rangle, \langle\text{Herman, David}\rangle\}$$

where $f(x)$ is defined as:

$$\{\langle\text{Ernie, Saul}\rangle, \langle\text{Herman, David}\rangle\}$$

The upshot, then, is that the referent of 'schmi' is sensitive both to the context of utterance and to the choice of object picked out by the universal quantifier.

If, on the other hand, we had assigned 'schmi' the matrix $[+C, +A]$, then its free variable position would have been unavailable for binding by the universal quantifier and would have remained free. How, then, are we to understand a sentence such as (2), where 'schmi' is tagged $+A$? As a rough suggestion, suppose that any variables which are free after final semantic evaluation of a sentence inherit a reference to the context, or to some aspect of the context. This hypothesis would explain why the removal of the initial quantifier from:

(14)   Every philosopher is such that he admires logicians.

yields the context-sensitive:

(15)   He admires logicians.

The term 'he', absent a binding quantifier, remains a free variable through every level of semantic evaluation, and thus finally inherits a referent from context.

Terms which have the evaluation matrix [+C, −A] have a certain similarity to Kaplan's 'dthat' terms. Kaplan allows 'dthat' to bind any term to form a new term that inherits its world and time of evaluation from the context. Kaplan never considers any cases in which 'dthat' is applied to a term containing a free variable, such as:

dthat(the x Rxy)

but his formal language certainly generates such expressions, which would then be semantically influenced by quantifiers binding the locally free variable. However, there are two important differences between 'dthat' terms and [+C, −A] terms.

(i)   A term which is [+C, −A] engages, despite its context-sensitivity, quite generally in semantic interaction with its surrounding operators. Thus, not only can that term have component free variables bound by quantifiers elsewhere in the sentence, it can also have component predicates modally or temporally influenced by operators elsewhere in the sentence. 'dthat' terms, on the other hand, are unaffected in their evaluation by modal and temporal operators, and thus enjoy a partial autonomy (giving them a mixed status which is oddly unmotivated, in my opinion).

(ii)   Furthermore, the type of modal and temporal insensitivity enjoyed by 'dthat' terms is different from that enjoyed by +A-terms in my system. +A terms have their predicates evaluated at whatever world and time the sentence is evaluated with respect to, and then provide the appropriate extension oblivious to modal and temporal operators elsewhere in the sentence. 'dthat' terms, on the other hand, have content assigned to them by evaluation at the actual world and present time (as provided by the context). The semantic escape of 'dthat' terms, then, is more analogous to that induced by the addition of "actually" and "presently" operators than that induced by autonomous semantic evaluation.[5]

---

5 There is a complex issue here regarding the comparative counterfactual truth conditions of sentences involving dthat-terms and sentences involving +A-terms. Thus compare the following:

(FN 1)   Dthat(the speaker) is a philosopher.

(FN 2)   (The speaker)$_{+A}$ is a philosopher.

Suppose that I am actually the speaker of both of these utterances, and that we want to know whether each of these claims are true relative to a world w in which George W. Bush is the speaker of the utterances. In the case of the first sentence, involving 'dthat,' the answer is unambiguously yes, since 'dthat(the speaker)' picks out the speaker in the actual world, or me. On the other hand, (the speaker)+A, when evaluated at world w, picks out George W. Bush, and thus yields a false claim. This appears to be a bad result, but I think it really points out the need to distinguish between two notions:

• The evaluation of a content with respect to a possible world.

• The evaluation of a character (more broadly, the meaning of a sentence) with respect to a possible world.

The content of both of the above claims is the same, because by the time content has been reached, both dthat-terms and +A-terms have been assigned their reference. Thus the counterfactual truth conditions of the contents of the two claims are identical. However, the counterfactual evaluations of the characters of the two claims differ, so when character is evaluated with respect to w, different contents result, each of which has its own set of truth conditions and counterfactual truth conditions.

III.iii. Monsters and Victims

In "Demonstratives," Kaplan considers and rejects the possibility of what he calls "monsters" – operators that "attempt to operate on context" (1977, 510), as in:

(16)   In some contexts it is true that I am not tired now.

in which the operator 'in some contexts' attempts (and fails) to bind the context-sensitive elements 'I' and 'now'. Am I just proposing introducing monsters to the semantics, and do Kaplan's arguments against monsters then show that my proposal as well should be rejected? The answer to both questions is, I think, "No."

My proposal differs crucially from Kaplan's rejected monsters in that I am not suggesting that there is a special class of operators that have the ability to bind the contribution of context (i.e., to bind into character). Rather, I am suggesting that there is a special class of expressions that have the special feature that their character-level semantic values are capable of being bound (or, more broadly, semantically impacted) by operators (generically speaking, without requiring any special feature on the part of the operator). If Kaplan's rejected context-binding operators are monsters, devouring all in their path, my expressions bindable-in-character are the most hapless of victims, easily falling prey to even the most humble of binding operators.

Semantic binding is a binary relation which holds between an operator and a target of that operator; accounting for unusual cases of binding can thus be done either by attributing special features to the operator (as in Kaplan's monsters) or by attributing special features to the target expression (as in my [+C, −A] expressions). I am thus free to agree with Kaplan that (16) does not have a context-shifting interpretation. On the flip side, my view commits me to the claim that when a context-sensitive expression is able to be affected by a particular operator, it is (potentially) affected by all operators. Kaplan's rejected monsters would not have that consequence – the fact that a context-sensitive expression was bindable by a monster would not entail that it was bindable by any non-monstrous operators.

The two strategies are not equivalent. Positing monsters commits one to the view that all context-sensitive expressions will be bound by monsters. As Kaplan observes, this result is problematic, since indexicals like 'I' seem unavoidably to pick out the speaker in the actual context, and hence seem immune to influence by putative monsters. Positing [+C, −A] expressions, on the other hand, does not commit one to the view that there are any operators that affect all context-sensitive terms. It is perfectly compatible with my view that there are some indexical expressions (perhaps including 'I') which are [+C, +A] and hence which are unaffected in their evaluation by other operators. Kaplan says of monsters:

> I am not saying we could not construct a language with such operators, just that English is not one. And such operators *could not be added to it.* (1977, 510)

He thus adopts an intermediary position between one which says that monsters are simply a logical impossibility and one which says that it's merely an accidental feature of English that it contains no monsters. While the nature of this intermediary is not fully explicit in Kaplan, I take it that the view is that it's a robust, empirical generalization about English that the class of context-sensitive terms and the class of operator-insensitive terms coincide, and hence that the most explanatorily adequate logic for English is one which builds it in that these two features come together (in Kaplan's case, by placing context sensitivity in character, and placing character outside the range of operators). Kaplan's analysis of character, and his concomitant rejection of monsters, is thus based on the following empirical thesis:

> (K) In natural languages, context-sensitive terms cannot be bound by operators.

Given this perspective on Kaplan's project, the following challenge to my separation of the features *A* and *C* arises:

> Surely it's no surprise that such a separation is possible, just as monsters are possible. The question is whether it's profitable – whether there's any point in having a logic for natural languages that allows the possibility of a separation that, as an empirical matter, never occurs.

This challenge is, I think, a fair one, but I think it is also one which can be met. In the next section, I will suggest that abandoning the AT, and with it the NBP, allows us to see that both complex demonstratives and unarticulated constituents are arguably context-sensitive expressions which are bindable by operators, and which hence falsify thesis K. But one needn't go so far afield to find compelling examples. In fact, Kaplan gives a suitable example early in "Demonstratives":

> (17)   For what is a man profited, if he shall gain the whole world, and lose his own soul? (1977, 490)

Kaplan claims that 'he' in this sentence is "used not as [a] demonstrative but as [a] bound variable" (1977, 489), but this assertion begs the question. It's true, of course, that the semantic contribution of 'he' in this sentence derives not from context but rather from the binding operator 'a man', but if binding into character does occur,[6] it's an unavoidable consequence of such binding that the bound expression will no longer be context-sensitive, since its innate context-sensitivity has, via binding, become operator-sensitivity. To say that 'he' in (17) does not count as a demonstrative (and hence not as a context-sensitive term) is simply to assume in advance that there can be no binding of character.

Dropping that *a priori* assumption, we can hold that 'he' is a generically context-sensitive expression, perhaps with character:

the x (male x and salient-in-c x)

In constructions like (17), the context-variable c is bound by an earlier operator associated with 'a man'[7], and 'he' thus inherits its meaning

---

6   Where the operator in question binds the context-variable in the character of the context-sensitive expression.

7   I'm supposing something like an event-analysis here, in which each verb phrase is associated with an event quantifier, which can then serve to bind context-variables in characters of expressions. The net effect is as if the noun phrase associated with the verb phrase providing the event quantifier were directly binding the indexical 'he' *tout court*.

from the lexical context, rather than from the utterance context. The bindability of 'he' is thus direct evidence that K is not correct, and that a correlation between context-sensitivity and autonomy-from-binding should not be built into the semantics. We see a similar phenomenon with the context-sensitive 'that', which can also act as a bound variable, as in:

(18)   Every time a philosopher gets into an argument with a linguist, that philosopher ends up wishing he hadn't.

I would suggest that Kaplan fails to see these counterexamples to K because he is thinking of exceptions to K in terms of monsters – putting the capacity to violate K in the operator rather than in the indexical. It's true that trying to bind 'he' by an explicit shift in context seems ineffective; consider:

(19)   In every context, he is the tallest man around.

in which 'he' acts demonstratively, picking out some salient individual in the current context. But this, on my view, is because 'he' doesn't require some special monstrous operator to be bound – it is bound by ordinary operators like 'a man'.[8] Similar effects can be achieved with 'we':

(20)   Every time I talk to some linguists, we disagree about everything.

and with 'you':

(21)   Every time I teach this class, fewer and fewer of you get a passing grade.

and with 'yesterday':

---

8   Or, as in footnote 6 above, by an event quantifier associated with 'a man'.

(23)   Hammer was worried. Just yesterday, the client had entered his office, a smoking gun in his hand.[9]

It's true that some indexicals seem highly resistant to binding. 'I' persists in picking out the actual speaker, no matter what operators it is placed within.[10] 'Here' and 'now' are similarly persistent. But this is to be expected, on my view, since the abandonment of AT, coupled with the explicit tagging of expressions as $+A$ or $-A$, allows us to treat different indexicals differently. If 'I' and 'here' and 'now' are in fact incapable of being bound, this simply shows that they are $+A$, but does nothing to undermine the evidence against K and hence the case for abandoning AT as a generic principle governing indexicals.

IV. Context Sensitivity Without Escape From Content: Re-evaluating the Dever and Stanley Arguments

Having replaced Kaplan's character–content with the more versatile, two-dimensional $+/-C$ and $+/-A$ distinction, we can now return to the two arguments which I earlier suggested presupposed the NBP, and re-evaluate their prospects in a semantic framework which lacks the constraint of the NBP.

Consider first the case of complex demonstratives. Suppose we adopt the following general semantic rule:

'that φ' is interpreted as 'the x: $\varphi(x)$ and x is salient in c' (where c is the context of utterance), and given the evaluation matrix $[+C, -A]$

---

9   Note that 'yesterday' here is controlled by the past tense operator, and picks out the day before Hammer's worrying, not the day before the telling of the story. This holds true even if one prefaces the story with an explicit present-tense introduction. 'Let me tell you about what happened to Hammer....'

10   Although there is a worry about cases like Nunberg's:

(FN 3)   You should be more careful. I might have been a thief.

in which 'I' is arguably controlled by the epistemic modality 'I'. Complex issues about the behaviour of referential expressions in propositional attitude contexts come into play here, though, making the issue hard to evaluate clearly.

Because a complex demonstrative is tagged as +C, it can continue to exhibit a sensitivity to context (even without overt reference to context in the complex demonstrative). However, since it is also tagged –A, it can interact semantically with its lexical environment, thus allowing the possibility of binding into such a demonstrative. The hope is that the difficulties that the Braun–Borg account had with the Binding Principle can thus be avoided.

The full prospect of this modification of the character-based approach to complex demonstratives depends on how some of the details of the move to the two-dimensional A/C system are implemented. As I've set up the semantics above, there are two immediate problems with the proposal:

> (i) While complex demonstratives, interpreted as bearing descriptive meaning tagged [+C, –A], no longer prove completely inaccessible to binding (as they did on the character-based account), they are now instead *too* accessible. As the Binding Principle notes, binding in to a complex demonstrative is semantically accessible only when the binding acts in the typical cross-clausal manner, allowing an undistributed reading on which the interpretation of the anaphoric term is settled entirely by the restricting descriptive material in the binding quantified noun phrase, and not by the particular determiner used. However, once the descriptive material of a complex demonstrative is tagged –A, it enters into binding relations in the normal way. This would then entail the acceptability of constructions like:

> (4) *Every boy$_i$ read this book he$_i$ liked.

> and the impossibility of an undistributed reading in:

> (5) Several eyewitnesses$_i$ described that assailant they$_i$ saw.

However, there is still room to maneuver, here – perhaps a case can be made for suggesting that when a term is tagged [+C, –A], its relation to operators in the lexical environment is like that of anaphoric terms to binders not *c*-commanding them.

(ii) Once an expression is tagged as –*A*, to allow it to enter into binding relations with quantifiers elsewhere in the sentence, it also becomes susceptible to the intensional influence of modal operators elsewhere in the environment. Complex demonstratives, construed as –*A* expressions, would thus provide an example of modally ductile, directly referential terms. They would still make a non-predicative contribution to content – now a function from worlds to objects – and hence be unaltered in their semantic behaviour when considering the counterfactual truth conditions of content, but what specific object they picked out would depend on the particular influence of any modal operators in the lexical environment.

However, we expect complex demonstratives to be immune to such influence; thus, the absence of a trivially true reading of:

(24) Necessarily, that dog with a blue collar is wearing a blue collar.

Again, there are prospects still open for the modified character-based analysis of complex demonstratives. Perhaps it could be suggested that autonomy from quantifiers and autonomy from intensional operators are two separate issues, and that the two-dimensional evaluative matrix currently proposed needs to be expanded to a three-dimensional one.

I have grouped quantificational and intensional semantic influence together on the broad assumption that the two have some deep similarity in their mode of semantic operation, but that assumption is little more than speculation, at this point. Alternatively, if the suggestion of (i) is followed, and [+*C*, –*A*] terms are seen as analogous to donkey pronouns in their binding relations to the environmental context, we could argue for the appropriate intensional escape on the grounds that intensional operators do not extend beyond their local domain in semantic impact.

There are a number of subtle issues involved here, and I certainly don't think the matter is settled one way or another. All I want to claim here is that my earlier conclusion, that the transfer of descriptive content to character invalidated a certain theory of complex demonstratives by blocking appropriate binding, was too quick, by relying uncritically on the NBP. Abandoning the NBP puts character-based accounts of complex demonstratives back on the table, and then opens up a debate about whether or not the details of binding into character can be motivated in a way that properly meshes with the empirical data concerning complex demonstratives.

Turning next to Stanley's argument against unarticulated constituents, suppose we give the following semantic rule for 'rains':

> 'rains' is interpreted as 'rains(the $x(x$ is the time of $c)$, the $y(y$ is the location of $c)$' (where c is the context of utterance) and assigned the evaluation matrix $[+C, -A]$

In a sentence like:

> It's raining.

we start with the structural entity:

> $\langle$RAINS, $\langle$the $x(x$ is the time of $c)$, the $y(y$ is the location of $c)\rangle\rangle$

which after contextual evaluation yields:

> $\langle$RAINS, $\langle t, l\rangle\rangle$

where t and l are the time and location, respectively, of the context.

To handle Stanley's example:

> (8) Every time John lights a cigarette, it rains.

we invoke the earlier thought that context-indicators can be thought of as variables which, when free, referred to context or aspects of context. Suppose we think of the context indicator c above as such a variable. When c is unbound, it picks out context; however, we can also bind c, since 'rains' is tagged $-A$. If we take 'every time John lights a cigarette' to introduce a quantification over events (cigarette-lightings by John), we get a structured entity corresponding to:

$\forall e(e$ is a cigarette lighting by John $\rightarrow$ Rains(the $x(x$ is the time of $e)$, the $y(y$ is the location of $e))$

This structured entity then yields exactly the truth conditions that Stanley suggests for (8):

(8') Every time John lights a cigarette, it rains where John lights the cigarette.

If, on the other hand, we assign the component 'the $y(y$ is the location of $c)$' of the meaning of 'rains' the evaluation matrix $[+C, +A]$, then that particular occurrence of c will be inaccessible for binding and will refer to context. This gives an alternative reading to (8):

(8'') Every time John lights a cigarette, it rains here.

(8'') is, to my ears, a permissible reading of (8).

Depending on the flexibility of the semantic rule associated with 'rains', we may be able to get even more readings of (8). Suppose we use the following rule:

'rains' is interpreted as 'rains(the $x(x$ is a time R-related to $c)$, the $y(y$ is a location S-related of $c)$' (where c is the context of utterance) and assigned the evaluation matrix $[+C, -A]$

and allow contextual factors to supply the particular relations R and S. Then we can get readings in which, while the time and place of the raining vary with the cigarette-lighting, they are not simply identical to the location of that lighting. Thus consider the following cases:

(25) There's some sort of strange connection between John's smoking and the city he's thinking about as he smokes. I've been in many of those cities while he was smoking, and I've noticed something. Every time John lights a cigarette, it rains.

(26) John's usual strange ability to cause rain seems to be running behind schedule. Every time John lights a cigarette, it rains – but it often takes a day or two for the rain to begin.

In the first case, the correct reading is achieved by supplying for S the relation 'is the location of the city John is thinking about during c'. In the second case, the correct reading is achieved by supplying for R the relation 'is a day or two after c'. These readings are admittedly not the most robust imaginable, but if they are available, it is unclear to me whether Stanley can provide a satisfactory analysis of them.

As with the case of complex demonstratives, I don't want to claim that the introduction of the two-dimensional A/C distinction settles the issue. Stanley's cases are, in my opinion, handled quite smoothly by placing unarticulated constituents into the setting of the type of modified-character account I have given. However, the demands that Stanley's cases place on the account are, in important cases, inconsistent with the demands that a modified-character account of complex demonstratives places. Thus, note the following:

(i) The $-A$ expressions in cases of unarticulated constituents, unlike in the case of complex demonstratives, are sensitive to modal operators elsewhere in the linguistic environment. In:

(27)   Necessarily, every time John lights a cigarette it rains.

it is required that, in each world w, it rains every time John lights a cigarette in that world, and at the place where the lighting occurs in that world. Thus, the descriptive content of the unarticulated location specifier, as built into the character with a $-A$ tag, must be sensitive to the initial 'necessarily' operator.

(ii) The $-A$ expressions in cases of unarticulated constituents, unlike in the case of complex demonstratives, require quantificational binding of the intra-clausal, rather than the cross-clausal, type. Thus contrast the following:

(28)   Most times John lights a cigarette, it rains.
(29)   Most days, John lights a cigarette around noon. It rains shortly thereafter.

(29) has an undistributed reading on which it rains shortly after every cigarette lighting by John, not just the ones around noon. On this

reading, the anaphoric behaviour of the event variables in the meaning of 'rains', cross-clausally bound by the previous sentence, are indifferent to the choice of determiner governing 'days'. (20), however, has no such undistributed reading. There is no way of hearing (20) as *requiring* that it rain every time (and every place) that John lights a cigarette.

There remain, then, substantial open questions about what sort of two-dimensional *A*/*C*-type account of character can handle the optimal range of cases. But by acknowledging that context-sensitivity does not entail autonomy – by, that is, acknowledging [+C, –A] terms – the particular argumentative routes that Stanley and I used in our respective papers are, it seems to me, closed off.

V. Escape From Content Without Context-Sensitivity: Kripke's Modal Argument

The previous section centered around the applications of expressions which were tagged [+C, –A] – which retained context-sensitivity while abandoning autonomy of evaluation. The other "mixed category" made available by my rejection of the implicit Autonomy Thesis in the theory of character is that of terms tagged [–C, +A] – terms which are not context-sensitive, but which do have autonomy of evaluation. In this final section, I want to show how such terms can be used to resist Kripke's modal argument against descriptive theories of names.

V.i. The Modal Argument

In *Naming and Necessity*, Kripke deploys several arguments against what he calls the Frege–Russell theory of names, on which names are synonymous with some definite description, or some weighted cluster of definite descriptions. Prominent among these is the modal argument:[11]

---

11 Kripke's discussion, in the 1980 preface to *Naming and Necessity* (3–5), of the genesis of his ideas strongly suggests that the modal argument was the consideration that initially led him down the path that ended in *Naming and Necessity*. Certainly, as an autobiographical matter, the modal argument was the one which struck me most forcefully when I first read Kripke. However, a

Suppose the reference of a name is given by a description or a cluster of descriptions. If the name *means the same* as that description or cluster of descriptions, it will not be a rigid designator. It will not necessarily designate the same object in all possible worlds, since other objects might have had the given properties in other possible worlds, unless (of course) we happened to use essential properties in our description. So suppose we say, 'Aristotle is the greatest man who studied with Plato.' If we used that as a *definition*, the name 'Aristotle' is to mean 'the greatest man who studied with Plato.' Then of course in some other possible world that man might not have studied with Plato and some other man would have been Aristotle. (Kripke 1980, 57)

One way of putting the modal argument is this. Suppose that 'Aristotle' is synonymous with 'the greatest man who studied with Plato'. Then these two expressions can be intersubstituted *salva significatione*, and certainly *salva veritate*. But consider the pair:

(30) Aristotle might not have studied with Plato.
(31) The greatest man who studied with Plato might not have studied with Plato.

The first of these, one is tempted to say, is true, while the second is false. Thus, by *modus tollens*, the synonymy claim bruited above is incorrect. But analogous cases can be constructed for any description of Aristotle that does not specify an essence of him (and, tacitly, specifying an essence for Aristotle is difficult-to-impossible), so the descriptive theory is to be rejected.

---

rejection of the modal argument does not entail the defeat of Kripke's rejection of the Frege–Russell theory of names. Even in the absence of the modal argument, I find that the epistemological argument (that based on the possibility of referential continuity in the face of misdescription) is decisive against descriptive theories of names.

V.ii. Wide-Scope Response to the Modal Argument

However, this way of putting the argument is too fast (Kripke himself is more careful). The obvious counter-move at this point is to observe that (31) is not so obviously false as one might think. There is an available reading of (31) on which it says something true – and plausibly the same true thing that (30) says, namely, that some particular person (Aristotle, the greatest man who studied with Plato) is such that he might not have studied with Plato. We can make this reading explicit by appealing to Russell's Theory of Descriptions and its concomitant tool of scope distinctions. (31) thus yields two distinct readings:

(31a) $\Diamond$[the *x*: greatest-man-who-studied-with-Plato *x*] ¬studied-with-Plato *x*

(31b) [the *x*: greatest-man-who-studied-with-Plato *x*] $\Diamond$¬studied-with-Plato *x*

Reading (31b) is true, since the relevant object (Aristotle) is first found as the unique object satisfying *in the actual world* the description 'greatest man who studied with Plato', and then is, after being picked out, considered *in himself* (not under a description) in other possible situations.

These considerations lead Dummett (1973), in perhaps the most famous response to the modal argument, to suggest that names are indeed descriptive, but that the distinctions of scope allow an adequate response to Kripke's argument. Dummett argues that while (31b) captures the most natural sense of (31), (31a) captures another possible reading of (31), one which is most readily brought out in examples such as:

(32) St. Anne might not have been the mother of Mary.

which, says Dummett, has a false reading. Dummett then holds that Kripke implausibly posits distinct mechanisms for the ambiguities in the two cases – scope ambiguities in the case of definite descriptions, an ambiguity between alethic and epistemic modalities in the case of names – and that instead he should acknowledge that the both the phenomena and the mechanism are the same for both names and definite descriptions, and hence that the modal argument gains no ground against the Frege–Russell theory of names. Alternatively, for those (like me) who find Dummett's rejection of the distinction between alethic and epistemic readings of the modality unacceptable, it could be posited that the descriptive meaning of a name takes, by convention, wide scope in any sentence.

Kripke responds to Dummett's scope argument in the 1980 preface to *Naming and Necessity* by raising[12] the issue of the comparative behaviour of names and definite descriptions in simple sentences. Thus, compare:

(33)   Aristotle was fond of dogs.
(34)   The last great philosopher of antiquity was fond of dogs.

As Kripke points out, while (33) and (34) have the same truth value in the actual world, they have differing counterfactual truth conditions. What is said by (33) is true with respect to a world in which:

Aristotle is fond of dogs.
The last great philosopher of antiquity is Parmenides
Parmenides is not fond of dogs.

However, what is said by (34) is false with respect to that same world, since (34) would require Parmenides, rather than Aristotle, to be fond of dogs in that world. The difference between (33) and (34), suggests Kripke, cannot be accounted for by appealing to any sort of wide scope reading for the definite description, because – since (33) is a simple sentence – there is no modal operator for the definite description to take wide scope over. (34) has only one reading, and it is the wrong reading for matching (33).

---

12 Re-raising, really. A close reading of the passage given above in which the modal argument is stated in the text shows that Kripke was characterizing the issue in terms of counterfactual truth conditions of simple sentences from the beginning.

V.iii. Refinements of the Wide Scope Response

Attempts to salvage the wide-scope defense of the Frege–Russell theory of names can now take the direction of searching for some larger context containing a modal operator over which the descriptive content of the name can take wide scope.[13] I will sketch two such positions here: that of Dummett and that of Sosa.

Dummett, in *The Interpretation of Frege's Philosophy* (1981), responds to Kripke's critique of his earlier argument as follows:

(P1) The counterfactual truth conditions of a sentence are part of the *grade two* or *ingredient* sense (specifying how it is to be understood when imbedded in larger sentential contexts) and not a part of the *grade one* or *content* sense of that sentence.

(C1) Thus, if 'Aristotle' and 'the last great philosopher of antiquity' differ in meaning, they differ only in their ingredient sense.

(P2) If a speaker associates different senses with different expressions, he must be able to manifest his possession of those different senses.

(P3) Manifestation of possession of a particular ingredient sense is possible only through judgment of modal statements and counterfactual conditionals.

(C2) Thus, if 'Aristotle' and 'the last great philosopher of antiquity' differ in meaning, speakers must judge differentially modal statements and counterfactual conditionals involving those two expressions.

(P4) Any apparent differences between speakers' judgments of modal statements and counterfactual conditionals involving 'Aristotle' and 'the last great philosopher of antiquity' can be accounted for by appeal to scope ambiguities

---

13 In response to Kripke's simple-sentence argument, some have also been tempted to hold that the rigidity of descriptive names is to be achieved by the rigidification of the descriptive content by way of an actuality operator, rather than by scope effects. I find that such approaches go wrong by inappropriately building the notion of actuality into the content of names (a criticism worked out in detail in Soames, 1998), and will not further consider them here.

involving the descriptive content of the names and the
modal operators in the judgment.

(C3) 'Aristotle' and 'the last great philosopher of antiquity' do
not differ in meaning.

By insisting that a grasp of counterfactual truth conditions is inelim-
inably connected to a grasp of the simple truth conditions of modal
statements, Dummett forces a new modal operator onto the scene,
over which descriptive content can take wide scope to ensure rigidity.
Thus, Kripke's argument from simple sentences is defused.

Sosa (2001) uses a broadly similar strategy for escaping Kripke's
anti-scopal argument. Sosa argues that any scope ambiguity that
exists in the material mode statement:

> Had it been the case that *S*, the last great philosopher of antiq-
> uity would have been fond of dogs.

persist in the corresponding formal mode statement:

> The sentence 'The last great philosopher of antiquity is fond of
> dogs' is true with respect to the counterfactual situation *that S*.

on, broadly, the grounds that the material and formal mode should
give two ways of saying the same thing. Kripke suggests that that
when we shift from consideration of the actual truth-conditions of the
explicitly modalized statement:

(35) Aristotle/the last great philosopher of antiquity might
have been fond of dogs.

to consideration of the counterfactual truth conditions of the simple
sentence:

(36) Aristotle/the last great philosopher of antiquity is fond of
dogs.

we remove the possibility of a scope ambiguity. Sosa, in effect, suggests that Kripke is focusing too narrowly on the sentence in question.

Were he to consider the general semantic context of the rules for determining counterfactual truth conditions, he would find that these rules contain a mention of the simple sentence imbedded in the scope of a modal operator:

> (37) With respect to counterfactual situation S, 'Aristotle/the last great philosopher of antiquity is fond of dogs' is true.

Should we allow any definite descriptions in the simple sentence to broaden their scope all the way out of their original sentence, across the quotation marks, and out through the rule for ascription of counterfactual truth conditions, we would regain the wide-scope reading and thereby the desired rigidity of proper names, even when descriptively understood.

The underlying thought in both the Dummett and the Sosa strategy is nicely summarized in a comment by David Lewis that Sosa quotes:

> If a description is eager enough for wide scope, its scope may cross sentence boundaries and also boundaries of quotation and disquotation. You think – and I agree – that it's fair to treat the following alike; and in each case to say that 'Aristotle' may take wide enough scope to cover all the rest.
>
> (a) With respect to [counterfactual situation] S, Aristotle was fond of dogs.
> (b) This is the case with respect to S: Aristotle was fond of dogs.
> (c) Consider the simple sentence 'Aristotle was fond of dogs.' That sentence is true with respect to S.
>
> ... wide-scopers [have been accused] of solving the problem of (a) while ignoring (c). Our reply is that (c) functions as a mere stylistic variant of (a). (2001, n. 7)

However, I find myself wary of both the Dummett and the Sosa strategy. In both cases, the methods of introducing the broader modal context strike me as suspect. Dummett's premises (P2) and (P3) above both seem to me to derive from a broadly verificationist approach to meaning, and both, I would suggest, are incorrect – grasp of a sense does not require the capacity to manifest that grasp, and furthermore manifestation of an ingredient sense can be achieved otherwise than through judgement of complex sentences. Sosa's approach requires that quantifiers be able to cross quotational boundaries,[14] a suggestion

---

14 Strictly speaking, what Sosa needs is for sentences of the form:

(FN 4)   'The F is G' is true with respect to S if and only if with respect to S, the F is G.

to be true on both disambiguations of the scope of the used description 'the F':

(FN 5)   'The F is G' is true with respect to S if and only if [the x: Fx] (with respect to S, Gx).

(FN 6)   'The F is G' is true with respect to S if and only if with respect to S, [the x: Fx]Gx.

Assuming sentences like (FN 5) and (FN 6) are to be derived from a compositional truth theory, we would then need two axioms for the counterfactual truth conditions of definite descriptions:

$\forall\Phi\forall\Psi\forall\sigma\forall i\forall w$(with respect to w, σ satisfies '[the x_i: $\Phi(x_i)$]$\Psi(x_i)$' $\leftrightarrow$ [the σ^*: $\forall j(j \neq i \rightarrow \sigma^*(j) = \sigma(j))$ & σ^* satisfies $\Phi(xi)$](σ^* satisfies $\Psi(x_i)$))

$\forall\Phi\forall\Psi\forall\sigma\forall i\forall w$[the σ^*: $\forall j(j \neq i \rightarrow \sigma^*(j) = \sigma(j))$ & σ^* satisfies $\Phi(x_i)$](with respect to w, σ satisfies '[the x_i: $\Phi(x_i)$]$\Psi(x_i)$' $\leftrightarrow$ (σ^* satisfies $\Psi(x_i)$))

Setting aside the fact that these axioms seem to me to yield incorrect counterfactual truth conditions, it seems to me that there are two serious difficulties here:

• First, the axioms as they stand are inconsistent, since each purports to give necessary and sufficient truth conditions for the sentence '[the x_i: $\Phi(x_i)$]$\Psi(x_i)$,' but they do not give the same necessary and sufficient conditions. The biconditionals in each axiom would thus have to be weakened to right-to-left conditionals, which would then result in the biconditionals in the statement of the counterfactual truth conditions also being weakened to right-to-left conditionals. We would then be left with a partial statement of sufficient conditions for the truth of 'The F is G' with respect to S, but no statement of necessary and sufficient conditions. This is, of course, a symptom of a general problem of dealing with ambiguity in a semantic theory, but it's worth noting that one traditional route to dealing with ambiguity – namely, assigning different structures or different lexical contents to the various disambiguations of the target sentence – is not available to Sosa here.

I find it hard to make sense of and one which (a) (as Sosa notes[15]) encourages the idea that "'The *F* is *G*' is not true" is similarly ambiguous between a wide and narrow scope reading, and (b) makes it extremely difficult to see how a compositional procedure, performed in a language with scopes marked unambiguously, will be able to produce both the wide and narrow scope readings of (28). In both cases, the search for wide-scope options seems too severe a desirable connection between the semantic scope behaviour of an expression and the syntactic domain of that expression.

V.iv. Autonomy and Rigidity

I think, though, that I can offer the fan of the wide-scope analysis something much like what he wants without the side-effects. Suppose that proper names are assigned descriptive meanings, but that those meanings are then tagged [–*C*, +*A*]. Evaluation of a sentence involving such a name will thus begin by extensionalizing the proper name, replacing its descriptive contribution to character (broadly conceived)

• Second, the existence of a pair of axioms for the counterfactual satisfaction conditions induced by definite descriptions means that a certain attractively simple picture of the nature of counterfactual semantic rules must be abandoned. It is, I think, attractive to suppose that semantic knowledge consists in an appropriately formulated theory of simple truth conditions, and that our knowledge of counterfactual truth conditions is derived from that prior knowledge, via the generic assumption that if it is a semantic principle that Φ, it is also a semantic principle that with respect to S, Φ. Thus, for example, if we know that the referent of 'Aristotle' is Aristotle, then we also know that (for any conditions S), the referent of 'Aristotle' with respect to S is Aristotle, and that knowledge is derived from the knowledge of the simple reference conditions. But this minimalist picture of the source of knowledge of counterfactual truth conditions will yield only a single axiom for the counterfactual satisfaction conditions induced by definite descriptions (the first (and in my view only correct) of the two above), and thus must be rejected by Sosa.

15 Sosa resists this implication of his view, holding that the relevant ambiguity does not arise in the case of negation and other extensional operators. However, no reason for this differential scopal escape from quotation is given beyond a professed inability to hear the wide scope reading in the case of negation. Since I can't hear it in either case, I find the response unsatisfactory.

by an objectual contribution to content. Since the descriptive content of the name is tagged –*A*, it does not interact with its linguistic environment – specifically, with any modal operators in the sentence – in the process of being extensionalized. Thus rigidity is guaranteed.

When evaluating the claim:

(38)   Aristotle might not have been a philosopher.

where 'Aristotle' is assigned 'the last great philosopher of antiquity' as its meaning, tagged [–*C*, +*A*], we first obtain content from character by extensionalizing the meaning 'the last great philosopher of antiquity' to obtain:

⟨POSSIBLY, ⟨NOT, ⟨Aristotle, PHILOSOPHER⟩⟩⟩

which will be true, since Aristotle (that is, that very guy) might not have been a philosopher. The descriptive meaning is still there, on the level of character, but it is flushed out, independent of modal operators in the environment, before content is reached. And when we consider counterfactual truth conditions of the simple claim:

(39)   Aristotle is not a philosopher.

we first take the character of that statement:

⟨NOT, ⟨the last great philosopher of antiquity, PHILOSOPHER⟩⟩

and use it find the content:

⟨NOT, ⟨Aristotle, PHILOSOPHER⟩⟩

which is then evaluated (and evaluated correctly) for counterfactual truth conditions.

Fans of the wide-scope analysis, then, are right in thinking that the descriptive meaning of the name needs somehow to be pulled away from the linguistic context in which that name is used. However, they are pulling in the wrong direction. They pull *outward*, to a wider scope position, and then find themselves impelled continually to pull further and further out as the modal nature of the dialogue is located further and further from the name. Instead, they should be pulling *upward* – moving the descriptive meaning into character, where it is, as a consequence of its +*A* tagging and the graduated manner in which content is derived from meaning in a context of use, in principle immune to any modal considerations in play.

Here is a broad way of putting the central point:

> Once you acknowledge that indexicals ('I', 'now') have descriptive meaning and acknowledge that indexicals are rigid referring expressions, you've implicitly abandoned the modal argument.

This point tends to get lost because the descriptive meanings of indexicals are specifically context-sensitive, which bumps them up to the level of character and secures their rigidity by their evaluation prior to the level of content. Once the connection between autonomy and context-sensitivity is dropped, the point is easier to see. Another way of putting the central point:

> Once you've got 'dthat,' you've got all you need to defeat the modal argument.

> Once the autonomy-granting function of 'dthat' is isolated from the context-sensitivizing function of that, rigid, descriptive names are again clearly on the table.

Put so baldly, the point seems, I think, rather obvious and unavoidable. Yet it also seems rarely to have been grasped in the literature. Kripke makes brief mention of Kaplan's 'dthat' in *Naming and Necessity* (construing it as an operator actualizing a description), but gives no hint that it in any way threatens his modal argument.[16] Dummett actually makes the central point in his 1981 discussion of Kripke:

> The conception that [the dthat operator] is possible is, of course, precisely the conception that being a rigid designator is a feature of a term which need not depend upon its lacking a sense. (1981, 562)

---

16 Kripke seems to construe 'dthat' as an actualizing operator:

"It is indeed useful to have an operator which transforms each description into a term which rigidly designates the object actually satisfying the description. David Kaplan has proposed such an operator and calls it 'Dthat'" (1980, 60).

But he then goes on to spend another fifty-one pages setting out a wide scope response to Kripke – a response unnecessary if his remark about 'dthat' is correct. The connection between 'dthat' and the modal argument is, however, characterized very much as I've characterized it here by Recanati (1993). Recanati proposes a semantic feature REF which "indicates that the truth-condition (or, more generally, satisfaction-condition) of the utterance where it occurs is singular" (1993, 17). The connection between REF and 'dthat' is explicit in Recanati's discussion:

> Kaplan has devised an operator, DTHAT, which prevents the mode of presentation of the reference from going into the content, in such a way that the content of an expression within the scope of DTHAT can only be its reference. REF does exactly the same job as DTHAT; the difference between them is simply that I take REF to be a semantic feature of natural language while DTHAT is an operator in an artificial language. (1993, 31)

Recanati then suggests that the REF feature is part of the meaning of proper names, thereby accounting for their modal rigidity even if they have descriptive content. REF is thus in effect a special case of my semantic feature –*A*, applying only to NP-type expressions. The more general framework I give here allows us to capture the virtues of Recanati's suggestion without having to stipulate specifically that REF yields a singular proposition – on my account, singularity falls out as a consequence of the fact that NPs take objects as their extensions combined with the fact that the +*A* feature prevents the character of an NP from interacting with its lexical context prior to extensionalization. While my approach fully agrees with Recanati's when restricted

---

Reading 'dthat' as an actualizer, I think, stands in the way of seeing how 'dthat' offers a solution to the modal argument. This reading of 'dthat' encourages an approach to the modal argument on which one "bulks up" the definite description giving the sense of the name until that definite description is itself *de facto* rigid, and hence encourages responses such as that of Soames (1998), which bring out problems in the bulk accumulated. On the understanding of 'dthat' which I am favouring here, 'dthat' does not add content (such as an actuality operator) to a definite description, but changes the status of the content that is there, making it autonomous from its surrounding lexical context.

to the specific question of the rigidity of proper names, it grants extra flexibility by allowing us to designate expressions other than NPs as +*A* and have their operator-impervious semantic contribution fall out of the generic procedure of extensionalization (thus, for example, a +*A* predicate will contribute a set of individuals to content).

V.v. Dthat, Indexicals, Descriptive Meaning, and Names

While I've suggested that the 'dthat' operator contains the seed of a response to the modal argument, and tried to track the potential growth of that seed, I see no sign in Kaplan that he intends 'dthat' to address the modal argument. Nowhere either in "Dthat" (1978) or in "Demonstratives" (1977) does Kaplan consider the applicability of 'dthat' to the understanding of descriptive names or to Kripke's modal argument.[17] Kaplan does, however, have an interesting discussion of "dthat" in his "Afterthoughts," where he takes up the question of whether "dthat-terms are directly referential." Here Kaplan distinguishes an operator interpretation from a demonstrative-surrogate interpretation of 'dthat', preferring in the end the latter. Of the demonstrative-surrogate interpretation, he says:

> The word "dthat" was intended to be a surrogate for a true demonstrative, and the description which completes it was intended to be a surrogate for the completing demonstration. On this interpretation "dthat" is a syntactically complete singular term that requires no syntactical completion by an operand. (A 'pointing,' being extra-linguistic, could hardly be a part of syntax.) The description completes the character of the associated occurrence of "dthat," but makes no contribution to content. Like a whispered aside or a gesture, the description is thought of as off-the-record (i.e., off the content record). It determines and directs attention to what is being said, but the manner in which it does so is not strictly part of what is asserted. The

---

17 "Dthat," was, of course, written in 1970, presumably before Kaplan was aware of Kripke's argument. However, it was not published until eight years later, and the published version includes no updates to demonstrate an awareness of the potential applicability to Kripke's modal argument.

semantic role of the description is pre-propositional; it induces no complex, descriptive element into content. (1989, 581)

Note first the intimate connection Kaplan sees between 'dthat' and context-sensitivity – 'dthat' terms are essentially a formal realization of the pre-theoretic category of the demonstrative, the term whose referent depends on its use in context. Again, this linking of context-sensitivity and autonomy (lack of descriptive contribution to content, in this case) may be partly responsible for making the application to the modal argument hard to see.

Furthermore, note the odd way in which Kaplan does characterize the role of the description accompanying the 'dthat'. The description is:

(i) like a whispered aside or a gesture
      thought of as being off-the-record
      pre-propositional
(ii) making no contribution to content
      inducing no complex, descriptive element into content

The characterizations listed under (i), however, are rather stronger in isolating the descriptive meaning than are those in (ii). (ii) says only what the theory of the character–content distinction commits Kaplan to saying: that descriptive meanings which feature in character are isolated to character, and provide only an object to the level of content (thus allowing rigidity of indexicals). (i), however, makes character surprisingly remote. If the descriptive complement to a 'dthat' term is just a pragmatic cue to finding the right referent, a whispered aside off the record, then it is not clear that the "solution" to the modal argument that I am proposing actually goes against Kripke's own picture.

Strictly speaking, Kripke does not commit himself to names having no descriptive content. In *Naming and Necessity*, he argues against a descriptive theory of names characterized by quite explicit principles:

(1) To every name or designating expression 'X,' there corresponds a cluster of properties, namely the family of those properties φ such that A believes 'φX.'
(2) One of the properties, or some conjointly, are believed by A to pick out some individual uniquely.

    (3)   If most, or a weighted most, of the φ's are satisfied by one unique object γ, then γ is the referent of '*X*.'

    (4)   If the vote yields no unique object, '*X*' does not refer.

    (5)   The statement, 'If *X* exists, then *X* has most of the φ's' is known a priori by the speaker.

    (6)   The statement, 'If *X* exists, then *X* has most of the φ's' expresses a necessary truth (in the idiolect of the speaker).

(C) For any successful theory, the account must not be circular. (1980, 71)

To the extent that the modal argument consists merely of observing that Kripke's thesis (6) commits one to the wrong truth conditions for sentences like:

    (38)   Aristotle might not have been a philosopher.

and then rejecting the theory characterized by (1)–(6) and (C), then the considerations I've offered do not touch the argument. Neither do wide-scope analyses, since neither touches the fact that a theory including (6) yields the wrong truth conditions. It is only when we take the broader argument as suggesting the auxiliary premise:

    (P)   A descriptive theory of names will be committed to (1)-(6) above.

that the modal argument can be turned against descriptive theories of names as a general target. The analysis of proper names as having autonomous descriptive character then provides a route to the denial of (P).

    Assessment of the modal argument with (P) added, however, raises the crucial question of what it takes for a theory to *count* as a descriptive theory of names. Kripke, after all, has a role for descriptions to play in the general linguistic behaviour of names. A description can be used to fix the referent of a proper name – the description is used to pick out (descriptively) some object, which then becomes the referent of the name. The descriptive content is then discarded, and plays no role in the semantic evaluation of the name. Kaplan's comments on the role of the description in a 'dthat' term – especially those comments which I placed in category (*I*) above – seem to rest on a picture very similar to Kripke's reference-fixing picture: the description is semantically disposable; it does some scene-setting work, and then vanishes before the serious semantic work begins. If this is all character amounts to, then placing descriptive meaning in the character of a proper name does nothing to evade the force of Kripke's modal argument – it amounts, instead, to an endorsement of a notational variant of his own view.

This, then, is what I take to be the central residual question, and the question for which I don't have an adequate answer: Supposing that we are motivated to replace a naïve, single-tiered theory of meaning with one that recognizes that meanings of claims are built up in stages. We then have a way of accommodating the rigidity of descriptive names, and a way which seems to me to match our pre-theoretic impulse: names don't change their referents in counterfactual circumstances because the first thing we do when we get around to evaluating a claim is figure out who or what is being talked about (descriptively, if a descriptive theory of names is right), and then go on to build up a claim about those entities. But what we don't have, and need, is a way of determining what the *significances* of the various levels of semantic interpretation are to be. Making this determination requires settling very broad issues about the goal of a theory of meaning. Absent such a goal, all we can conclude is that descriptive content can indeed be put *somewhere* (for example, in character, or more broadly, in some modally-autonomous domain, or in the then-discarded reference-fixer) in the semantics of proper names – a point on which it seems all sides must agree – without being able to decide whether or not it matters where we put such content.[18]

---

18 This paper was presented at the Language, Mind, and World conference in Tlaxcala, México, where it benefited greatly from comments and questions from David Chalmers, Jeff King, Jason Stanley, and Zoltan Szabo. Thanks also to David Sosa for valuable comments.

Joshua Dever

References

Almog, J., Perry, J., and Wettstein, H, eds. 1989. *Themes From Kaplan*. Oxford: Oxford University Press.

Borg, E. 2000. "Complex Demonstratives." *Philosophical Studies* 97: 229–49.

Braun, D. 1994. "Structured Characters and Complex Demonstratives." *Philosophical Studies* 74: 193–219.

———. 1995. "What is Character?" *Journal of Philosophical Logic* 24: 227–40.

Dever, J. 2001. "Complex Demonstratives." *Linguistics and Philosophy* 24:271-330.

Dummett, M. 1973. *Frege: Philosophy of Language*. Cambridge, MA: Harvard University Press.

———. 1981. *The Interpretation of Frege's Philosophy*. Harvard: Harvard University Press.

Kaplan, D. 1977. "Demonstratives." In Almog, *et al.*, 1989, 481–563.

———. 1978. "Dthat." In Ludlow 1997, 669–92.

———. 1989. "Afterthoughts. In Almog, *et al.*, 1989, 564–614.

Kripke, S. 1980. *Naming and Necessity*. Cambridge, MA: Harvard University Press.

Ludlow, P. 1997. *Readings in the Philosophy of Language*. Cambridge, MA: The MIT Press.

Perry, J. 1986. "Thought Without Representation." *Supplementary Proceedings of the Aristotelian Society* 60: 137–52.

Recanati, F. 1993. *Direct Reference*. Oxford: Blackwell Publishers.

Soames, S. 1998. "The Modal Argument: Wide Scope and Rigidified Descriptions." *Noûs* 32: 1–22.

Sosa, D. 2001. "Rigidity in the Scope of Russell's Theory." *Noûs* 35: 1-38.

Stanley, J. 2000. "Context and Logical Form." *Linguistics and Philosophy* 24: 391–434.

CANADIAN JOURNAL OF PHILOSOPHY
Supplementary Volume 30

What is a Change?

GUILLERMO HURTADO

In this paper I offer an ontological elucidation of change. In the first part, I examine two conceptions of change that can be found in Aristotle's *Physics* and I hold that one of them is more basic than the other. In the second part, I offer an ontological model of change according to which a change is a kind of conjunction of states and times.

I. Two Notions of Change

According to Aristotle a change, *metabolé*, is *from* something *to* something else.[1] He distinguishes three kinds of changes. One of them is what he calls motion – *kinesis* – i.e., the transition from a positive term *A* to a negative term *B*. Motion in respect to quality is called alteration, in respect to quantity it is known either as increase or as decrease, and in respect to place it is designated by the name of locomotion.[2] Although Aristotle affirms that motion is just a case of change – the others are *coming to be* and *perishing* – there are occasions in which he uses 'change' and 'motion' as synonyms. A reading of *Physics* VI gives the impression that Aristotle's view of change is ruled by his conception of motion and, in particular, of locomotion.

Aristotle's view of motion in *Physics* VI is intimately connected to his theory of activity and potentiality. In Ross' translation, motion is defined as the *fulfilment of what exists potentially*.[3] This fulfilment is the

---

1 Aristotle 1936, 225a.

2 Ibid., 226a.

3 Ibid., 201a.

process by which what is potential becomes actual. Hence, a motion exists only during the period of time in which a particular potency is becoming actual. Before this process begins, there is no motion, it has not begun; and when that which was potential is fully actual, it ceases.

Waterlow[4] has emphasized the difference between the Aristotelian notions of change and motion and has claimed that they imply different ways in which changes can be individuated.[5] The first one is that the change from a state A of x to a state B of x is the *emergence* of B. The change does not happen before or after the actual emergence of B. The second one is that change from a state A of x to a state B of x is a *process* between A and B. According to this view, the change happens before the emergence of B. Following Waterlow, I will distinguish between change-M (for *metabolé*) and change-K (for *kínesis*). I define the former in this way:

> An object x changes-M iff, for every property F and every property G such that F and G are incompatible (or F is $\sim G$ or G is $\sim F$):
>
> (i) x is F at $t1$.
> (ii) x is G at $t2$

A change-M of x is x's acquisition of G at $t2$ after having F at $t1$. Property F can be $\sim G$ or property G can be $\sim F$ in order to include cases such as that in which x changes from not having G or F to having F or from having F to not having F or G.

This conception of change can be found in *Physics* III and VIII, but is not the one defended in book VI. What is proposed in that book is rather what I will call change-K, which I define as follows:

> An object x changes-K iff, for every property F and every property G, such that F and G are incompatible:

---

4 Now S. Broadie.

5 See Waterlow 1982.

(i) x is F at $t1$
(ii) x is G at $t2$.
(iii) x is becoming G during a tx such that tx is between $t1$ and $t2$.

A change-K of x is the *process* by which x obtains property G. To change-K is to *be changing*.
From the previous definitions it follows that every change-K is a change-M, but that there could be a change-M that is not a change-K, i.e., a change that would not fall under condition (iii) of the previous definition.
Some defenders of the thesis that events are changes have claimed that *all* changes, and hence all events, are changes-K.[6] According to L. Lombard, for example, the notion of change is a *dynamic* notion and this is another way of saying that all change is change-K. It is this notion of change, he claims, that we have to adopt in order to understand the thesis that events are changes.[7]
The point of difference between change-M and change-K is (iii). But what does it mean that x is becoming G? A way to explain this is as follows:

An object x is becoming G during tx iff:

(i) x has a property H at tx
(ii) x does not have H at $t1$ nor at $t2$.
(iii) x has property G at $t2$ in virtue of having property H at tx.

One could say, from a neoaristotelian perspective, that H is what makes a potency of x actualized: a kind of catalyst. This actualization,

---

6   The thesis that events are changes has been defended by L. Lombard (1986) and, to some extent, by B. Taylor (1985). The idea that an event is a change is also well seen by other authors who defend theories of events different from those of Lombard or Taylor. D. Davidson (1980, 173), for instance, has said that he finds probable that the concept of an event depends on the idea of a change in a substance. And J. Kim (1993) accepts that the notion of an event implies that of a change in a substance, and that although he takes events to be sorts of states of affairs, the difference between these notions should not bother us.

7   Lombard, 1986, p. 109.

i.e., H, is itself an actual property of x, which is different from G, as a potential or actual property of x and also from G as a property that is being actualized. H is also distinct from F. Behind the contemporary claims that change requires something like H, we find a version of the Aristotelian doctrine of actuality and potentiality reformulated in a more or less novel vocabulary. Lombard, for instance, calls properties like H 'dynamic properties', i.e., properties that, so to speak, drive x from having one static property to another, i.e., from one state to another.[8]

Kim's and J. Bennett's conceptions of change (i.e., events) are analogous to the one just described, since they hold that for x to change is for x to have a certain property.[9] The main difference between states and events, according to these theories, depends on what kind of properties constitutes them. Whereas events are constituted by dynamic properties, like H, states are constituted by static properties, like F or G.

It seems to me that the conception of events as constituted by dynamic properties is mistaken, and that the source of this mistake is the doctrine of change as change-K.

Against the doctrine that all changes can be changes-K we can provide the following argument. If H is a property that x actually has while becoming G, the passage from not having H – as it is the case when x has F – to having H is another change of x. Hence, according to the definition of change-K, there must be a property H^* that makes x pass from not having H to having it. But for the same reason, there should be another property, H^{**}, that makes x pass from not having H^* to having it, and so on. If we want to avoid this regress we have to accept that it is possible that x acquires a new property without the intermediation of a property like H, and hence that not all changes are changes-K.

A reply to this argument is that it is a version of Zeno's paradox, for it attempts to show that change is impossible under certain assumptions. And since Zeno's paradox is supposed to be harmless, so would be my argument. My response is that the infinite regress obtained in

---

8   Lombard, 1986, p. 104.

9   See J. Bennett 1988, and J. Kim, op. cit.

my argument is not a case of Zeno's paradox, for it has nothing to do with the infinite divisibility of a sequence and does not conclude that x could never reach property G. Let us remember that although not all infinite regresses are harmful, some of them are; for example, the third man argument, or the so-called Bradley's paradox. According to Russell, regresses are vicious when obtained from an infinite analysis and not vicious when obtained from an infinite chain of inferences.[10] It seems to me that my argument belongs to the first sort. The change from x having F to x having G is analyzed by means of x having property H. Since this analysis is what produces the regress, we would have here a case of a truly vicious regress.

A different reply to my argument could be to claim that even if not all changes require dynamic properties, it does not follow from this that all changes are not changes-K. In order to defend this view, one would have to accept that the condition that x *is becoming* G is not equivalent to the fact that x has a property such as H. But this comes very close to saying that the sentence 'x is becoming G' is a mere *flatus vocis*, i.e., that there is nothing in the world concerning x that makes the former sentence true or false, and this is something which I doubt defenders of the doctrine of change as change-K would be eager to accept. It could be replied that it is possible that an object x may be changing at tx even if retains all the properties it had before it began to change, given that at the same time there is a different object y engaged in a process that will result in the emergence of a new property in x. But in this case I could produce another version of my argument if the process in which y is engaged requires a property like H and like H^*, and like H^{**}, etc. If the process in which y is engaged does not trigger an endless regress of properties of the H kind, then one can accept that sometimes the change of an x is the result of something that happens to y (for instance, a woman is becoming a widow while her husband dies).

We can then conclude that not all changes are changes-K. If there are changes, some must be changes-M.

A corollary of this conclusion is that there can be changes that take no time at all. Let us remember that a change-K from a state A to a

---

10 See B. Russell 1903, 167–68.

state *B* is what happens *between A* and *B*. But according to the conception of change as change-*M*, there may be no time at all, not even an instant, between the end of *A* and the beginning of *B*

The thesis that there are changes that take no time at all has been rejected on the basis of some considerations concerning the nature of time. In *Physics* VI, Aristotle supports his view of change as change-*K* by appeal to a conception of time as continuous.[11] Although I have offered an argument that shows that if there are changes at least some must be changes-*M*, it is worth examining Aristotle's arguments. He argued that:

> (T1) It is necessary that every change lasts more than one instant.
>
> (T2) It is necessary that every change lasts a period of time composed of an infinite number of instants.

The argument for (T1) is as follows. Let's suppose that *x* changes at an instant *tx* and that *tx* cannot be divided into further instants. If this is so, *x* will have and *not* have a property at *tx*. However, this would go against the law of non-contradiction, that claims that no object can have and not have, in the same instant, a certain property. Therefore, change must last more than one instant. This period of time between the two states of a change is what allows reality to escape – as von Wright said – from the contradiction with which change threatens it.[12]

Let us consider now the argument for (T2). If *x* changes at an instant, it follows, Aristotle says, that there must be a previous instant and a subsequent instant in which *x* also changes, and this is because he believed that time is *continuous*.

What can be said about the arguments in favour of (T1) and (T2)?

Concerning (T1) it is obvious that the initial state and the final state of a change cannot both happen in one and the same instant, for that would violate the law of non-contradiction. Nevertheless, we can

---

11 It is important to recall that in other parts of his *Physics*, Aristotle accepts changes with no duration. See, for example, VIII.3, 253b21–30 and I86a15–16.

12 See G. H. von Wright 1967, 21.

accept that there can be changes-M in which the initial and final states happen in different instants such that there is no instant between them and hence they do not overlap in time. On the other hand, we could also say that a change-K could last just one instant if, in that instant, x does not have F nor G but only H. Hence, in the single instant during which x is changing, it is neither F nor G – for H is neither one of them – and so there is no contradiction at all.

In order to respond to (T2) we have to consider the difficult question of whether time is continuous. There seems to be some *a posteriori* evidence against this hypothesis.[13] However, I believe that one might propose an *a priori* argument in favour of the thesis that time is not continuous. Let us assume that between the initial and the final state of every change there is always a space of time. Consider now a change-M in which the initial state is that x has F and the final state that x does not have F. According to our assumption, there must be a space of time beween the initial state and the final state of this change-M. In that space of time, x would not have F – for x is no longer in the initial state – but neither would it have not-F – for it is not yet in the final state. And it would not have a property such as H, for it is supposed that it is not a change-K. But if the law of excluded middle is *ontologically* true, the case described could not be possible: x must always have F or not-F. Hence either there is no change at all or there are no changes-M in which there is a space of time between their initial and final states. If we opt for the latter – and, as we know, there could be no change without changes-M – we can conclude, given that there is change, that time is not continous.[14]

To sum up: the doctrine of change as change-K is mistaken. Although many of the changes that matter to us may be changes-K, change rests on change-M. The essential temporality of change does

---

13 It has been claimed that Bell's theorem shows that there are changes that take no time.

14 It could be objected that the law of excluded middle cannot be ontologically true, for there is fuzziness in the world. I will not deal here with the difficult question of whether the world is fuzzy in itself. I will simply assume that it is not, yet I accept that if it were fuzzy or vague, many of the claims I make here may turn out to be false.

not imply that changes must always have a duration, and this seems to imply that time is not continuous. Against what Aristotle thought, there are changes in which their initial and final states are contiguous.

II. The Form of Change

In this section I wish to propose an ontological model of change based on the conclusions of the previous section. I will claim that a change is a kind of conjunctive fact, namely, a conjunction of temporally delimited states.

Let us begin our research with the examination of what may be the smallest of possible worlds.

Imagine a world, which I will call 'world-1', in which there is only one thing, say a black sphere. From the beginning to the end of this world the only thing there is in it is that black sphere, which I will call 'e'.[15]

Is world-1 identical to e? World-1 is not identical to e, because there could be another world where e was blue and there was nothing else in that world. Hence, in order to determine the identity of world-1, one must consider that e is black.

Can we then say that world-1 is identical to the class of e and the properties of being black, being a sphere, etc. $\{e, B, S, \ldots$ etc.$\}$? World-1 is not identical to the class of e and its properties, since the existence of that class does not imply the existence of the *facts* that e is black, e is a sphere, etc. World-1 is, like any other world, the totality of its facts.

Facts have a structure that can be depicted with a logical form. For example, the fact that an object has a property has the form Fa.

Is world-1 a class of facts of the form Fa? I do not think so. Even a small world like world-1 has facts of several ontological structures. In world-1, we find the singular fact that e is black – Be – but also the

---

15 I am not worried by the objection that nothing could be black or white or of any other colour if it was the only object in the world because I assume that the example could be made using other properties. What would require a rather more solid argument is the objection that if an object were the only existent, it could have no properties – is this what a resemblance nominalist would claim? – or that it is really impossible.

relational fact that e is identical to itself – $e = e$ – the conjunctive fact that e is black and e is spherical – i.e., Be & Se –, and the general fact that everything is black – (x) Bx – among others.[16]

Let us now imagine another world, which I will call 'world-2', where there is only that same sphere which is black up to a point of time and then becomes white and stays like that until the world ends.

The difference between world-1 and world-2 is that in the latter, there is a change. What ontological concepts are needed in order to narrate the history of world-2? Can we describe world-2 with the same kinds of facts found in world-1?

In order to describe world-2, we have to say that one and the same thing, i.e., e, is black and white. It would seem, therefore, that it is a fact of world-2 that:

(1) Be & We.

Let us remember that in world-1 there is also the conjunctive fact that e is black and spheric:

(2) Be & Se

At first sight there is no significant difference between (1) and (2). In both it is claimed that e has one property and has another property. And both, it would be said, are true of world-2. But the fundamental difference between (1) and (2) – and, hence, between *states* and *changes* – is that whereas the fact expressed by (2) is logically innocuous, the putative fact expressed by (1) violates the principle of non-contradiction. What this shows is that (1) is not really a fact of world-2 – which may be small, but not contradictory. What is missing in (1) is the proviso that e is black and white in a very different manner from which it is black and spheric. In other words, what is missing in (1), but not in (2), is a way of expressing the condition that the fact that e is black has an *end* and the fact that e is white has a *beginning*, and that the end

---

16 I have examined the nature of facts in Hurtado1988. The model of change that I offer in this paper can be seen as an extension of the ontological system that I proposed in that book.

of the fact that e is black is *previous* to the beginning of the fact that e is white.

I want to stress that it is not enough to say that these facts happen at different times. We have to settle the *order* in which they happen. A world where e is originally white and then turns black is different from world-2, even if both satisfy – in an extensional way – the description (1). What this shows is that temporal order is not only required to protect world-2 from contradiction, but also to determine its identity.

However, it is not enough to claim that e is black before it is white in order to determine the identity of world-2, for there could be a world where the *durations* of Be and We could be different. Let us say that in world-2, e becomes black at ta and ceases to be black at tb, and becomes white at $tb+1$ and ceases to be white at tc. In order to distinguish world-2 from a world in which e is black and then white but in different periods, one has to indicate in the description of world-2 the exact duration of states Be and We:

(3)   Be (from ta to tb) & We (from $tb+1$ to tc)

So we can now say that the difference between world-1 and world-2 is that among the facts that constitute world-2 we must include the conjunctive fact expressed by (3). What distinguishes (3) from the conjunctive facts of world-1 is temporal order and the exact determination of the duration of each one of the conjuncts of (3). Aristotle famously claimed that time is the form of change. I would say that time gives change a form on top of its primary conjunctive form. Perhaps it would be more exact to say that the form of change is logically temporal.

It is important to stress the difference between the order and the duration of a state. Consider the proposition:

(3)*   Be (between ta and tb) & We (between $tb+1$ and tc)

It would seem that there is no major difference between (3) and (3)*, yet they determine different worlds. If the arrow of time ran from the future to the past, (3)* would be true. The direction of time is determined in the temporal indexes of (3) by the form '(*from* ... *to* ...)' in a way in which is not in the temporal indexes of (3)* which have the form '(*between* ... *and* ...)'.

This is the moment to raise a crucial question: is the fact expressed by (3) identical to the change that happens in world-2? Or is this change supervenient on the fact expressed by (3), but not identical to it?

My hypothesis – which I reckon coincides with the intuition that lies underneath the definition of change-*M* – is that this change is identical to the fact expressed by (3). Changes are, I believe, conjunctive facts like (3) or, as we shall see, conjunctive facts of more complexity which have as constituents changes like (3).

This conception of change elucidates the close connection between change and time, although in a different way from how it is explained by traditional doctrines. There is no change without time for the simple reason that particular changes are *constituted* by particular times. In other words, changes not only *are in time*, but are, at least, partly *made of times* – i.e., of time particles inside an ontological structure.

I admit that I have not answered questions such as what is time, or what are times, duration, or the beggining or the end of a state. Is there time in world-1? Are the moments of time in world-2 the same in number as the states that are in it? My answer is evasive: in the model of change that I offer here, time plays the role of a *primitive* notion. This does not mean that I believe that one can fully understand what change is without knowing more about time, but I trust that this task may belong to a future stage of research, where we can explore the elements of this model in a more substantial manner.

Let us now consider a world-3. Here the sphere becomes grey during a space of time before becoming white. To put it in a more precise way: e is black from ta to tb, grey from from $tb+1$ to tc and white from $tc+1$ to td.

A description of world-3 requires, therefore, the following two changes:

(4) *Be* (from ta to tb) & *Ge* (from $tb+1$ to tc)
(5) *Ge* (from $tb+1$ to tc) & *We* (from $tc+1$ to td)

But it could be said that this way of describing world-3 ignores a third change, namely, the one in which the black sphere becomes grey and then white. This change happens during a period of time. It is the change that allows us to say, between $tb+1$ and tc that e is *becoming white* – at a time in which it is neither black nor white. This is what we can call the *process* by which *e* goes from being black to being white. This process is:

(6)   (*Be* (from *ta* to *tb*) & *Ge* (from *tb*+1 to *tc*)) & (*Ge* (from *tb*+1 to *tc*) & *We* (from *tc*+1 to *td*))

Processes are, according to this view, conjunctions of consecutive changes. Some types of processes happen regularly in nature. When we talk about these regularities – which can be laws of nature – we do not talk about this or that process in particular, but of a common *structure* found in them. For example if we abstract '*e*' from (6) and substitute it for a variable "*x*" what we obtain is a propositional function:

(7)   (*Bx* (from *ta* to *tb*) & *Gx* (from *tb*+1 to *tc*)) & (*Gx* (from *tb*+1 to *tc*) & *Wx* (from *tc*+1 to *td*))

This propositional function can be satisfied by different objects. Now, if we substitute the temporal indexes for temporal variables, the propositional function thus obtained could be satisfied by different objects at different times:

(8)   (*Bx* (from *tx* to *ty*) & *Gx* (from *ty*+1 to *tz*)) & (*Gx* (from *ty*+1 to *tz*) & *Wx* (from *tz*+1 to *tw*))

I believe that (8) is the closest thing to a *universal* that we can have concerning changes. But it is important to notice that (8) is not a change, but a change-structure that can be shared by many changes and that can be predicated, truly or falsely, of different suitable objects.

If we add existential quantifiers to (8), so that all the variables are bound, we would get the following general and conjunctive fact:

(9)   ($\exists x$) ($\exists tx$) ($\exists ty$) ($\exists tz$) ($\exists tw$) ((*Bx* (from *tx* to *ty*) & *Gx* (from *ty*+1 to *tz*)) & (*Gx* (from *ty*+1 to *tz*) & *Wx* (from *tz*+1 to *tw*)))

The fact expressed by (8) is that something changes from being black to being white through becoming grey, following a temporal pattern. Perhaps this is not what we normally would call a change, but it is, I think, what we would call an event of a certain kind. A causal law, if we see things in this way, would be a general fact in which two propositional functions of the form (8) would be connected by the primitive relation of causality, and all the variables found in those propositional functions would be bound by universal quantifiers.

What can we conclude from our examination of worlds 1, 2 and 3?

A complete description of a dynamic world such as ours requires three ontological subcategories of facts: states, changes, and processes.

Changes are a type of conjunction of states (although we have to keep in mind that not every conjunction of states is a change) and processes are a type of conjunction of changes (without forgetting that not every conjunction of changes is a process).

The relations of dependence between these categories are the following: there can be states without changes, but there can be no changes without states and no processes without changes.

From the previous laws some philosophical consequences may be inferred. One of them – just to mention one – is that Davidson seems to be mistaken when he claims that the world has no facts (i.e., what I have called states),[17] but has events (i.e., what I have called changes).[18] Without states, there can be no changes.

In what follows I will consider some possible objections to the model that I have proposed.

It could be said that a problem with this model is that it is too formal, for it does not include causality, teleology, laws of nature, etc. My response is brief. The model is *ontological*, i.e., it is concerned with the fundamental question of what is a change, and it is not *metaphysical*, i.e., it is not concerned with the way in which changes are organized and directed. What matters in this case is the *form* of change, not its origin, ending, or norm, and at this point my theory moves in a very different direction from a strictly Aristotelian theory of change.

Another objection to my model is that it does not take into account – as other recent studies do – the grammatical form of sentences that

---

17 See D. Davidson 1984.

18 See D. Davidson 1980.

express or talk about changes. My response is that the grammatical form of a sentence of an ordinary language with which we express a change is rarely equivalent to the form of that change.[19] Take, for example, the descriptive phrase 'The conquest of México'. Has this small phrase the same structure or even a similar one to the one had by the enormous and complex chain of changes denoted by it? My guess is that it does not have the same structure, and I would not say that this is a defect of ordinary languages, but on the contrary, it is what allows us to narrate the flux of change with the limited resources we possess. Although I have not offered here an analysis of the sentences with which we talk about changes, I would dare to say that my ontological analysis of change is similar to the Russellian analysis of the facts expressed by sentences with definite descriptions. In my analysis, as in Russell's, the proposed ontological structure is more complex than it would seem from the grammatical structure of the sentences that express those facts, and the proposed analysis allows us to reject certain entities – in the Russellian cases, nonexistent objects such as the present king of France, and in the cases I examine, dynamic properties.

I finish this essay with a suspicion that, if correct, will force us to reconsider the basis of my proposal.

It has been claimed that the symbolism of formal logic can be used to depict the ultimate structure of facts. Following this tradition – which can be traced back to the origins of analytic philosophy – I have attempted to offer the general form of change using quantificational calculus. However, I sometimes suspect – somewhat in the line of the Mexican philosopher José Vasconcelos – that a language closer to musical notation would represent more perspicuously the form of change.[20] Let me explain myself. In a musical score, the flux of the melody is expressed by each one of the notes that have to be played by the instruments. In the same way, the representation of a complex change should show in symbolism each one of the objects, proper-

---

19 Nonetheless, it seems that the conjunctive structure of changes (or events) can be reached at by a strictly semantical analysis. Vid., e.g., James Higginbotham 2000.

20 See J. Vasconcelos 1959.

ties, states, transitions, and chains of simple changes that constitute it. Let us remember that in scores one can indicate rhythm and speed. Just as one sequence of notes can be played with different rhythms and speeds, the same may happen with the speed and rhythm of an event; for example, one can open a door more or less quickly, or with one or another rhythm. These features of changes may be expressed with some kinds of logical symbolism, but not others. Let us take into account that the score is not only made of notes on a staff, but that in it, one can also indicate the *mode* in which those notes ought to be played: cheerfuly, sadly, agitatedly, etc. In an analogous way, changes made of the same constituents could have different modes of realisation. A person x can open a door y respectfully, clumsily, elegantly, etc.

How can we choose between the model of music and the model of logic, between the metaphor of the world as a score and the metaphor of the world as a book? I still believe that in a last level of analysis the structure of change is conjunctive, but I do not know how to answer this question. And it troubles me that, ultimately, the choice would have to be between two *metaphors*.[21]

References

Aristotle. 1936. *Physics*. Oxford: Oxford University Press.

Bennett, J. 1988. *Events and Their Names*. Indianapolis: Hackett Publishing Company.

Davidson, D. 1980. "The Individuation of Events." In *Essays on Actions and Events*, 163-180. Oxford: Oxford University Press, Oxford.

———. 1984. "True to the Facts." In *Inquiries into Truth and Interpretation*, 37-54. Oxford: Oxford University Press.

Higginbotham, J. 2000. "On Events in Linguistic Semantics." In *Speaking of Events*, eds. J. Higginbotham, F. Pianesi, and A. Varzi, 49-80. Oxford: Oxford University Press.

Hurtado, G. 1998. *Proposiciones russellianas*. Mexico: UNAM.

---

21 I thank Axel Barceló, Dorit Bar-On, Sarah Broadie, Patricia Díaz, José Díez, Maite Ezcurdia, Alberto Fonseca, Ricardo Salles, Richard Sorabji and Robert Stainton for their comments on previous versions of this paper.

Kim, J. 1993. "Events as Property Exemplifications". In *Supervenience and Mind*, 33-52. Cambridge: Cambridge University Press.

Lombard. J. L. 1986. *Events: A Metaphysical Study*. London: Routledge.

Russell, B. 1903. *The Principles of Mathematics*. Cambridge: Cambridge University Press.

Taylor, B. 1985. *Modes of Occurrence: Verbs, Adverbs and Events*. Oxford: Blackwell.

Vasconcelos, J. 1959. "Estética." In *Obras Completas*, Volume 3. Mexico: Libreros mexicanos unidos.

Waterlow, S. 1982. *Nature, Change and Agency in Aristotle's Pysics: A Philosophical Study*. Oxford: Clarendon Press.

Wright, G. H. von. 1967. *Time, Change and Contradiction*. Cambridge: Cambridge University Press.

CANADIAN JOURNAL OF PHILOSOPHY
Supplementary Volume 30

Context Dependent Quantifiers
and Donkey Anaphora

JEFFREY C. KING

It is generally agreed that some anaphoric pronouns with (what appear to be) quantifier antecedents occur outside the syntactic scope (i.e., the c-command domain) of their antecedents. First, there is "donkey anaphora," of both the conditional and relative clause varieties:

> (1) If Sarah owns a donkey, she beats it.[1]
> (2) Every woman who owns a donkey beats it.

Without going through the details, let me just assert that there is good reason to think that the pronouns in (1) and (2) do not occur in the syntactic scope of the quantifier 'a donkey'.[2]

---

1 I intend these sentences on readings on which 'it' in each sentence is anaphoric on 'a donkey' and on which 'she' in 1 is anaphoric on 'Sarah'. Throughout, I generally avoid co indexing to indicate intended anaphoric relations because it reduces clutter and it is obvious which anaphoric relations are intended.

2 A sketch of the details: all independent evidence available suggests that a quantifier can't take wide scope over a conditional and bind variables in its consequent (*'If John owns every donkey$_i$ he beats it$_i$'). Further, even if 'a donkey' could magically do this in 1, assuming it is an existential quantifier, we still wouldn't get the intuitive truth conditions of 1, which require that Sarah beats every donkey she owns. Similarly, the independent evidence available suggests that quantifiers can't scope out of relative clauses (*'A man who owns every donkey$_i$ beats it$_i$'), and so again the pronoun in 2 is not within the scope of its quantifier antecedent. Though all agree that the pronouns in 1 and 2 are not in the *syntactic* scope of 'a donkey', on some theories 'a donkey' nonetheless *semantically* binds

A second sort of case in which a pronoun with a quantified antecedent occurs outside the syntactic scope of its quantifier antecedent is one in which the pronoun and its antecedent occur in different sentences. Examples of such "discourse anaphora," from the very simple to the slightly complex, include:

(3) A man is following Sarah. He is from the Internal Revenue Service.
(4) A man is following Sarah. Melanie believes he is from the Internal Revenue Service.
(5) It is possible that several students flunked at most five exams. Melanie believes they didn't study for them.
(6) Suzi ought to apologize to most of Ann's dinner guests. It is certain that she insulted them. But it is unclear whether they noticed.

Because in these two sorts of cases pronouns occur outside the syntactic scopes of their antecedents, given standard assumptions, they cannot be viewed semantically as variables bound by their quantifier antecedents. Let us call such pronouns instances of *unbound anaphora*. In the last twenty years, a number of semantic theories of unbound anaphora have arisen. These include E type/D type analyses (Evans 1977, Heim 1990, Neale 1990), Discourse Representation Theory (Kamp 1981, Heim 1982), Dynamic Logic accounts (Groenendijk and Stokhof 1991, Chierchia 1995), and the Context Dependent Quantifier account (Wilson 1984; King 1987, 1993, 1994). I hasten to add that on some of these accounts, instances of unbound anaphora *are* semantically bound by their antecedents or by "higher" quantifiers. So perhaps the term 'unbound anaphora' is unfortunate here, and perhaps something like the melodic *non-c-command anaphora* would be better. Nonetheless, since on my view the pronouns in question are syntactically and semantically unbound, I shall stick with the term 'unbound anaphora'.

---

the pronoun. This is mentioned below. I should add that according to DRT theorists such as Kamp (1981) and Heim (1982), indefinites like 'a donkey' are not quantifiers. However, I will be assuming they are.

The account of unbound anaphora I favour, the Context Dependent Quantifier, or CDQ account, to this point has been presented only as an account of discourse anaphora. The question arises as to how it would treat donkey anaphora. As we shall see, there initially appear to be difficulties with applying the CDQ account to donkey anaphora. The present paper has two goals. First, I shall argue that the difficulties in applying CDQ to donkey anaphora are merely apparent, and that by adapting techniques employed by Heim (1990) and others, CDQ can give an account of donkey anaphora. Second, along the way I shall gesture at certain methodological advantages that CDQ enjoys over various competitors.

I shall begin by giving an informal overview of the CDQ theory, and the data to which it has been applied.

The CDQ account of discourse anaphora was originally motivated by a felt analogy between the semantics of discourse anaphora and the semantics of "instantial terms" that figure in quantificational reasoning in natural languages and in derivations of systems of natural deduction for first order predicate logic. An example of an instantial term in natural language would be occurrences of 'n' when one supposes that n is an arbitrary prime number and, on the basis of subsequently establishing the claim that n is F, one concludes that all prime numbers are F. Or given that some prime number is F, one might let n be "a prime that is F" and go on to establish certain other claims "about" n. In systems of natural deduction, instantial terms are the singular terms that are introduced in applications of existential instantiation and eliminated in applications of universal generalization.

CDQ has been applied to the instantial terms of a certain range of systems of natural deduction. In these applications, occurrences of formulas containing instantial terms in derivations are assigned truth conditions. The truth conditions assigned depend on the structure of the derivation containing the occurrence of the formula. Thus, given an occurrence of a formula A in derivation D, one defines the truth conditions of A in context c, where c encodes the structural features of derivation D that are relevant to the truth conditions of the occurrence of A in D. The assignment of truth conditions to occurrences of formulas in derivations delivered by CDQ allows one to prove a theorem to the effect that if in derivation D formula A was inferred from $B_1, \ldots, B_n$, then for any model M, if the relevant occurrences in D of $B_1, \ldots, B_n$

are true in their contexts under M, then the relevant occurrence in D of A is true in its context under M. Call this theorem *line soundness*.[3] Classical soundness is a trivial consequence of this theorem.

To those not familiar with the application of CDQ to instantial terms in natural deduction, line soundness may be mildly surprising. For it entails that if in a derivation D there is an application of existential instantiation as follows:[4]

$$(\exists x)P(x)$$
$$a \quad \Big|$$
$$\Big| \quad P(a)$$

.
.
.

then if this occurrence of '$(\exists x)P(x)$' is true in its context under model M, this occurrence of '$P(a)$' is true in its context under M. Obviously, if that is true, and if the existential quantifier is given its standard semantics, the instantial term 'a' in '$P(a)$' must itself be in some way expressing generality as quantifiers do. And indeed, CDQ treats it in just this way. But of course, exactly what sort of generality (universal vs. existential, etc.) a given instantial term in an occurrence of a formula expresses will depend on features of the derivation containing the occurrence of the formula. That is, what sort of generality an instantial term expresses is determined by the derivational context in which the occurrence of the formula occurs. For example, 'a' in the above "derivation" has the force of an existential quantifier. However, in another derivation we might have an occurrence of 'a' in an application of universal generalization as follows:

---

3 See King 1991 for a proof of this result.

4 I am assuming here that the rule of existential instantiation is formulated in such a way that '$P(a)$' is inferred from '$(\exists x)P(x)$'.

.
.
.

$$a \ \mid \ P(a)$$

$$(x)P(x)$$

Here, in order that the truth of '$P(a)$' in its context forces the truth of '$(x)P(x)$' in its context, 'a' must have the force of a universal quantifier. So again, what sort of quantificational force an occurrence of an instantial term has is determined by the derivational context in which it occurs. It is for this reason that I called these expressions *context dependent quantifiers*.

Now the idea underlying the application of CDQ to discourse anaphora is that these expressions, too, look like expressions of generality, where the precise nature of the generality they express is determined by features of the linguistic context in which they occur. Thus, on the CDQ account, instantial terms and anaphoric pronouns with quantifier antecedents in discourse anaphora are contextually sensitive devices of quantification. That is, these instantial terms and anaphoric pronouns express *quantifications*, and *which* quantifications they express is partly a function of the *linguistic environments* in which they are embedded.

Before spelling this out a bit more, let me informally motivate the idea that the pronouns in discourse anaphora are devices of quantification that are sensitive to linguistic context. Consider the following discourses:

(7) A man from Sweden climbed Mt. Everest alone. He used no oxygen.

(8) Every player is dealt five cards. He passes one card to the player on his left.

(9) Most students passed the exam. They didn't get scores below 70 percent.

Imagine that I were to utter (7). Suppose now that in fact at least one Swede has climbed Mt. Everest alone without oxygen. Then it would seem that in uttering (7) I have spoken truly. If this is correct, then it appears that the second sentence of (7) expresses a (existentially) *general* claim. If the pronoun 'He' in the second sentence is itself a quantifier, we would have an easy explanation as to why the second sentence expresses a general claim: the generality is a result of the presence of this quantifier in the sentence. Similar remarks apply to (8) and (9). Further, consider the following discourse:

(10) A man killed Alan last night. Michelle believes he used a knife to kill him.

It seems to me that the second sentence has two different readings. On one reading, it asserts that, concerning the man who killed Alan last night, Michelle believes of *that very man* that he used a knife. This would be the case if, for example, Michelle knew the man who killed Alan, believed that he killed Alan and, based on his well-known fondness of knives, believed he used this sort of weapon. But the second sentence has another reading, on which it ascribes to Michelle the general belief to the effect that a man killed Alan with a knife last night. On this reading, the sentence would be true if, for example, on the basis of conversations with personnel at the hospital and having no particular person in mind, Michelle believed that a man fatally stabbed Alan last night.

Again, these facts would be easily explained if we held that the pronoun in the second sentence is a quantifier. For we might then expect that, like other quantifiers, it could take wide or narrow scope relative to 'Michelle believes'. On the wide scope reading of the pronoun/ quantifier, the second sentence attributes to Michelle a belief regarding a particular person. On the narrow scope reading, it attributes to Michelle a general belief.

To summarize, then, sentences containing pronouns with quantifier antecedents in other sentences appear to make *general claims* (7, 8, 9) and appear to admit of scope ambiguities (10). These facts would be most straightforwardly explained on the hypothesis that the anaphoric pronouns in question are quantificational.

Occurrences of "ordinary quantifiers," such as 'every man', have what we might call a *force*, in this case universal; what we might call a *restriction*, in this case the set of men; and *scope* relative to other occurrences of quantifiers, verbs of propositional attitude, and so on.

CDQ claims that the anaphoric pronouns in question also have *forces* (universal, existential, etc.), *restrictions* ("domains over which they quantify") and *scopes* relative to each other, verbs of propositional attitude, etc. However, unlike "ordinary" quantifiers, these anaphoric pronouns *qua* quantifiers have their forces, restrictions, and relative scopes determined by features of their linguistic environments. So again, it should be clear why I call them *context dependent quantifiers* (henceforth, cdqs).

I have already indicated that the CDQ account has been applied to instantial terms in reasoning in natural language and in systems of natural deduction. I have also indicated that the account has been applied to discourse anaphora. Before turning to other matters, I wish to note an advantage CDQ has over dynamic or DRT approaches in application to some discourse anaphora. As the discussion of sentence (10) above may have suggested, CDQ has been applied to discourses in which anaphoric pronouns combine with verbs of propositional attitude and modal, epistemic, and deontic operators ('it is certain that'; 'it ought to be the case that').[5] Examples of such data, including some moderately complicated cases, are as follows:

(11) Sarah believes several students flunked the exam. They are in my office.

(12) Sarah knows that several students flunked the exam. They are in my office.

(13) A man killed Alan last night. Michelle believes he used a knife to kill him.

(14) At most four students passed the exam. Elizabeth believes they are smart.

(15) Glenn hopes some woman will go out with him. Brad regrets she is from Kansas.

(16) Hob believes a witch has blighted Bob's mare. Nob believes she killed Cob's cow.

(17) Winston believes every successful movie stars a famous female actress. Emmet believes that she is responsible for its success.

---

5 See King 1993 and 1994 for such applications.

As (16) makes clear, the data to which CDQ has been applied here includes Geach "intentional identity" examples, as well as more complex examples of the sort illustrated by (17), which I call *Generalized Geach sentences*. Now as I've already indicated, CDQ predicts that some of the sentences in these discourses have more than one reading, (e.g., the second sentences of (13) and (14)). This is due to the fact that the CDQ account predicts that cdqs, since they are quantifiers, can sometimes take wide or narrow scope with respect to verbs of propositional attitude (and other operators). So, for example, as mentioned earlier, the second sentence of (13) can either attribute a general belief to Michelle, or a belief about a specific man.

This highlights what I take to be the methodological advantage that CDQ enjoys over DRT and dynamic approaches to data in which anaphoric pronouns mix with attitude verbs and operators of various sorts. Namely, since CDQ holds that the anaphoric expressions are quantificational, it predicts that they will take varying scope with respect to verbs of attitude and other operators, yielding multiple readings in some cases. This prediction is clearly correct. By contrast, since DRT approaches and dynamic approaches take anaphoric pronouns of the sort under consideration to be (semantically) bound variables, they only predict readings on which there is binding *into* the verb of attitude or operator. That is, they only predict readings corresponding to our wide scope readings. Thus, to account for what we call the narrow scope readings, which are clearly present in certain cases (e.g., (13) above, on the reading on which a general belief is attributed to Michelle), DRT and dynamic approaches must invoke some completely different semantic mechanism.

It seems to me a methodological advantage of CDQ that it holds that a single semantic mechanism generates the multiple readings present in examples of the sort we have been considering. Since we are about to turn to donkey anaphora, let me point out that even here there are readings of donkey sentences that DRT and dynamic approaches cannot explain. Consider the following sentences:

(18) Every woman who has a secret admirer thinks he is stalking her.

(19) If a woman has a secret admirer, usually she thinks he is stalking her.

These sentences certainly appear to have readings on which they attribute *de dicto* beliefs to the women in question. That is, they have readings on which they attribute to the women in question *general* beliefs to the effect that they are being stalked by secret admirers. This is why these sentences can be true even though the women in question don't know who their secret admirers are, and so have no beliefs about *particular* persons stalking them. Hence these readings can't result from the pronouns' being bound from outside the verb of attitude 'thinks'. Hence, here again, DRT and dynamic approaches must posit some other mechanism to capture these readings.

In any case, I hope this overview of the CDQ account makes clear *both* roughly what the account is *and* the rather wide range of data to which it has been applied.

Let us now turn to donkey anaphora. Before getting to that, one aspect of the CDQ account must be further articulated. First, let's recall what a symmetric monotone increasing quantifier is. Let D be a determiner, and let A, B, and C be predicates. Very informally, we can say that a determiner D is *symmetric monotone increasing* iff for predicates A, B, and C:

    i. $D(A)$ is B iff $D(B)$ is A (e.g., some man is happy iff some happy thing is a man)

and

    ii. The following inference is valid:

$D(A)$ is B	(e.g., some man is under six feet tall)
Every B is C	(every man who is under six feet tall is under seven feet tall)
----------	------------
$D[A]$ is C	(some man is under seven feet tall)

Thus, e.g., 'a(n)', 'some', and 'several' are symmetric monotone increasing determiners. A *quantifier* (e.g., 'some man') is symmetric monotone increasing iff its determiner is.

Now on the CDQ account, a cdq with a symmetric monotone increasing antecedent has the same quantificational force as its antecedent. Further, the restriction on such a cdq is determined by the predicative material in the sentence in which its antecedent occurs as follows. Consider a discourse of the following form:

An *F* is *G*. He/she/it is *H*.

The cdq 'he/she/it' here has the force of the quantifier 'An *F* that is *G*'. So the cdq here has existential force, and its restriction is *F*'s that are *G*'s.[6]

With this in mind, we turn to donkey sentences. Because the treatment of conditional donkey sentences is somewhat more involved, let us consider relative clause donkey sentences first. Thus consider again:

(2)   Every woman who owns a donkey beats it.

Let's assume that the syntactic structure of 2 is *very* roughly something like:

(2b)   [Every x: [x is a woman & [[a y: y is a donkey & x owns y]]]
       [x beats y]

Now let's suppose that the "pronoun" 'y' following 'beats' in (2b) (i.e., the pronoun 'it' in (2)) is a cdq, since, given standard assumptions, it is anaphoric on, but not bound by, its quantifier antecedent. The CDQ theory then predicts that the pronoun is an existential quantifier whose restriction is the set of donkeys owned by x. That is, 'y' ('it') expresses the quantification that could be expressed by the quantifier phrase 'a donkey x/she owns'. If we add to the CDQ theory the claim that when a cdq occurs in the syntactic scope of a quantifier that takes wide scope over the cdq's antecedent, the cdq is interpreted semantically as taking narrow scope with respect to the quantifier in question, we have the result that the cdq 'y'/'it' in (2b)/(2) expresses an existen-

---

6 In more complex, multi-sentence discourses, the restriction of a cdq with a symmetric monotone increasing antecedent is determined in a more complex manner. See, e.g,. King 1994, 224 for details. This additional complexity is not relevant for present purposes, so I suppress it.

tial quantification over donkeys x/she owns that takes narrow scope with respect to 'Every woman who owns a donkey'. Thus the account predicts that the sentence is true iff every donkey owning woman beats at least one donkey she owns.

Now there is a debate in the literature as to what are the proper truth conditions of 2 and similar sentences such as:

> (2′)   Most women who own a donkey beat it.
> (2″)   No woman who owns a donkey beats it.
> (2‴)   Some woman who owns a donkey beats it.

Some think that the truth of (2) and (2′) require every donkey-owning woman to beat *every* donkey she owns, and most donkey owning women to beat *every* donkey they own, respectively. Let us call these the (alleged) *universal readings* of (2) and (2′). Others think that (2) and (2′) require for their truth merely that every donkey owning woman beats *some* donkey she owns, and that most donkey owning women beat *some* donkey that they own, respectively. Let us call these the (alleged) *existential readings* of (2) and (2′), (these, of course, are the readings CDQ assigns to these sentences). Still others think that (2) and (2′) are ambiguous and have both readings.

The view that (2) and (2′) only have universal readings seems very doubtful. First, an observation due to Rooth (1987) and noted by Heim (1990) casts doubt on the claim that (2) has (only) a universal reading. Consider the following sentences:

> (2)   Every woman who owns a donkey beats it.
> (2a) Every donkey that is owned by a woman is beaten by her.

When informants (who aren't linguists and philosophers of language working on donkey anaphora) are presented with these sentences and asked whether they would be true if one woman owns ten donkeys and beats nine of them, whereas every other woman beats every donkey she owns, many hesitate to judge (2) false, but do not hesitate to judge (2a) false. If both sentences had only the universal reading, this would be hard to explain. For if that were so, the sentences would be truth conditionally equivalent. Second, it seems clear that some sentences relevantly like (2) and (2′) have existential readings:

Every person who had a credit card paid his bill with it.
Most women who have a dime will put it in the meter.

It seems pretty clear that the truth of these sentences require only that every person who has a credit card paid his bill with *some* credit card he has, and that most women who have a dime put *some* dime she has in the meter, respectively.

As indicated above, CDQ as formulated to this point assigns only existential readings to all of (2)–(2‴). In the case of (2‴), this is all to the good, since sentences of this sort always seem to have only existential readings (on which the truth of (2‴) requires that some woman who owns a donkey beats some donkey she owns). Further, as already indicated for (2) and (2'), the following examples show that sentences relevantly like (2)–(2″) possess the existential reading:

(20) Existential Readings:
  (a) Every person who had a credit card paid his bill with it.
  (b) Most women who have a dime will put it in the meter.
  (c) No man with a teenage son lets him drive the car on the weekend.

(The truth of (20c) requires that no man with a teenage son lets *some* teenage son of his drive the car on the weekend.) Because of these facts, I am tempted to think that all relative clause donkey sentences possess only the existential readings assigned to them by CDQ, and to give a Gricean explanation of the appearance of universal readings in some cases. But I have to confess that in certain cases, the universal reading is so robust that it is hard to believe that it results from Gricean mechanisms. The following example from Kanazawa 1994 illustrates this: 'Every student who borrowed a book from Peter eventually returned it'.

What, then, about the view that relative clause donkey sentences have both universal and existential readings? First, as already mentioned, sentences such as (2‴) never seem to have universal readings. So some explanation needs to be given of this fact. However, in the other cases (where the wide scope quantifiers are formed from the determiners 'every', 'most', and 'no') it does seem as though on can find examples in which the universal reading is favoured, and examples in which the existential reading is favoured (I repeat (20) above):

(20) Existential Readings:
 (a) Every person who had a credit card paid his bill with it.
 (b) Most women who have a dime will put it in the meter.
 (c) No man with a teenage son lets him drive the car on the weekend.

(21) Universal Readings:
 (a) Every student who borrowed a book from Peter eventually returned it.
 (b) Most parents who have a teenage son allow him to go out on the weekend.
 (c) No man with an umbrella leaves it home on a day like this.

These examples and others suggest that whether a given relative clause donkey sentence appears to favour the universal reading or the existential reading seems to be influenced by a variety of factors, including the monotonicity properties of the determiner on the wide scope quantifier, the lexical semantics of the predicates occurring in the sentence, and general background assumptions concerning the situations in which we are to consider the truth or falsity of the sentences. It is very hard to find significant generalizations regarding under what conditions a given reading is favoured.[7] Further, it is

---

7 Kanazawa (1994) discusses how the montonicity properties of the determiner on the wide scope quantifier in a relative clause donkey sentence ('Every', 'Most', and 'No' in (20a–c), respectively) affect whether a universal or existential reading for the sentence is favoured. Though Kanazawa admits that other factors also contribute to making one or the other reading favoured in particular cases (see p. 124), he claims that certain monotonicity properties of the determiners on the wide scope quantifier result in only one reading being possible. Thus, he claims that when the wide scope quantifier has a determiner that is upward monotone on both arguments (e.g., 'some'), only the existential reading (which Kanazawa calls the "weak reading") is possible (120, 124). As I've indicated in discussing (2‴), I agree with this (see also my (26) below and surrounding discussion). However, Kanazawa also claims that when the wide scope quantifier has a determiner that is monotone down on both arguments (e.g. 'no') only the existential (weak) reading is possible (120, 124). Though such sentences favour existential readings, sentences like 21 c cast doubt on the claim that they

very hard to find sentences that clearly allow both a universal and an existential reading. This makes the view that the sentences actually possess both readings as a matter of their semantics at least somewhat suspect. If they really do possess both readings, why is it so hard to find sentences that clearly allow both readings?

In any case, the main point here is that an extremely straightforward and natural extension of the CDQ theory yields the existential readings for (2), (2'), (2"), and (2'''). I find these readings the most natural readings of (2') and especially (2") and (2'''); and I think a plausible case can be made that (2) possesses the existential reading as well. However, as I have indicated in discussing (21a–c), sentences relevantly like (2)–(2") seem to possess quite robust universal readings. Thus, I simply note that there is a controversy concerning what the truth conditions of relative clause donkey sentences are, and that CDQ straightforwardly delivers one set of truth conditions for these sentences, which some claim are the only truth conditions they possess.

It is important to note that most approaches to donkey anaphora (e.g., the DRT approaches of Kamp (1981) and Heim (1982), the *E* type approach of (Neale 1990), the dynamic approach of Groenendijk and Stokhof 1991) yield only the universal readings of donkey sentences.[8] So in not delivering both readings as currently formulated, CDQ is no worse off than these accounts. Further, the only theories known to me that deliver *both* the existential and universal readings do so by

---

only allow existential readings. In any case, the important point is that though Kanazawa is concerned with how monotonicity properties of the determiners on the wide scope quantifiers in relative clause donkey sentences affect which readings are favoured or available, he agrees that in the general case factors other than such monotonicity properties affect which readings are favoured. See also Guerts (2002) for interesting data on factors affecting which readings are favoured for donkey sentences.

8 Actually Neale's (1990) account also assigns readings to donkey sentences on which the truth of e.g., (2) and (2') require that every man owns exactly one donkey, and most men own exactly one donkey, respectively (see 237–41). However, this is not the existential reading, and I find it very implausible that the sentences have these readings. So here Neale's account is worse off than CDQ.

positing some sort of ambiguity.[9] CDQ could capture both readings by positing some sort of ambiguity, but I am suspicious of this move and so I shall not follow that strategy here. I believe more thought needs to be given to the alleged universal and existential readings of relative clause donkey sentences, and the relations between the alleged readings.

Let us now turn to conditional donkey sentences such as (1) repeated here:

(1)   If Sarah owns a donkey, she beats it.

In contrast to the relative clause donkey sentences we've considered, (1)'s truth conditions seem quite clear: (1)'s truth (on at least one of its

---

9   Kanazawa (1994) captures the universal and existential readings by defining a strong and a weak dynamic generalized quantifier for each determiner (see 138). This appears to amount to claiming that determiners are ambiguous. However, Kanazawa appears to take himself to be simply "modeling" the readings of donkey sentences and not actually proposing a semantics. Thus, in introducing his dynamic predicate logic with generalized quantifiers, he consistently talks of using the framework to "model" or "represent readings of" donkey sentences (see 132, 137, 138, 139); and after discussing the framework, he writes: "So far, we have not proposed any concrete model of the mechanism that assigns interpretations to donkey sentences. Although it would not be difficult to extract a compositional semantics from my treatment of donkey sentences in dynamic predicate logic with generalized quantifiers, our interest in this paper is not in finding the right set of compositional semantic rules that give donkey sentences the interpretation that they actually have (in the default case)" (150). But the point is that if one were to turn Kanazawa's approach into a semantics, it seems that it would posit an ambiguity in determiners. Kanazawa himself seems to recognize this when, in discussing Chierchia's approach and contrasting it with his own, he writes "So he [Chierchia] shifts the locus of ambiguity from the determiner to the pronoun" (155). On the other hand, as Kanazawa's remarks just suggested, Chierchia (1994) attempts to capture the universal and existential readings by positing an ambiguity in the pronouns in donkey sentences. Chierchia holds that such pronouns are interpreted either as dynamically bound variables or E type pronouns (see 110–22). Chierchia denies that the (alleged) fact that donkey pronouns can be interpreted in these two ways amounts to postulating an ambiguity in these pronouns (see 117). However, I don't find what he says on this matter persuasive.

readings) requires Sarah to beat every donkey she owns.[10] Let's call the fact that (1)'s truth requires that Sarah beat every donkey she owns the *universality requirement*. I begin with a pedestrian observation. In

(1a)   Sarah owns a donkey. She beats it.

the second sentence has no reading on which it requires that Sarah beats every donkey she owns. The universality requirement is absent here. But as we have seen, as soon as we form a conditional from our two sentences, the universality requirement appears. This strongly suggests to me that in donkey conditionals some other factor (e.g., the semantics of conditionals) is interacting with the semantics of unbound anaphora to produce the universality requirement. And of course, some approaches to conditional donkey sentences do hold that the universality requirement in donkey conditionals results from the interaction of the semantics of anaphora and the semantics of conditionals (e.g., DRT approaches). But some approaches try to squeeze the universality requirement in donkey conditionals out of the semantics of unbound anaphora alone. I believe such approaches are wrong

---

10   Most discussions of conditional donkey sentences such as (1) assume that they have only what we might call *universal readings* (on analogy with universal readings of relative clause donkey sentences), according to which, e.g., (1) requires that Sarah beats every donkey she owns. However, particularly if one uses 'will', one can formulate conditional donkey sentences that appear not to have universal readings: 'If Leroy has a quarter, he will put it in the meter'. The truth of this sentence does not seem to require that Leroy puts every quarter he has in the meter. It is perhaps harder to find present tense conditional donkey sentences that lack the universal reading (or favour a reading that is not the universal reading). The results of trying to construct examples mimicking present tense relative clause donkey sentences that favour readings other than the universal reading are unclear: 'If a man has a nice hat, he wears it to church'; 'If a man has a credit card, he pays his bill with it'. I am inclined to think that the former *does* require every man who has a nice hat to wear each of his nice hats to church. My intuitions about the latter are unclear. I am not sure why it appears easier to formulate conditional donkey sentences lacking the universal reading (or favouring a reading other than it) with 'will', and what role the semantics of 'will' plays here. The data here seem quite complex, and I shall in the present paper simply follow the majority in assuming that conditional donkey sentences have only universal readings. However, I believe much more work is required on these issues.

headed. Before explaining how CDQ handles donkey conditionals, let me illustrate why I think such approaches *are* wrong headed.

The main account of donkey anaphora that tries to get the universality requirement in donkey conditionals only from the semantics of unbound anaphora is that of Stephen Neale (1990a, b). So let me briefly explain Neale's account of donkey sentences and why I think it is incorrect.

Neale's view is that in a discourse such as:

(22)   John bought a donkey. Harry vaccinated it.

the pronoun 'it' "goes proxy for" the definite description 'the donkey John bought'. Hence the second sentence of such a discourse is equivalent to the sentence 'Harry vaccinated the donkey John bought' with the description understood in standard Russellian fashion. Within a generalized quantifier-type framework, where 'the' is treated as a determiner that, like other determiners, combines with a set term to form a quantified NP, the evaluation clause for sentences containing a singular description (with wide scope) can be given as follows

(23)   'the $(F)^\wedge x[Y]$' is true iff $|F|=1$ and $|F|-|^\wedge x[Y]|=0$

(where 'F' is a term denoting a set, 'Y' is an open formula with free occurrences of 'x', '$^\wedge x[Y]$' is a lambda expression denoting the set of things that satisfy 'Y' when assigned to 'x', $|F|$ is the cardinality of the set denoted by 'F' and $|^\wedge x[Y]|$ is the cardinality of the set denoted by '$^\wedge x[Y]$' – I suppress reference to models, etc.). So the second sentence of (22) is true iff Harry vaccinated the unique donkey John bought. Thus far, then, the view is that pronouns anaphoric on singular indefinites are interpreted as Russellian definite descriptions.

There is, however, a further complication in Neale's theory. For a variety of reasons, Neale introduces what he calls a "numberless description": a description that, unlike semantically singular descriptions, puts no cardinality constraint on the denotation of the set term that combines with the determiner to form the quantified NP (other than that it must be nonempty – note above how in the singular case $|F|$ is constrained to equal one). Following Neale, let 'whe' be the determiner (corresponding to 'the') used to form "numberless descriptions." Then the evaluation clause for sentences containing numberless descriptions, analogous to (23) above, would be

(24) 'whe$(F)^\wedge x[Y]$' is true iff $|F| \geq 1$ and $|F| - |^\wedge x[Y]| = 0$

Thus numberless descriptions are in effect universal quantifiers.

In addition to going proxy for Russellian singular descriptions in the way we have seen, Neale claims that anaphoric pronouns sometimes go proxy for numberless descriptions. In particular, Neale holds that pronouns anaphoric on singular existential quantifiers (but outside of their scope) can be interpreted *either* as standard Russellian descriptions *or* as numberless descriptions. Now if the pronoun in (1) is interpreted as a numberless description, (1) asserts that if Sarah owns a donkey, she beats all the donkeys she owns. So treating the pronoun as a proxy for a numberless description yields the correct result that at least on one of its readings (1) entails that Sarah beats every donkey she owns. Note that the semantics of the alleged numberless description in (1) by itself yields the universality requirement in (1).

The obvious question concerning an account like this, that allows pronouns anaphoric on singular existential quantifiers to go proxy for both Russellian and numberless descriptions, is: what determines whether such a pronoun is going proxy for a Russellian, as opposed to a numberless, description? This question is pressing, since there will be a substantial difference in the truth conditions of a pronoun-containing sentence depending on whether the pronoun receives a numberless or Russellian interpretation. In his most explicit statement about the matter, Neale (1990, 237) makes clear that it is primarily whether the utterer had a particular individual in mind in uttering the indefinite description that determines whether a pronoun anaphoric on it receives a Russellian or a numberless interpretation.[11]

---

11 Actually, Neale mentions another factor as well. Concerning the sentence 'Every man who has a daughter thinks she is the most beautiful girl in the world' Neale writes: "… it is arguable that a singular [Russellian] interpretation of the pronoun is preferred. A reasonable explanation is that immediate linguistic context, and lexical and background knowledge, conspire to defeat the numberless interpretation. (In the normal run of things, there cannot be *two*

If this is correct, then discourses of the form

(25)   A(n) *F* is *G*. He/she/it is *H*.

generally ought to display both readings (in the suitable contexts), depending on whether the utterer of the discourse had a particular individual in mind in uttering 'A(n) *F'*. So the second sentences of discourses of the form of (25) ought to have readings on which they mean the unique *F* that is *G* is *H* (Russellian) *and* on which they mean every *F* that is *G* is *H* (numberless). But this simply does not seem to be the case. In particular, such discourses do not have readings corresponding to the numberless interpretation of the pronoun. Recall my pedestrian observation concerning (1a):

(1a)   Sarah owns a donkey. She beats it.

It seems clear to me that this discourse has no reading on which the second sentence means that Sarah beats every donkey she owns, even if we imagine that the utterer of the discourse had no particular donkey in mind when she uttered the first sentence. Suppose, for example, that the Homeland Security and Donkey Care Bureau comes to town and wants information about local donkey ownership and beating. I tell them that I really don't know how many donkeys anybody owns, and I have never seen or had any other contact with particular local donkeys. But I tell them that I have received some information from reliable sources and it has been "deemed credible." I then say:

For example, Sarah owns a donkey and she beats it.

Even though I have no particular donkey in mind in uttering these sentences, we simply don't get a numberless reading here. If Sarah

---

most beautiful girls in the world" (238). It is odd to me that Neale here talks of factors conspiring to "defeat" the numberless interpretation, since in the very next paragraph he suggests that the Russellian ("singular") interpretation is the default interpretation. If that were so, then one would think that a numberless interpretation would not have to be defeated to be absent. In any case, I suppress this factor affecting which reading an anaphoric pronoun has. For the examples I consider in which an anaphoric pronoun lacks a numberless reading there are no factors such as the impossibility of there being two most beautiful girls in the world that would "defeat" the numberless reading.

beats some donkey she owns, I have spoken truly even if she owns others she fails to beat. Or again, suppose we are debating whether anybody has an eight track tape player any more, and I say, "I'll bet the following is true: some guy with a '68 Camaro owns an eight-track player and he still uses it." Again, there is no numberless reading for the pronoun in the second sentence, even though I clearly have no particular eight-track player in mind. If some '68 Camaro driving guy owns and uses an eight-track player, I have spoken truly even if he owns other eight track players that aren't used.[12]

So Neale has no explanation of why the pronouns in discourses like (1a) never have numberless readings.[13] I should add that Neale has similar problems with sentences like:

(26)   Some woman who owns a donkey beats it.

Here again, Neale's theory predicts that this sentence has a reading on which its truth requires that some woman beats every donkey she owns. And again, even if we imagine the sentence being uttered without any particular woman or donkey in mind, we don't get this reading of the sentence predicted by Neale's theory, (say we are discussing women's tendencies towards animals they own, and I utter (26) simply thinking it is statistically likely to be true). So Neale has no explanation as to why the second sentence of discourse (1a) and sentence (26) lack the relevant readings assigned to those sentences by his theory.

The problem with this sort of approach to conditional donkey sentences should be clear. If you claim that pronouns anaphoric on singular existential quantifiers can go proxy for standard Russellian descriptions *or* numberless descriptions in order to get the right truth

---

12 Note that nothing like the impossibility of there being two most beautiful girls in the world is present in this case to defeat the numberless reading. Sarah could beat more than one donkey and the Camaro driver could use more than one eight-track player. See previous note.

13 Since Chierchia (1995) thinks that pronouns on singular indefinites can be interpreted in an *E* type way, and that when they are they can be interpreted as "number neutral" (i.e., the pronoun in (1a) can be interpreted as having "the maximal set of donkeys" owned by Sarah as its value), this criticism applies to Chierchia, too.

conditions for donkey sentences, then you are committed to the claim that the pronouns in discourses like (1a) have readings resulting from their going proxy for numberless descriptions. Since the pronouns do not have such readings, one has to come up with some pragmatic mechanism that stifles these readings *when the pronouns occur in a discourse like (1a) but not when they occur in a conditional like (1)*. But as the flaws with Neale's attempted explanation shows, it is not easy to think of a mechanism that *always* stifles the relevant readings in discourses like (1a) and *always* allows the reading to come through in conditionals like (1). Further, the claim that there is a pragmatic mechanism that *always* stifles the relevant reading in one construction and *always* allows it to come through in another seems very *ad hoc*. And this is why I think trying to get the universality requirement present in donkey conditionals out of the semantics of unbound anaphora *alone* is wrong headed. Inevitably, such a theory will generate readings for the sentences in discourses like (1a) that they simply don't have, and so force one to posit a mechanism that always stifles the readings in these constructions.

A more promising strategy for explaining all these facts is to suppose that the anaphoric pronouns in (1a) and (1) have the same, single semantics, and that in (1), this semantics interacts with the semantics of the conditional to produce the implication that Sarah beats all the donkeys she owns. Thus, the universality requirement is present in donkey conditionals, but not in simple "donkey discourses" such as (1a). Let us see how we might pursue this strategy, assuming that CDQ is the correct theory of the semantics of the pronouns in (1a) and (1).

Unadorned, CDQ predicts that 'she' in the consequent of (1) expresses an existential quantification over donkeys Sarah owns, so that (1) apparently ought to be equivalent to

(1b) If Sarah owns a donkey, she beats a donkey she owns.

Obviously, this isn't right.

But suppose we adopt the idea, found in many writers, that a conditional is true iff any way of making the antecedent true can be extended to a way of making the consequent true (relatives of this idea, apparently inspired by Lewis 1988 [1975], are in Kamp 1981, Heim 1982, 1990, and Berman 1987, among many other places). Further, suppose we implement this more precisely as follows. First, we need the notion of a *situation*. A situation is just objects possessing properties and standing in relations to one another. Situations can be of various sizes, but the "smallest" situation consists of a single object possessing a single property. We can use sets of n-tuples to represent situations.

Consider the situation consisting of a single object a possessing the property P. We shall represent this situation by the set $\{\langle P,a \rangle\}$. A situation consisting of n objects $a_1, \ldots, a_n$ standing in the n-place relation R will be represented by the set $\{\langle R,a_1, \ldots, a_n \rangle\}$. Bigger situations will be represented by sets with more members. In general, any set each of whose members is an $n+1$-tuple whose first element is an n-place relation and whose next n elements are objects represents a situation.[14]

Now consider the following way of implementing the idea that a conditional is true just in case any way of making the antecedent true can be extended to a way of making the consequent true, which is due to Berman (1987):

(C)   'If A then B' is true iff for any minimal situation s_1 in which 'A' is true, there is a situation s_2 such that s_1 is a part of s_2 and 'B' is true in s_2.

A minimal situation in which 'A' is true is a situation in which 'A' is true but which has no situation that is a proper part of it (i.e., subset of it) in which 'A' is true. So it is a "smallest" true-making situation for 'A.' I should mention that if we were talking about conditionals other than donkey conditionals, I would have to give a more complicated characterization of a minimal situation. But since we are talking about donkey conditionals, I'll go with this simple formulation.[15]

---

14   For present purposes, we aren't considering, e.g., situations in which an individual stands in a relation to a property. Thus our sets that represent situations don't have as members, e.g., n-tuples whose first member is a relation and whose next two members are an object and a property.

15   I am worried about sentences like 'If Steve loses most sets, Jill will be happy'. We don't want minimal situations here to be the smallest situations in which Steve loses most sets, since presumably these would be situations in which Steve plays and loses a single set. I ignore such worries here.

Note that (C) makes it part of the semantics of conditionals that they quantify over situations.[16] The usual way of thinking of this is that bare conditionals of the sort governed by (C) contain an "invisible" quantifier over situations; and sometimes conditionals have explicit quantifiers over situations in them, such as:

If A, then always/usually/often/etc. B.

As (C) makes clear, the invisible quantifier over situations in bare conditionals has universal force. When conditionals contain overt quantifiers over situations such as 'usually', etc., these determine the force of the quantification over situations for the conditional.

In any case, if we apply (C) to (1), we get the result that it is true iff every situation consisting of Sarah owning a single donkey (the smallest situation that makes 'Sarah owns a donkey' true) is part of a larger situation in which Sarah beats a donkey she owns. This still isn't right for (1). For it would make (1) true if, e.g., Sarah owns ten donkeys and beats one of them. In this case, there are ten minimal situations consisting of Sarah owning a single donkey, and each is part of a larger situation in which Sarah beats a donkey she owns.

Of course, these truth conditions are right for (1b). The problem is that they aren't right for (1), and CDQ seems to make (1) and (1b) equivalent. So is there a way for CDQ to assign different truth conditions to (1) and (1b)?

At first this seems impossible, since CDQ holds that 'she' in the consequent of (1) expresses the same quantifier as does 'a donkey she owns' in the consequent of (1b). But there is a difference between (1) and (1b). In particular, 'it' in the consequent of (1) is a definite NP and is anaphoric on 'a donkey' in the antecedent, whereas 'a donkey she owns' in the consequent of (1b) is indefinite and not anaphoric on

---

16   It is important to see that the idea that conditionals quantify over situations is motivated independently of donkey conditionals. First, conditionals such as 'If John sneezes, he laughs' seem to (universally? generically?) quantify over situations in which John sneezes. Second, adverbs of quantification seem to quantify over something like situations in both non-conditionals and non-donkey conditionals ('A good ski run is usually very steep'; 'If John wins every set, he usually gloats').

anything. Admittedly, we classify NP's as definite or indefinite on the basis of their *semantics*, but presumably this is based on their "typical" or "usual" or "basic" semantic function (e.g., indefinite NP's occur in generic statements – 'A whale is a mammal' – but are they *semantically* indefinite here?).

Now definite NP's are often thought to involve some sort of "familiarity" condition (they must be used to "talk about" something already introduced), and indefinites are thought to involve a "novelty" condition (they must be used to "introduce" something new). Suppose that we thought that the *definiteness* and anaphoricness of the NP in the consequent of (1) and the *indefiniteness* and non-anaphoricness of the NP in the consequent of (1b) make a difference to truth conditions, even though both NP's express the same quantification. Here's the idea. In the case of (1b), (C) applies and works in the way indicated. In particular, any (minimal) s_1 in which the antecedent is true must be part of an s_2 in which the consequent is true. Since the non-anaphoric indefinite in the consequent induces some sort of novelty condition, there is no requirement that the donkey owned in the "smaller" s_1 be the donkey beaten in the "bigger" s_2.

By contrast, the "familiarity" condition induced by the definite, anaphoric 'it' in (1) changes things slightly. In particular, for any (minimal) s_1 in which the antecedent is true, there must be an s_2 that s_1 is part of, in which the consequent (understood as expressing the claim that Sarah beats a donkey she owns) is true. But *in addition*, because of the "familiarity" condition induced by the anaphoric definite, there must be a donkey in s_2 that is also in s_1 and that makes the consequent true. In other words, familiarity requires that a donkey that makes the cdq-containing consequent true in s_2 also be present in s_1.

To see what this means, consider a situation s_1 that is a minimal situation in which the antecedent is true. s_1 consists of Sarah owning a single donkey. If, e.g., Sarah owns ten donkeys, there are ten such minimal situations. For (1) to be true, each such s_1 must be part of a situation s_2 such that s_2 is a situation in which Sarah beats a donkey that she owns and that is in s_1. Now the only way that every minimal s_1 in which Sarah owns a donkey can be part of an s_2 in which Sarah beats a donkey she owns in s_1 is if Sarah beats every donkey she owns. To repeat, in the case of (1), intuitively "familiarity" requires that for each s_1 in which the antecedent is true, we find an s_2 that s_1 is a part of, in which the consequent is true and in which a donkey that makes the consequent true in s_2 is in s_1. So intuitively, "familiarity," triggered by the definite anaphoric cdq 'it' in (1), amounts to not allowing "new" owned donkeys to be brought in to s_2 to make the consequent of (1) true there, whereas "novelty," triggered by the non-anaphoric indefinite in (1b) allows this. Thus, familiarity in effect constrains the s_2's quantified over in (C) ('there is an s_2 such that ...') in the case of (1), but not (1b).[17] (Actually, things may have to be a bit more complicated than this to handle more complex examples.)

This gives (1) the proper truth conditions, and they are different from (1b)'s. Now suppose we wanted to generalize this treatment to conditionals containing explicit adverbs of quantification, such as:

(27)   Usually, if a woman owns a donkey, she beats it.

Further, suppose we assume, as discussed above, that such conditionals differ from bare conditionals such as (1) only in that bare conditionals involve universal quantification over situations, whereas in (27) the explicit adverb expresses the force of the quantification over situations. Given this, the most straightforward extension to (27) of the approach I have outlined here would run into what is called in the literature "the proportion problem."

Here is the problem. I have treated 'usually' as a quantifier over situations in sentences like (27). Now consider a minimal situation s_1 in which the antecedent is true. It will contain a single woman owning a single donkey. Now for (27) to be true, most such s_1's must be parts of an s_2 in which a woman who was in s_1 beats a donkey she owned

---

17 A different way of getting the same result here would be to say that the familiarity and anaphoricness of the cdq in (1) results in that cdq having its domain of quantification restricted to s_1, whereas the indefinite in (1b) quantifies over things in s_2. Thus (1) is true iff for every minimal situation s_1 of Sarah owning a single donkey, there is an s_2 such that s_1 is part of s_2 and a donkey owned by Sarah in s_1 is beaten by Sarah in s_2. And (1b) is true iff for every minimal situation s_1 of Sarah owning a single donkey, there is an s_2 such that s_1 is part of s_2 and a donkey owned by Sarah in s_2 is beaten by Sarah in s_2. I am unsure as to the relative merits of this way of assigning the proper truth conditions to (1) and (1b) and the way discussed in the body of the paper.

in s_1 (again, the familiarity and anaphoricness of 'she' and 'it' in the consequent of (27) trigger this additional restriction on the s_2's). But this predicts that in a world in which one woman owns one hundred donkeys and beats them, and eighty women own a donkey each and fail to beat them, the sentence is true. This does not seem correct to most people. Intuitively, (27) makes a claim about most donkey owning women (i.e., most situations consisting of a woman and all the donkeys she owns), not a claim about most pairs of a woman and a donkey she owns (i.e., most situations consisting of a woman and a single donkey she owns).

Now it looks like it is the fact that 'a woman' is in subject position in the antecedent of (27) that makes the quantification in (27), on its most natural reading, over situations consisting of a woman and all the donkeys she owns, and not over situations consisting of a woman and a single donkey she owns. For consider the following:

(28)   Usually, if a donkey is owned by a woman, it is beaten by her.

In contrast to (27), most people find the most natural reading of (28) to be the one on which in a world in which one woman owns one hundred donkeys and beats them, and eighty women own a donkey each and fail to beat them, the sentence is true. So here it looks like we are quantifying over donkeys owned by women, and not pairs of a woman and a donkey she owns.

If things were this simple, it would be easy to fix our account to avoid the proportion problem. We would just have to complicate our account of a minimal situation so that what constitutes a minimal situation in which a sentence like 'A woman owns a donkey' is true is determined in part by the expression in subject position. So, the minimal situations in which 'A woman owns a donkey' is true are the situations consisting of a woman and all the donkeys she owns. Whereas, the minimal situations in which 'A donkey is owned by a woman' is true consist of a donkey and (all?) the women who own it.

However, many think that the situation is more complex than this. They think that a variety of factors, including which indefinite is in subject position in the antecedent, which indefinites in the antecedent are picked up by anaphoric elements in the consequent, topic, focus, and so on affect the truth conditions of donkey conditionals. Consider this example from Chierchia (1995):

(29) Dolphins are truly remarkable. Usually, if a trainer trains a dolphin, she makes it do incredible things.

Most people think that in a circumstance in which most trained dolphins do incredible things, (29) is true, even if most trainers don't get dolphins to do incredible things (there are three out of seven trainers who get dolphins to do incredible things, and they've trained more dolphins) and most dolphin-trainer pairs aren't such that the trainer gets the dolphin to do incredible things (there are a couple of "bad seed" dolphins who were trained over and over by different trainers and did nothing incredible). So the quantification here is over minimal situations consisting of a single trained dolphin (and all of its trainers). But what we said before about expressions in subject position in the antecedent would predict that for (29), minimal situations would consist of a single trainer and all the dolphins she trained, so that (29) would be true iff most trainers who train dolphins make dolphins they train do incredible things. Thus if most people's judgments about (29) are right, it isn't just what expression is in subject position that determines what the minimal situations are, and so what the truth conditions of the sentence are. That the first sentence of (29) makes dolphins the *topic* of the discourse is relevant to determining what counts as a minimal situation. Similarly, the contrast between the following sentences suggests that focus also determines what counts as a minimal situation (capitals indicate focal stress):[18]

(30) Usually, if A SKIER (as opposed to a surfer) lives in an apartment complex, it is near a ski hill.

(31) Usually, if a skier lives in AN APARTMENT COMPLEX (as opposed to a house), it is near a ski hill.

---

18 Of course this may be because, as suggested by Chierchia (1995, 69), focus (sometimes) indicates what the topic is (in 30 and 31, what is *not* focused – apartment complexes and skiers, respectively). If that is right, then all of (29), (30) and (31) show that what the topic is helps determine what counts as a minimal situation.

Again, many people think intuitively that in (30) we are quantifying over apartment complexes inhabited by skiers, so that a minimal situation is one apartment complex inhabited by at least one skier. Thus, it is true iff most apartment complexes where at least one skier lives are near a ski hill. By contrast, in (31) intuitively we seem to be quantifying over skiers who live in apartment complexes, so that a minimal situation is one skier who inhabits an apartment complex. Thus it is true iff most skiers who inhabit an apartment complex inhabit one near a ski hill. Thus, in a situation in which there are three apartment complexes, two of which have exactly one skier-tenant and are near a ski hill and the third of which has ten skier-tenants and is far from a ski hill, intuitively (30) is true and (31) is false.

These judgments about (29), (30) and (31) are subtle, and I am not sure that they are correct (though I am inclined to think they are). But even if they are, and the readings of donkey sentences are affected by a variety of factors, our account can handle this. We have seen how to handle the idea that which expression is in subject position in the antecedent can affect the truth conditions of a donkey conditional. It just determines what counts as a minimal situation. And then our account applies as before. Similarly, if a complex variety of factors affect the truth conditions of donkey sentences in the same way, we simply need to hold that this complex of factors together determine what counts as a minimal situation. And once this is determined, we apply our account as before. This, again, really just is an employment of devices found in Heim 1990.[19] So I don't think that the proportion problem, and the varying readings of donkey conditionals, are a problem for us.[20]

---

19 Heim (1990) discusses avoiding the proportion problem by holding that what counts as a minimal situation depends on various features of the context of utterance (150–51). She attributes the idea to Berman 1987. Of course Heim is here assuming that donkey pronouns are *E* type.

20 There is an interesting point about the readings of conditionals containing only a single indefinite, such as 'If a donkey is owned by Sarah, she beats it'. Here, the only things that can be minimal situations are situations consisting of Sarah owning a single donkey. If, e.g., Sarah and all the donkeys she owned could be a minimal situation, then given the other things I have said, CDQ would predict that the sentence has a reading equivalent to (1b). It seems reasonable that the

This brings me to a final point. We have just seen that to deal with the proportion problem and related issues within a framework of the sort I am employing, we must hold that various factors put constraints on the nature of the situations quantified over by conditionals. In effect, various factors, including which indefinites in the antecedent are picked up by anaphoric elements in the consequent, topic, focus, and so on, affect what counts as a minimal situation in a given context, and then a given donkey conditional quantifies over those minimal situations. I wish to emphasize that this way of dealing with the proportion problem and related issues was already embraced by those employing the type of account of the semantics of conditionals I am appealing to here. Thus the idea that the *nature* of the situations

---

situation constituted by Sarah owning all her donkeys can't be minimal here, because there is only one such situation and so universally quantifying over all such "situations" would be quantification over the one situation. So perhaps a strong preference to have the universal quantification be over more than one situation (when possible – Sarah may only own one donkey!) prevents the situation of Sarah owning all her donkeys from being minimal. Interestingly, however, when we consider examples in which the predicate in the antecedent is less stative and more episodic, we at least *seem* to get different things counting as minimal situations. Consider 'Usually, if a man walks through that door, he turns on the light'. I *think* I can hear two readings of this sentence. On one, we are quantifying over instances of a man walking through the door, and so a minimal situation is an episode of a man walking through the door. On this reading, the sentence would be true if, e.g., one man walked through the door ten times and turned on the light each time, and nine other (distinct) men walked through the door once each and didn't turn the light on. On another reading, we are quantifying over men who walked through the door. A minimal situation here would be something like a man and all of his entries through the door. On this reading, the sentence would be *false* if, e.g., one man walked through the door ten times and turned on the light each time, and nine other (distinct) men walked through the door once each and didn't turn the light on. (On this reading, it is unclear what happens if trouble makers sometimes turned on the light and sometimes didn't.) *Very* cryptic notes I took at the time suggest that perhaps Peter Ludlow raised something like this point in the question session when I gave an earlier version of this paper at a conference at the University of Cincinnati in 2001. At any rate, my notes consisted of the sentence 'Usually, if a man walks through that door, he turns on the light' with "proportion problem" and "Ludlow" written next to it. Over a year later, finding this "note" and puzzling over what it could possibly mean, I was led to these thoughts.

quantified over by conditionals can be affected by various factors is already embraced by some within the framework I am employing. But consider my explanation as to why, on the CDQ account, (1) can have the correct reading, and a different reading from (1b). It is that a cdq, being a definite and anaphoric, triggers a familiarity condition that constrains the nature of the situations in which the consequent of (1) must be true for the conditional to be true. But then this is just another case of some factor constraining the nature of the situations quantified over by conditionals (in particular, those quantified over by the phrase '... there is a situation s_2 ...' in (C) above).[21] Thus, my explanation of the truth conditions of (1) invokes a mechanism that is already employed in frameworks of the sort I am employing. But then I don't believe my explanation here can be viewed as some *ad hoc* trick, appealing as it does only to mechanisms already employed by the framework to which I appeal.

In conclusion, I have tried to give you an overview of the wide range of "non-donkey" data covered by the CDQ theory. I have also tried to gesture at certain methodological advantages the theory has over certain competitors. Finally, I have explained how the theory can handle donkey anaphora, by appealing to independently motivated accounts of the semantics of conditionals and adverbs of quantification. As a result of this, I hope to have convinced you that the CDQ account of anaphora and instantial terms is a promising one.[22]

---

21 The only difference in the two cases is that when factors affect what counts as a minimal situation, they constrain the nature of the situations quantified over by the phrase '... for any minimal situation s_1 in which ...' in (C), whereas the familiarity and anaphoricness of a cdq in the consequent of a donkey conditional constrain the nature of the situations quantified over by the phrase '... there is a situation s_2 such that ...' in (C). This difference hardly seems significant enough to warrant embracing the former mechanism and rejecting the latter.

22 An earlier version of this paper was given at the Conference on Contextual Sensitivity in Semantics at the University of Cincinnati on November 15–18, 2001. I thank the audience on that occasion for their helpful questions and comments.

References

Berman, S. 1987. "Situation-Based Semantics for Adverbs of Quantification." In *University of Massachusetts Occasional Papers 12*, ed. J. Blevins and A. Vainikka. Amherst: University of Massachusetts.

Chierchia, G. 1995. *Dynamics of Meaning*. Chicago: University of Chicago Press.

Evans, G. 1977. "Pronouns, Quantifiers and Relative Clauses (I)." *Canadian Journal of Philosophy* 8 (3): 467–536.

Groenendijk, J., and Stokhof, M.. 1991. "Dynamic Predicate Logic." *Linguistics and Philosophy* 14: 39–100.

Guerts, B. 2002. "Donkey Business." *Linguistics and Philosophy* 25: 129–56.

Heim, I. 1982. *The Semantics of Definite and Indefinite Noun Phrases*. Doctoral Thesis, University of Massachusetts, Amherst.

———. 1990. "E-Type Pronouns and Donkey Anaphora." *Linguistics and Philosophy* 13: 137–77.

Kamp, H. 1981. "A Theory of Truth and Semantic Representation." In *Formal Methods in the Study of Language*, ed. J. Groenendijk, *et al*. Amsterdam: Amsterdam Centre.

Kanazawa, M. 1994. "Weak vs. Strong Readings of Donkey Sentences and Monotonicity Inference in a Dynamic Setting." *Linguistics and Philosophy* 17: 109–58.

King, J. C. 1987. "Pronouns, Descriptions and the Semantics of Discourse." *Philosophical Studies* 51: 341–363.

———. 1991. "Instantial Terms, Anaphora and Arbitrary Objects." *Philosophical Studies* 61: 239–265.

———.1993. "Intentional Identity Generalized." *Journal of Philosophical Logic* 22: 61–93.

———. 1994. "Anaphora and Operators." *Philosophical Perspectives, 8: Logic and Language*.

Lewis, D. 1988 [1975]. "Adverbs of Quantification." In *Papers in Philosophical Logic*, 5-20. Cambridge: Cambridge University Press.

Neale, S. 1990. *Descriptions*. Cambridge, MA: MIT Press.

Rooth, M. 1987. "NP Interpretation in Montague Grammar, File Change Semantics, and Situation Semantics." In *Generalized Quantifiers*, ed. P. Gardenfors, 237-268. Dordrecht: Reidel.

Wilson, G. 1984. "Pronouns and Pronomial Descriptions: A New Semantical Category." *Philosophical Studies* 45: 1–30.

CANADIAN JOURNAL OF PHILOSOPHY
Supplementary Volume 30

Proper Names: Ideas and Chains

JOSEP MACIÀ

Chains, well I can't break away from these chains [...]
And they ain't the kind that you can see.
("Chains," Gerry Goffin and Carole King)

The main aim of this paper is to present a certain notion – that of *Coordination* – and an associated requirement – the *Coordination Requirement* (CR) –, and to show how they help us to better understand the communicative role of proper names. A second aim of the paper is to use these notions to defend the kind of view I favour regarding the meaning of proper names – a certain kind of descriptivist theory – by showing that this view is not subject to two seemingly powerful considerations against it that have been provided from two different camps: one from the anti-descriptivist camp (by Saul Kripke in *Naming and Necessity*), another from the neo-Fregean camp (by Richard Heck in *The Sense of Communication*). In dealing with these matters, I will have to discuss the role that complex individual concepts (or *ideas*) play in allowing us to understand and use proper names.

In *Naming and Necessity* (1980), Saul Kripke provides a number of arguments against descriptivist theories of proper names. He suggests that beyond these specific arguments, we know that descriptivism cannot be correct since it is based on a wrong picture of how proper names work. He claims that descriptivism is not compatible with the very plausible general picture about how proper names work that he presents. Against this, I will argue that, because of the *Coordination Requirement*, even if descriptivism is correct, something very much like a Kripkean picture must still obtain.

On the other hand, Richard Heck's *The Sense of Communication* (1995) presents a complex argument for the view that successful linguistic communication using proper names requires the transmission of senses associated with the names. On my understanding of it, the argument is based on the claim that the only explanation for certain facts is that names have associated senses. I will argue that the existence of the Coordination Requirement provides an alternative and better explanation of those same facts.

In Section I, I present Kripke's general argument against descriptivism. In Section II, I present the sort of descriptivist theory I favour. Section III is the central section of the paper; in it, I introduce the notion of *Coordination* and the associated *Coordination Requirement* (CR). In Section IV, I show how (CR) can be used to resist Kripke's general consideration against descriptivism. In Section V, I consider two versions of an argument by Richard Heck in favour of a kind of descriptivism incompatible with the one I favour. I contend that, again, (CR) can be used to resist this argument. In the course of the discussion of Heck's argument I refine my characterization of the notion of *Coordination* and of its corresponding *Coordination Requirement*.

I. Introduction: Kripke Against Descriptivism

One of the aims of Kripke's *Naming and Necessity* is to show that it is very implausible that any descriptivist theory of proper names be correct. Another one of the aims is to present an alternative picture of how proper names work.

According to Kripke's characterization in *Naming and Necessity*, a descriptivist theory of proper names (DT) holds that a name has an associated description or cluster of descriptions, and that if an object fits the description or most of the descriptions in the cluster, the name refers to that object, and if nothing fits the description, the name does not refer. What I will call a *meaning descriptivist theory* holds that the associated description is synonymous with the name; what I will call a *reference-fixing descriptivist theory* holds that the associated description only fixes the referent of the name.

Kripke acknowledges that there are some very powerful reasons in favour of a descriptive theory of proper names. One of them is that a descriptivist theory can explain how the reference of a proper name is determined, whereas for a non-descriptivist theory, it would seem mysterious how a name can *reach* its referent. "If there is *not* such a descriptive content to the name, then how do people ever use names to refer to things at all?" (1980, 28). There is a deeply felt intuition that in order to be speaking about something by using a name one must have, as Wettstein (1989, 318) puts it, a "*cognitive fix* on the thing in question," "something in one's thought must correctly distinguish the relevant item from everything else in the universe."

The advantages of descriptivism notwithstanding, Kripke claims that descriptivism regarding proper names is clearly false. He presents a number of very serious difficulties for a DT:

(I) The modal argument: if we substitute any of the most plausible candidates for the description associated with 'Aristotle' for 'the *X*' in 'Aristotle might not have been the *x*', we obtain a true statement.

(II) Non-necessity (of the associated description): In the Gödel/Schmidt example, 'Gödel' will refer to Gödel, who is not the person who proved the theorem.

(III) Non-sufficiency (of the associated description): in the Gödel/Schmidt example, 'Gödel' will not refer to Schmidt, who is the person who proved the theorem.

(IV) The epistemic argument: if we substitute any of the most plausible candidates for the description associated with 'Aristotle' for 'the *X*' in 'Aristotle is the *X*', we obtain a statement that is not an *a priori* truth.

(V) Circularity: this objection applies to those DT's that appeal to meta-linguistic descriptions such as 'the object named "Socrates"'.

Naming and Necessity also presents a different kind of consideration against descriptivism. It provides a reason for not holding any DT, even if one thinks that the friend of descriptivism might be able to offer a reply to some of the objections in (I)–(V). It is a consideration of a much more general sort:

(GenCon) Descriptivism is based on the wrong general picture: Kripke presents in *Naming and Necessity* a very plausible picture of how the reference of a proper name is determined; this picture is incompatible with descriptivism.

The well-known Kripkean picture of proper names is roughly the following: what a name refers to in one specific use is determined by a chain that goes from the object named to the speaker of that specific use; the chain starts with an initial "baptism," where the name is introduced by some people (by naming the object either by ostention or by identifying it through some description); the chain then continues with those who learned the name from the ones participating in the initial baptism, and those who learned it from them, and so on. What is essential for me to appropriately use the name 'Feynman' is not that I appeal to some description such as 'the one that introduced the theory of pair production and annihilation' that uniquely picks out Feynman independently of the community in which I am using the name; rather, what it is essential is that I am appropriately placed in the chain that started with Feynman himself and an initial baptism and that has reached me through my community.

(One observation regarding what counts as "my community": the community for the use of a particular name does not need to coincide with the community for most of the other words in my language (i.e., with a community such as the English speakers, the Swahili speakers, etc.) 'Eva Peron' is a name for Eva Peron beyond the Spanish speaking community. Is it the case that the community for any name is the whole of humanity? Certainly not; consider, for instance, the word 'Monaco', which is a name in the Italian speaking community for the city that in German is called 'München', whereas in, say, German, 'Monaco' is the name of a certain tiny European country. Also: A few of us might decide, for instance, to call Elisabeth Anscombe 'Elians'. Then the community for the name 'Elians' will be just those of us who agreed to use 'Elians' as a name for Anscombe.)

The erroneous picture that Kripke (1980, 91) believes is behind a DT is the following: someone alone in her room decides to use a certain name, e.g., 'Gödel', to refer to, say, whoever proved that arithmetic is incomplete. Then, if Schmidt was the one that proved the theorem, it is clear that the person does not refer to Gödel when she tells herself, e.g., 'Gödel was a genius'. Whom does the person refer to when she uses the name when talking to other people (who took no part in her introduction of the name 'Gödel' and who are in no other way connected with her in their use of 'Gödel')? It is not clear what we should answer here. (Most of our puzzlement arises, I believe, from the fact that the person would be acting in an irrational way, since if she knows that 'Gödel' is a name that she introduced while alone in her room, it would be irrational for her to try to use it in front of others who were not there in the room and who, she should believe, know nothing about this name). I would say that our intuitions are that if she refers at all, she would refer to Schmidt, and not to Gödel. And whether we want to say that she refers or not, it is clear that we must say that she does not communicate the thought she intends to express to the people who are listening to her; it seems clear that we must say that they do not understand what she wanted to say.

Is this really a correct description of the descriptivist picture regarding proper names? I think it is not. I will explain why in section III, where we will consider related examples. Before that, though, in the next section I will present the particular sort of descriptivist theory I favour. This theory is different from, and incompatible with, both the anti-descriptivist view of Kripke and the descriptivist, neo-Fregean view of Heck. So if one wants to defend the sort of descriptivist theory I favour, it is essential that one has a way of replying both to the general considerations against descriptivism by Kripke and the argument in favour of Heck's particular sort of neo-Fregeanism. The Coordination Requirement will allow us to reply to both arguments. So, the notion of *Coordination* and its associated requirement are useful to anyone interested in resisting either one of these arguments (it can, for instance, be used by the Kripkean to resist Heck's argument). Still, the notion of *Coordination* and its associated (CR) are of *particular* interest if one holds a descriptivist theory of the kind I hold.

II. A Descriptivist Theory

In addition to the distinction between a *meaning descriptivist theory* and a *reference-fixing descriptivist theory*, there is another distinction among DT's that is lurking in the discussion in *Naming and Necessity*: the description (or cluster) might be associated with the name for the entire community, or it might be so associated only for a specific user, or even just for a particular use by a specific user. I will call a DT of the first kind a *community-level* DT, and a theory of the second kind an *individual-level* DT.

We have then four kinds of DT's:

133

(a)   Community-level meaning DT
(b)   Community-level reference-fixing DT
(c)   Individual-level meaning DT
(d)   Individual-level reference-fixing DT

I will now proceed to describe a particular theory of type (d). This is the kind of theory I favour regarding the semantics of proper names. I will not make much use of this theory in the later sections of the paper (I will only go back to it at the end Section IV). My main reason for sketching this theory here is to show what my motivation is to reply both to an argument against descriptivism and an argument in favour of a Neo-Fregean view. As pointed out above, (CR) is of particular interest in order to defend this theory.

As a theory of type (d), i.e., as a reference-fixing individual-level theory of proper names, our theory is a sort of descriptivist theory about proper names that holds that the (cluster of) description(s) associated with a name fixes the name's reference but is not synonymous with it, and that each name has an associated (cluster of) description(s) for each individual speaker and each use of the name.

Our theory holds the following principle (DR) (*Direct Reference*):

(DR)   The semantic contribution of a name to what is expressed
       by a sentence where the name occurs consists in providing
       a certain individual.

Is (DR) compatible with a descriptivist theory of proper names? A DT of the kind in (d) can be perfectly compatible with the direct-reference view of proper names. An individual-use reference-fixing theory can claim that the semantic function of a name is to provide an individual, while being at the same time sensitive to the intuition that in order to talk about an individual one needs to be able to intellectually reach the individual, or as we said above, to be able to have a cognitive fix on that individual. All a name does is to refer to some individual, but in order to be able to competently use a name, a speaker must have a cognitive fix on the individual, and he can do so if the speaker in each one of his uses of the name has an associated "description" (more in a moment about what exactly can be part of this "description") that applies uniquely to the individual that is the referent of the name.

Each person in a community might identify an individual in a different way, but if they all identify the same individual and are justified in believing that they all identify the same individual, then they can agree to use a certain expression as a name for that individual.

Even if each speaker is able to identify the referent of the name, whatever information he has associated with the name is not part of the meaning of the name, and need not be shared by other speakers. Being able to identify the referent of the name is just a condition on being able to understand the convention governing the use of the name (i.e., that people in the community have agreed to use such an expression as a name of such an individual), and this does not alter the fact that the sole semantic function of the name is to provide some individual.

Now, there are some necessary conditions that are to be met if some person A is to be a competent user of a name N that refers to X: One requirement, for instance, will be that A knows N as a syntactic object. This will require, among other things, that A is able to identify tokens of N under normal circumstances, and that A knows N's syntactic possibilities of combination.

A must also (tacitly!) know that N is an expression whose meaning is of the kind that satisfies condition (DT).

In the spirit of what Evans (1982) calls 'Russell's Principle', A must also know that the individual that N provides is X. In order to know this it is not necessary for A to have any special acquaintance with X. All that is required is that A is able to identify X some way or other. It is enough that A has some description that uniquely picks out X; in this way A will be able to "intellectually reach" X, and so A will be able to believe that N is a name of the object that is the so-and-so.

Different speakers might, and most likely will, of course, use different "descriptions" to identify the object they all refer to with the name N.

The information one speaker uses to identify the referent of a name will usually not be a single description, but a whole cluster of information – including non-linguistically codified information such as how a person looks. Each such cluster of information that a subject binds together as identifying one, single object is what I will call an *idea*. It might be that not all the "descriptions" in an idea apply to the individual to which the idea applies. Also, not all the information in an idea has the same weight. An idea applies to a certain individual if the individual satisfies a weighted majority of the information in the idea. The relative weight of each "description" in an idea associated with a name N might depend on contextual factors.

An idea is an individual concept. Any individual concept includes as part of it that there is a single individual satisfying certain conditions. An idea, then, includes as part of it that there is a single individual to which a weighted majority of certain items of information apply.

The idea associated with a name N will typically contain information such as "the individual that those I learned the name N from referred to with N" or "the individual that other people in this community refer to with N," or "the individual that up to now has being called N."

Is not the descriptivist theory I am describing obviously subject to the circularity objection I pointed out in (V) above? The kind of "description" that one person A *cannot* use to identify an individual X is the sort of description that appeals, one way or another, to the fact that A is able to identify X using that description. This would be circular. There is no circularity involved, though, if the description appeals to what others are able to identify, if they are able to identify the object without appealing to what A is able to identify (either in a direct or "indirect" way: they would appeal indirectly to what A is able to identify if they were to appeal to someone else who, in turn, directly relies on what A is able to identify, or directly relies on someone else who indirectly relies on what A is able to identify).

If an individual is already named α and I know it, then that the individual is named α will be part of my idea of that individual. It would not be possible for a group of us to first introduce some name β by identifying the individual that is to be called β as 'the individual that is called β' (or 'that will be called β'). But, of course, if an individual is already named α, and I know that there is an individual named α, and if that is the only such individual, I can think of it as 'the only individual named α'.

That this is possible, and that there is no circularity involved, here, might be easier to appreciate if we consider an analogous case in which there is some convention involving some individual which is not a convention about the use of names. Suppose that a group of individuals have the convention of jumping twice every time they meet some particular individual. If I learn about this fact, even without knowing anything else about the individual in front of whom people jump I am able to intellectually reach this individual, knowing that he is 'the one about whom there is the jumping-convention'. (Just with this information I would not, of course, be able to follow the jumping-convention because being able to follow this convention requires knowing who the individual is in a way that allows one to realize [in normal conditions] that one is in front of that particular individual. But in order to take part in a convention of naming something or someone, what is needed is not to be able to realize whether one is in front of the object, but simply to be able to intellectually reach the object, and to do this it is enough that one has an idea that applies uniquely to that individual.)

I pointed out above that the different "descriptions" in an idea might not have the same weight, and that the relative weight of some description in an idea might depend on the context. Metalinguistic descriptions are usually the ones that have the most weight. One way of seeing that this must be so is by appeal to the following test: Suppose that some person X uses a certain name, say 'Plato', and is told that some of the information that she is associating with the name does not apply to the individual she wants to talk about. Suppose that we ask X which of the descriptions she is associating with 'Plato' she is more willing to give up. It will usually be the case that she will be much more willing to give up descriptions like 'the teacher of Aristotle' rather than metalinguistic descriptions such as 'the individual that those I learned the name from referred to with "Plato"'.[1]

III. Coordination

Suppose there are two villages in a distant forest whose inhabitants speak the same language, say, English. There has been frequent contact between the two communities: the two villages are only some 10 km apart, though there is a mountain between them. Suppose that

---

1 For a more detailed discussion of the theory introduced in this section see Macià 1998. For other metalinguistic descriptivist theories of proper names substantially different from the one presented in this paper see, for instance, Loar 1976, Bach 1987, Recanati 1993, and García-Carpintero 2000.

a number of planes, say twenty, start flying daily in the aerial space around the mountain, and so can be seen by the people in both villages. Assume that during the whole period in which the flying takes place there is no communication at all between the people in one of the villages and the people in the other, and no communication at all between anyone in one of the villages and someone from somewhere else (in particular, people are not able to listen to the radio or use the Internet). Suppose that in each of the villages, people start recognizing the planes and give names to them (say each plane is painted in bright, distinctive colours). Suppose that something extremely unlikely happens: people in both villages give the same name to one of the planes: both communities call a certain plane 'Cratacrota' (even though, as it should be expected, they give of course different names to the other nineteen planes). Suppose now that one day two people, *A* and *B*, one from each village, meet in the mountains and, not realizing they are from different villages, *A* tells *B*, "Cratacrota did not do any flying this morning." Did *B* understand what *A* told her? Did *A* and *B* successfully communicate?

I think we should say that they did not, even if *B* formed the same belief she would have formed had she really understood *A*. We can aid our direct intuitions regarding this case by appealing to the following principle, that I will call the *Transmission of Knowledge requirement* (TOK)[2]

(TOK) For a speaker *X* to successfully communicate by means of an utterance *U* with a speaker *Y*, it is necessary that *Y* gains knowledge (by testimony) of what *X* intended to say by uttering *U* (providing that *Y* is justified in believing that *X* is to be trusted as regarding the truth of what *X* attempts to say by using *U*, and furthermore *X* is to be so trusted, and what he intends to communicate is true).

TOK tell us, then, that successful communication has to be able to give rise to transmission of knowledge. The condition in TOK is not

---

2 Different versions of the same requirement can be found in Evans 1982, 310–11 and Heck 1995, 92.

met in the case of the two villagers A and B: even if A's utterance results in B forming a belief with the same content as the belief that A wanted to communicate, our intuitions are that B does not *know* that Cratacrota had not been flying in the morning, even if B is completely justified in trusting A's testimony, and furthermore A's testimony is accurate. The reason that B does not acquire knowledge is that it is only by chance that she ends up forming the right belief. (Similarly, I do not gain the knowledge that it is now 11:23 p.m. by looking at a clock which, unknown to me, is broken and is always indicating '11:23 p.m.', even if it now happens to be 11:23 p.m.) Given that B did not come to *know* what A intended to communicate, we can apply (TOK) to conclude that in the case of the two villagers, there was no successful communication between A and B.

What went wrong? I would like to suggest that what was missing in this case is that A and B were not *coordinated* in their use of 'Cratacrota'. I will try to characterize the notion more precisely in a moment, but to give a preliminary, rough idea of what our characterization will try to capture: the notion of *being coordinated in the use of an expression* is intended to be one that applies to those uses of an expression by a speaker that, unlike the use of 'Cratacrota' by A, are not independent or disconnected from what the other speakers do.

In the remainder of this section I will, first, give a characterization of this notion of coordination for the particular case where the expression under consideration is a proper name; I will then introduce the *coordination requirement*; then, I will suggest how the characterization of the notion of *coordination* might be generalized.

We can recursively define *being coordinated*, in terms of *being immediately coordinated* in the following way:

> I am *coordinated* with an individual A in my possession of the name N to refer to X if and only if I am *immediately coordinated* with A or I am coordinated with someone who is immediately coordinated with A. I am *immediately coordinated* with A in my possession of the name N to refer to X if one of the following three conditions obtains:
>
> (i) I learned the name (at least in part) from A. That is, I learned from A that the expression N is used in some community

as a name in accordance with (DR) to determine *X*. The qualification "at least in part" is meant to include the case where I realized that there is the relevant kind of convention by observing how some individuals who included *A* were using the expression *N*, and to include also the case where by observing *A* I would have *some* evidence that there is the relevant kind of convention, but not enough evidence as to allow me to *know* that *N* is used to determine *X* in accordance with (DR), and so I also rely on other sources of evidence – when each by itself is not sufficient to provide me with knowledge of the relevant convention, even though taken all together they do provide me with enough evidence to give me *knowledge* of the convention;

(ii)   *A* learned the name (at least in part) from me,

(iii) We both took part in the introduction of the name. We might have done so by explicitly saying, "Let's use *N* as a name of such-and-such individual." The such-and-such individual might have being specified by means of some descriptions, or might have being identified using a demonstrative and relying on the fact that each of us were able to identify it and that, furthermore, each of us knew that the other was identifying the same individual as we did. Or we can both be part of the introduction of a name if we agreed on following a certain general rule for the introduction of names (like the one governing the assignment of number-names to the streets in certain cities). There could possibly be still other ways of two people participating together in the introduction of a name.

Using the notion of coordination, we can explicitly introduce the following *coordination requirement* (CR)

(CR)   For two speakers *S* and *S'* to be able to successfully communicate using a proper name, it is necessary that *S* and *S'* be coordinated in their use of the name.

In the 'Cratacrota' example, (CR) was not met, and that explains why there was no successful communication between *A* and *B*.

The notion of coordination applies beyond the use of proper names. Consider the following case, similar to the 'Cratacrota' example. There are two communities that speak two different languages and that have never been in contact with each other (either directly or indirectly). It so happens that, by pure chance, they use the same expression, say 'kaumam', to express that it rains. Suppose that one day a man from one of the communities meets a woman from the other and, not knowing that they are from different communities, says to her, "Kaumam." As in the previous example, the intuition seems to be that something went wrong and that there was no successful communication between the two people. This intuition can, again, be supported by appealing to (TOK): even if the hearer formed the same belief she would had formed if she had understood what the speaker said, she did not gain knowledge of what he said. And so, it follows from (TOK) that there was no successful communication between the two people.

As in the 'Cratacrota' example, it seems that the correct explanation of what went wrong is that the two people were not *coordinated* in their use of 'kaumam'.

We can try to give a rough generalization of our characterization of the notion of *coordination*, so that it applies to any sort of (simple) expression, in the following way:

I am *coordinated* with an individual *A* in my possession of an expression *E* to mean *Y* if and only if I am immediately coordinated with *A* or I am coordinated with someone who is immediately coordinated with *A*.

I am *immediately coordinated* with *A* in my possession of the expression *E* to mean *Y* if one of the following obtains:

(1) I learned the expression (at least in part) from *A*. That is, I learned from *A* that the expression *E* is used in a certain community in some specific way to contribute certain sort of meaning to the complex expressions where it appears, and that furthermore *E* has such-and-such syntactic category and enjoys such-and-such possibilities of combination with other expressions.

(2) *A* learned the expression *E* (at least in part) from me.

(3)   We both took part in the introduction of the expression. We might have done so by explicitly saying, "Let's use *E* as an expression of such-and-such syntactic category to make such-and-such contribution to what is expressed by the more complex expressions that contain it." There could possibly be still other ways of two people participating together in the introduction of an expression.

What explains why there was not successful communication in the 'kaumam' example is that the two people involved were not coordinated in their use of 'kaumam'.

Notice that an example involving two completely isolated linguistic communities and a very unlikely coincidence between them could involve *any* expression (for instance, a sentence containing words such as 'bachelor', 'fortnight', or any other expression we wish). A generalization of the *Coordination Requirement* applies to any sort of expression, not just to proper names.

IV. A Reply To Kripke's (GenCon)

In the light of (CR) and the examples discussed in Section III, it should be clear that what Kripke regarded as the erroneous picture about proper names is not just erroneous about proper names but about any sort of expression at all. No one can communicate using an expression that one has endowed with meaning by an act performed when alone in one's room.

It is hard to deny, on the other hand, that expressions such as 'bachelor' or 'fortnight' do have some sort of "descriptivist meaning" (knowing their meaning requires knowing some sort of condition associated with them). The picture that Kripke associates with descriptivism does not even apply to these kind of expressions. Kripke has presented an inadequate picture of descriptivism.

Beyond the fact that Kripke presents a distorted picture of descriptivism, we can ask: Is descriptivism incompatible with the Kripkean picture of proper names (as (GenCon) claimed)? It is not. Descriptivism *is* perfectly compatible with the Kripkean picture. What is more, because of (CR), if a descriptivist theory is correct then something very much like a Kripkean picture of proper names should also be the case. If speakers A and B are to successfully communicate using a proper name N, then they must be coordinated in their use of N. That means that there is going to be what we might call 'a *coordination chain*' linking each one of them with those they learned the name from, and linking those people in turn to the ones *they* learned the name from, and so on. At one end this chain will lead to the object itself. On the other hand, we have that if there is a coordination chain linking A and B with the other speakers and with the object itself, then there will also be what we might call 'a *Kripkean chain*' linking A and B and those they learned the name from, and so on, and ultimately linking them to the object itself. Why is that so? Because Kripkean chains are part of coordination chains. Let's justify this last claim. Whenever there is what we might call a *coordination link* in a chain, then that link is also (what we might call) a *Kripkean link* in the chain: According to *Naming and Necessity*, for there to be a successful transmission of a proper name involving two individuals (i.e., for it to be the case that two speakers constitute one link in a Kripkean chain) it has to be the case that one of them "hears the name" from the other and, also[3], that when he learns the name he intends to use it with the same reference as the person from whom he heard it. Now, if *any* descriptivist theory is correct, then the following has to be the case: if there is a coordination link between A and B (i.e., if A and B are immediately coordinated with respect to the name), then one of them will have learned the name from the other (say, B learned from A). What is required for B to learn the name N from A will vary depending on which descriptivist theory we consider. Whatever descriptivist theory we consider, though, it will be the case that if B learned the name from A, then he "heard it from A" and he has the intention of using it in the same way that those whom he learned it from did (if a descriptivist theory of, say, type (a) is correct, then one additional requirement will be that B associates with the name the same description that A associates with the name, etc.). And so, the fact that A and B are immediately coordinated with respect to the name (i.e., the fact that they constitute one link in a coordination chain) will imply that they constitute one link in a *Kripkean chain*.

---

3 Quite often, the fact that Kripke places this restriction on when there is a link in a chain is overlooked. See Kripke 1980, 96.

So, even if a descriptivist theory is correct, because of (CR) it will be the case that a Kripkean picture obtains. The strong intuitive plausibility of the Kripkean picture cannot be used, then, as an additional consideration against descriptivism.

Maybe one could try to raise the following objection to what I just proposed. Claiming that a Kripkean picture of proper names obtains does not just involve claiming that it is *necessary* that there is a Kripkean chain (or rather *net*) linking the speakers to each other and to the object they refer to. It also involves claiming that it is *sufficient* that there is such a net for it to be the case that a speaker successfully refers to a certain individual. My reply is that if that was what was involved in it being the case that a Kripkean picture obtains, then the Kripkean picture would not be correct and so it would not be a problem for a descriptivist theory that it is not compatible with this sufficiency condition of the "Kripkean picture." Let's see why this is so by considering an example. (This example will also be of use in dispelling another possible objection to the descriptivist theory that I have presented in Section II. The worry is: Given that the descriptivist theory that I favour holds that there is metalinguistic information associated with a name, and also holds that this information is usually that which has the most weight in determining which individual [if any] we refer to by a use of a name, is there any substantial difference between our view of proper names and Kripke's view?) [4]

Consider the name 'Aristotle'. It is clear that we could learn that some of the information that we have associated with 'Aristotle' is not correct and that this would not change the fact that with 'Aristotle' we have been referring to Aristotle. We might learn, for instance, that he did not actually write the *Nicomachean Ethics*, or that he was not the teacher of Alexander the Great. This would not prevent us from referring to him with the name 'Aristotle'. Now, could we learn that, unbeknown to us until now, with the name 'Aristotle' we have been referring to a column in the Parthenon? The answer to this question in obviously "No." We could certainly learn that at the origin of the

---

4 Kripke considers (88) the possibility of a metalinguistic descriptivist theory that would be trivially correct if his views on proper names are correct. He credits Robert Nozick with pointing out that there is such a possibility.

name 'Aristotle' there is certain column of the Parthenon (imagine that two people that used to meet next to the column gave it the name 'Aristotle', and other people then learned the name from them; later on, some people came to believe that the column Aristotle had the power of inspiring poets to write good poems, then someone was gullible enough to believe that some poems in a manuscript that someone left next to the column had magically been written by the column itself; other people later on attributed to the column Aristotle the authorship of some philosophy works – which were actually written by several different authors – and so on ...; while all this being the case, each new person learning the name intended to use the name in the same way as those whom she learned the name from). Even if it so happened that, unbeknown to us, at the origin of the name 'Aristotle' (at the origin of the Kripkean chain) there was a certain column in the Parthenon, that would not make it the case that with the name 'Aristotle' we had all along been referring to the column in the Parthenon. Nevertheless, if the Kripkean picture implied that it is a sufficient condition for a speaker to refer to a certain object that there is a Kripkean chain linking the speaker and the object, then the Kripkean picture would wrongly predict that in the hypothetical case we are considering, 'Aristotle' would refer to the column.

Notice that this case does not present a problem for the kind of descriptivist theory that I favour: even if each speaker associates with the name some metalinguistic information, such as 'the object that those that I learned the name from referred to with "Aristotle"', he also has other information in the idea associated with the name. And this other information (a person, author of such and such works, teacher of Alexander, etc.) is so massively false of the column that it makes it the case that (even if the metalinguistic information were to lead to the column in the Parthenon) the idea as a whole does not apply to any individual. And so the prediction of our theory is that the name does not refer. This is in accordance with our intuitions regarding this hypothetical situation.

V. Chains and Senses

Heck (1995) offers a complex and very interesting argument for a neo-Fregean view of proper names. According to this kind of view, names would have conventionally associated "descriptions" that would provide their meaning. This would be, then, a community-level descriptive theory of proper names. Even if it is a descriptivist theory, this theory is in opposition to the individual-level descriptivist theory that I favour.

There is some difficulty in establishing what exactly the details of Heck's complex argument are[5]. We will consider two versions of an argument for the existence of senses that provide the meaning of a name. It might well be that neither of these two versions of the argument fully corresponds to the arguments in Heck 1995. Even so, I think that both versions of the argument that we will consider are interesting in their own right, and present a serious difficulty for all non-Fregean views of proper names. I will use our discussion of the two versions of the argument to further develop the characterization of the notion of *coordination* that I introduced in section III. I will call the two versions of the argument *Heckian argument-1* and *Heckian argument-2*.

Heck's argumentation is based on an example similar to our 'Cratacrota' example.

Heckian argument-1: A new patient who suffers from amnesia arrives at a clinic. His doctor, Alex, names him 'George Orwell'. Unknown to everyone in the clinic, the patient happens to be George Orwell, the writer. Toni, who doesn't know about the new patient but who knows about the writer, tells Alex, "George Orwell wrote *1984*." Alex takes Toni as intending to refer to the new patient. The name 'George Orwell' has the same syntax and the same referent for both Alex and Toni. Even so, it seems clear that there was some failure of communication between them. The neo-Fregean has an easy explanation of what went wrong: Successful communication using proper names requires not just the transmission of the referent of the name, but also of the appropriate sense expressed by the name. Alex did not grasp the sense associated with 'George Orwell' in Toni's use of it.

This conclusion would, if correct, pose a problem not just for a Kripkean non-descriptivist view of proper names, but also for the DT of type (d) that I want to defend.

---

5 This can also be seen in the exchange with Byrne and Thau (see Byrne and Thau 1996 and Heck 1996). García-Carpintero (2000) also expresses some doubts regarding what exactly the argument in Heck 1995 is.

The notion of coordination that we have introduced provides us, though, with an alternative explanation of what went wrong in the exchange between Toni and Alex that does not require subscribing to the neo-Fregean thesis: there was no successful communication between Toni and Alex because they were not coordinated and, so, (CR) was not met.

Heckian argument-2: Consider a situation just like the one in *Heckian argument-1* except that now Toni also knows that there is a new patient who the people in the clinic call 'George Orwell'. Toni, though, like everyone else in the clinic, does not know that the patient and the writer are the same person. As in the previous case, Toni says to Alex, intending to refer to the writer, "George Orwell wrote *1984*." Alex takes Toni as intending to refer to the new patient. Again, the intuitions are that there is a failure of communication between Toni and Alex, even if they share the referent of the name. (We can supplement our intuitions by appealing to (TOK) and observing that the belief that Alex formed as a result of listening to Toni does not constitute knowledge – it was just by chance that Alex formed a belief about the right person). And again, the neo-Fregean seems able to explain why there was a failure in communication by appealing to the fact that Alex did not grasp the appropriate sense that was associated with the name.

It would seem, though, that unlike *Heckian argument-1*, we cannot explain what went wrong by appealing to (CR): in this case, Alex and Toni *are* coordinated, both in their use of 'George Orwell' to refer to the writer and in their use of 'George Orwell' to refer to the patient.

What this example shows is that the notion of coordination should not be taken to apply to speakers and names in general, but rather to specific uses of a name by a speaker. We should not ask whether or not you and I are in general coordinated with respect to the name N, but rather whether or not my use now of N is one with respect to which you and I are coordinated.

Regarding the 'George Orwell' example, we would like to say that Toni and Alex were not *coordinated with respect to the specific use of 'George Orwell'* that Alex made: like in the 'Cratacrota' example above, it was just by chance that Toni and Alex ended up thinking about the same individual. We would like to have a notion of *coordination* that accounts for the intuition that Alex's uses of 'George Orwell' when Alex intends to refer to the person whom he identifies as the famous writer are coordinated with Toni's uses of 'George Orwell' when Toni intends to refer to the person whom Toni identifies as the famous writer, but *not* with Toni's uses when Toni intends to refer to the person whom Toni identifies as the new patient; and Alex's uses of 'George Orwell' to refer to the person whom he identifies as the new patient are coordinated with Toni's uses of 'George Orwell' to refer to the person whom Toni identifies as the new patient, but *not* with Toni's uses to refer to person whom Toni identifies as the famous writer.

What is essential for coordination in the use of a name is not (as the example just given might lead one into thinking) that both speakers associate the same information with the name in that use of the name, but rather that there is the right sort of connection between the fact that the first speaker associates the idea (information) i with the name and the fact that the second speaker associates the idea i' with the name (whether i and i' are similar or not).

We thus need a new characterization of the notion of *coordination* that is defined with respect to specific uses of a name. Since the characterization of this new notion of *coordination* is technically more complex than the one we have so far, it will be helpful to consider first a simplified case: one in which there are only two speakers involved and one learned the name from the other (we will furthermore consider first just a *sufficient* condition). Suppose that A learned the name N from B, and that at a certain point A uses the name N while addressing B. What would be sufficient for it to be the case that A and B are coordinated in this specific use of N?

In order to answer this question, we need to introduce first the notion of an *idea being a predecessor of another idea*. I believe that this notion has a clear, intuitive content. For our present purposes we will rest content with the following rough characterization[6]:

If i and i^* are ideas that some individual X has or has had, then i^* is a ***predecessor*** of i, if i resulted from i^* as a result of a process of adding or subtracting information from i^*. Each operation of adding or sub-

---

6 Some of the notions that we use in the characterization would themselves, of course, also call for a clarification. We will not pursue here, though, the task of providing such a clarification.

tracting information was made assuming that the original idea and the idea that resulted from it applied to the same individual[7].

We will by stipulation consider any idea to be a predecessor of itself (this stipulation is harmless and will simplify some definitions).

Now consider again the case in which A learned the name N from B, and is now using it when talking to B. We have that:

A is coordinated with B in this specific use of N if

there is an idea, idea-a, that A has associated with N (and which is what allows A to identify the referent of N, and so to be a competent user of N),[8] and there is an idea, idea-b, that B has associated with N, and there is an idea-a* that A has or has had associated with N, and there is an idea idea-b* that B has or has had associated with N, and

(i)   idea-a* is a predecessor of idea-a
(ii)   idea-b* is a predecessor of idea-b
(iii) idea-a* has no predecessor (other than itself) that A associated with N
(iv) A came to have idea-a* associated with N as a result of B having idea-b* associated with N (for instance, A might come to associate idea-a* with N because of his observation of B using N, and in those uses B was able to make a competent use of the name because B was associating idea-b* to N).

---

7   We could give a characterization of *coordination* that would be equivalent to the one that we will provide which would not appeal to this notion of *an idea being a predecessor of another*. We could instead have identity conditions for ideas that allowed them to undergo changes in the information they contain. Then, instead of talking about one idea being a predecessor of another, we would talk about one stage of an idea preceding in time another stage of the same idea.

8   From now on we will omit the clause between brackets. Every time we say that some speaker S has an idea-s associated with a name N, it has to be understood that having the idea-s associated with N is what allows the speaker to "intellectually reach" the individual the name refers to, and so it is part of what allows the speaker to be a competent user of the name.

Notice that according to this characterization, what makes it the case that A and B are coordinated in the present use of N by A, is that there is the right kind of relationship between two ideas that are predecessors of the two ideas that A and B are now associating with N and that allow them to be competent users of the name.

The situation described in the clauses (i)–(iv) is represented in the following diagram:

Figure 1.

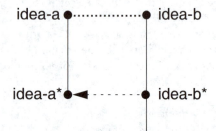

Now we can address the more complex task of characterizing in general what it means to say that two speakers are coordinated in some particular use of a name. I will proceed as follows: I will first give the definition of *coordination in a particular use of a name*; this definition will make use of the notion of *coordination**; I will then define *coordination**; this definition of coordination* will make use of the notion of *being immediately coordinated**; I will then give the definition of *being immediately coordinated**; this will complete our definition of *coordination in a particular use of a name*.

A and B are coordinated with respect to some specific use U of a name N if and only if

> there is some idea idea-a that A has associated with N in his use U of N (and which is what allows A to be a competent user of N *in U*),

and

and

> there is some idea idea-*b* that *B* has associated with *N* in his
> use *U* of *N* (and which ... etc.),

> *A* associating idea-*a* with *N* is *coordinated** with *B* associat-
> ing idea-*b* with *N*.

Now let's recursively define *coordination** in terms of *immediate coordination**:

Speaker *X* having the idea idea-*x* associated with the name *N* is *coordinated** with speaker *Y* having the idea idea-*y* associated with *N* iff

(i)   Speaker *X* having the idea idea-*x* associated with the name
      N is *immediately coordinated** with speaker *Y* having the
      idea idea-*y* associated with *N*, or
(ii) There is a speaker *Z* that has an idea idea-*z* associated with
      N, and speaker *X* having idea-*x* associated with the name
      N is *coordinated** with speaker *Z* having idea-*z* associated to
      N, and speaker *Z* having idea-*z* associated to *N* is *immedi-
      ately coordinated** with speaker *Y* having idea-*y* associated
      with *N*.

Speaker *X* having idea-*x* associated with a name *N* is *immediately coordinated** with speaker *Y* having idea-*y* associated with the name *N* iff

(i)   There is some idea idea-*x** that *X* has or has had associated
       with *N*, such that idea-*x** is a predecessor of idea-*x* or idea-
       x is a predecessor of idea-*x**, and
(ii)   There is some idea idea-*y** that *Y* has or has had associated
       with *N*, such that idea-*y** is a predecessor of idea-*y* or idea-
       y is a predecessor of idea-*y**, and
(iii) One of the following three clauses obtains:

(a) idea-x^* does not have any predecessor (other than itself) that X associated with N, and idea-x^* came to be associated to N by X, because Y associated idea-y^* to N (this might be so because, e.g., X came to associate idea-x^* to N after observing some uses of N by Y, and in those uses Y was associating idea-y^* to N)

(b) (same as (a), exchanging the roles of X and Y): idea-y^* does not have any predecessor (other than itself) that y associated with N, and idea-y^* came to be associated to N by y, because X associated idea-x^* to N

(c) X and Y knew that it was mutual knowledge among them that they were both identifying the same object, and decided to introduce the name N as a name of that object. In that introduction of the name, X associated with the name the idea idea-x^*, and Y associated with the name the idea idea-y^*.

Consider the following diagram:

Figure 2.

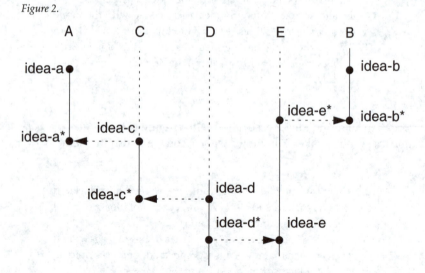

We have, according to the diagram, that A's use of a name N (when A is associating idea-a with N) is coordinated with B's use of the name (as a hearer) (when B is associating idea-b with the name). This is so because, in this specific use of N that we are considering, A is associating idea-a with N, and B is associating idea-b with N, and A's associating idea-a with N is coordinated* with B's associating idea-b with N. And this is so, in turn, because there is the right kind of relationship between the fact that A associates idea-a with N and the fact that B associates idea-b with N.

We can also have now a version of (CR) that applies to specific uses of names:

> (CR)* For two speakers S and S' to be able to successfully communicate with some specific use of a proper name it is necessary that S and S' be coordinated in that specific use of the name.

We can now consider again *Heckian argument-2*, and see how (CR)* allows us to explain the lack of successful communication between Toni and Alex. Toni and Alex are not coordinated in the specific use of 'George Orwell' that we consider. In that use, Toni associates with the name 'George Orwell' an idea I-t (that will contain, among other bits of information, for instance, 'He is my favourite writer'). When listening to Toni, Alex associates with the name an idea I-a (that will contain, among other bits of information, for instance, 'He is the patient I just saw'). Toni having the idea I-t associated with the name 'George Orwell' is not coordinated* with Alex having the idea I-a associated with the name (even if Toni having the idea I-t associated with the name *is* coordinated* with Alex having some *other* idea associated with 'George Orwell' – the idea that allows Alex to use the name 'George Orwell' when he intends to be talking about the patient).

Another way of putting the matter is: the fact that Toni associates a certain idea with 'George Orwell' when he uses the name intending to refer to the author is not connected (in the appropriate way) with the fact that Alex associates a certain idea with 'George Orwell' when he intends to refer to the patient. The lack of coordination is not due to the fact that the two ideas do not contain the same information, but rather to the fact that one speaker associating *his* idea with the name is not appropriately connected with the fact that the other speaker associates his (other) idea with the name.

Given that Alex and Toni are not coordinated in this specific use of 'George Orwell' in *Heckian argument-2* we have that in this situation (CR)* is violated. We have, then, a way of explaining what went wrong in this situation that does not require us to accept, with the neo-Fregean, that there are senses associated with the names that must be grasped in order for successful communication to take place.

Notice, finally, that our 'kaumam' example (or analogous ones – we could provide other examples involving the word 'grandmother' or 'fortnight') shows that sharing, in addition to the referent of an expression (the contribution to the truth conditions expressed by the sentences that contain the name), the descriptive material or sense associated with it, is not sufficient either for successful communication. We could even devise a case similar to our 'kaumam' example but involving proper names, where the two individuals X and Y, one from each of the communities, assign not just the same referent to the name, but also exactly the same descriptive material, the same sense. Even so, if there was no previous contact (either direct or indirect) between the two communities, there would not be successful communication between X and Y. And so, we can conclude, postulating senses conventionally associated with the name is not only not necessary for explaining what went wrong between X and Y (as shown in our discussion of *Heckian argument-1* and -2), it is not sufficient either.

The main aim of this paper has been to introduce the notion of *Coordination* and its associated *Coordination Requirement* and to make the case for their interest, usefulness, and potential in helping us to better understand the communicative role of proper names. As part of showing the interest of these notions, I showed how they can be used to reply to two otherwise powerful arguments: Kripke's General Consideration against descriptivism, and Heck's arguments for neo-Fregeanism. A secondary aim of the paper has been to present and defend a certain specific theory about proper names: an individual-level reference-fixing descriptivist theory.[9]

---

9 Research for this paper was supported by the Spanish Government's MCyT research grants BFF2003-08335-C03-03 and BFF2002-10164 (within the framework of the European Science Foundation EUROCORES program "The Origin of Man, Language and Languages"), and by the Catalan Government's DURSI research grant SGR01-0018. Different versions of this paper have been presented

References

Bach, K. 1987. *Thought and Reference*. Oxford: Oxford University Press.

Byrne, A., and M. Thau. 1996. "In Defense of the Hybrid View." *Mind* 105: 139–49.

Evans, G. 1982. *The Varieties of Reference*. Oxford: Clarendon Press.

García-Carpintero, M. 2000. "Fregean Sense and the Proper Function of Assertion: Comments on Textor." *Theoria* 15: 303–16.

Heck, R.G. Jnr. 1995. "The Sense of Communication." *Mind* 104: 79–106.

———. 1996. "Communication and Knowledge: Rejoinder to Byrne and Thau." *Mind* 105: 151–56.

Kripke, S. 1980. *Naming and Necessity*. Cambridge, MA: Harvard University Press.

Loar, B. 1976. "The Semantics of Singular Terms." *Philosophical Studies* 30: 353–77.

Macià, J. 1998. "Does *Naming and Necessity* Refute Descriptivism?" *Theoria* 13: 445–76.

Recanati, F. 1993. *Direct reference: From Language to Thought*. Oxford: Blackwell.

Wettstein, H. 1989. "Turning the Tables on Frege or How is it That 'Hesperus is Hesperus' is Trivial?" *Philosophical Perspectives* 3: 317-339.

at several conferences; I wish to thank the audiences for their questions and comments. I also wish to thank Ignasi Jané, Kirk Ludwig, Genoveva Martí, and Ignacio Vicario for their comments on earlier versions of this paper, and Manuel Garcia-Carpintero for many helpful discussions of the topic of proper names. I am grateful to Mark Textor and Marco Santambrogio, who acted as commentators on two different workshops where I presented parts of this paper and provided me with many insightful comments and challenging objections. Special thanks are due to Rob Stainton for his many useful comments.

PART B

Language and Mind

CANADIAN JOURNAL OF PHILOSOPHY
Supplementary Volume 30

Semantic Eliminativism and the Theory-Theory of Linguistic Understanding

DORIT BAR-ON

Suppose, familiarly, that you and a friend have landed in an alien territory, amidst people who speak a language you do not know. Upon seeing you, one of them starts yelling, seemingly alarmed. You say to your friend, "She thinks we want to hurt her. She's scared. We must seem very strange to her." Your friend, who is facing you, says, "No, I think she's actually trying to warn you: there's a snake right above your head, on that tree. You see the sling in her hand? I think she's going to try to shoot it down."

On a prevalent view, much discussed in recent years, you and your friend have engaged in a mini-theoretical enterprise. Using certain observations of the alien's behaviour as your data, and deploying certain generalizations and principles concerning human behaviour, you advance hypotheses regarding the internal psychological states which issued in her observed behaviour. You attribute to the alien the *belief* that you want to hurt her, the *feeling* of being scared, the *perception* that you are strange-looking, the *intention* to warn you, the *meaning-to-say* that there is a snake on the tree above you, the *desire* to rescue you by shooting down the snake, and so on. These psychological attributions are all part of a theoretical effort to explain and predict her behaviour.

According to the so-called *Theory-Theory* of commonsense psychological attributions, the foregoing characterizes what we regularly do at home as well as abroad. Our everyday notions of belief, desire, intention, etc., form part of a naïve (and for the most part tacit) psychological theory, a so-called folk psychology. These notions are proto-theoretical notions that the folk use to point to internal, contentful mental states as part of their causal-explanatory and predictive account of the behaviour of certain highly complex objects (paradigmatically, fellow human beings). They serve the folk much in the same way that the notions of, e.g., fragility, weight, molecular structure, and so on, have served them in their naïve attempts to account for the behaviour of inanimate objects.[1]

Now, the folk have been wrong about many things. They have been wrong about lightning and thunder being signs from angry gods, about the existence of witches and phlogiston, about the effects of the configuration of stars on human character and action, and about countless other things. A consequence of the Theory-Theory is that the folk may turn out to be wrong in their psychological theory, too; and not just wrong about particular details, but wrong in the main. A sophisticated, properly scientific theory of mind might be able to offer causal explanations and systematic predictions of human behaviour without appealing to contentful mental states such as mentioned above. The folk's psychological notions of beliefs, desires, etc. – and with them all commonsense psychological attributions – might then prove entirely obsolete. Such is the Theory-Theory's commitment to the possibility of *eliminativism*.

A good deal of the current debate on the status of 'folk psychology' has centered around the actual prospects for its elimination.[2] Some friends of commonsense intentional attributions have been moved to argue that, at least in outline, folk psychology is a rather good and successful theory, so there is no serious danger of its being completely superseded by a scientific psychology. These friends have rejected psychological eliminativism while still embracing the Theory-Theory of commonsense psychological attributions. But other friends have chosen a less conservative option: rather than claim that folk psychology is a good theory, and so unlikely to be entirely replaced by a better

---

1 For earlier articulations, see, e.g., Lewis 1966, Fodor 1968, and Churchland 1988. For more recent articulations, see relevant articles in Davies and Stone 1995a and 1995b, and in Carruthers and Smith 1996.

2 For a brief "map of the area," see the Introduction to Carruthers and Smith 1996), Section 2.

scientific theory, they have suggested that it may not be a theory at all, thereby denying that it is a potential candidate for elimination.

There are different ways to reject the Theory-Theory. One can maintain that our ordinary psychological terms are not like theoretical terms but are more like observation terms. Alternatively, one can maintain that folk psychology is not in the business of offering causal explanations and predictions of behaviour, like ordinary scientific theories, but is rather in the business of offering rationalizing or systematizing explanations. As evidence for this claim, one might point out that folk attributions of psychological states and propositional attitudes are governed by normative principles the likes of which have no place in science, principles such as "Charity," "Humanity," or "Rationality."[3] Finally, one can argue that folk-psychological explanations do not fit the format of scientific explanation, but rather deploy strategies such as 'simulation,' 'replication,' or 'mimicking'.[4]

In this paper I am not directly interested in psychological eliminativism, but rather in a related form of eliminativism: *semantic* eliminativism. More specifically, I am interested in the possibility of denying semantic eliminativism by rejecting what I dub the Theory-Theory of *linguistic understanding*. Semantic eliminativism is the view that the central notions of "folk semantics," such as *the* meaning of a linguistic expression, sameness and difference of meaning, correct translation, etc., lack objective status. These notions will find no room in a properly scientific theory of language. On one way of looking at things, this view is an immediate consequence of psychological eliminativism. This is so if folk semantics is seen as simply a proper part of folk psychology, and semantic notions are taken to belong with other psychological notions used by the folk in their naïve attempts to theorize about their fellows' behaviour. On another way of looking at things,

---

3 For some discussion of these principles and references, see Ramberg 1989 and Bar-On and Risjord 1992. Some support for the idea may be found in Collingwood, and in the European Verstehen tradition (represented by Max Weber and Wilhelm Dilthey), which maintains that the social sciences in general differ from the natural sciences in requiring a different sort of understanding.

4 For defenses of this view, see, e.g., Heal 1986,1995; Goldman 1989, 1992,1993; and Gordon 1986, 1992, 1995.

it is rather psychological eliminativism – at least eliminativism about the propositional attitudes – that is itself a consequence of semantic eliminativism.[5] On this second way of thinking, it is *because* there is no hope of making objective sense of the notions of meaning, sameness of meaning, etc., that there can be no hope of making objective sense of contentful mental states (beliefs/desires/intentions/hopes *that p*) which can be genuine causes of observable behaviour.

Either way, semantic eliminativism can be directly linked to a Theory-Theory about linguistic understanding, as I argue in Section I below. Furthermore, I argue in Section II that adhering to a genuine Theory-Theory of linguistic understanding makes it very difficult to avoid some form of semantic eliminativism. In Section III, I offer reasons for rejecting the Theory-Theory conception of understanding. I conclude by speculating on what we might put in its place.

I. Linguistic Understanding, Translation, and the Theory-Theory

We all have a remarkable ability to understand each other's linguistic utterances. We exercise it all the time, and with great facility. What is involved in having this ability? And how do we come to possess it in the first place? A natural first pass is to take linguistic understanding to involve the ability to make judgments regarding what linguistic expressions mean. Coming to possess this ability is a matter of somehow learning to make these judgments. According to what I shall describe as the Theory-Theory of linguistic understanding, becoming a competent language-speaker is a matter of tacitly developing, or coming to know, or "internalizing," a finite, recursive theory of the relevant language, which issues in assignments of meanings to infinitely many linguistic expressions. The theory determines the conditions under which expressions mean such-and-such, the conditions under which expressions mean the same, and so on. One has achieved mastery of the language when one has successfully figured

---

5 See Quine 1960, especially Chapter IV.

out in some way what these conditions are, on the basis of input from the relevant linguistic environment.[6]

On this conception, understanding what other speakers say and mean, at home as well as abroad, can be seen as the outcome of theory construction, however tacit. Our entry into others' speech – even as complete linguistic novices – is provided by *observation* of their behaviour; the behaviour serves as the *data* or *evidence* on the basis of which, with the help of various *hypotheses*, we *infer* what they mean, think, etc. We have achieved understanding of what they mean when we have matched with the sounds that come out of their mouths the interpretation dictated by our theory. Our access to the meanings of others' utterances is thus mediated by an implicitly held theory about the structure of their speech behaviour, overt or covert; it is the deliverances of this theory that allows us to assign semantic content to their speech. My present aim is to show how this conception of linguistic understanding conspires, along with certain other claims, to threaten us with semantic eliminativism. Toward that end, I invite the patient reader to revisit a familiar thought experiment designed to convince us of semantic eliminativism – Quine's famous thought experiment of radical translation. (See Quine 1960, Chapter II).

I.i. Quine's Indeterminacy and Semantic Eliminativism

Suppose, after being rescued from the snake by the kind native, you and your friend decide to learn her language. As Quine's story goes, you might notice, first, that volunteered utterances of certain sequences of sounds – say, [*bagbu*] – are systematically correlated with the presence of snakes. You can then try actively to determine the conditions under which native speakers assent to and dissent from the relevant sound sequence when *you* utter it. On the basis of all such data, you might form the following inductive hypothesis:

> [*Bagbu*], *as a one-word sentence*, matches our English one-word sentence 'Snake!'

---

6 Whether or not one must also be able to recognize when the conditions obtain is a matter for debate. For relevant discussion, see my 1996.

And similarly for other native utterances. To achieve a complete translation manual between the alien language and English, however, you would have to go beyond such simple correlations of one-word sentences. You must find a way to break down single utterances into recurring parts – words and phrases – identify various grammatical constructions, and correlate them with English words, phrases and constructions. For instance, you must decide whether, as a *term*, [*bagbu*] should be correlated with the English term 'snake,' or with 'an attached snake part', or with 'a momentary snake appearance'. These sorts of correlations cannot be determined simply by observing patterns of assent to/dissent from whole sentences. They also cannot be determined on the basis of simple ostension. (Point to a snake, and you've pointed to its attached parts, as well as to momentary snake appearances). These correlations are what Quine calls "analytical hypotheses." A complete translation manual is a set of analytical hypotheses that would enable us to give for each sentence of "Bagbuese" a translation into English.

As is well known, Quine has taken his thought experiment to issue in the *thesis of the indeterminacy of translation*, which says: Given any two languages, it is objectively indeterminate which of mutually incompatible sets of analytical hypotheses for translating between them is the correct one.[7] This claim can be broken down into two. The claim of *translational underdetermination* says that, for any given source language and target language, one can devise distinct sets of analytical hypotheses that would both fit all objective evidence and yield translations that we would recognize as mutually incompatible.[8] The claim of *translational indeterminacy* is that "there is not even ... an objec-

---

7 In 1960, Chapter II, Quine suggested that no such incompatibility could arise with respect to what he calls "stimulus meanings." Accordingly, he restricted the indeterminacy thesis to non-observation sentences. For reasons I discuss in my 1987, Chapter II, this restriction is misleading at best. I shall in any event ignore it in what follows, since it has no bearing on anything important to the present discussion.

8 If we think of a translation manual as a recursive function for mapping sentences of a source-language into sentences of a target-language, the thesis says that, for any two languages, there can be two recursive functions, f_1 and f_2, for mapping the source- into the target- language, such that f_1 will map some given

tive matter to be right or wrong about" (Quine 1960, 73) concerning which translation manual is the correct one. Quine seems to think that the former claim provides support for the latter claim.

As Quine and his followers have stressed over the years, the indeterminacy thesis has far-reaching consequences.[9] Pretheoretically, we take it that our task in developing a translation manual for the native's language is to produce translations that capture the *native's understanding* of her own language. But the thesis of translational indeterminacy is antithetical to the idea that there is a prior understanding of the natives' (non-observation) sentences – ours *or* theirs – that a translation manual can capture correctly or incorrectly. Any understanding of the natives' sentences is an artifact of – rather than a precondition for – the production of a translation manual. And, where manuals conflict, there is no uniquely correct "prior" understanding by reference to which conflict could even in principle be settled. Relatedly, since a translation manual is a way of specifying the meanings of source sentences, it would follow from the indeterminacy thesis that there is no objective fact concerning what the sentences of any language mean.[10]

In short, the indeterminacy thesis issues in the view earlier called "semantic eliminativism." Given indeterminacy, linguistics as an objective science cannot take itself to be treating of meanings ordinarily conceived. The central notions of what Quine calls "intuitive semantics" – meaning, sameness/difference of meaning, etc. – would all have to go by the wayside; they will have no room in a scientific theory of language. Moreover, linguists' frequent appeals to speakers' intuitive semantic *judgments* as data to be accounted for, or evidence to be accommodated by linguistic theories, would have to be eliminated. This is because, if the indeterminacy thesis is right, these judgments themselves lack objective status.

---

source sentence S onto a target sentence p and f_2 will map it onto q, where p and q would be judged (semantically) non-equivalent. See my 1993, Section 2 for discussion.

9 For references and discussion of these consequences, see my 1986, 1990, 1992b, 1993.

10 Beyond a limited range; see Note 7.

Following Chomsky,[11] many critics of Quine have challenged his apparent inference from translational underdetermination to translational indeterminacy. They have insisted that we have no reason to regard underdetermination as different, or more damaging, in the case of linguistics than it is in the case of other special sciences. After all, they have pointed out, Quine himself believes that underdetermination infects *all* scientific theories: even given all possible evidence, there could always be rival theories in physics, chemistry, etc. tying for first place. Yet Quine was never prepared to conclude on that basis that there are no objective physical, chemical, etc. facts.[12]

Addressing Chomsky's challenge, Quine has said:

> The indeterminacy of translation differs from the underdetermination of science in that there is only the natives' verbal behavior for the manuals of translation to be right or wrong about; ... In the case of natural science, ... there is a fact of the matter, even if all possible observations are insufficient to reveal it uniquely. The facts of nature outrun our theories as well as all possible observations. (1987, 9 f.)

We may be able to see the point behind Quine's response if we recognize a distinction between two different levels at which underdetermination could arise in the case of linguistics, corresponding to two types of judgments concerning language. Focusing on semantics, at the *ground level* we have unreflective semantic judgments made by

---

11 See, e.g., his 1975a.

12 Quine has argued (see his 1970) that a science of linguistics would suffer from a "second-order underdetermination." (See also his 1986, 1990.) Like physics, it would be underdetermined relative to all possible evidence, but, in addition, it would be underdetermined even relative to a fixed physical theory. However, Quine's critics have pointed out that the same holds of all other special sciences; only physics may enjoy a privileged status. Below, I offer a reconstruction of Quine's reasoning which provides an alternative way of understanding the claim about "second-order underdetermination." Putnam, for one, has accepted Quine's inference from underdetermination to indeterminacy in "the special case of indeterminacy of translation" (Putnam 1975, 182), for reasons not unrelated to the ones I give below. But Putnam does not draw the crucial distinction on which my reconstruction relies.

ordinary language users. These are intuitive judgments about what expressions mean (e.g., that the word 'futile' means such-and-such), about sameness and difference of meanings of expressions (that the word 'snake' and the phrase 'attached snake part' do not mean the same; or that in such-and-such a context, expression *a* is interchangeable with expression *b*, etc.), as well as about various other semantic features of linguistic expressions and semantic relations among them. Speakers may explicitly articulate intuitive semantic judgments when they teach the use of linguistic expressions to novices, when they volunteer pronouncements about meanings of expressions, or when they answer directly questions about various semantic features of expressions. Semantic judgments can also be articulated less explicitly, as when a speaker volunteers a paraphrase of what someone else (or she herself) has said.[13] And sometimes semantic judgments are only indirectly evidenced, as when we elicit speakers' responses concerning the applicability of expressions in various counterfactual situations.[14]

There is wide disagreement about the nature and correct characterization of such intuitive semantic judgments, as well as about their centrality to a philosophical understanding of language.[15] But I think it would be hard to dispute the relatively modest claim that such judgments are regularly made by competent speakers, and are often used as a measure or test of a speaker's linguistic competence. Clearly, these judgments are recognized as importantly relevant for linguistic theory by Chomskian linguists, insofar as they take speakers' intuitive interpretations of linguistic expressions to provide crucial *data* for linguistic theory. As for the Quineans, it is arguable that *Quine's*

---

13 See Platts 1979, 236.

14 This is one natural way to understand the point of the familiar twin earth thought experiments proposed in, e.g., Punam 1975 and Burge 1979.

15 For a skeptical view, see Devitt 1991, 14.6. Devitt appears to hold that semantic competence in a language in no essential way requires ability to make judgments of the sort mentioned here. Devitt connects this claim to another claim (which I believe to be separate), namely, that the semantic vocabulary of a language is just like, say, the theoretical vocabulary of chemistry: it is fully detachable from the language without damage to a speaker's semantic competence. For discussion of Devitt's view, see my 1997.

own arguments for indeterminacy require acknowledging that we make ground-level semantic judgments of sameness and difference of meaning, if only as a step toward undermining the objective status of such judgments.[16]

We should separate semantic judgments made at the ground level from judgments *about* the semantics of a language made at the *theoretical level*. The relevant judgments here are the empirical semanticist's claims regarding the correct representation or systematization of the semantic facts about any given language. There is as yet no agreed-upon canonical form for such theoretical claims. What I have in mind here is whatever will turn out to be the semantic analogue of the abstract rules offered by contemporary linguists to capture the phonological and syntactic facts of a language. The axioms of a Davidsonian truth-theoretic semantics may qualify as an example. Still at the theoretical level (perhaps more on the psycholinguistic side), we may find various explanatory claims made by a complete empirical semantics as to the actual processes by which speakers arrive at their ground-level semantic judgments.

We are now in a position to distinguish two possible claims of underdetermination in the semantic case. The claim of *ground-level underdetermination* would say that ground-level semantic judgments are underdetermined in roughly the following sense: given the linguistic data to which language learners are exposed, they could come up with conflicting sets of ground-level semantic judgments.[17] The claim

---

16 See my 1986, 1993 for arguments to this effect, and my 1994, 1997, and below for further relevant discussion. Quine himself would no doubt refuse to regard speakers' judgments about semantic features of expressions (as opposed to their observable dispositions to use expressions in various ways and to assent to/dissent from sentences which use them) as relevant to a theory of language. However, even he can be seen as at least obliquely recognizing ground-level semantic judgments. Witness, for instance, his talk of "intuitive" or "uncritical" semantics (in, e.g., 1960, Chapter II; 1969, 27; 1986, 74), or of our "acquiescing in our mother tongue, taking its terms at face-value" (1969, 49). On the reconstruction I offer below, such recognition plays an essential role in the Quinean reasoning behind indeterminacy.

17 Strictly speaking, this is ambiguous between 'different speakers could come up with conflicting ground-level judgments' and 'a given single speaker might have come up with ground-level judgments which conflict with those she actually

of *theoretical underdetermination* would say that the empirical semanticist's theory is underdetermined: the evidence on which she bases her theory may be compatible with conflicting semantic theories.

Using the 'ground-level'–'theoretical level' distinction, we can reconstruct the argument for indeterminacy as follows.[18] Recall that the semantic eliminativist position is *not* that we might not be able to *tell* what alien speakers mean by their words; rather, it is that there is no fact of the matter about what they mean. In my terminology, this is the claim that there is indeterminacy of meaning *at the ground level*. If such indeterminacy can be established, then empirical semantics ordinarily conceived would indeed lack a legitimate subject matter. Now, on my proposed reconstruction, if there is ground-level indeterminacy, it must be not because of *our* limitations as theorists probing their language, but rather because *their* semantic judgments are not apt to support unique interpretations for expressions of their own language. In other words, it must be because there is *ground-level* underdetermination – underdetermination of the native speakers' own interpretive, semantic judgments. And the thought experiment of radical translation can be seen as attempting to convince us of the following. Given that underdetermination inevitably afflicts *our* attempts at specifying what the natives mean (since we could come up with alternative translation manuals for their language), the natives' *own* judgments concerning what expressions of their language mean must also be underdetermined.

Committed Quineans may balk at this talk of speakers' semantic judgments. However, I think appeal to speakers' judgment is crucial for at least one compelling way of arguing for translational

came up with'. Nothing in what follows hangs on disambiguating here. Also, there is a question about the status of the modal element in this claim. What sort of possibility is claimed here – logical? Metaphysical? Epistemic? Psychological? Though I do not think the question is unimportant, I do not attempt to settle it here.

18 The argument I reconstruct below uses familiar, distinctively Quinean materials. The reconstruction is in part designed to illuminate aspects of Quine's own reasoning about indeterminacy. However, it may involve elements which Quine himself would find objectionable. (See Notes 16 and 20.) Strict exegesis is not my concern, here.

indeterminacy. On the present construal, the argument moves from ground-level semantic underdetermination to (ground-level) semantic indeterminacy. But underdetermination requires the possibility of conflicting theories, or sets of judgments, relative to given evidence or data. If one disallows all talk of ground-level semantic judgments, and confines oneself to talk of speakers' brute dispositions to verbal behaviour, there can be no room to talk of underdetermination at the ground level. The present reconstruction does, however, allow us to take account of Quine's insistence that linguistic facts are facts about speakers' behavioural dispositions, for it enables us to see his preference for 'linguistic behaviourism' over its most prominent alternative – Chomskian mentalism – as a consequence of a *reductio* argument. According to this argument, the Chomskian mentalist is bound to construe linguistic facts in terms of mental (ground-level) judgments made by speakers. But such judgments (Quine would argue) must be underdetermined, thus ultimately making "intuitive" ground-level meaning indeterminate.[19]

We can now take the thought experiment of radical translation as aiming to establish, first, theoretical underdetermination. Theoretical underdetermination is then supposed to lead to ground-level underdetermination. Finally, ground-level underdetermination is used to convince us of ground-level indeterminacy. Schematically, we have:

> (1) Theoretical underdetermination → (2) Ground-level underdetermination → (3) Ground-level indeterminacy

The dialectic between Quinean indeterminists and their Chomskian opponents can then be seen as follows. Chomskians accept (1) but reject (3). They argue that theoretical underdetermination should be no more damaging to the study of language than it is to other scientific pursuits. And they may well be right about this. But simply calling attention to underdetermination in other special sciences is not enough. One must show either that the link between (1) → (2) fails, or that the link between (2) → (3) fails. If there are reasons to insist on *both* these links, the Chomskian objection would fail.

---

19 For a fuller development of this reading, see my 1992, 97 ff. and Section 2).

I.ii. Linguistic Underdetermination and the Theory-Theory of Understanding

Let us first consider the link between (1) – the theoretical underdetermination of empirical semantics – and (2) – the underdetermination of ground-level semantic judgments. Suppose, as seems naïvely plausible, that we think of empirical semantics as attempting to systematize and explain the ground-level semantic judgments made by speakers of a given language.[20] Empirical semantics so conceived seems different from special sciences like chemistry or biology in that it ultimately concerns ground-level *judgments* of speakers. It is in this sense "second-order," whereas chemistry, biology, or the theory of human physiology, are "first-order" – they concern, if you will, ground-level natural phenomena (whether those involve human subjects or not). Notice that when it comes to "first-order" natural sciences, the ground-level–theoretical-level distinction has no application. Thus, the distinction can be used to mark a certain methodological difference between natural sciences, on the one hand, and cognitive and social sciences, on the other. Like empirical linguistics, theories that study cognitive or social phenomena, such as the study of visual perception, moral psychology, economics, and various social sciences, involve the systematization, explanation, and prediction of ground-level judgments made by subjects.

Recently, Fodor has made a closely similar observation. Contrasting the physicist's job with the psychologist's, Fodor remarks that:

> ... the intentional sciences are different. When a psychologist says 'blah, blah, blah, because the child represents the snail as an agent ... ,' the property of *being an agent-representation* (*viz.*

---

20 This would be consonant with the way Chomsky at least used to think of linguistic theory (see, e.g., 1965, Section 1). Once again, one would expect Quineans to balk at this mentalistic-sounding characterization of empirical semantics and to insist on a characterization in terms of the systematization and explanation of dispositions to verbal behaviour. But as I have explained, on my reconstruction the preference for linguistic behaviourism should be seen as a consequence of the sorts of considerations discussed here, rather than as an unargued assumption.

> *being a symbol that means* agent) is appealed to in the explana-
> tion, and the psychologist owes an account of what property
> that is…. Both the physicist and the psychologist is required to
> theorize about the properties he ascribes, and neither is required
> to theorize about the properties of the language he uses to
> ascribe them. The difference is that the psychologist is working
> *one level up.* (Fodor 1998, 59, my emphasis)

Ordinary folk may have all sorts of naïve beliefs – "folk theories" –
about the phenomena described and explained by "first-order" theories. But such folk theories in no way concern people's judgments or
beliefs. Assuming the "second-order" character of empirical semantic is acknowledged, however, it is far from obvious what we should
regard as "folk semantic theory." Is there an identifiable body of beliefs
– a recognizable set of platitudes – held by the folk concerning speakers' semantic judgments? Granted, the folk all make various semantic
judgments. But, on their face, such judgments concern features of linguistic expressions – what they mean, when they mean the same, etc.
They *constitute* speakers' ground-level semantic judgments; they do
not appear to be *about* speakers' ground-level judgments. (Later on,
we shall return to this point, which I think is important but potentially
confusing.)

Now consider another theoretical enterprise that does directly concern (ground-level) beliefs: what has been called (following Quine)
"naturalized epistemology." Naturalized epistemology seeks to systematize and explain the beliefs human subjects arrive at regarding
the external world, and so, to that extent, it is also "second-order." If,
as many believe, any serious special science is bound to suffer from
theoretical underdetermination, both the naturalized study of human
external-world beliefs and the naturalized study of human linguistic judgments would issue in underdetermined theories. In addition,
however, the naturalistic study of humans' beliefs about the world
would likely reveal a certain gap between the relevant data available
to human subjects (their worldly observations) and their external-
world beliefs. One might argue that there is such a gap by pointing
out the possibility of alternative world theories. In this way, we can see
that there is ground-level underdetermination of our external-world
beliefs. In such a case, we can speak of 'second-order underdetermina-

tion': it is the underdeterminination of a theory whose subject-matter is someone's underdetermined set of beliefs.

In the case of empirical semantics, the Quinean claim is that there is ground-level semantic underdetermination – underdetermination of the unreflective, intuitive semantic judgments that ordinary language-users come to make in the course of acquiring their language. (To repeat, these are judgments concerning the interpretation of linguistic expressions, synonymy relations among expressions, and so on.) For this claim to make sense, we need to think of the ground-level semantic judgments as, in some sense, *theoretical* judgments – judgments that represent the result of theorizing (if only tacit), and which together, perhaps loosely, form a theory. Empirical semantics – thought of as the empirical study of semantic judgments – would then constitute an underdetermined theory of underdetermined ground-level judgments; it would exhibit second-order underdetermination, just as Quine has claimed.[21]

Now, in general, underdetermination of theory by evidence does not imply indeterminacy of fact. In particular, underdetermination of ground-level beliefs or judgments need not imply indeterminacy in the relevant domain. Thus, our empirical epistemologist could legitimately maintain that, where her subjects' external-world beliefs are underdetermined, there could still be "facts of nature" which "outrun" all of her subjects' beliefs, and which could in principle determine the truth or falsity of their underdetermined beliefs. That is, the empirical epistemologist need not ultimately take the ground-level beliefs she investigates at face value. Once her theory is complete, the epistemologist may go on to ask: Are human subjects *right* in their beliefs about the external world? And she may legitimately suppose that there is an objectively determinate (even if unknown) answer to this question.

Turning to our empirical semanticist, we may ask: Are there semantic facts which could "outrun" the systematized speakers' judgments and against which we could measure the adequacy of those judgments? Once the semanticist has completed the task of systematizing and explaining ground-level semantic judgments, is there room for her to ask: Are the users of the language *right* in their ground-level

---

21 See, e.g., Quine 1970.

judgments? If the answer to these questions is "No," then it would seem as though the subject-matter of empirical semantics "bottoms out" in the judgments speakers make (explicitly or implicitly) about expressions of their language. But, if this is so, then *underdetermination in speakers' ground-level semantic judgments would indeed imply ground-level semantic indeterminacy*, that is, indeterminacy of semantic facts. This would give credence to Quine's idea that there is something special about empirical semantics (and linguistics generally). Empirical semantics – conceived as the study of ground-level semantic judgments – would concern ground-level judgments that *cannot* themselves be underdetermined, on pain of indeterminacy.

Recall our reconstructed argument for indeterminacy:

(1) Theoretical underdetermination → (2) Ground-level underdetermination → (3) Ground-level indeterminacy

If ground-level semantic underdetermination indeed brings semantic indeterminacy in its train, the inference from (2) to (3) would be secured. We shall return to this inference later on. Right now, however, our concern is with the inference from (1) to (2). This inference, I would now like to argue, is implicitly supported by a certain view shared by *both* proponents of semantic eliminativism *and* their Chomskian opponents: what I shall call the Theory-Theory of linguistic understanding.

Both Quine and Chomsky, for instance, invite us to think of a child learning a first language as, in crucial respects, like an amateur theorist of the language spoken in his community. In probing a language, Quine tells us, both child and radical linguist use as their data "the concomitances of ... utterance and observable ... situation" (1969, 81).[22] And Chomsky presents "[t]he problem for the linguist, as well

---

22 Quine also points out that, just as the radical translator, restricted to such meager evidence, cannot determine purely inductively what the native means by the word [gavagai], so a child hearing our word 'rabbit' uttered in conjunction with a gesture pointing to rabbits cannot learn by pure conditioning whether the word refers to rabbits or, on the contrary, to their undetached parts or stages. Quine has claimed that the indeterminacy thesis is "of a piece" with the doctrine that "conditioning is insufficient to explain language learning" (1976, 58). For some discussion and further references, see my 1992b, 97 ff.

as for the child learning the language" as that of "determin[ing] from the data of performance the underlying system of the rules" that govern the language, which requires having "a method for devising an appropriate grammar, given primary linguistic data" (1975b, 4, 25). On this picture, the task for both the child and the linguist is to settle on a theory of the language at hand. In the child's case, this (obviously tacit) theory is expressible in the more or less stable set of linguistic judgments which can serve to characterize her as a competent speaker. In the linguist's case, the theory may be explicitly expressed in terms of a set of rules for the language under study.[23]

More recently, Quine has explicitly endorsed the child-linguist analogy:

> I agree with Chomsky on the learner as theorist. That is the way to look at both the field linguist and the learning child. It is instructive thus to intellectualize the child's behavior. He is picking up data and conjecturing, performing induction. Deliberate induction is more of the same; it is just that we get more conscious of what we are doing and more refined in how we do it. (1990, 291)

One feature of the analogy is that it requires seeing the child as being in principle able to *represent* to herself various alternative hypotheses regarding adult speech. Seizing upon this feature, Jerry Fodor has advanced an argument for the existence of a *language of thought*. Fodor thinks learning a language *must* involve constructing hypotheses about (at least) the extensions of predicates of the language learned. And this, in turn, requires that the first-language learner possess a system rich and complex enough to represent "the predicates of [the learned language] *and their extensions*" (1975, 64). Hence, Fodor argues, to *learn* a language one must already *have* a language. And, on pain of regress, that language cannot itself be learned, so it must

---

23 For early articulations of this 'Theory'-theory by these authors, see Chomsky 1975, Chapters 1 and 2, and Quine 1960, Chapter II; 1974; 1976, 57 f. In more recent writings, Chomsky has gradually moved away from describing the task for the first-language learner as that of selecting among alternative grammars on some basis. I discuss the shift below, in Section II.iii.

be innate. This picture is directly carried over by Fodor from first-language learning to adult linguistic understanding and interpretation. A mature hearer's understanding of an utterance made by a speaker consists in a *translation* of the utterance into the hearer's language of thought. And determining what is the appropriate translation is a matter of deciding "which hypothesis about the speaker's [communicative] intentions best explains his (the speaker's) verbal behavior" (1975, 108 Note 7). Fodor remarks that this is just a "special case" of the view that "attributions of mental states to others are, in general, to be analyzed as inferences to the best explanation of their behavior" (1975, 108 Note 7).[24]

Davidson, who follows Quine in endorsing semantic indeterminacy, has made some very similar remarks.[25] A hearer's interpretation of a speaker's words represents her best attempt at figuring out the speaker's intention. And the process by which the hearer does that, Davidson thinks, is best described in terms of the interpreter con-

---

24 With this, Fodor invites us to return to the classical mentalist model of linguistic communication. This model, with its "museum myth," is Quine's major target of attack in his discussions of indeterminacy. On the mentalist model, the speaker in a linguistic transaction has a particular message in mind, which she "encodes" in a conventional linguistic form. The hearer's job is to use her knowledge of linguistic conventions to "decode" the message. Communication succeeds when decoded and encoded messages converge. As Fodor puts it:

> A speaker is a mapping from messages onto wave forms, and a hearer is a mapping from wave forms onto messages. The character of each mapping is determined, inter alia, by the conventions of the language that the speaker and hearer share. Verbal communication is possible because the speaker and hearer both know what the conventions are and how to use them: ... The exercise of their knowledge ... effects a certain correspondence between the mental states of speaker and hearer.... The speaker ... has a certain [message] in mind and the hearer can tell [what message] it is. (1975, 108)

25 This may seem surprising, since it is well known that Davidson would have no truck with Fodor's language of thought, or with most other major aspects of Fodor's views on language, mind, metaphysics, or epistemology. But it should be recognized that the agreement I am identifying between these two authors concerns the epistemology of language. It leaves plenty of room for disagreement between them on other major aspects of the conception of language.

structing a *theory* of the speaker's speech: "A person's ability to interpret or speak to another person", Davidson says, "consists... [in] the ability that permits him to construct a correct, that is, convergent, ... theory for speech transactions with that person" (1986, 445).[26] What the interpreter constructs, he says,

> really is like a theory at least in this, that it is derived by wit, luck and wisdom from a private vocabulary and grammar, knowledge of the ways people get their point across, and rules of thumb for figuring out what deviations from the dictionary are most likely ... [This is like] the process of creating new theories to cope with new data in any field – for that is what this process involves. (1986, 446)[27]

Leading indeterminists and their chief opponents, then, appear to converge on a general conception of what goes into linguistic understanding. On this conception, to recapitulate, the process of coming to understand other speakers' speech is assimilated to the process of theory construction – making observations, assessing relevant evidence, drawing inferences, framing hypotheses (allowing, of course, that the process is unconscious). Once this assimilation is made, it is natural to see the ground-level intuitive judgments in which the acquisition of a first language culminates as themselves comprising a theory, of sorts. Moreover, on the Theory-Theory of linguistic understanding, our adult access to others' speech is mediated by the theory we have implicitly constructed or internalized on the basis of data about their speech behaviour to which we have been exposed.

---

26 Davidson distinguishes in this connection a "prior" theory from a "passing" theory:

> For the hearer, the prior theory expresses how he is prepared in advance to interpret an utterance of the speaker, while the passing theory is how he does interpret the utterance. For the speaker, the prior theory is how he believes the interpreter's prior theory to be, while his passing theory is the theory he intends the interpreter to use. (1986, 442)

27 The 'Theory'-Theory of linguistic understanding is shared by at least two other Quinean "indeterminists," Paul Churchland (1988) and Stephen Stich (1983) (although Stich has more recently recanted [see his 1996]).

Now, the thought experiment of radical translation is supposed to convince us, first, that any theorist's attempt to construct a theory of meaning for a language is bound to be underdetermined. With the Theory-Theory conception brought to the foreground, we can now see that this result would have direct impact on the ground-level: *inasmuch as ground-level semantic judgments are the outcome of theorizing, they too must be recognized as underdetermined*; hence the inference from (1) to (2). If one accepts that empirical theories in general, and linguistic theories in particular, are underdetermined, and one further holds that speakers' ground-level semantic judgments constitute a theory, then one will be committed to the claim of ground-level semantic underdetermination. But then, to avoid the threat of semantic eliminativism, one would have to insist that semantic underdetermination does *not* imply semantic indeterminacy; that is, one would have to deny the inference from (2) to (3).[28]

II. Underdetermination, the Linguistic Theory-Theory, and Semantic Facts

The inference from (2) to (3) is to the effect that *if* the semantic judgments of speakers constitute an underdetermined theory, then linguistic meaning is *in*determinate. As noted earlier (in Section I.ii), accepting the inference requires accepting that the semantic facts of a language cannot, in general, outrun the semantic judgments systematically made by the speakers of the language. In other words, it requires accepting a certain dependence of semantic facts on speakers' (ground-level) semantic judgments. We now turn to a closer examination of this dependence claim.

---

28 There is an additional option here, to be discussed in Section II.iv: It is to insist that the ground-level judgments, though in some sense theoretical, are nevertheless not really underdetermined, in the sense that there are no real alternatives to them, given the speakers' mental equipment/constitution. But note that this requires either reneging on the claim that all theories are truly underdetermined by their data, or heavily qualifying the claim that ground-level judgments form a theory in anything but the most "promiscuous" sense. (See Blackburn [1995].)

II.i The Public Accessibility of Semantic Facts

Here are some considerations one might invoke in support of the dependence claim. As realists often observe, naïvely speaking, it seems to make perfect sense (though it is quite probably false) to suggest that no one has ever known the real chemical structure of iron, or that people have everywhere and always taken two substances which are really distinct to be the same (or vice versa). But it seems to make little sense to suggest that the word 'elephant' has *always* been mispronounced by all (or even most) English speakers; it seems to make equally little sense to say that English speakers have always used the wrong word order or extracted a relative clause in the wrong way, etc. Similarly, it would be very odd (at best) to suggest that English speakers have *always* misunderstood, or misused, say, the word 'chair', or that *no* English speaker has ever understood what, say, the word 'tomorrow' really meant, or that, contrary to the judgments of all English speakers (ever), two expressions really do (or do not) mean the same.[29] Further, suppose that, due to some cosmic happening, everyone in the English speaking community suddenly came to think the sentence 'Break a leg!' meant what the sentence 'Watch your step!' now means. Wouldn't the sentence thereby come to have that meaning?

In view of this, one could argue that, ultimately, the semantic distinctions drawn and the interpretive judgments made by the speakers of a language are the final arbiter for an empirical semantic theory. Semantic distinctions that are not somehow discernible or drawn by speakers of the language *can have no objective semantic status*; they have no title to being among the semantic facts of the language. Conversely, features of expressions that are of semantic relevance should be in principle discernible or recoverable by speakers of the language. In general, it may seem that semantic facts – facts about what expressions mean, about sameness and difference of meaning, etc. – cannot be hidden from speakers of the language in the way that we think facts about the chemical structure of substances can be. These sorts of

---

29 Jonathan Bennett, for instance, describes as "ludicrous" the suggestion that "no one has ever known what any part of our language really means," and connects this observation with the idea that "what an expression means in language L is logically connected with what the users of L generally mean by it" (1976, 8).

facts must be in principle *publicly accessible*. This places what we may call a *Publicity Requirement* on our conception of meaning:

> The correct understanding of linguistic expressions by their users must be in principle possible. Semantic (and other linguistic) features of expressions must be *publicly available* to and *discernible* by users of a language.[30]

II.ii Semantic Verificationism

It is natural to read the Publicity Requirement as expressing a form of verificationism – verificationism about meaning, or *semantic verificationism*. Semantic verificationism, like other verificationisms, forges a link between the metaphysical and the epistemic – between the facts and our ability to discover, know, or make correct judgments about them – in a specific domain. A semantic verificationist maintains that there cannot be semantic facts of a language that are beyond the epistemic reach of the speakers of the language. Semantic facts (ordinarily conceived) cannot be metaphysically independent of ("cannot outrun," in Quine's phrase) speakers' explicit and implicit semantic judgments.[31]

---

30 Quine has often linked his linguistic behaviourism to an observation about the public nature of language. For instance: "... My aversion [to the mental], within its limits, has a reason: the want of intersubjective checkpoints. It is Wittgenstein's rejection of private language. It is this, and not mentality as such, that disqualifies any irreducibly intuitive notion of meaning or synonymy or semantic relevance ..." (1986, 74, my emphases). And see also Quine's 1969, 26 ff.; 1970, 1987.

Donald Davidson (echoing Quine) has articulated the Publicity Requirement as follows: "Mental phenomena in general may or may not be private, but the correct interpretation of one person's speech by another must in principle be possible.... That meanings are decipherable is not a matter of luck; public availability is a constitutive aspect of language" (1990, 314). Versions of the Publicity Requirement can be also found in Frege, Wittgenstein, Dummett, and Putnam (among others). For some discussion of Publicity, see Follesdal (1990), Stjernberg (1991), and Bar-On (1992b, 1994, 1997). For a rejection of the idea that Publicity provides support for behaviourism over mentalism, see Fodor and Lepore (1992, 80 ff.).

31 I think this is the natural reading when we take the requirement as intended to separate the domain of language from other domains. And it is the reading

We should note that being a semantic verificationist in the sense described here is not the same as maintaining a verificationist theory of meaning. Semantic verificationism holds that semantic facts – facts of the kind expressed by, e.g. 'Expression *E* means [such-and-such] ...,' or 'Expression E_1 and expression E_2 have the same / different meaning' (in a given language) – cannot go beyond speakers' semantic judgments. The verification theory of meaning, on the other hand, is a particular view of the nature of meaning: it identifies the meaning of a statement – *any* statement – with the procedures by which the statement can be verified or falsified. Endorsing the verification theory of meaning may be tantamount to espousing a Dummett-style, wholesale verificationism: the view that *no* facts can in principle outrun our judgments. And one may find this implausible, whereas semantic verificationism can arguably co-exist with non-verificationist (or realist) views concerning non-semantic facts.[32]

Semantic verificationism as presented here is intended to be compatible with a variety of views on meaning. Of particular interest here would be the popular "causal theory" of reference determination, since it seems, on its face, to conflict with semantic verificationism. The semantic verificationist insists that facts about the meanings of expressions depend on the systematic semantic judgments of speakers of the language. And this idea would seem to go against the claim made by proponents of the causal theory that "meanings ain't in

---

needed to allow the reconstructed argument for indeterminacy to go through. (For a much weaker reading, see Fodor and Lepore 1992, 80 ff.) Semantic verification could be seen as a form of anti-realism about meaning, inasmuch as it uphold the judgment-dependence of semantic facts. On the other hand, it could be seen as a realist thesis about the metaphysical constitution of semantic facts. Whether or not the thesis qualifies as realist or anti-realist will depend on how one draws the realism–anti-realism distinction, a matter which I cannot take up here. (But see relevant discussion below, in Section II.iii.)

32 I discuss this issue at length in my (1994). Quine has in several places expressed allegiance to the verification theory of meaning (see, e.g., 1969, 80). On the face of it, however, this view of meaning would seem in tension with his claim that the truths of objective science could "outrun our theories as well as all possible observation" (1987, 10).

speakers' heads."[33] What we should notice, however, is that the "judgment-dependence" of meaning maintained by semantic verificationism does *not* imply that a set of necessary and sufficient descriptions "in the head" of any (or even all) of the speakers can serve to fix the extensions of all terms. Equally, however, to say that causal relations between speakers and worldly items feature essentially in determining the extension of certain terms cannot imply the elimination of the role of speakers' semantic judgments in determining the meaning of those terms. It is this role that semantic verificationism highlights.

Thus, consider again the hypothetical cosmic happenings mentioned earlier. There seems to be no reason why one could not maintain a causal theory about extension determination of relevant terms yet agree that such cosmic happenings would indeed lead to a change of meaning. To remain faithful to the causal theory, one would simply have to deny that we should understand any change in the extension of terms that might result from the change of meaning merely in terms of changes in the descriptive contents speakers have come to associate with the terms. In fact, as far as I can see, accepting the insights of the causal theory is consistent even with the view that the semantic rules for determining the extension of those terms are still "in speakers' heads," in the sense that the character of the rules is itself dependent on speakers' judgments. (Again, this is, of course, not to say that the relevant rules can be specified in terms of descriptive necessary and sufficient conditions.)[34]

Finally, notice that semantic verificationism by itself does not entail that semantic judgments are illusory, and hence that there really are no semantic facts. All it claims is a certain dependence of semantic

---

33 See Putnam 1975. As a brief reminder, the core idea of the causal theory is that it is facts about objective causal relationships between speakers and actual items in the world (individuals, natural kinds, etc.), and not anything purely "in speakers' heads" (such as descriptive contents, or analytic definitions) that determine the reference of, e.g., proper names, or the extension of terms such as 'gold' or 'water'. This is what may seem to go against the idea that the meanings of linguistic expressions depend in some essential way on what speakers of the relevant language judge those meanings to be.

34 For relevant discussion, see my 1992a, Section 4.

facts on the systematic semantic judgments speakers make. (It may be taken, in effect, as the claim that semantic facts are "logical constructions" out of the systematic semantic judgments of speakers.) Semantic verificationism implies that *where ground-level semantic judgments do not determine the correct interpretation* of some term, *there can be no fact of the matter* about what the term means.[35]

If semantic verificationism is right, then semantic facts would be different from, say, chemical facts, in that (barring wholesale verificationism) chemical facts *could* in principle outrun all possible verification by human speakers. And empirical semantics would differ from other empirical theories, in that – as suggested before – it would concern ground-level judgments which cannot themselves be underdetermined (on pain of indeterminacy). Indeed, empirical semantics would turn out to be different even from some theories that, unlike chemistry, do concern ground-level judgments. Take again the empirical theory of our beliefs about the external world; the beliefs it studies themselves concern facts which may in principle outrun all possible verification by believers. We can allow these ground-level beliefs to be underdetermined without risk of indeterminacy, since there is no reason (again, barring wholesale verificationism) to take the facts about the external world to be dependent on our beliefs. In this way, semantic verificationism would support the inference from ground-level semantic underdetermination (2) to semantic indeterminacy (3), and would vindicate a Quinean separation of linguistics from other sciences (including other special sciences).

However, while semantic verificationism would show the indeterminists to be right in thinking that a certain kind of underdetermination cannot be tolerated in linguistics, by itself it does not allow us to affirm that there *is* ground-level semantic underdetermination. On the present reconstruction, the Chomskians are also right about something: they are right in thinking that indeterminacy does not follow *simply* from the fact that linguistics, as an empirical theory, is (like any other science) bound to be underdetermined. Indeterminacy would only follow from *ground-level* underdetermination. But I have argued

---

35 I consider and reject various reasons for denying semantic verificationism in Bar-On 1997, Section III.

that the claim that there is ground-level underdetermination is supported by a view accepted by Chomskians: the view that speakers' ground-level judgments are similar to the judgments arrived at by linguists in forming a *theory* of the relevant language. So, if Chomskians accept that linguistic theories (like all theories) are indeed underdetermined by their evidence, and they further accept that the acquisition of a first language is a matter of devising a theory for which adult speech behaviour provides the evidence, then they appear saddled with the claim of ground-level underdetermination. But then it looks as though the only avenue open to the Chomskian who wishes to deny indeterminacy is to attack semantic verificationism, since, as we saw, it is this claim that leads from ground-level underdetermination to indeterminacy.

II.iii. Chomskian Mentalism: "Ground-Level" Underdetermination, Semantic Verificationism, and Theory-Theory[36]

As I have presented the dialectics between Quinean eliminativists and their opponents so far, there is a certain convergence between them on a Theory-Theory conception of language. This convergence can be seen to represent agreement on central aspects of the *epistemology* of language acquisition and understanding. However, the agreement appears to leave plenty of room for wide disagreement between them on the *metaphysics* of language. For the Quinean eliminativist, linguistic facts must be different from ordinary scientific facts about which we may theorize. Linguistic facts, such as there are, must be recoverable from publicly available evidence; they cannot consist in facts that are potentially hidden. Since, in addition, they believe that the public evidence leaves undetermined certain semantic matters that we intuitively tend to think *are* determinate, they adopt eliminativism about so-called "intuitive semantics."

Realist opponents of Quinean eliminativism, on the other hand, will try to portray the metaphysics of language as fully on a par with realist metaphysics in other domains, and will insist that there is no

---

36 In what follows, I present a summary of an argument I offer in Bar-On 1997, Section IV.

more room for skeptical anxiety in the study of language than there is in any other area. When we study language, as novices, as ordinary adults, or as empirical linguists, we try to arrive at correct judgments concerning the meanings of expressions in people's speech. Our aim is to figure out certain facts: linguistic facts. These are the facts we regularly hypothesize about, and which would render our judgments true. Any theory we reach in studying language will be underdetermined, but such underdetermination should not be regarded as implying indeterminacy in this domain any more than in any other domain. As in other domains, here, too, the facts are one thing; people's knowledge of the facts is another.

But the question for the realist opponent is this: What *are* the facts in the linguistic domain such that they might systematically go beyond all relevant evidence, or outrun theorists' best judgments (be they linguists or children)? In this section, our interest is in the Chomskian answer to this question, and its success in fending off the line of reasoning to indeterminacy presented earlier. I will be arguing that, insofar as the Chomskian answer succeeds in rebutting indeterminacy, it does *not*, as its advocates often present it, succeed by placing linguistic facts on a par with other facts that can go beyond speakers' epistemic reach, thereby rejecting semantic verificationism. Rather, it is by, in effect, departing from the Theory-Theory conception of language acquisition and understanding.

The most common Chomskian response to Quinean skepticism about language has been to charge Quineans with adherence to a dated and objectionable form of linguistic behaviourism. In its place, Chomskians have advocated thoroughgoing *mentalism*. Chomskian mentalism is usually presented as escaping Quinean eliminativism about language through the rejection of the verificationist move from underdetermination to indeterminacy. However, I think this should be seen as misleadingly oversimplified, once our earlier distinction between ground-level and theoretical underdetermination is properly appreciated. As we have seen, it is one thing to accept that all the evidence that *linguists* can gather regarding speakers may underdetermine their theory of language. It is another to accept that speakers' linguistic judgments are themselves underdetermined. It is the latter claim that threatens to bring indeterminacy in its train. The critical question is whether adopting Chomskian mentalism allows us to adhere to the idea that there is ground-level underdetermination – that speakers' ground-level linguistic judgments comprise a theory that is underdetermined by its evidence – while at the same time denying that this implies any kind of Quinean indeterminacy. For this is what it would take to reject semantic verificationism.

On the picture suggested by the Chomsky of *Syntactic Structures* (1957), we are to think of a child acquiring a first language as facing the task of developing a theory about the language spoken in the linguistic community into which she is born. The linguistic representations the child comes to associate with linguistic expressions are thought of *as hypotheses about a certain public language*. Assuming that all theory is underdetermined by evidence, the child's theory (if that is what it is) would be, too: there would be competing sets of semantic hypotheses equally compatible with the linguistic evidence available to the child. The problem of underdetermination can then be presented as a version of "the poverty of stimulus" problem: How is it possible for the child to settle on a single set of linguistic hypotheses (and converge with other learners on the *same* set of hypotheses), thereby achieving knowledge of her language, given that the evidence vastly underdetermines linguistic theory? Empirical linguistics, as conceived by Chomsky, is designed to provide an answer to this question.

The mentalist answer is that children bring to the task of language acquisition some very sophisticated, innate mental endowment. Although the linguistic evidence leaves open a choice among a wide array of competing sets of linguistic hypotheses, the child's choice is determined innately. Innate mental contribution serves to determine what would otherwise have been underdetermined. The mind bridges over the gaps found in the observable behavioural evidence. The appearance of rejecting semantic verificationism is generated by adding the idea that the relevant facts in the case of language consist in internal, mental goings-on of which we, as ordinary speakers, may be as ignorant as we are of other internal goings-on (say, in our stomachs). These internal goings-on are what we try to latch onto in our ordinary ascriptions of meaning.

On the mentalist picture, we should regard everyday episodes of understanding and ground-level semantic judgments as conjectural; they involve making hypotheses about hidden goings-on. The mentalist's contribution is to provide a stable subject-matter for these hypotheses, an "underlying reality," or domain of facts: the inner workings of speakers' minds. It is by reference to these inner workings that interpretive hypotheses would be ultimately verifiable or falsifiable. The mentalist proposal seems to be that we can construe semantic facts – the *real* semantic facts – on the model of ordinary scientific facts, which may very well be hidden from ordinary public view and may outrun speakers' judgments. This is what appears to go against the Publicity Requirement and the attendant semantic verificationism.

However, this appearance is misleading. For, as I will now argue, a closer look at the Chomskian mentalist conception as it has developed over the years reveals that this conception, far from rejecting semantic verificationism, is strongly committed to a version of it. To see this, consider the more developed Chomskian picture, according to which the child's innate "universal grammar" places heavy constraints on the set of possible grammars the child can acquire, leaving undetermined only certain superficial linguistic features. These features, dubbed "parameters," become "fixed" upon exposure to the idiosyncratic linguistic input of the particular language the child ends up acquiring. (See, e.g., Chomsky 1980). The point of enriching the innate universal grammar is to leave very little unsettled before the child begins the process of language acquisition, so as to make it possible for the child to construct a theory of the language he is acquiring, despite the limited amount of data he has to work with. (This is Chomsky's way of solving the "poverty of the stimuli" problem.) The association of particular sets of mental representations with linguistic expressions is no longer thought to be a matter of choice for the child. Luckily for the child, it is innately determined.

This way of thinking of the child's situation could be seen as offering a way of avoiding the problem of underdetermination. But if it does, it is only by moving away from seeing the child's task as truly similar to that of the linguist's. On the above picture, it is no longer clear that we should think of the linguistic input received by the child as *evidence* or *data* on the basis of which the child is to *determine* (however unconsciously) the facts of a certain public language. Instead, it seems as though adult speech merely serves as a psychological trigger enabling the child to become a speaker of a particular language. The process as described does not leave much room for thinking of the stable linguistic judgments the child arrives at as forming a body of knowledge – a set of true and warranted beliefs – that is similar in any interesting way to theoretical knowledge in other domains. (One way of putting the point: on the revised Chomskian picture, there seems to be very little reason to think of the relation between child's linguistic "data" and her ensuing linguistic judgment as a *rational* rather than merely *causal* relation.)

If this is so, then we must conclude that the linguist and the child are in very different businesses, much to the detriment of the child–linguist analogy. Whereas the child's task is to reach a stable set of mappings from sounds to meanings upon sufficient exposure to linguistic input, the linguist's is to discover the facts about *which* set of mappings the child has settled on, on the basis of her observations of the child's speech behaviour (and other evidence). The linguist's relation to the semantic facts may well be just like that of any empirical theorist to the facts in her domain of investigation. And we can make sense of the possibility of underdetermination *for the linguist*, since the evidence available to her may well underdetermine the correct theoretical decision concerning which set of representations (from among competing alternatives) any given speaker associates with expressions. But the child's relation to the relevant facts is different. This is because the mental representations that constitute the child's linguistic judgments are not *for him* a matter for discovery or choice. He simply *comes to have* these representations. And there can be no further question about whether or not his so-called hypotheses are correct. Rather, the linguistic judgments he comes to have are *what determine which language he ends up speaking*. Whereas the linguist's judgments concern *which* language the speaker speaks, the speaker's judgments constitute the language he speaks.

So far, I have argued that if, as mentalism maintains, linguistic facts consist in certain facts about speakers' mental representations, we must recognize a difference between the child's and the linguist's relation to the linguistic facts. The difference that matters most to our discussion is this: it is not clear what sense can be made of a potential problem of underdetermination *for the child*. In that case, the linguist's theory is not an underdetermined theory of an underdetermined (ground-level) theory. So Chomskian mentalism has not provided us with a way of adhering to a Theory-Theory and ground-level underdetermination while rejecting indeterminacy. If Chomskian mentalism allows us to reject indeterminacy, it is, in effect, by denying that there is (ground-level) underdetermination in the first place.

Now, Chomsky is well known for insisting that the representations which a linguistic theory attributes to speakers are some kinds of beliefs, or cognitive judgments. This is part and parcel of the standard Chomskian proposal that we understand linguistic competence in terms of *what speakers know*. A true linguistic theory will attribute to the speakers all and only the linguistic rules or representations which the speaker *can be said to know*.[37] Speakers, we are told, "tacitly believe" the truths used by a linguistic theory to describe their competence.[38] Now, Chomsky has dismissed objections to construing tacit linguistic belief as a species of ordinary belief as mere pedantic quibble. But he has also remarked that "[s]ince a language has no objective existence apart from its mental representation, *we need not distinguish between 'system of beliefs' and 'knowledge,' in this case*" (1972, 169, my emphasis).[39] So, although Chomsky wants to preserve the connection between linguistic knowledge and ordinary knowledge, he seems to recognize that when it comes to language, individuals *must* be in a position to possess the relevant knowledge. But then it *is* the case after all that speakers must be in a position to know the semantic facts of

---

37 When discussing psychological theories of concepts, Fodor complains that psychologists too often ignore this requirement. "When Pinker says that the child represents the snail as an agent, 'agent' isn't just a term of art that's being used to express a concept of the theorist's; it's also, simultaneously, being used to express a concept that the theorist is attributing to the child. It serves as part of the de dicto characterization of the intentional content of the child's state of mind, and the burden of the theory is that it's the child's being in a state of mind with that content that explains the behavioral data" (1998, 58). For relevant discussion (as well as references to Chomsky and Fodor), see Devitt and Sterelny 1989, Section 3.

38 For discussion of tacit linguistic knowledge, see the articles by Davies and by Higginbotham in George 1989.

39 See also: "One could perhaps take the intuitionist view of mathematics as being not unlike the linguistic view of grammar" (1982, 16), and, "Knowing everything about the mind/brain ... there is not the slightest reason to suppose that there are truths of language that would still escape our grasp" (1986, 33). This last pronouncement is, however, probably best understood as a statement of metaphysical supervenience, despite the epistemological guise.

their language, though they may be ignorant of ordinary empirical facts. Semantic facts, unlike other empirical facts, would be strongly dependent on speakers' judgments. We are back with a version of semantic verificationism.

Notice that the semantic verificationism I am attributing to the Chomskian mentalist concerns the relation of speakers to the semantic facts of their *own* language – i.e., to their idiolects. It does not concern their relation to public languages. However, Chomsky (as well as Fodor) has little patience with public languages, and little desire to secure an objective status for them. It would not be unfair to say that the Chomskian position with respect to public languages is eliminativist. *A fortiori*, then, it does not escape eliminativism by rejecting verificationism when it comes to public languages. Finally, it still remains possible for the Chomskian mentalist to reject semantic verificationism concerning the relation of speakers to the semantic facts of *others'* idiolects. If Chomskian mentalism is right, speakers' interpretation of *others'* speech may well be on an epistemic par with their other empirical investigations. The earlier point, concerning a speaker's own language, remains, however. Chomskian mentalism must acknowledge that the facts about a speaker's *own* idiolect do not "outrun" the speaker's linguistic judgments. Insofar as there is an epistemic relation at all between speakers and the facts of their idiolects, it is very different from the epistemic relations they have to other empirical facts, *or* to the semantic facts of others' language.

III. Between Mentalism and Semantic Eliminativism: A No-Theory Theory?

A possible conclusion from our discussion of Chomskian mentalism would be that we should no longer think of the child acquiring a first language as being in the predicament of a linguist studying a language. Speaking on the issue of the child's epistemic situation, Fodor and Lepore say:

> [The child] differs from the linguist in that his background assumptions aren't justified by bootstrapping. In fact, they aren't justified *at all*. A fortiori, his choice of a T-theory on the basis of the observational evidence together with theses assumptions

does not yield justified true belief, and thus does not yield *knowledge*.... But then, there is no reason to suppose that children (or anybody except, maybe, a few linguists) *do* have knowledge of their language in *that* sense. What is truistic is only that children know their language in the sense that they are able to talk it. (Fodor and Lepore 1992, 77)

What is here proposed is a rather un-Chomskian separation between the child's linguistic *competence* – her ability to talk – and her *judgments* or beliefs about her language.[40] This separation would seem to go against a crucial aspect of the Theory-Theory of language acquisition: the idea that acquiring language is in important, non-trivial ways like the forming (or internalizing) of a theory. And this would offer a way of breaking out of the reasoning to indeterminacy offered earlier. For, on the reconstruction developed in this paper, a crucial step on the way to semantic eliminativism is the claim that ground-level speakers' judgments are underdetermined by linguistic evidence. This step can be undermined if we cease altogether to think of the linguistic input to which children are exposed as evidence or data for the child, and of their linguistic judgments as (quasi-) theoretical beliefs that somehow represent the *theory* of language they construct – however unconsciously – *on the basis of* linguistic evidence. (This is of course not to say that there may not be other arguments for indeterminacy.)

In the previous section, we have seen some reasons internal to the Chomskian conception to abandon the view of the child as theorist. The view requires that we take the child to be in a position to make a choice (however tacitly and arbitrarily) among alternative semantic hypotheses. Being able to make such a choice, in turn, requires that the various alternatives – the candidates for selection – be, in some

---

40 See also Fodor's more recent attempt at resolving the indeterminacy problem by denying that public linguistic evidence underdetermines translational hypotheses, instead of appealing to Chomskian innate constraints (see Fodor 1994, Lecture 3).

There is a strand in Chomsky's own writings that leads in the same direction. It is the claim that language learning is akin to the development of a biological organ. Needless to say, this strand is in tension with the more "cognitivist" pronouncements, which place emphasis on the idea of linguistic knowledge as an internalization of a theory of language.

way, available to the choice-maker. But even if we allow that children do already have a language in which the relevant alternatives *could* be represented – an unacquired language of thought – it is still not clear how to make sense of the idea that the child makes a theoretical (or even "quasi-theoretical") choice among these alternatives.

The difficulty is in seeing how to give substantive content to the idea of a genuine choice on the child's part, over and above the claim that she actually acquires one particular set of semantic judgments rather than another one. More important, perhaps, is the difficulty in maintaining that the child's selection is significantly similar to the kind of *rational* choices made by a linguist theorizing about a language. To speak of a tacit choice, here (as Chomskians are often moved to do), does nothing more than signal an explanatory gap. (Notice that the present point does not depend on challenging the Chomsky/Fodor idea that there is a fact of the matter about which set of hypotheses best characterizes the child's semantic competence – which one is "psychologically real" – or the idea that semantic competence involves associating linguistic sounds with some items in a language of thought.)

Given these peculiarities, and given the consequences discussed in this paper of endorsing the child–linguist analogy, I believe we would do well to abandon the analogy. Abandoning the analogy would mean ceasing to think of the linguistic judgments speakers come to make in the course of acquiring their language as beliefs or hypotheses assessed in light of evidence and selected in preference to alternatives (albeit unconsciously). But if this Theory-Theory conception goes, what shall we put in its place?

Here is one possibility, due to Michael Devitt (1996). At what (I am calling) the ground-level, we simply have speakers' linguistic competence – their ability to speak a particular public language. This ability is a purely practical ability, a matter of mere know-how, which requires no theoretical knowledge of facts *about* the language. Linguistic competence need involve no metalinguistic judgments; a speaker can know what words mean, for example, without forming any judgments about words or about meaning. To know what words mean is simply to be able to *do* certain things with them, to have certain linguistic skills. Ordinary speakers do, in fact, make various linguistic judgments – they have "linguistic intuitions." But such intuitive judgments are in no way implicated by their competence as speakers.

Rather, they constitute a "folk linguistic theory," on a par with folk chemistry, folk anatomy, etc. Folk linguistics is nothing more than a primitive theory about the symbols of a language.[41]

On Devitt's view, the semantic facts of English *can* be as far beyond the epistemic reach of speakers as ordinary empirical facts. There is no constitutive relation between speakers' judgments and the facts about the (public) language they speak. And he denies that speakers enjoy any more than an accidentally privileged knowledge of these facts. He says:

> [O]rdinary semantic intuitions are ... parts of an empirical, fallible, and certainly inadequate set of folk opinions or, more pretentiously, 'folk theory,' the linguistic wisdom of the ages. (1996, 54)

> From the naturalistic perspective, semantic intuitions are like intuitions in any other science: open to revision in the face of empirical theory. We could be wrong about what has a putative meaning. We could be wrong in thinking that anything has it. (1996, 80)

For Devitt, though semantic facts do depend on speakers' existence, in that speakers and their activities can be said to *produce* meanings, they do not exhibit any *epistemic* dependence on speakers. Presumably, speakers – even a whole linguistic community – could be largely wrong in their judgments concerning what their words mean. They could fail to know what words mean even while being competent users of them, and they need not even be in a position to discover what meanings expressions they use have. This is clearly in direct opposition to semantic verificationism.

Devitt's proposal diverges from Chomskian mentalism in two striking ways. First, it takes linguistics to be the empirical study of language, not of aspects of mind, or of psychology. Secondly, it takes speakers' linguistic knowledge to be not a matter of propositional knowledge of the truths delivered by a linguistic theory, but rather

---

41 See Devitt 1996, Section 2.2.

purely a matter of know-how, a practical skill. It is this combination of views that enables it to avoid semantic verificationism.

Now, I think Devitt is right to be suspicious of the Chomskian conception of linguistic knowledge in terms of propositional beliefs. However, I side with Dummett (and others) in thinking that the "mere know-how" view does not do justice to the nature of speakers' semantic competence, at least as long as we hold as a paradigm of such knowledge skills such as bicycle riding or swimming.[42] The skills Devitt himself does mention, such as the ability to make certain meaning-relevant inferences, "the skill of matching sentences and thoughts that are … alike [in meaning-relevant structures]" (Devitt and Sterelny 1989, 517), and the ability to use *that*-clauses, all appear suspiciously "propositional" and seem to involve at least tacit semantic judgments (e.g., regarding meaning similarities and relations of paraphrase). At the very least, one would like to see an explanation of these abilities which avoids all appeal to propositional beliefs, or to metalinguistic judgments. (My own suspicion is that such judgments *are* necessary to account for speakers' competence with propositional attitude ascriptions, which are central to Devitt's characterization. But this argument will have to wait for another occasion.)

I believe semantic judgments (and perhaps other cognitive judgments) are profitably thought of as lying between mere behavioural dispositions or practical skills, on the one hand, and theoretical beliefs or hypotheses, on the other.[43] In certain respects, they are like the perceptual judgments we make, for instance, when we see a certain configuration of lines on a piece of paper as (say) a duck at one time and a rabbit at another. While such judgments are systematically made in response to particular kinds of stimulations or elicitations, learning to make them is more than merely acquiring a discriminatory behavioural disposition, or a know-how capacity to perform some task. It is more than that, in that, for instance, it requires recognizing certain items – linguistic expressions in the linguistic case, or lines on

---

42 See Dummett 1991, passim.

43 See my 1996, especially Sections III and IV, for a closely related discussion of the special nature of linguistic knowledge as something in between purely practical know-how and full-fledged propositional/theoretical knowledge.

the paper, in the perceptual case – as having representational powers. Also, some of the judgments speakers learn to make in the process of learning a language appear to be articulable propositional judgments: e.g., judgments *that* expressions of the language have such-and-such meanings. (As pointed out earlier, such judgments may be expressed by speakers directly or indirectly.) Such judgments can enter into logical inferences and can serve as reasons for intentional actions. It is, in good part, these facts about the nature of semantic judgments that makes a purely behaviouristic, as well as a pure "know-how," conception of language acquisition philosophically unattractive.

On the other hand, acquiring semantic judgments also seems different from learning to make observations, or forming ordinary factual beliefs, or drawing conclusions, or framing hypotheses on the basis of evidence. This is in part because such judgments (again, like the perceptual judgments mentioned above) involve a crucial constructive element. For instance, there is a sense in which it is much more appropriate to think of the truth-conditions assigned by a speaker to an utterly novel sentence as "laid down" or constructed, rather than discovered or hypothesized.[44]

Semantic judgments can, then, be seen as "responsive/constructive." I believe such judgments, when fully characterized, will turn out to be interestingly different from the sorts of beliefs that we paradigmatically think of as forming theories. If this is so, then it is misguided to regard speakers' piecemeal and unreflective interpretive judgments, their judgments of synonymy, heteronomy and so on, as together forming a "folk semantic theory." Unlike folk chemistry, folk biology, or even so-called folk psychology, these judgments do not collectively represent a repository of beliefs and pat-explanations *about* a given domain. Rather, they partially constitute a domain: the domain for empirical semantics. What Quine calls "intuitive" or "uncritical" semantics, then, is not a naïve and failed theory, like phlogiston theory, which ought to be replaced by an appropriately purged scientific theory of language. For, it is not a theory at all.

There may be something that deserves the title 'folk semantic theory.' Folk semantic theory, to the extent that it exists, would be a

---

44 See my 1996 for some discussion of this idea.

set of folk beliefs about the correct characterization, systematization and explanation of ground-level semantic judgments made by speakers. And this folk theory should probably be expected to be no closer to the truth than folk anatomy or folk theory of vision or memory.

Once an appropriate no-theory conception of language acquisition is developed, we could perhaps kick away the ladder of radical translation. The thought experiment of radical translation can now be seen as attempting to articulate what would be involved in the empirical study of a language. What it purports to describe is, at bottom, a process of theory construction which (if I am right) is different from the process of ground-level language acquisition. But on a no-theory conception, a first-language learner is not fruitfully thought of as an amateur theorist of the language spoken around her, passively observing (at least initially) other speakers' behaviour and hypothesizing about the underlying structure and causes of their linguistic emissions, with an eye to producing a systematic representation of the language they speak. Rather, she is an initiated *user* of the language, a soon-to-be active participant in an ongoing, ever-evolving system of communicative practices, linguistic transactions, judgments, and interpretations. Once this is accepted, we can go back to the naïve conception, according to which language acquisition is the more fundamental phenomenon that forms the basis for theorizing about language. For the radical translator to have a job, there must already be a language in place, acquired and used by native speakers, and sustained by their linguistic practices and judgments. In pursuing her project, the radical translator is responsible to those practices and judgments. In a sense I have tried to expound, they form the ultimate court of appeal in matters linguistic.

A no-theory conception as I envisage it could accept the Publicity Requirement and reject (with Quine) the "museum myth," for it would refuse to see the semantic facts of language as determinate beyond the systematic semantic judgments of speakers of the language; it would insist that there is ultimately *no more* to semantic acts than what the language speakers can make of them. But, at the same time, it would stop short of Quine's skepticism about so-called intuitive semantics. This is because it would insist that the semantic facts of a language are also *no less* than what the speakers of that language make of them. In opposition to Quinean skepticism, it would find a proper place for the intuitive (and non-theoretical) semantic judgments that speakers make as a crucial part of the subject-matter for linguistic theory.

References

Bar-On, D. 1986. "Semantic Indeterminacy and Scientific Underdetermination." *Pacific Philosophical Quarterly* 67: 245–63.

———. 1990. "Scepticism: The External World and Meaning." *Philosophical Studies* 60: 207–31.

———.1992a. "On the Possibility of a Solitary Language." *Noûs* 26: 27–46.

———. 1992b. "Semantic Verificationism, Linguistic Behaviorism, and Translation." *Philosophical Studies* 66: 95–119.

———. 1993. "Indeterminacy of Translation: Theory and Practice." *Philosophy and Phenomenological Research* 53: 781–810.

———. 1996. "Anti-Realism and Speaker Knowledge." *Synthèse* 106: 139–66.

———. 1997. "'Natural' Semantic Facts – Between Eliminativism and Hyper-Realism." In *The Maribor Papers in Naturalized Semantics*, ed. D. Jutronic, 99–117. Maribor: Pedagoska Faculteta Maribor.

Bar-On, D. and Risjord, M. 1992. "Is There Such a Thing as a Language?" *Canadian Journal of Philosophy* 22: 163–90.

Barrett, R. and Gibson, R., eds.. 1990. *Perspectives on Quine*. Oxford and Cambridge, MA: Blackwell.

Bennett, J. 1976. *Linguistic Behavior*. Cambridge, MA: Cambridge University Press.

Blackburn, S. 1995. "Theory, Observation, and Drama." Reprinted in M. Davies and T. Stone 1995a, 274–90.

Burge, T. 1979. "Individualism and the Mental." *Midwest Studies in Philosophy 4*, 73–122 Minneapolis: University of Minnesota Press.

Carruthers P., and Smith, P. K., eds.. 1996. *Theories of Theories of Mind*. Cambridge University Press.

Chomsky, N. 1957. *Syntactic Structures*. The Hague: Mouton.

———. 1965. *Aspects of the Theory of Syntax*. Cambridge, MA: MIT Press.

———. 1972. *Language and Mind*. New York: Harcourt Brace Jovanovich.

———. 1975a. "Quine's Empirical Assumptions." In *Words and Objections*, ed. Davidson and Harman, 53–68. Dordrecht, Holland: D. Reidel.

———. 1975b. *Reflections on Language*. New York: Pantheon.

————.1980. *Rules and Representations*. New York: Columbia University Press.

————.1982. *The Generative Enterprise*. Dordrecht: Foris.

————.1986. *Knowledge of Language: Its Nature, Origin, and Use*. New York: Praeger.

Churchland, Paul, 1988. *Matter and Consciousness* (revised edition). Cambridge, MA: MIT Press.

Davidson, D. 1986. *A Nice Derangement of Epitaphs*. In *Truth and Interpretation*, ed. E. Lepore, 433–46. Oxford and Cambridge, MA: Blackwell.

————. 1990. "The Structure and Content of Truth." *The Journal of Philosophy* 87: 279–328.

Davies, M., and Stone, T., eds. 1995a. *Folk Psychology: The Theory of Mind Debate*. Oxford: Blackwell.

————. 1995b. *Mental Simulation*. Oxford: Blackwell.

Devitt, M. 1991. *Realism and Truth* (2nd ed.). Oxford and Cambridge, MA: Blackwell.

————. 1996. *Coming to Our Senses*. Cambridge, MA: Cambridge University Press.

Devitt, M. and Sterelny, K.1989. "What is Wrong with 'the Right View.'" In *Philosophical Perspectives 3*, ed. J. Tomberlin, 497–581. Atascadero, CA: Ridgeview.

Dummett, M. 1991. *The Logical Basis of Metaphysics*. Cambridge, MA: Harvard University Press.

Fodor, J.1968. *Psychological Explanation*. New York: Random House.

————. 1975. *The Language of Thought*. Cambridge, MA: Harvard University Press.

————.1994. *The Elm and The Expert*. Cambridge, MA: MIT Press.

————. 1998. *Concepts: Where Cognitive Science Went Wrong*. Oxford: Clarendon Press.

Fodor, J., and Lepore, E. 1992. *Holism*. Oxford and Cambridge, MA: Blackwell.

Follesdal, D. 1990. *Indeterminacy and Mental States*. In Barrett and Gibson 1990, 98–109.

George, A., ed. 1989. *Reflections on Chomsky*. Oxford and Cambridge, MA: Blackwell.

Lewis, D. 1966. "An Argument for the Identity Theory." *The Journal of Philosophy* 63: 17-25.

Platts, Mark, 1979. *The Ways of Meaning*. London: Routledge & Kegan Paul.

Putnam, H. 1975. "The Meaning of 'Meaning'." In *Mind, Language and Reality*, 215-271. Cambridge MA: Cambridge University Press.

Quine, W.V.1960. *Word and Object*. Cambridge, MA: MIT Press.

———. 1969. *Ontological Relativity and Other Essays*. New York: Columbia University Press.

———. 1970. "Philosophical Progress in Language Theory." *Metaphilosophy* 1: 2–19.

———. 1974. *The Roots of Reference*. La Salle, Ill.: Open Court.

———. 1976. *The Ways of Paradox and Other Essays* (revised and enlarged edition). Cambridge, MA and London: Harvard University Press.

———. 1986. "Reply to Alston." In *The Philosophy of W.V. Quine*, ed. L.E. Hahn and P.A. Schilpp, 73–75. La Salle, Ill.: Open Court.

———. 1987. "Indeterminacy of Translation Again." *Journal of Philosophy* 84: 5–11.

———. 1990. *Pursuit of Truth*. Cambridge, MA: Cambridge University Press.

Ramberg, B. 1989. *Donald Davidson's Philosophy of Language*. Oxford: Basil Blackwell.

Stich, S. 1983. *From Folk Psychology to Cognitive Science*. Cambridge and London: A Bradford Book; MIT Press.

———. 1996. *Deconstructing the Mind*. Oxford: Oxford University Press.

Stjernberg, F. 1991. *The Public Nature of Meaning*. Stockholm: Almqvist & Wiksell International (doctoral dissertation).

CANADIAN JOURNAL OF PHILOSOPHY
Supplementary Volume 30

Mental Concepts as Natural Kind Concepts

DIANA I. PÉREZ

The aim of this paper is to explore the hypothesis that mental concepts are natural kind concepts.[1] By 'mental concepts' I mean the ordinary words belonging to our everyday languages (English, Spanish, and so on) that we use in order to describe our mental life. The plan of the paper is as follows. In the first part, I shall present the hypothesis: firstly, I shall present a theory about the meaning of natural kind concepts following Putnam's 1975 proposal, with some modifications; secondly, I shall present a taxonomy of mental concepts and, thirdly, I shall explain what the meaning of each kind of mental concept would be on the hypothesis defended in this paper. In the second part of the paper, I shall present two interesting consequences of the hypothesis proposed: first, that it is preferable to avoid a certain way of conceiving phenomenal concepts which does not fit with the hypothesis proposed; second, that folk psychology could fruitfully be considered a theory, and why, ultimately, it will not be eliminated.

I. Natural Kinds, Essences and Stereotypes

According to Putnam's proposal, the meaning of natural kind terms is a n-tuple constituted by syntactic markers, semantic markers, a stereotype, and an indexical component which points to the extension of the term.[2] This account for the meaning of natural kind terms tends

---

1 In this paper I shall use 'concept' and 'term' interchangeably.

2 Putnam presents this account of the meaning of many more types of words than natural kind terms. I shall only be concerned with this specific type, i.e., with words such as 'tiger', 'water', etc., which belong to our everyday language, and

to include in the meaning of natural kind terms two elements that traditional semantic theories left aside: the contribution of the real world, and the contribution of society. The actual world contributes to the meaning of natural kind terms through the indexical component implicit in all natural kind terms. In the case of 'water', its indexical component points to a given substance in the actual world whose correct description has been discovered by chemistry: t is the substance whose scientific description is 'H_2O'. This idea is complemented by Putnam with a realistic metaphysics. He holds: "In the view I am advocating, when Archimedes asserted that something was gold he was not saying that it had the superficial characteristics of gold … he was saying that it had the same general *hidden structure* (the same 'essence', so to speak) as any normal piece of local gold" (Putnam 1975, 235). However, in spite of his explicit realistic commitment, Putnam is aware that even if all natural kind terms point to a hidden structure, the world does not contribute to the meaning of the terms in the same way in all the cases: in certain cases, science will in fact discover the hidden structure which was indicated by the ordinary term, like in the 'water' case, but there are other, different cases; for example, (i) some diseases turned out to have no hidden structure at all (there are cases where the only thing in common between the members of the extension is a cluster of symptoms), (ii) there are other diseases where the only hidden structure found was an etiology, and finally (iii) there are some cases where it was found that there is not a single hidden structure but two, like in the 'jade' case. For this reason, Putnam is only able to make a conditional claim: "if there is a hidden structure, then generally it determines what it is to be a member of the natural kind" (1975, 241), but he does not say what happens in the other possible (and even actual) cases mentioned.

In my opinion, a better understanding of this component of natural kind terms is achieved if we accept that what contributes to the meaning of natural kind terms is not an essence in the world, but a certain "psychological essentialism" (Medin 1989). According to this proposal, in order to classify things under natural kind terms we presup-

---

according to which we classify things whose "deep nature" has been scientifically explained through postulating new theories throughout the history of science.

pose the existence of hidden mechanisms that contribute to the actual classification. And this same presupposition drives people to propose new theories in order to give an account of those mechanisms. In fact, we could say that what occurs in the 'water' case is that in order to give an account of the nature of that substance, science had to create a new set of concepts, such as 'oxygen' and 'hydrogen', etc. and a new set of laws connecting them; briefly, it had to generate a new theory about a certain domain of phenomena. When this new theory can identify (in its own terms) a certain substance that behaves in the same way as the unknown substance referred to by the natural kind term, a theoretical identity is stated (water = H_2O). In the 'water' case, the theory offered is a microstructural theory, but in other cases, a different kind of theory could do the job: the properties postulated by those theories do not have to be intrinsic/categoric, but they can be relational, or functional, or historic properties (for example, the hidden essence of 'red' could be a certain relation between the physical world and our eye, the hidden essence of 'tiger' could be its evolutionary history,[3] the hidden structure of 'heart' could be the function of pumping blood).

According to the view I am proposing, this component highlights an incompleteness of the meaning of the term, which could be completed with the growth of knowledge, with the postulation of new explanatory concepts of the phenomena.[4] This account of the meaning of natural kind terms, as many people have remarked (Boyd 1991, Griffiths 1997), does not imply an essentialist commitment. On the contrary, it only implies that people (in many cases the specialists, i.e., scientists) will formulate new theories, employing new concepts,

---

3 There is no agreement among philosophers of biology on this issue, but there is a school of systematics known as "cladistics" that defends this position (See Griffiths 1997, Chapter 8).

4 Even Putnam 1975 admits an interpretation less realistic like this, if we pay attention to paragraphs like the following: "It is beyond question that scientists use terms AS IF the associated criteria were not *necessary and sufficient conditions*, but rather *approximately* correct characterizations of some world of theory-independent entities, and that they talk AS IF later theories in a mature science were, in general, *better* descriptions of the *same* entities that earlier theories referred to" (Putnam 1975, 237; his italics, my capitals). Here, realism seems to be in the speakers' intention/mind.

in order to understand the macrophenomena observed in everyday life. This proposal aims to be in accordance with the spirit of Quine's theory of natural kinds, and it is quite far from any metaphysical essentialism whatsoever.[5]

Returning to Putnam, the meaning of a natural kind term is not only constituted by the extension of the term, but also partly constituted by the stereotype. As I said above, the stereotype is something that could be added to the semantic marker in order to give a description of the meaning of a natural kind term. It is the part of meaning where the contribution of all society (i.e., the linguistic community as a whole) is manifested.

According to Putnam, the stereotype is first of all something that allows people to communicate (Putnam 1975, 247–49) – for, together with the syntactic and semantic marker, it represents the linguistic knowledge that guides the speaker' s use of the term; hence, the possession of the stereotype presupposes a set of common beliefs shared by the community, a body of knowledge about the extension of the term. In the second place, the stereotype is constituted by criteria, the features that in normal situations allow people to recognize that a given entity belongs to a given class. Finally, the features assigned to the objects by the stereotype are only features of the paradigmatic (normal) objects of the extension, they indicate the usual features of X – how it behaves, or what it looks like[6] – but they are not necessary features of all the objects of the class. Therefore, the links between a term and the features that constitute their stereotype are not analytical. Thus, the information contained in the stereotype cannot be known

---

5 Quine (1969) affirms that young children usually classify things according to superficial similarities, but with the growth of knowledge, people (even older children) tend to categorize things according to theory-based similarities. This idea was adopted by developmental psychologists, who empirically tested Quine's intuition with success, giving rise to the "theory-view" or "explanatory-view" of concepts (see Keil 1989).

6 Note that Putnam does not say that stereotypes are constituted exclusively of phenomenal properties of things, nor of functional properties. They are constituted of those features indispensable in order to acquire the words of our everyday language, whichever they turn out to be in each case.

a priori,[7] it depends upon the actual features that certain paradigmatic members of the extension possess, and hence, the stereotype is not enough to decide whether a given term could be correctly applied *in every possible situation*. To have the mastery of terms is simply to apply them correctly to the paradigmatic members of the extension; when queer situations obtain, there is not a definite answer to give.

It seems to me that we can develop an idea of 'stereotype' appealing to the Wittgensteinian notion of 'criteria'.[8] The idea is that there exists a peculiar relation between sentences – the criterial relation – which contributes to determine the meaning of the words involved in those sentences. This "criterial" relation is not a necessary condition relation or an entailment relation, nor a merely inductive/empirical relation. It is an "in between" relation, stronger than the merely inductive relation but weaker than the logical relation, because it is defeasible. When we learn our language, we learn how to use the words 'tiger', 'red', 'pain' or whatever, learning the normal circumstances under which we are justified to utter a (big, and in principle indeterminate) set of sentences where the considered word occurs.[9] This is the set of sentences that contributes to the meaning of the given word.

I am not trying to defend a Wittgensteinian theory of meaning (if there exists something like that); I am only indicating some similarities between Putnam's stereotypes and some Wittgensteinian ideas about the grammar of words, because in the third section, I will use some of the criterial (grammatical) considerations that Wittgenstein proposed to understand mental concepts in order to make clear what could constitute the stereotype of mental concepts if they are conceived as natural kind concepts.[10]

---

7 By 'a priori' here I mean something that we could know without considering peculiar features of our actual world, i.e., something we could know merely by considering all possible worlds, without knowing which is actual.

8 Following Hacker's (1972, Ch. X) interpretation.

9 And we also learn in which kind of cases no justification is needed: some words are such that their meaning is constituted by the fact that certain sentences where the word in question occurs could be asserted without criterion, like 'I am in pain' in the case of 'pain'.

10 I would like to note that there is strong empirical support for the account of the semantics of natural kind terms that I am proposing in this paper. As I said

II. Mental Concepts: A Taxonomy

There are many words in our everyday languages that are used in reference to our mental lives (words like 'pain', 'belief', 'desire', 'thought', 'anger', 'fear', 'love', 'hate', etc.). As I said above, in this paper I will refer to these words with the expression 'mental/ psychological concepts' (or 'mental/psychological terms'). They are a subset of the ordinary concepts expressed in our natural languages and, consequently, they have a history, they may differ from culture to culture, and they may change over the history of mankind. However, there are also some concepts that seem to be constant among cultures and over the ages, for example sensation concepts such as 'pain', the basic emotion concepts such as 'fear', 'anger', 'surprise', and the basic propositional attitude concepts such as 'desire' and 'belief'. I shall concentrate on these constant concepts. These mental concepts form a kind of network; they are interconnected and the possession of each one seems to presuppose the possession of many others. This network of everyday psychological concepts is usually called 'folk psychology': the network of concepts by means of which normal adult human beings interpret, predict and explain our own and other people's behaviour.[11] Nevertheless, not all of these ordinary terms function in a similar way,

---

above, the idea of "psychological essentialism" is a well-developed empirical hypothesis in recent works on concepts (Murphy and Medin 1985, Medin 1989). That said, a crude psychological essentialism (or, in other terms, a pure causal theory of meaning) is not appropriate for natural kind terms. For instance, in recent research (Malt 1994) it is noted that people will accept labeling some stuff 'water' not only according to the simple presence (or absence) of H_2O, but also bearing in mind the use, source, location and phenomenal features of the stuff under consideration. In my terms, people will take into account not only the extension but also the stereotype of the term in order to classify things under a natural kind term or other. (I thank J. Ezquerro, who provided the reference to Malt's paper)

11   At this point, I want to remain neutral on the debate about the theory-theory vs. the theory of simulation view of folk psychology; this is the reason why I prefer to talk about a 'network of concepts' rather than about a 'theory' while referring to folk psychology: both sides of the debate admit that normal adult human beings are in possession of a network of mental concepts.

they do not seem to refer to the same type of entities,[12] and it is difficult to maintain that all of them share a common feature beyond belonging to folk psychology. Moreover, it is not clear that every occurrence of a single word, for example 'belief', refers to the same kind of entities in every case.[13]

It is a well-established fact that our mental lives have at least two different aspects. On the one hand, some mental states are intentional (in Brentano's sense); they are about something, about an intentional object or a proposition. These mental states are thought of as having a representational aspect; they are states where a given individual holds a relation with a mental representation with semantic properties, a state that carries information (true or false information) about the world. The paradigmatic cases of intentional states are beliefs and desires. On the other hand, there are some mental states that seem to possess an ineliminable qualitative aspect, i.e., a certain quality that allows us to distinguish a given state from another, for example, a pain from an itch. The paradigmatic cases of qualitative states are sensations, for example 'pain', 'having an experience of red', 'seeing green', etc.

Ordinary terms used in order to refer to emotions are difficult to classify. Some of them clearly have an intentional object; for example, we might be afraid of lions but not of spiders. But there are some emotional states that do not seem to refer to any object or state, like anguish. Some emotions clearly possess a qualitative aspect, like

---

12 Some of them seem to refer to events, others to states, dispositions, processes, and so on.

13 Goldman (1970) distinguishes between occurrent versus standing beliefs. An occurrent belief is, for example, the belief I am having now that my room is cold, which causes me to turn on the heat. A standing belief is something that I believe, for example that the Earth revolves around the Sun, but about which I am not thinking right now, and as a consequence does not cause any of my present behaviours. Occurrent beliefs are better thought of as events; standing beliefs are better understood as dispositions. Occurrent beliefs are usually accompanied by our awareness of being in that belief-state, but standing beliefs are such that we might not be aware of them at any time, but nevertheless it is right to say that we possess them, such as the belief that zebras do not use clothes, about which Dennett once made us think.

fear, but it is not clear that all of them possess it, like shame or love, emotional states that I can entertain without being aware of them, so without having any qualitative subjective experience associated.[14] Moreover, many emotional concepts, for example 'fear', point not only to a certain quality (the "sensation of fear") and a certain functional/ representational state, but also to a certain physical state, described in terms of levels of adrenaline, the increase of our heart rate, etc. As W. James (1890) wisely wrote:

> What kind of an emotion would be left if the feeling neither quickened heart-beats nor of shallow breathing, neither of trembling lips nor of weakened limbs, neither of gooseflesh nor of visceral stirrings, were present, it is quite impossible for me to think. Can one fancy the state of rage and picture no ebullition in the chest, no flushing of the face, no dilatation of the nostrils, no clenching of the teeth, no impulse to vigorous action, but in their stead limp muscles, calm breathing, and a placid face? (quoted in Damasio 1994)

On the other hand, sensation concepts and propositional attitude concepts are more distant from their physical manifestations: it is usually claimed that there is only a contingent link between beliefs or pains and their behavioural/physical manifestation. (We cannot discover that someone believes that snow is white by looking at her face, nor discover if someone is truly in pain by looking at her face, for she could be an actress on the stage.)[15]

Summing up, it seems to me that we can clearly distinguish three different kinds of mental concepts: sensation concepts, emotion concepts and propositional attitude concepts,[16] which are intercon-

---

14 Think about the fact that many times a good friend could know your feelings better than you do.

15 Note that the claim that there is only a contingent link between a qualitative state and a physical /behavioural state is the first step in the standard arguments for qualia, such as the inverted spectrum and the zombies arguments.

16 I know that this classification is not exhaustive; there are also moods and personality traits that I will not take into account in this paper. (I thank P. Rychter for making me think about this point.)

nected[17] and constitute the network of our "folk psychology." So conceived, folk psychology is a network of mental concepts. The aim of this paper is to explore the idea that mental concepts are natural kind concepts; therefore, in the next section, I shall show what happens if we consider emotion concepts, sensation concepts, and propositional attitude concepts as natural kind concepts.

III. Mental Concepts as Natural Kind Concepts[18]

Griffiths (1997) is devoted to the hypothesis that our ordinary emotion terms are natural kind terms. He explains some of our ordinary emotion concepts – in particular the six basic emotions: fear, surprise, anger, disgust, sadness, and happiness – in terms of the idea of "affect program" that belongs to a biological theory proposed by Ekman.[19] In the case of these basic emotions, according to Griffiths,

---

17 By 'interconnected' I mean that the stereotype of each of these words includes specific relations with words referring to other types of mental states. For example, 'being afraid' usually presupposes 'having the sensation of fear', 'having a pain in the stomach', 'believing that oneself is in danger', 'desiring not to be in that situation', and so on.

18 Nagel (1986, Chapter 2, Section 3) is an important antecedent of the idea developed here. He considers the word 'I' as the main example in order to apply Putnam's semantics to mental concepts, but I think that it is a bad choice, because (1) it is not clear if the stereotype of this word is shared by the different speakers of a given language, and (2) because the reference of this word is a token, not a type which could be scientifically studied. My examples are more adequate to develop the hypothesis proposed. McGinn 1991 also argues for the existence of a "hidden essence" of consciousness (and other mental states as well), but he rejects the idea that this hidden structure could be phenomenological or physical; he holds – in accordance with his "Trascendental Naturalism" (McGinn 1993) – that we will never know the real nature of that deep essence, although it exists. Hill 1991 adopts the idea that certain limited groups of mental terms such as "pain" are natural kind concepts.

19 "The central idea of affect program theory is that emotional responses are complex, coordinated and automated. They are complex because they involve several elements. These are usually taken to include (a) expressive facial changes, (b) musculoskeletal responses such as flinching and orienting, (c) expressive vocal changes, (d) endocrine system changes in the level of hormones, and (e) autonomic

there is a well-established biological theory that identifies the deep structure (the affect program) that explains the co-occurrence of the behavioural properties (including facial expressions) and the physical properties (increasing heart rate, paleness, trembling, etc.) associated with our ordinary emotion terms, i.e., the stereotypical macroproperties associated with each emotion term.[20] But the other ordinary emotion concepts, such as "love," "guilt" and "envy" for example, cannot be identified with affect programs. In Griffiths' words: "the general category of emotion subsumes three different kinds of psychological states. The best understood of these are affect programs. The second, more speculative kind are irruptive motivational complexes in higher cognition. The third kind are disclaimed actions" (1997, 245). As a consequence, he holds that our ordinary concept of emotion (in general) has to be eliminated from our language, and replaced by three, more specific concepts, because 'emotion', as we have found empirically, has partial reference, i.e., it refers to different phenomena with nothing in common among them; but the particular emotion concepts, such as 'fear', 'happiness', 'love', etc., will be preserved as long as their "hidden structure" can be found by one scientific theory or another: biology, psychology, or anthropology.

---

nervous system changes. Emotion feelings and cognitive phenomena such as the directing of attention are obvious candidates to be added to the list. The affect responses are coordinated because the various elements occur together in recognizable patterns or sequences. They are automated because they unfold in this coordinated fashion without the need for conscious direction. Ekman sometimes conceives affect programs as literal neural programs which coordinate the various elements in the emotional response. However, the phrase can be used in a more noncommittal fashion. The affect program is the coordinated set of changes that constitute the emotional response. I use the phrase in this sense" (Griffiths, 1997, 77).

20 Griffiths 1997 48–50 reproduces the facial and musculoskeletal expression of basic emotions, which were first formulated by Darwin 1872. Griffiths 1997, Section 3.2. is devoted to more recent formulations of emotional expressions. These emotional expressions constitute an important item among the criteria according to which we learn emotion words. (More details regarding the "grammar" of emotion concepts may be found in Wittgenstein 1967, Section 488 ff.) In any case, as I said in the last paragraph, facial expression, bodily alterations, and behaviour are among the criteria which constitute the stereotype of emotion terms.

There are, in sum, two interesting question we could address, inspired by Griffiths' book: (1) Is 'mental concept' a natural kind concept? and (2) Are individual mental concepts, e.g. 'fear', 'pain', 'belief', natural kind concepts? I tried to show in the second section that the answer to the first question is negative, and Griffiths' book gives a similar answer for general mental terms, such as 'emotion'. In the rest of this paper I shall be focused on the second question, which is answered by a "Yes" for the case of individual emotion terms by Griffiths. I shall expand his proposal to the other individual mental concepts such as 'belief', 'desire', and so on, i.e., propositional attitude concepts, and also to 'pain', 'seeing red', and so on, i.e., sensation concepts.

What would happen if we seriously considered the idea that ordinary sensation concepts, such as 'pain', are natural kind concepts? In my opinion, this possibility is highly plausible. The stereotypical part of the meaning of these terms is constituted by what Wittgenstein called the "grammar" of these terms. Wittgenstein (1953, 1967) is, in my view, one of the most important sources for a description of the "grammar," i.e., the relational aspects, the stereotype, of our everyday sensation concepts (and many others). There are many remarks that Wittgenstein made about this topic. I would like to recall a few of them, which will be useful in what follows.

First, Wittgenstein clearly distinguishes between the first- and the third person ascription of mental states. According to Wittgenstein, the criteria for third person ascriptions are behavioural, while first person ascriptions are criterionless (1953, 289–90; 1967, 576, 591, 539–64; see Wittgenstein 1967, 472 for a generalization of these ideas for all mental concepts). But what is attributed in both cases is the same concept (Wittgenstein 1967, 220).[21] Second, there are many things we have to know before acquiring mental concepts such as 'pain' (1953, 257): the grammar of pain is presupposed before learning the word. Without a general agreement about how the world is, there are no concepts at all (1967, 351–2, 430–31).[22] The expression of pain and its manifest behaviour are relevant while learning the word, and also relevant for

---

21 See footnotes 9 and 10 above.

22 See the features of stereotypes mentioned in section 1.

successful communication. But what is "in the box" (1953, 293) is irrelevant in both cases. Translated into my words, this means that the stereotype does not include the essence of 'pain'; for communicative purposes, public criteria are enough. But this claim is compatible with the idea that the essence – what is "in the box" – could be scientifically studied, although I am not defending the claim that Wittgenstein himself accepted this idea.

The indexical part of the meaning of sensation concepts is, in my view, what scientific research is looking for nowadays: the "neural correlate" of consciousness. In my opinion, we may reconsider the old psychophysical identity thesis defended forty years ago by J.J.C. Smart in light of this idea: the identity between pain and a neurophysiological state ("C-fiber's firings") will be stated when a new neurophysiological theory is formulated in terms of which we might describe the indexical element that was always part of the meaning of our everyday mental concepts.

Let us briefly remember the central theses of type-type identity theory, in the spirit of Smart.[23] According to this theory, there are no mere nomic correlations between qualitative phenomena of our mental life and physiological phenomena (or some other more basic phenomena); they are simply identical. Mental concepts, like 'pain', and physical concepts, like 'C-fiber's stimulation', express different concepts without any conceptual/*a priori* connection between them but, following Frege's distinction, these two concepts share the same reference: they point to the same property in our world. This same thesis can be restated in light of the idea that our sensation concepts behave as natural kind concepts.

According to this proposal, 'pain' is associated on the one hand with the relational/functional properties that constitute the "grammar" of pain, and, on the other hand, 'pain' has an indexical com-

---

23 It is interesting to remark that the original formulation of the Identity Theory involved, precisely, the qualitative states of our mental life: the identity was established between sensations and brain processes. (Smart 1959) Identity theorists thought that the rest of mental phenomena, like belief, understanding, wanting, etc. could be adequately handled by a behaviouristic approach. However, they later extended the identity thesis to all kinds of mental phenomena. (I owe this historical point to E. Rabossi.)

ponent that will be described by neurophysiology. This neurophysiological description will be formulated in a new scientific vocabulary. The neurophysiological description will identify the reference that the concept of pain has today, i.e., the indexical component of the concept of pain, but this description will be formulated with a new vocabulary, so we will not find a conceptual link between the stereotype of pain and the description of the deep structure of pain (the neurophysiological state identified with pain); they will just be two alternative descriptions of the same stuff in the world. In the same way 'water' and 'H_2O' are different (conceptually independent) concepts, one of them is constituted by the stereotype of water and its indexical component, and the other one is a description of the extension of the term 'water' in a new scientific vocabulary. This account of 'water' as a natural kind concept is not incompatible with the idea held by the type-identity theorists according to which 'water = H_2O' is an *a posteriori* identity, discovered by scientific progress.

Propositional attitude concepts seem to pose certain problems if the hypothesis I am proposing is to accommodate them. In this case, it seems empirically impossible to find a categorical property, or a unique neurophysiological property, with which we can identify a propositional attitude concept, because of the well-known multiple realizability argument. Nevertheless, it is widely accepted that propositional attitudes are functional states: their "essence" is functional, relational, and not microstructural (as in the case of chemical properties). Beliefs are states that carry information about the world. And it is usually thought that these informational states are exactly those postulated by cognitive psychology while trying to explain psychological phenomena such as memory, decision-making, problem-solving, text comprehension, etc.: the new scientific description of these phenomena proposed nowadays is given in functional terms, but it is a legitimate essence after all (on my own reading of psychological essentialism proposed in the first paragraph of this paper). Thus we consider propositional attitude concepts to be natural kind concepts, with a functional essence (which could be multiply realized, as the orthodoxy claims).

As we can see, the hypothesis that mental concepts are natural kind concepts coheres with the taxonomy of mental concepts proposed in the last paragraph. As we saw above, there is a certain heterogeneity among mental concepts: not all of them behave in the same way, and it is difficult to find a common feature shared by all mental states (in fact, it seems to me that mental concepts are bound together only in virtue of certain family resemblance, and that is all; there are no further reasons to put them all together). On the other hand, philosophical discussions about the qualitative usually take neuroscience as the basic science in terms of which reduction, elimination, and so on have to be thought; but the parallel discussions about the intentional always take cognitive science as the basic science (and the case of emotions is in between). If we accept the idea that mental concepts are natural kind concepts, this difference could be easily explained: it is true not only that there are differences in stereotype between one kind of concept and the others (as we saw above, basic emotions stereotypes include physical changes, while propositional attitudes' stereotype does not), but also, there are differences in their "essences": while the best set of concepts in order to describe the "essence" of the qualitative are neurophysiological concepts, the "essence" of the intentional is best explained by a cognitive theory, a higher-level theory. The heterogeneity that we find in the stereotype of mental concepts tracks the difference in essences that they possess.

IV. First Consequence: Phenomenal Concepts are Dispensable

Understanding mental concepts as natural kind concepts entails many interesting philosophical consequences. To begin with, the notion of 'phenomenal concept' supposed in recent discussions about *qualia* turns out to be a dispensable notion. All we need in order to explain the phenomena are *sensation concepts*: 'pain', 'colour sensations', and the like. Phenomenal concepts are supposed to be those that refer to the phenomenal properties of our mental lives, to our subjective experience, to our *qualia* (i.e., to what is beyond the functional, the relational, and the cognitive). They refer to the intrinsic character of our minds. The well-known thought experiments of zombies and inverted spectra are designed to set apart the functional features of our mind from the non-functionalizable part of our mind: the qualitative features, referred to by phenomenal concepts. I will set aside the question of the very existence of these *qualia*. In what follows, I will only be concerned with the idea of phenomenal concepts, and with whether it makes sense to consider these phenomenal concepts as natural kind concepts. In the first place, it is not clear that our everyday language contains phenomenal concepts in the sense outlined above. In fact, our ordinary language contains sensation concepts such as 'pain', 'sensation of red', etc., but these ordinary concepts have a relational side, a functional aspect (and in the opinion of some philosophers, this functional aspect exhausts the meaning of these terms Lewis 1966, 1972). As Chalmers (1996, 17) acknowledges, "we might say that the notion of pain is ambiguous between the phenomenal and the psychological [functional] concept, or we might say that both of these are components of a single rich concept." In my view, the first of these options involves the hypothesis that there are two concepts behind our ordinary word 'pain', a phenomenal concept of pain (which refers to an intrinsic property of our experience, known from the first person perspective), and a psychological concept of pain (which refers to the cause of our observable pain-behaviour, exclusively known from the third person perspective). In any case, this would be a philosophical distinction, not an ordinary one, because it is based on the thought experiments mentioned above. The second option is, in my view, the right one concerning our everyday language. Our ordinary mental concepts are complex, rich; they have different application criteria for the first and the third person. That is the "grammar" of our ordinary mental concepts. If we try to take apart the first- and the third person aspects of our mental lives, the phenomenal and the behavioural aspects of the mental concepts, we fracture our ordinary concepts, and this move has to be justified. I am not claiming that our ordinary concepts cannot change, but that any change we introduce has to be justified in one way or another.

In the second place, even if phenomenal concepts are accepted as a consequence of a *philosophical* distinction, there is a problem with their individuation. In a recent paper, Chalmers (2003) affirms that when we are having a red experience and we think that we are having a red experience, there are at least four phenomenal concepts involved in that thought: (1) the community relational concept: red_C ('the quality caused in normal observers in my community by red things'), (2) the individual relational concept: red_I ('the quality normally caused in me by red things'), (3) the indexical concept: E ('the quality I am experiencing now') and (4) the qualitative concept: R. But, according to Chalmers, the same property makes true the different statements involving all of these concepts, that is to say that it is *a posteriori* necessary that $red_C = red_I = E = R$. My claim is that (1)–(4) are all constituents of the ordinary concept 'sensation of red'. If by 'concept' we mean the content of ordinary terms, I think my claim is right.

In the third place, it is not clear what R could be. In order to explain the distinction between a phenomenal and a functional ("psychological," in Chalmers' words) concept, Chalmers introduces some technical notions about the meaning of words. For him, the meaning or intension of a given term is composed of two different intensions, the primary intension of the term and the secondary intension of that same term. The primary intension of a term is a function from worlds to extensions according to the way the actual-world reference is fixed: it picks out the features that H_2O of our Earth, and XYZ of Twin Earth, have in common. The secondary intension picks out the same substance in all worlds; given the fact that water turns out to be H_2O in our actual world, the secondary intension of 'water' picks out H_2O in every possible world. The primary intension picks out the stereotype, the relational, phenomenal features of the substance referred to by the natural kind term. The primary intensions of the concepts are determined by conceptual analysis; they are absolutely *a priori*, they are independent of the way our world is.

Phenomenal concepts, according to Chalmers, are those where primary and secondary intensions collapse, or, more accurately, they are those that lack primary intension; they lack a stereotype, they do not have any relational or functional features. However, if this is true, they cannot be natural kind concepts, because natural kind concepts require a stereotype constituting their meaning. And according to what I have said above, our ordinary sensation concepts do not seem to behave this way; they do have a functional or relational side/aspect: our ordinary sensation concepts are not concepts like R.

Finally, Chalmers explicitly argues against the analogy between phenomenal concepts and natural kind concepts. His argument goes as follows:

> But here we see a strong disanalogy. Once Oscar acquires the chemical concept H_2O and Twin Oscar acquires XYZ, they will

no longer be twins: their functional properties will differ significantly. By contrast, at the corresponding point Mary and Inverted Mary are still twins. Even though Mary has a pure phenomenal concept **R** and inverted Mary has **G**, their functional properties are just the same. So the difference between the concepts **R** and **G** across functional twins is something that has no counterpart in the standard Twin Earth story. (2003, 231)

I have two worries with this argument. First, we can consider this same passage as a *reductio ad absurdum* of the idea that R and G (pure phenomenal concepts) are *concepts* at all. If something doesn't make a difference in the beliefs that it constitutes, it is not a concept. Second, if phenomenal concepts are concepts, in the sense that they do make a difference in the beliefs that they constitute,[24] then *there really is* a functional difference between Mary and Twin Mary if they have different phenomenal concepts because of their different experiences, and so the analogy with the H_2O case is re-established. The only way to avoid this objection is to accept a difference among beliefs without a correlative functional difference – but if this is the case, beliefs do not supervene logically on the functional, and the very distinction between the "easy problem" and the "hard problem" of consciousness disappears (see Chalmers 1996, 1997).

Summing up, supposed qualitative concepts (purely phenomenal concepts) are not natural kind concepts; our folk psychology is constituted by mental concepts that are natural kind concepts; thus, there is no reason to accept this kind of concept, because all the phenomena of our mental life which could be scientifically explained are exactly those phenomena that are already referred to by our ordinary mental concepts.

---

24 It is worth mentioning that this is exactly the thesis that Chalmers is defending in this paper: his idea is that phenomenal beliefs are a special kind of belief not completely functional, but partly constituted by these phenomenal concepts, which obviously cannot be functionalized.

V. Second Consequence: Folk Psychology is Ineliminable

In the last thirty years, many papers have been written in order to clarify the status and nature of folk psychology. Since Lewis 1972 and Churchland 1981, the idea that folk psychology is a theory was widely discussed. And since Churchland 1981 and Stich 1983, the fate of folk psychology has been inextricably linked to its theoretical status. Nowadays, there are many different issues concerning folk psychology that are discussed in the philosophical and the psychological literature; I do not want to examine the whole discussion. On the contrary, I want to take as a starting point the idea of folk psychology as this network of everyday psychological concepts by means of which (at least sometimes) normal adult human beings interpret, predict, and explain our own and other people's behaviour.[25] In light of the hypothesis proposed in this paper (i.e., that mental concepts are natural kind concepts in the sense specified in Sections I–III), I shall try to show that there is a legitimate sense according to which folk psychology is to be considered as a theory but, in spite of being a theory, it makes no sense to discuss whether or not it will be eliminated because of scientific progress; to the contrary, the sense of 'theory' involved in this proposal will prevent it from being eliminated. In order to do that I shall, firstly, present the general form of the eliminativist's argument, and I shall make some remarks about the most famous exemplifications of it; then, I shall explain the sense in which folk psychology is a theory within the framework proposed in this paper, and I shall show why this theory will not be eliminated.

---

25 I will not consider the cases (if there are any) where it is possible to make predictions or explanations of human behaviour without using mental concepts (as it seems to be possible according to the "simulation theory"). I will not take into account the discussions about the acquisition of mental concepts (or the so-called "theory of mind"), i.e., the discussions on whether there exists an innate module containing this theory of the mind, or if it is the result of a general-purpose mechanism that we use in order to generate general theories about the world, or if it is acquired by enculturation. And finally, I will not be concerned with the empirical question about the information-processing mechanisms that need to be postulated in order to provide an explanation of the actual human practice usually called "folk psychology."

The general form of the argument for eliminativism is simple. The first premise affirms that folk psychology is a theory. The second premise is that it is a bad theory. Many different particular arguments for this premise take different facts as a starting point. Churchland's (1981) version of the argument maintains that folk psychology is a bad theory because it cannot explain certain phenomena, because it is not a "progressive" research program, and because it is in conflict with other well-established theories, especially with neuroscience. Stich's (1983, 1996, Chapter 2) argument is based on the idea that the understanding of beliefs provided by folk psychology is in conflict with mature cognitive science. This bad theory, so the general argument continues, will be replaced by a better (scientific) theory. Therefore, the ontology presupposed in the rejected theory has to be rejected too: after all, there are no beliefs, desires, and so on.

The first premise of this argument has been repeatedly discussed in the last twenty years. What kind of "theory" is it supposed that folk psychology is? The idea shared by Stich, Churchland, Lewis (following Sellars), and many others is that folk psychology is a set of causal laws that are used in order to explain and predict behaviour. These laws connect perceptual and other inputs with behavioural outputs, postulating a special kind of theoretical entity – mental states – which have, within this folk theory, the same status as other theoretical entities in other scientific theories; they are, for example, like "atoms": non-observable entities assumed in order to explain observable facts.

I want to make some remarks on some instances of this general argument form. The sense of "theory" Churchland adopts is quite clear: he assumes that folk psychology is an empirical theory like any other scientific theory; the empirical theories that he uses in order to exemplify the idea that the ontology of a false theory has to be eliminated are alchemy and the phlogiston theory (Churchland 1981, 12–14). It is remarkable that he does not compare our folk psychology with our commonsense conception of physical phenomena – our folk or "intuitive" physics (McCloskey 1983) –, but with two particular physical theories proposed by a special community, i.e., the physicists' community at that time.

In the second place, Churchland's criticisms of folk psychology are focused on a special part of it, the part concerned with propositional attitudes – which, he says, are "the principal elements of common

sense psychology" (Churchland 1981, 1). He explicitly ignores emotions and sensations. Stich's (1983) arguments for eliminativism are
also focused on propositional attitudes. There are also eliminativist
arguments that are concerned with *qualia* (Dennett 1988) or emotions
(Griffiths 1997). But there do not seem to be general arguments against
folk psychology as a whole. And, as I said above, it seems obvious to
me that our commonsense conception of ourselves includes emotions
and sensations as well as beliefs and desires. Our behaviour is usually explained in terms of propositional attitudes, but also in terms of
the emotions and sensations we possess. And the worst consequence
of the partial understanding of our folk psychology that Churchland
assumes is that it has infected all the discussions thereafter about the
status, nature, and future of folk psychology.[26]

I believe that the hypothesis I propose in this paper allows us to
preserve the theoretical status of folk psychology in a fruitful way,
avoiding its elimination. According to the hypothesis that mental concepts are natural kind concepts, and following the account of natural
kind concepts I proposed (in Section I), folk psychology – the set of
our ordinary mental concepts – is a network of concepts, including
at least three kinds of mental concepts: sensation concepts, emotion
concepts and propositional attitude concepts. As I said above, each of
these concepts has a "grammar," a theory or body of knowledge that
includes many other mental concepts, some behavioural facts (both
linguistic and non-verbal), some facial manifestations, etc.

This theory is our folk psychology, the stereotypical component of
our psychological natural kind concepts. Learning the meaning of our
ordinary mental concepts is having the mastery of this theory, being
able to use it in order to communicate our mental states and to explain
and predict our own and others' behaviour.

In my opinion, we can distinguish at least two different senses in
which we could say that folk psychology is a theory. On the one hand,
we could suppose that it is a theory because we accept the idea that
mental states are postulated on the basis of observable behaviour, in

---

26 See, for example, Greenwood 1991, Introduction, where he restricts the
discussions about the future of folk psychology to those conceptions that involve
psychological states that are contentful and causally efficacious.

order to explain and predict human action. This is the original sense in which Lewis and Churchland affirmed that folk psychology is a theory. But there is another (wider) sense of theory: it is the idea that any coherent set of beliefs about a certain subject is a theory, and this is the sense in which we accept that before knowing the scientific structure of water, we already had a "theory of water." In this second sense, I want to affirm that folk psychology is a theory. But this claim does not commit us to the idea that we can only observe behaviour. To the contrary, it is plainly compatible with the idea that we could observe directly our own as well as other people' s mental sates, and that we do not "infer" other people's mental states on the basis of their behaviour, or facial expression.[27]

According to the account of natural kind concepts that I proposed above, mental concepts also have an "indexical" component. This component, understood in terms of psychological essentialism, has to be filled in with more theories, such as those proposed in order to discover the hidden essence of these mental concepts. But these theories are continuous with our folk theories, given the fact that they are built in order to explain more deeply the facts already explained by the theory that constitutes the grammar of these concepts. Folk psychology and scientific psychology are (as a consequence of my view) in the same relation as our folk theory about water with chemistry, which grounds the identity water = H_2O.

According to the hypothesis I am defending, the eliminativist position is untenable because our folk psychology is the basic understanding of our mental lives, the initial point for undertaking our scientific research. Our commonsense and our scientific knowledge form a continuum, and scientific research can explain some commonsense phenomena. Of course, our commonsense understanding can change

---

27 In my opinion, the passage always quoted from Wittgenstein (1967, 225) in order to argue that he did not accept that folk psychology is a kind of theory is only adequate in order to reject the first sense of theory, but not the second one, which is compatible with the idea that our common knowledge about our mental life, the kind that makes possible our mental concepts, is in fact a certain kind of theory (although not entirely empirical, but for someone like me who rejects the two dogmas of empiricism, the question if it is an empirical or a conceptual theory is not important).

because of scientific findings, but, in the end, the very same phenomena that constitute our ordinary understanding of the world and of ourselves have to be included in the scientific image of the world, for they cannot contradict it.[28]

Comparing the folk psychology case with the water case, what scientific researchers look for is the "essence" of water; when they discover that water is H_2O, they do not eliminate 'water', but they incorporate 'water' into the scientific image of the world. If we pretend that psychology, while dealing with informational states or with neurophysiological states, can eventually change into something where there is no place for notions such as 'belief', 'desire', 'pain', 'fear'," and so on, then there is a change of subject, and we are not dealing any more with our psychology.

Moreover, as I suggested above, the eliminativist arguments that we find in the philosophical literature are, in general, partial, i.e., restricted to the idea of eliminating propositional attitudes (Churchland 1981, Stich 1983, Greenwood 1991) *or* qualia (Dennett 1988) *or* emotion (Griffiths 1997), but not all of them by a single argument. And even accepting those arguments for their respective cases, it is risky to extend the same argument to other cases, because they are usually based on peculiar features of the mental involved in the particular cases considered, and they cannot be extended to other cases

---

28 The strategy I am defending against eliminativism is not the same as that proposed by Lycan, who opposed the philosophical thesis of eliminativism with a bunch of "Moorean facts" such as that Granny wants a beer. The opposition I am trying to draw here is not simply between philosophy and common sense, but between the idea that scientific research can ignore common sense versus the idea that scientific inquiry is continuous with common sense; and, because of that, that commonsensical psychology will not be eliminated. I am congenial to Moore's and Wittgenstein's defense of commonsense certainties against the idealist (and the skeptic), but a direct application of this strategy to the problem of the status of folk psychology (Rabossi 2000 is an example of this move) drives one, in my opinion, to a position which denies any possible change in folk psychology. That is, I want to make a weaker claim: many things could change in our folk understanding of ourselves, and probably scientific research and philosophy will have to do a lot with those changes, but there will always be some basic psychological concepts used in order to understand ourselves that will not be abandoned. See Pérez (forthcoming) for further arguments along these lines.

easily: the arguments for the elimination of propositional attitudes presuppose that they are relational, and that the agent involved is related to a sentence-like item (Churchland 1981, Stich 1983), whereas the argument for the elimination of qualia presupposes their intrinsicality, directness, privacy, and so on (see Dennett 1988). But, if there is no interest in extending the argument proposed for a subset of mental concepts to the other mental concepts, then the problem is that the argument involves an inadequate understanding of folk psychology. The set of ordinary mental concepts that constitutes folk psychology combine in a framework that is impossible to divide: the interactions among them are so strong that it is artificial to set apart a subset and treat it independently of the remaining concepts, pretending that they do not exist.[29]

References

Boyd, R. 1991. "Realism, Anti-foundationalism and the Enthusiasm for Natural Kinds. *Philosophical Studies* 61: 127–148.

Carey, S. 1985. "Knowledge Acquisition: Enrichment or Conceptual Change?" Reprinted in Laurence and Margolis 1998.

Chalmers, D. 1993. "Self-ascription Without Qualia: A Case Study." *Behavioral and Brain Sciences* 16: 35–36.

———. 1996. *The Conscious Mind*. Oxford: Oxford University Press.

———. 1997. Facing Up the Problem of Consciousness." In *Explaining Consciousnes*, ed. J. Shear, 9–30. Cambridge, MA: MIT Press.

---

29 Some of the ideas proposed in this paper were previously presented to the group LOGOS, Universitat de Barcelona, Spain, February, 2002, at the XI Congreso Nacional de Filosofía, Salta, Argentina, November 2001, Coloquio de filosofía teórica y filosofía de la ciencia, SADAF, Buenos Aires, Argentina, July 2001, and Seventh International Colloquium on Cognitive Science, San Sebastián, Spain, May 2001. I want to thank many people for useful discussion, including J. Biro, J. Corbí, J.A. Diez Calzada, J. Ezquerro, M. Garcia Carpintero, C. Gonzalez, D. Justo, D. Pineda, E. Rabossi, P. Rychter, M. Sabatés, L. Skidelsky, R. Stainton, J. Vergara and many other participants of the mentioned events. Financial support was provided by the Fundación Antorchas.

————. 2003. "The Content and Epistemology of Phenomenal Beliefs." In *Consciousness. New Philosophical Perspectives*, ed. Q. Smith and A. Jokic, 220–272. Oxford: Oxford University Press.

Churchland, P. 1981. "Eliminative Materialism and the Propositional Attitudes." In Churchland 1989. *A Neurocomputational Perspective*. Cambridge, MA: MIT Press.

————. 1998. *On the Contrary*. Cambridge, MA: MIT Press.

Damasio, A. 1994. *Descartes' Error*. New York: Avon Books.

Dennett, D. 1988. "Quining Qualia." In *Consciousness in Contemporary Science*, eds. Marcel, A., and E. Bisiach, 43–77. Oxford: Oxford University Press,

Goldman, A. 1970. *A Theory of Human Action*. Princeton: Princeton University Press.

————. 1993. "The Psychology of Folk Psychology." *Behavioral and Brain Science* 16: 15–28.

Greenwood, J. 1991. *The Future of Folk Psychology*. Cambridge: Cambridge University Press.

Griffiths, P. 1997. *What Emotions Really Are*. Chicago: Chicago University Press.

Hacker , P.M.S. 1972. *Insight and Illusion*. Oxford: Clarendon Press.

Hill, C. 1991. *Sensantions. A Defense of Type Materialism*. Cambridge: Cambridge University Press.

Jackson, J. 1993. "Qualia for Propositional Attitudes?" *Behavioral and Brain Science* 16: 52.

Keil, F. 1989. *Concepts, Kinds and Cognitive Development*. Cambridge, MA: MIT Press.

Laurence, E. and Margolis, S. 1988. *Concepts. Core Readings*. Cambridge, MA: MIT Press.

Lewis, D. 1966. "An Argument for the Identity Theory." *Journal of Philosophy* 63: 17–25.

————. 1972. "Psychophysical and Theoretical Identifications." *Australasian Journal of Philosophy* 50: 249–58.

Lycan, W. (Unpublished Manuscript) "A Particularly Compelling Refutation of Eliminative Materialism."

McKlosky, M. 1983. "Intuitive Physics." *Scientific American* 248: 122–30.

McGinn, C. 1991. "The Hidden Structure of Consciousness." In *The Problem of Consciousness*, ed. C. McGinn, 89 - 125. Oxford: Blackwell.

————. 1993. *Problems in Philosophy*. Oxford: Blackwell.

Malt, B. 1994. "Water is not H$_2$O." *Cognitive Psychology* 27: 41–70.

Margolis, E. and Laurence, S. 1998. *Concepts: Core Readings*. Cambridge, MA: MIT Press.

Medin, D. 1989. "Concepts and Conceptual Structure." *American Psychologist* 44: 1469–81.

Murphy, G. and Medin, D. 1985. "The Role of Theories in Conceptual Coherence." In Laurence and Margolis 1998, 425–458.

Nagel, T.1986. *The View from Nowhere*. Oxford: Oxford University Press.

Pérez, D. (2004) "Repensando la *Folk Psychology* desde el barco de Neurath." In *La mente y sus problemas. Temas actuales de filosofia de la psicologia*, ed. E. Rabossi, 41–74. Buenos Aires: Catalogos.

Putnam, H. 1975. "The Meaning of 'Meaning.'" In *Mind, Language and Reality. Philosophical Papers. Vol 2*, 215–271. Cambridge: Cambridge University Press.

Quine, W.V.O. 1969. "Natural Kinds." In *Ontological Relativity and Other Essays*, 114–138. New York: Columbia University Press.

Rabossi, E. 2000. "La filosofía de sentido común y la teoría de la teoría. Algunas reflexiones criticas." *Endoxa* 12: 643–55.

Rorty, R. 1979. *Philosophy and the Mirror of Nature*. Princeton: Princeton University Press.

Shear, J. 1998. *Explaining Consciousness. The Hard Problem*. Cambridge: MIT Press.

Smart, J.J.C. 1959. "Sensations and Brain Processes." *Philosophical Review* 68, 41–56.

Stich, S. 1983. *From Folk Psychology to Cognitive Science*. Cambridge, MA: MIT Press.

———. 1996. *Deconstructing the Mind*. Oxford: Oxford University Press.

Wittgenstein, L. 1953. *Philosophical Investigations*. Oxford: Basil Blackwell.

———. 1969. *On Certainty*. New York: Harper Torchbooks.

———. 1967. *Zettel*. Oxford: Basil Blackwell.

CANADIAN JOURNAL OF PHILOSOPHY
Supplementary Volume 30

The Rashness of Traditional Rationalism and Empiricism

GEORGES REY

I was brought up to believe that, in the "great debate" with the Rationalists, the Empiricists had largely won, particularly in view of Quine's holistic conception of justification, whereby even the claims of logic, though remote from experience, are indirectly tested by it. But some years ago I awoke to the possibility that there was something fishy in all this, and that the fallibilistic banalities that have played such a large role in driving the Quinean conception couldn't plausibly have such dramatic consequences. "Everything can be revised in the light of experience" is good advice for someone who hasn't noticed just how rich, complex and indirect our reasonings about any issue, including logic and mathematics, can be; but does it really tell against what Kant and the others had in mind when they believed that there were some claims *whose justification needn't appeal to experience* (which, it's crucial to remember, is how he and others thought of it, until the Positivists and Quine revised it to "unrevisability")?

One thing that soon struck me was the uncharacteristic casualness of Quine's actual account of empirical knowledge (see Quine and Ullian 1970/78). Simplicity, modesty, conservativism, and generality are all, no doubt, sterling virtues of an entire belief system, but they are hardly serious, substantive proposals about how scientists do, or ought to, assess rival hypotheses. When criticized about the vagueness of these virtues, Quine replied, "I have treated the matter mainly at that level because I have known little to say of it that was not pretty much common knowledge" (1986, 493). But if that is really all he has to say, what is supposed to rule out *a priori* knowledge? Kant himself could agree that we ought to opt for the simplest, most general, etc., hypotheses, proceeding cheerfully to add: "Just so; that is what leads me to posit *a priori* transcendental conditions for the possibility of experience." The point is that methods of justification needn't be *exclusive*: that we *sometimes* might reason holistically in terms of overall simplicity, generality, etc., might only camouflage whether the resulting whole involves more local justificatory means. It's seldom noticed that Quine claims not only that our beliefs confront the tribunal of experience as a corporate body, but that they confront it *"only* as a corporate body" (Quine 1953b, 41; my emphasis). Where did he get this 'only'?

As a result of this awakening from my Quinian slumbers, I began to reconsider the possibility of *a priori* knowledge, and to read contemporary proponents of it, such as George Bealer, Chris Peacocke, Jerry Katz, and Laurence Bonjour. I'm afraid, however, that I've found most of what they say surprisingly disappointing. What I find surprising is that the account they offer seems to be precisely the one that led philosophers like Quine to be wary of the *a priori* in the first place.

What I want to do in this paper is, first, to reiterate the one *good* reason Quine advanced for his wariness, but then go on to sketch what seems to me a more promising defense of the *a priori* that seems to me to respond to his good reason. I then want to call attention to a problem that seems to me to be shared by both Quine and his traditional Rationalist opponents, *viz.*, a disregard of the potential depth and relative inaccessibility of the *a priori*, and a consequent impatience about an account of it. Both proponents and opponents seem to me to assume that, if there is *a priori* knowledge, its existence *as a priori* knowledge should be relatively ready to hand, establishable either by introspective or behavioural test. Philosophers like Katz and Bonjour rely on such tests to establish such knowledge, and philosophers like Quine, finding the tests inadequate, deny such knowledge exists. I find both views rash. The assumption that a piece of our knowledge can be established as *a priori* by such readily available tests seems to me of a piece with a presumption about our minds that I have elsewhere (Rey 1994, 1997) called *superficialism*, or the view that facts about our minds must in general be available to us at either the introspective or behavioural surface of our lives. The view can be found in Cartesian claims about the deliverances of introspection, and also in Behaviourist ones about how "an inner process stands in need of an outward criterion."[1] If the last half-century of the "cognitive revolution" has taught us anything, it's that the structure of the mind is at least as unavailable to us as the structure of the rest of our bodies – actually, probably far more so, given its extreme abstractness – and that therefore we are going to have to be far more patient in drawing conclusions about it than either the Cartesian or the Behaviourist supposed. It's this sort of patience about the *a priori* that I want to urge here.

In Section I of the present paper I will review the claims and problems of the (roughly) Cartesian view of the *a priori* advocated by Katz and Bonjour.[2] In Section II, I'll indicate why I think we need to dig deeper, looking first (II.i) at what seems to still right about the challenge Quine raised against this Cartesianism, turning in II.ii to consider ways in which less superficialist approaches offer a better prospect of defending the possibility of formal *a priori* knowledge. In Section III, I'll take on the much more difficult issues of the possibility of *a priori* knowledge of analytic truths based on the existence of something like semantic rules. After admitting the difficulties (III.i), I want to draw attention to what I call the "analytic data" that such rules are supposed to explain (III.ii). There are other proposed explanations of these data; in III.iii and III.iv I'll say why I think at least two prominent ones, Quine's and Fodor's, are inadequate. In Section IV, I'll sketch what an internal rule account might look like, and how it can be defended – or defeated – only by the kind of intricate theorizing about the structure of our minds that Chomskian linguists have begun to provide about our language faculty. I emphasize that I want to establish, again, not that there *really is* a priori knowledge, but only that the question of whether or not there is requires far more detailed understanding of linguistics and psychology than any of us yet has, and consequently far more patience and empirical curiosity than most philosophers have displayed.

---

1 A view that did not die out with Wittgenstein (1953), but lives on in, e.g., McGinn (1991), Dennett (1991), and Hornsby (1997); see Rey 2001b for discussion.

2 I've discussed Peacocke's (1992, 1996, 1998) views at length elsewhere (e.g., Rey 1996, 1998).

I. Reasonable Worries

Jerrold Katz (1981, 200–16, and 1998, 32–61) offers "two thoughts" about "how to understand *a priori* knowledge of abstract objects" (1998, 39). The first is to avoid modeling such knowledge on the kind of causal contact that seems to be typical of perceptual knowledge; the second is that "our reason is an appropriate instrument for determining how things must be in that [abstract] realm" (1998, 9).

Why does Katz think reason is so appropriate? He considers a typical proof that two is the only even prime, which involves "reasoning so close-textured, so tight, that it excludes the possibility of the conclusion's being false" (1998, 40). Why should we have confidence in such "proofs"?

> In the formal sciences, it is common to refer to seeing that something is the case as "intuition" and to take such immediate apprehension as a source of basic mathematical knowledge. (Katz 1998, 43)

To the worry that such appeals to intuition have more than a whiff of "mysticism," he hastens to distinguish "mystery" from "mysticism":

> No one would deny that there is a mystery about how we can have knowledge of abstract objects.... But the obscurity of the rational mechanism is no grounds for dismissing the claim that pure reason does what, from the common-sense standpoint, it appears to do. (1998, 33)

On a more positive note, he adds:

> The relevant notion of intuition that is relevant to our rationalist epistemology is that of an immediate, i.e., non-inferential, purely rational apprehension that involves absolutely no connection to anything concrete.... Intuitions are apprehensions of structure that can reveal the limits of possibility with respect to the objects having the structure.... In [such cases] there is no explanation other than intuition for the fact that ordinary, unsophisticated people, without expert help, immediately grasp the truth. (1998, 44–45)

He adds to this claim a standard regress argument from A.C. Ewing (1947) that any inferential step must be justified by an interpolated argument or be seen immediately from intuition – "we must come to something which we see intuitively to be true, as the process of interpolation cannot go on *ad infinitum*" (Ewing 1947, 26, cited at Katz 1998, 46).

Katz seems to me here to be confusing serious *explanation* with a process of ordinary *justification*: it may well be that, especially in a necessarily finite bout of actual justification, there must be steps that are at least provisionally taken for granted in the discussion. And perhaps in an ideal justification, there have to be steps that are somehow intrinsically justified (although it seems to me that the topic of justification has yet to be sufficiently understood to insist on this demand). But none of this entails that there can be no *explanation* of why people might accept these steps, and that this explanation might not play an important role in justifying why that acceptance is justified. For example, it may be that the explanation of people's acceptance of these steps is one that also shows them to be terrifically *reliable*; or that the specific steps are ones someone would have to accept if they were to have rational beliefs at all. In any case, it is by no means clear that we need to rely on some mere unexplained (unexplainable?) *intuition* about the acceptabililty of those steps. Indeed, the question is why Katz thinks appealing to intuition is explanatory in the least.

Laurence Bonjour (1998) similarly regards *a priori* knowledge as based upon

> ... an act of *rational insight* or *rational intuition* ... [that] is seemingly (a) direct or immediate, non-discursive, and yet also (b) intellectual or reason-governed.... [It] depends upon nothing beyond an understanding of the propositional content itself... (1998, 102)

Of course, one might well wonder in what such a "direct" intuitive grasp of the necessity of a proposition could possibly consist. Here Bonjour goes a little further than Katz, and supplements his remarks with an account of a person's grasp of meaning:

> The key claim of such a view would be that it is a necessary, quasi-logical fact that a thought instantiating a complex

231

universal involving the universal triangularity in the appropriate way (about which much more would obviously need to be said) is about triangular things. In this way, the content of the thought would be non-contingently captured by the character of the mental act, and could accordingly be accessible to the thinker. (1998, 184)

Of course, the "appropriate way" that a thought "instantiates a universal" is obviously different from the way an *object* enjoying the universal does: after all, thoughts about triangularity aren't themselves triangular. By way of supplying what "more would need to be said," Bonjour invokes a distinction from Aquinas between "*esse intentionale*" and "*esse naturale*", whereby, e.g.,

... the form triangularity informs my mind in a special way that is different from the way in which it informs triangular things. (1998, 183)

These different ways actually give rise to "distinct, though presumably intimately related universals" (1998, 183). Bonjour does acknowledge the need of "some more articulate account ... of the two universals and the relation between them" (184), but confesses that, despite "the venerable history of this kind of view" (185), it is "not [to be] found in Aquinas – or, so far as I know, anywhere in that tradition" (184). I think I know what distinction Aquinas and Bonjour at least should have had in mind in the distinction between *naturale* and *intentionale*: it's the distinction between (genuine) properties and *concepts*. Bonjour, himself, gives concepts (as distinct from properties) short shrift, complaining that they would be "subjective entities, whose nature and metaphysical status would be extremely puzzling" (1998, 151). But, however puzzling such concepts may be, they do enjoy an independent role in psychological explanation, as, e.g., the constituents of the propositions towards which we have attitudes, a role that is importantly distinct from the further, independent role of (genuine) properties as, e.g., the relata of real causal interactions. Bonjour is presumably loath to distinguish these roles, since his account of *a priori* knowledge would then need to explain how we get from our ("direct"?) apprehension of concepts to any insight into genuine properties of a mind-independent world, and this problem would patently be just another way of raising the central problem of both semantics and epistemology: how does the mind manage to think and know about a mind-independent world?[3]

I want to stress what seems to me (but apparently not to everyone) an obvious point. Until someone supplies a good argument, *there is no particular reason that the world should conform to our conception of it*, that *esse intentionale* should match *esse naturale*. In particular, I see no reason to think that there's *a genuine property in the world* for every one of our concepts. This seems to me quite evident in the case of our complex concepts – [round square], [largest prime], or, lest there be any doubt, [property of all and only those properties that aren't properties of themselves] (where expressions in corner brackets refer to the content expressed by the expression). But I see no reason to think it's not true in the case of some primitive concepts as well: as many Rationalists since Plato have been fond of pointing out, the world of sensory experience could not possibly afford instances of the geometric objects corresponding to our Euclidean ideas of, e.g., line, circle, triangle. Nor, arguably, could any genuinely possible world afford instances of [phlogisticated], [magical], [soul], [freedom], [god], or of anything corresponding to our primitive ideas of [colour], [qualia], and [consciousness].[4] I suspect one thing that leads philosophers to think otherwise is a certain profligacy about properties that isn't usually tolerated for mere material objects: properties are thought to exist even un-instantiated, and so are apparently there just for the asking (or are presumed to exist until proven otherwise, an expectation about the powers of proof that I thought Gödel had dashed).[5] Against this

---

3 When pressed on this point, Bonjour has conceded that concepts are needed, but that "if such concepts are to make it possible for us to genuinely think about a mind-independent world, they must be tightly enough related to ... properties to serve as the vehicle for genuine insight into them (so that the resulting *a priori* knowledge would not pertain *merely* to the concepts" (2001, 683–84). That, of course, is the *conclusion* a Rationalist wants. The question is, what entitles him to it? I return to this issue at the end.

4 These last are, of course, more controversial; but, whatever the ultimate verdict, it seems inappropriate to decide them on semantic grounds alone.

5 It is interesting that this profligacy about properties is shared not only by "rationalists" like Bonjour, but by more "naturalistic" philosophers like Fodor

profligacy, I want to enter a certain methodological protest, or anyway, a plea for honest toil that I believe is honored in all other sciences:

> *Occam's Sharpened Razor*: Except as a last resort, do not introduce into your mental ontology entities for which there is no independent evidence.

Before we uncritically presume there is such a property as, say, [phlogisticated] or [magical], we need to ask whether or not, independent of our semantic desperation, there is any reason whatsoever to believe in it. Our best theories of the world – biology, chemistry, physics, cosmology – seem not to provide any. The presumption that there nevertheless are such properties seems simply a gratuitous projection of our semantic needs, one that, without independent evidence, only serves to obscure the explanatory problems at issue.

II. Digging Deeper

II.i. The Quinean Challenge

For lack of a satisfactory account of the *a priori*, many have, of course, wondered whether it exists at all. Quine raised the issue, but he rather overplayed his hand, linking his doubts to sweeping attacks on meaning, mentality, and modality that few still endorse. Despite his foibles in these respects, however, there is one serious challenge that is often missed:

> (C) How are we to distinguish such claims of *a priori* insight from merely deeply held empirical conviction?

(1990, 1998), whose theory of content requires there not only to be a property for every primitive predicate, but that this property actually figure in *laws*. Thus, there have to be laws relating god thoughts to a real property of *divinity*, thoughts about circles to genuine *circularity*. I would have thought that present physical theory provides abundant reason to doubt the existence of any such laws, a point to which we shall return (see note 15 below).

(C) survives as a challenge even for those of us who believe in mind, meaning, and modality, for we may raise it equally about claims in *those* domains as well: why shouldn't whatever claims we make about "unobserved" minds, mental contents, and even possible worlds be justified by the same methods, whatever they are, by which we justify claims about "unobserved" places and times? Remember Quine's own justification for belief in physicalistic rather than a phenomenalistic theory of the world:

> A physicalistic conceptual scheme, purporting to talk about external objects, offers great advantages in simplifying our over-all reports. By bringing together scattered sense events and treating them as perceptions of one object, we reduce the complexity of our stream of experience to a manageable conceptual simplicity. (1953a, 17)

Just so: by bringing together, e.g., scattered conditionals and treating them as false (or true) even if their antecedents happen to be false, we reduce the complexity of our understanding of the enduring (dispositional) traits of those objects – the poisonousness of the mushrooms doesn't pass in and out of existence depending upon someone (un)luckily sampling them. Anyway, this, I suspect, is precisely how your thoroughly modern Quinean, e.g., Devitt (1996, 2, 46–54; 1997), might argue for modality (and, *mutatis mutandis*, for meaning and mind). So we seem to have a standoff between Rationalism and Empiricism.

The only way I can think of moving beyond this standoff is to dig deeper into an explanatory account of our knowledge than Quine, Katz, or Bonjour do. Indeed, my complaint with Katz and Bonjour is in the end of a piece with my own complaint with Quine: along the lines of the superficialism I mentioned at the start, both confine themselves pretty much to the *surface appearances* of the *a priori*, and don't consider the deeper explanations of them that might be found "inside." In Quine, this superficialism plays a particularly crucial role in his dismissal of the *a priori*, since it leads him to replace, as I indicated at the start, the traditional conception of that category – "justifiability independent of experience" – with a behaviouristic *ersatz*, "immunity to revision." Of course, if *this latter* is the criterion, it's hardly surprising that one is hard put to distinguish the *a priori* from simply firmly held empirical convictions.

Katz and Bonjour, of course, are no behaviourists, and so are not *committed* to sticking to a *behavioural* surface. But in their emphasis upon "insight" and "rational intuition," they seem wedded to an introspective one. Bonjour does rightly dissociate the *a priori* from the *infallible* (1998, 115ff), noting some ways the surface could go wrong. But he underestimates the variety of the sources of fallibility, focusing largely on "irreparable bias or dogmatism" (1998, 137). The real problem raised by (C) is, again, distinguishing the *a priori* not merely from bias, but from other merely *empirical commitments* that might not deserve the name. After all, your (modern) Quinian might argue, if the claim that water is necessarily H_2O is not *a priori*, why should arithmetic or logic be so? Simply insisting upon the "directness" or "immediacy" of one's understanding that a proposition is necessary (1998, 103–6, 131) is insufficient to meet that challenge: without any account of this "immediacy" or "directness" the claim seems indistinguishable from mere table thumping – or simply finding certain things "obvious." Much in the ordinary perception of the world around us seems similarly "direct" and "immediate," but that alone should hardly daunt the psychologist from seeking intermediary mechanisms, or the skeptic from seeking intermediary justifications. Indeed, what one wants in the case of "rational insight" is precisely the kind of independent understanding we have of the visual system, whereby we can check the reliability – and particularly the variable reliability – of surface reports.[6]

What I am envisioning, of course, would amount to an empirical vindication of our claims to *a priori* knowledge. I like to think of this as a kind of "two-step": one steps back from one's claims and tries,

---

6 Nothing better illustrates both the problems I have in mind here, as well as the need of the approach I want to recommend, than Bonjour's parade example of an *a priori* truth, the justification of the claim that nothing can be red and green all over:

Given [my] understanding of the ingredients of the proposition, I am able to see or grasp in a seemingly direct and unmediated way that the claim in question cannot fail to be true – that the natures of redness and greenness are such as to preclude their being jointly realized (1998, 101).

à la Quine, to provide the most holistically reasonable theory of the world and our knowledge of it. But then, *in the light of that holistically confirmed theory*, it could turn out that we have every reason to believe that there are *also* entirely reliable, *local* justificatory means – perhaps, certain faculties of our minds. And so we could step forward again and take seriously our eyes and ears in the case of the spatiotemporal world, and perhaps certain faculties of our minds in the case of logic, mathematics and other "purely conceptual" issues. That is, one could try to give a Quinian justification for something like the "rational faculty" that Katz, Bonjour, and traditional Rationalists tried to secure for free, but then, with that meta-justification in hand, one could then reflect that people, including oneself, had been justified *a priori* in believing, e.g., the truths of logic and arithmetic all along. The meta-justification explains why something is a justification without being part of that justification itself.

Perhaps this is contrary to the spirit in which the *a priori* has traditionally been proposed, which was linked to a certain sort of self-justifying, immediate, introspective clarity with regards to which if it was *a priori* that *p*, then it was either introspectively obvious that *p*, or could be shown to follow by introspectively obvious steps from something that was introspectively obvious. For many, I suspect this was linked to a presumption that '*a priori*' iterated: if it was *a priori* that *p*, then it had to be *a priori* that it was *a priori* that *p*. But it's hard to see why any of these latter presumptions should be essential. *Idiots savants* who can accurately rattle off prime factors mightn't have a clue about how they do it, much less about whether or not they know them

---

Research on colour vision strongly suggests that the particular exclusion of red and green is due to "opponent processing": the firings of retinal cells sensitive to one of the pairs red/green, blue/yellow suppress the firings of ones sensitive to the other (see, e.g., Hardin 1988, 121ff). Since this is a quite basic and fixed feature of our visual system, it seems to prevent some people from even imagining something so coloured. But, if that's the explanation, then, *pace* Bonjour's (2001, 688) "clear insight" to the contrary, the impossibility is not as deep as it seems. Someone whose opponent processing was somehow overridden (as in the case of retinal fixation described in Hardin (1988, 124–25) might well be as prepared to find something red and green all over as we are to find something turquoise to be both green and blue.

a priori. Perhaps they couldn't engage in the specific activity of *explicit justification* that interests epistemologists; but it's not at all obvious that *that* specific activity is generally essential, or even interesting to anyone other than epistemologists.[7] *Idiot savant* children may know *a priori* that lots of numbers are prime nonetheless.

In any case, it's surely a *contingent* fact that we have any knowledge at all, whether empirical or *a priori.* Traditional epistemologies, whether rationalist or empiricist, have usually just slipped in empirical assumptions about our contingent psychological structure. I am merely suggesting that those assumptions be more informed by actual empirical theory in a way that Katz's and Bonjour's discussions seem to me to fail to be.

II.ii. A Logic Module?

By way of a contrast, and implementing the epistemic "two-step" I'm recommending, I have elsewhere (1993, 1998) raised the following possibility, by which I think one *could hope* to show something to be genuinely *a priori.* Along lines suggested by the currently influential computational-representational theory of thought, suppose it turns out that we have built into us a Gentzen-style natural deduction system of logic that is capable of producing the full infinitude of valid sentences of the predicate calculus, and suppose that it is the operation of this machine that is causally responsible for someone's belief in a specific logical truth, say:

> (R) Nothing bites all and only those things that do not bite themselves.

---

7 Perhaps it's also interesting to people struggling to settle deep-seated (e.g., religious) disputes. But, in general, it would seem a good idea not to burden a *theory* of knowledge with what may turn out to be a matter of local, pragmatic epistemics – or, for that matter, with the very special issues that arise in the case of first person justification, whose importance and privileges seem to me open as well to the challenge of (C). *Pace* Bonjour (1998, 203; 2001, 687) and Fodor (2004), I don't see any reason to presume that a thinker engages in any sort of *metarepresentation* of the nevertheless valid inferences she may make.

Then, I submit, we would have a genuine case of *a priori* knowledge: the belief in (R) would be the result of a process that was absolutely *reliable* (its sentences would be true no matter what external context the agent might be in), it would have been *justified* by rules that are *perfectly truth-preserving*, and that justification would involve no premises and, so, *a fortiori*, no premises about experience. Moreover, these properties of such a belief would be *no accident*: the rules that permit the generation of the theorems are ones that are patently sensitive to what seem to be the *validity-making properties of the sentences*, their *logical form* – it is because of the logical form of (R) that it is true in all possible worlds. One can even suppose that the little system is responsible for introspectively available "intuitions" about validity and other logical relations.

Now, why should we believe any of these standard claims about natural deduction? Well, let us suppose, our reasons are whatever reasons a Quinian has for believing anything: simplicity, conservativism, etc., of one's overall theory of the world, whatever these "virtues" may ultimately turn out to be. The crucial point is this: *if there is such a holistic, empirical justification of natural deduction, it will serve as a meta-justification of the processes of belief formation based upon it*, and since the system is in fact absolutely reliable and free of any (empirical) premises, the beliefs that issue from those processes alone satisfy at least Kant's condition on the *a priori* – someone's accepting (R) and having other logical intuitions on the basis of the operation of a Gentzen-style logic system would have a justification of (R) and those intuitions that was not dependent upon experience.

Of course, there's no reason to think such beliefs might satisfy Quine's condition of "unrevisability come what may": someone might have been led, even by thoroughly rational considerations, to *revise* such a belief in the light of experience, say, in the way that Putnam (1975) was once led to propose revising logic in the light of quantum mechanics. But, given the complexities of (rational) belief fixation, it's hard to see why we should burden an account of the *a priori* with any such further condition.

The extension of this epistemic two-step to domains beyond first-order logic, to perhaps even the "analytic" truths sought by linguistics and philosophy, is not at all obvious, and I want to address some of the difficulties of doing so in the next section.

III. Conceptual Truths and the Analytic

III.i. Problems with Analysis

Well, my opponent might concede, so there might be an empirical vindication of logic along these lines. Even Quine was ambivalent about how to regard logic.[8] But what about the more substantive claims of "philosophical analysis" regarding, e.g., the essential nature of number, geometry, thought, the good, the voluntary? Here we seem to have cases that appear not to be matters of "logical form" alone, but, notoriously, of claims of "synonymy" and "necessary connections among ideas," which seem especially susceptible to Quine's challenge (C).

Worse, in addition to Quine's challenges, there are the challenges from Wittgensteinians and "prototype" psychologists attacking the "necessary and sufficient" defining conditions that philosophical analysts typically sought. These latter conditions don't seem available to competent users, or, if the history of the enterprise is any indication, even to highly reflective philosophers. Instead, according to Wittgenstein, Quine, Kuhn and many of these psychologists, all that's available are prototypical "family resemblances" between exemplars, or fragments of theories in which the concepts are used. The unkindest cut of all is perhaps Jerry Fodor's recent (1998) arguments that the analytic, conceptual role semantics sought by philosophers and psychologists as constitutive of concepts – whether Classical, prototypical, or theoretical – is "where cognitive science went wrong."

There's a lot to address here, but for starters, I want to suggest that many of these criticisms also seem to me to arise from too superficialist a conception of the enterprise of "analysis." There is no question that many philosophers and psychologists have seriously underestimated the difficulty of producing these analyses, and that they do well to heed some of the skeptical challenges that have been raised against them. However, along the lines of my defense of the possible *a prioricity* of logic, I want to argue nevertheless that some kinds of

---

8 See, e.g., his "change of logic, change of subject" slip in his 1970, 80–81.

analyses may well be crucial to any cognitive psychology that will account not only for the superficial cognitive *performances* with which many of the above critics have been concerned, but with our conceptual *competence*.

III.ii. The Analytic Data

Such words bring to mind, of course, Chomsky's work on grammar, the analogy with which seems to me quite close. As in the case of grammar, we are confronted by regularities in spontaneous judgments that we need to explain. Many of them are, of course, the "intuitions" emphasized by Bonjour and Katz, but, unlike them, we don't need to regard them as *explanations* of any phenomena, but as *data* that any satisfactory explanation aims to explain – precisely as, in the case of grammar, people's intuitive "acceptability" judgments are merely data for linguistic (or, more broadly, psychological) theory.

It is worth pausing over the remarkable fact that people so much as *have* intuitions about these sorts of things. One of the many wonderful things that Chomsky brought to our attention was not merely that people have convergent judgments about the acceptability of various strings of English words, but that these judgments are to some extent *orthogonal* to their guesses about what someone might nevertheless intend by uttering such strings. For example, someone might utter:

(S1) *Who do you think that loves Mary?
(S2) *Who do you wanna go visit the pope on Thursday?
(S3) *He hopes John will win (he being John).

and a hearer would know perfectly well what was intended. If it were noticed at all, it would just "sound odd." As Chomsky has emphasized, facts such as these strongly suggest that we have a special faculty for the processing of natural language that is at least to some significant extent independent of the demands of communication or worldly understanding. It seems that our thoughts do not consist in the sort of "seamless web" of speech dispositions envisaged by Quine (1960). Significant portions of our minds appear to be "modularized," and the language system appears to be one such module (see Fodor 1983).

I think this is a useful perspective to take not only with regard to grammar, but with regard to conceptual investigations, and/or "semantics," as well (allowing provisionally that they are to be distinguished from syntax). Instead of treating the conceptual "intuitions" that interest the rationalists as some kind of direct acquaintance with *genuine possibilities* or *real properties*, as Katz and Bonjour would have us do, treat them instead merely as evidence about structures in our minds. These structures then may or may not provide us any insight into any (material or Platonistic) realities independent of our minds, depending upon how reliable in this regard our minds turn out to be.

Construed along these lines, let us call the "analytic data" the data that positing the analytic is supposed to explain (allowing that it might turn out to be "explained away"). It includes, *inter alia*, a non-negligible convergence in people's judgments with regard to particular concepts and/or lexical items, e.g. about synonymies, ambiguities, antonymies, entailments.[9] Ask speakers, as linguists do, whether 'bank,' or 'pride' are ambiguous; whether killings necessarily involve dyings; whether 'open' and 'closed' are antonyms; whether 'Jim boiled the water' implies 'The water boiled'; whether 'The square-root of a shadow is red' is anomalous. Ask people what things qualify as a bachelor, knowledge, coercion, a voluntary act, perception, water, brisket; elicit their considered judgments about hypothetical cases; ask them what they think *constitutes* being one of these things. I submit that one finds what philosophers have found since Socrates began casually doing this in his *agora*: that there is great deal of convergence about what one can and can't say, and about what clearly does and what clearly does not satisfy a concept; and that, although people can't readily provide adequate rules or definitions to capture these patterns, they soon *realize* they can't, and, despite disagreement, are quick to acknowledge at least *the cogency* of each others' cases and considerations.

By way of a further, important sort of evidence, consider also the famous *Euthyphro* question that, although it is a standard exercise in introductory philosophy, is insufficiently discussed in the context of the analytic:

---

9 See especially Katz 1972, 3–6 for a rich set of examples that seem to me to have been insufficiently discussed in the critical literature.

> Is something good because the gods say it is, or do they say it is
> because it is good?

Compare it with the similar question:

> Is something legal because the authorities say it is, or do they
> say it is because it is legal?

I take it that it is excellent evidence of having the concepts [good] vs.
merely [legal] that one finds one answering the questions differently:
the idea that the ultimate authorities could be wrong about legality
seems "unintelligible" in a way that the corresponding idea about the
gods failing to appreciate the good does not (note well that it may not
be *possible* for the gods to be wrong about the good, but it is still *intelligible*: for all his devotion to God, Abraham, poised with the dagger
over his son's throat, can still intelligibly wonder whether God has got
it quite right). Whatever the merits of the more "objective" account of
the good that this insight seems to recommend, I do think an examination of such Euthyphronic intuitions affords some insight into the concept of the good, as opposed to the merely legal, as well as into many
other concepts that we regularly employ.[10] And my suggestion here
is that traditional philosophical discussions of this sort, and attempts
at "conceptual analysis," can be regarded in this way as eliciting evidence and advancing hypotheses about such conceptual structures.

Alas, of course, these analytic intuitions are a lot more slippery
and elusive than the lovely cases of grammar, the rules a lot harder
to come by. As many people are fond of pointing out, philosophical
analysis is largely a history of failures (Fodor 1998, 69–70). Ironically
enough, however, this history of failure *could* be taken as actually an
argument *for*, not against, the project of analysis, or something like it.
(It's a little like the *combination* of success and failure in science that
argues for realism about its objects: we get enough success to think
we're on to something, and enough failure to think that it's not all

---

10 Note that the Euthyphronic question arises about merely the *concept* of the
good, whether or not goodness is an objective, mind-independent property of
the world (but especially if it isn't!).

wishful thinking, either). For what is it that leads us to *reject* proposed analyses? Why do we tend to agree about plausible candidates and also about their inadequacies? What do all of us know about 'know' that leads us to fall for 'justified true belief' and then to appreciate Edmund Gettier's (1963) counterexamples? Or about 'perception', or 'water', or 'brisket' that leads many of us to agree with Grice (1965), Putnam (1975) and Burge (1979) that we would defer to experts? Or about 'murder' and 'person', such that we understand why, e.g., abortion and euthanasia are difficult cases? That is to say, we should ask here exactly the question that Chomsky asked about syntax: *what explains the patterns and projections in peoples' judgments?*

III.iii. Quine's Bad Explanation

One way to appreciate the role of some kind of internal "semantical" rules is to notice the inadequacies of accounts of the analytic data that try to dispense with them. One of the earliest and most influential was Quine's own, according to which what was analytic was simply what was centrally or tenaciously believed by someone, capturing the idea that "no amount of evidence could refute the claim that bachelors are unmarried." Though it's certainly true that some (relatively trivial) analytic truths are tenaciously held in this way, the explanation doesn't really generalize. Notice, for example, that:

(1) Merely tenacious beliefs aren't regularly linked to claims of about synonymies, ambiguities, antonymies and or the specific logical entailments linguists note.

(2) Unlike the denials of analytic claims, denials of merely tenacious beliefs are easily *understood* by even their most committed adherents. Despite the fact that I'm as unlikely to believe anything as I am that people have never had noses, the situation is perfectly *imaginable*.

(3) Analytic claims are by and large *innocuous* in the way that tenacious beliefs are not: giving up 'The Earth has existed for many years' would be pretty disruptive in a way, where allowing female bachelors would be "merely verbal."

(4) Tenacity doesn't begin to explain the essentialist, Euthyphronic intuitions about constitutive conditions associated with concepts. This, of course, would not have bothered Quine, who might well dismiss such delicate modal questions as having no place in any ultimate science. But it should still bother those of us who, irrespective of the *correctness* of some set of thoughts, might still be interested in their *explanation*.

III.iv Fodor's Slightly Better Account

Although he of course doesn't share Quine's aversions to mind and meaning, Fodor (1998) has risen to the defense of Quine's skepticism about the analytic. He hopes to avoid the challenge that (C) presents to a theory of meaning by resorting to an "externalist" theory of content, whereby content is determined *not* by any psychological relation *internal* to a mind, which could be challenged by (C), but by relations states of the brain bear to external phenomena, particularly the kind of (possibly uninstantiated) properties we noted earlier.[11]

Fodor does recognize, however, that Quine's "centrality" explanation won't quite suffice to explain the analytic intuitions,[12] and so follows up a suggestion originally advanced by Hilary Putnam (1962): "analytic truths" are just examples of "one-criterion" concepts, or concepts like, e.g., [bachelor], [widow], [ophthalmologist], where there purportedly happens to be only one "way to tell" whether they apply.

Fodor (1998, 82) acknowledges that, so stated, this latter account won't suffice either, since the notion of "criteria" seems no better off

---

11 Briefly, a symbol S means P if non-P caused S-tokens depend upon P's causing S-tokens, but not *vice versa*. For general explication, defense, and criticisms of this "asymmetric dependency" theory, see Fodor 1987, 1990, Rey 1995, and many of the articles in Loewer and Rey 1991.

12 At any rate, he notes it doesn't work "for all the cases," suggesting it works for some (1998, 86). I actually don't find it works for any, except as a matter of pure coincidence, e.g., cases where the term involved just happens also to be central to our thought, as in 'Material objects are extended.'

than "analytic." In particular, if there were just *one* way to tell what's what, there would seem, trivially, to be indefinite numbers of different ways – for example, just ask someone who knows the one way; or ask someone who knows someone who knows; or … – and we would seem to have no better way to single out which way is "criterial" than we have to say which way is "analytic." But here Fodor offers a promising move, redolent of his general "asymmetric dependency" theory of content (see note 12 above): among the ways of telling what's what, some do and some don't asymmetrically depend upon the others; the one(s?) that *don't* are the ones that give rise to analytic intuitions. Thus, telling that someone is a bachelor by checking out his gender and marital status doesn't depend upon telling by asking his friends, but telling by asking his friends does depend upon telling by his gender and marital status; and so we have an explanation of why "bachelors are unmarried males" seems analytic – without it's actually being so.[13]

Such asymmetric dependence will "explain away" the analytic, however, only if the analytic isn't needed in an explanation of such asymmetric dependence. But it's hard to see how it wouldn't be. For notice that not just any such asymmetric dependencies give rise to analytic intuitions: the only way I know to tell whether something's an acid or not is to see whether it turns litmus paper red; other ways (asking my chemist friends) asymmetrically depend upon that way. But I haven't the slightest intuition that "acids turn litmus paper red" is analytic. Indeed, I fully expect that there are, or could be, better ways to test acidity, and that's because I believe 'acid' marks a relatively "deep" sort of thing, whose nature is not captured by what tests happen to be at hand. By contrast, I believe 'bachelor' marks a superficial kind, whose nature is pretty much exhausted by the linguistics of the matter: unlike the case of litmus paper and acidity, *the reason that gender and marital status are the best way to tell whether someone's a bachelor is that that's just what 'bachelor' means!*

On behalf of this contrast, note that should a chemist propose revising the test for acids in the light of better theory, this would not *per se*

---

13 Actually, one might wonder why Fodor's proposal is not a reductive explication rather than the eliminative "explaining away" of the analytic that he intends. One reason might be the very reason I will now suggest against its even being a successful elimination.

constitute a change in the meaning, whereas should, say, a feminist propose, in the light of better politics, revising 'bachelor' to include women, this obviously would. In any case, it should be clear that appeals to "one criterion" won't answer the explanatory challenge one might raise for the less obvious cases of the connections between, say, 'know' and 'justified', 'freedom' and 'spontaneity', since in each of these cases, although we seem to be on to some connections, it's notoriously difficult to specify even *one* genuinely adequate "way to tell."

VI. The Need for Internal Roles

IV.i. Empirical Theories of Competence

In order, then, to account for these sometimes fairly robust analytic intuitions, it appears that a theory of concepts will need to include some facts about a term's internal (e.g., inferential) role: [soul] plays a certain role in a person's thought, permitting the imagined (but probably not genuine) possibility of disembodied existence; [good] plays a role different from that of [legal]; [freedom] is tied to maybe impossible claims about spontaneity and moral responsibility; Euclidean [point], [line], [circle] form a cluster of inter-definable notions subject to certain axioms, and so forth.[14] Along lines suggested by, e.g., Heim (1989) and Recanati (1993), I think of concepts as *files*, especially (but not only) for lexical entries, whose syntactic and semantic deployment is governed by rules contained in the files.

As pressing as the need may be for this sort of account of concepts, there is, however, the immense difficulty of providing one. For starters, there's the fact that people seem to be able to believe most anything – Berkeley, for example, believed that trees are ideas, Pythagoreans that everything is numbers, contemporary literary theorists that everything's a text. Moreover, as we have noted that Quine (1953b)

---

14 I cite especially these examples, since if, per note 5 above, there really are no even *possible*, nomic phenomena that correspond to them (as arguably there aren't), then the need of a conceptual role account of their content would seem to be more than merely pressing; see Rey 1995 and forthcoming-b for discussion.

emphasized, all beliefs seem *revisable*: you can fool some of the people some of the time, and they can change their minds, about most anything, including even analyses (witness knowledge as "justified true belief").

However, although these considerations have been influential, they are hardly decisive. This is where we need to get past the superficialism that has, it seems to me, dominated too many of these discussions. The fact that we might revise what may in fact be in an analytic truth tells against the existence of the analytic only if our revision directly reflects our underlying linguistic or conceptual competence. But surely Berkeley was not linguistically challenged about material object terms: he knew perfectly well the presumptions of 'table' and 'chair' referring to concreta. He just had a *theory* that led him to assert something that at least seemed to go against the grain of his linguistic competence. He wasn't, after all, simply in the position of a confused foreigner, who misunderstood, e.g., 'table' and 'chair' to refer only to ideas.[15]

Indeed, in line with taking seriously Chomsky's competence–performance distinction, there is no reason to think that the actual sentences we *utter* need accord with linguistic rules.[16] In the first

---

15 Note, for example, that, unlike our confused foreigner, Berkeley does see the need to bring in God to capture at least the presumption that objects can exist unperceived by *us*.

16 Joe Levine reported to me what initially appeared to be a joke about just how extreme Chomsky could be in his public stances. Chomsky had apparently delivered some of his initial lectures on the "minimalist program," and a linguist had pointed out what seemed to be some problems for it with some example from Welsh. Without missing a beat, Chomsky apparently replied, "That just shows you that Welsh is not a natural language" – and then, after missing at most a beat, he added, "in fact, it's a common misunderstanding that people speak natural languages. There's not a shred of reason to think so." Although Chomsky is given to more than occasional hyperbole, this isn't an instance of it. If he is even roughly right about the existence of a linguistic competence underlying our usual performances as the proper object of linguistic study, then it would be as surprising that that competence were regularly displayed in our performance as it would be for the planets to be observed to obey Kepler's laws perfectly. In any complex macro-system, particularly one as intricate as the human mind, one expects systematic interaction between the wide variety of subsystems.

place, there is of course irony, understatement, implicature, impliciture, and acquiescence to one's audience's habits, needs, and expectations. But, as in the case of Berkeley and countless other philosophers, theory can also intervene and lead people to say things that may in fact violate linguistic rules.[17] As Chomsky often emphasizes, linguistic rules *incline*, but don't *compel*, and actual linguistic practice may sometimes serve other purposes than strict adherence to those rules. Hence the possible interest of Berkeley's and others' claims violating what may be analytic. All that may be essential to communication with a lexical item is that a hearer and speaker share a file containing a certain rule, even if the rule is violated in the speech exchange (which is what distinguishes Berkeley's usage from that of the confused foreigner).

IV.ii. The Analytic as Manifesting Linguistic Competence

But what about the *truth* of an analytic claim? What entitles us to think, e.g., that all killings are *in fact* necessarily dyings? Well, if the above assimilation of analyticity to grammaticality is correct, then whatever entitles speakers to know certain kinds of grammatical facts may entitle them to know the relevant semantic ones. Consider the grammatical cases first.

---

17 And not only philosophical theory can intervene. Subtle issues of verbal nuance, emphasis and "framing" can lead people to apparently contradictory attitudes. At any rate, consider:

(i) In a 1940 study, 54 per cent of Americans said we should "forbid" anti-democracy speeches, while 75 per cent said we should "not allow" them.

(ii) Doctors have been found more likely to recommend an operation with a 93 per cent survival rate than with a 7 per cent mortality rate.

(iii) People express more surprise when a 1/20 than when a 10/200 event occurs.

(iv) People averse to "smoking while praying" are not equally averse to "praying while smoking."

(See Myers 2004, 125–6, 279–80 for discussion and references.)

The data of linguistic inquiry are largely based upon the spontaneous reactions of native speakers of a language to certain (purported)
strings of that language. Speakers find the strings intelligible, puzzling, or unacceptable, and can report on various of their properties,
e.g., ambiguity, antonymony, anomaly, purported co-reference. Now
perhaps, as Devitt (forthcoming) proposes, they do this on the basis of
the kind of empirical evidence that serves them in other domains, for
example, in learning statistical facts about plants and animals, facts
about social history, or the kind of verbal niceties taught in "grammar" school (e.g., "Sentences have subjects and predicates; pronouns
have antecedents.")[18] But, as Chomsky has emphasized, this seems
extremely unlikely for most of the interesting facts of linguistic structure, which are remarkably abstract, subtle, and not the objects of
ordinary attention or instruction – only linguists, for example, will
have noticed the unacceptability of (S1)–(S3). People's intuitions
seem largely to be not empirical inferences, but merely *manifestations*
of their competence: someone's *not* finding anything strange about
(S1)–(S3) would be strong *prima facie* evidence not for some inferential
deficiency, but rather that their competence just diverged from that of
ordinary English speakers.

Of course, merely that the intuitions manifest a competence doesn't
alone make them *knowledge*: intuitions about biological kinds may
manifest an underlying competence with a folk biology without counting as genuine biological knowledge. But here the mind-dependence
of language can play a crucial role. Insofar as a language (or idiolect
– what Chomsky calls an "I-language") is *constituted* by a person's
language faculty, then there is no issue of correctness independent of
the principles of that faculty. Consequently, if a person's intuitions
were genuine manifestations of that faculty, then they would possess
a certain freedom from error not present in the case of competencies
regarding mind-independent domains.

One might worry about the domain of language being items in
space and time. But it is part and parcel of the conception of I-language

---

18 Though I disagree with Devitt most emphatically on this issue, I am much
    indebted to him for discussions of it and, indeed (counter-suggestible as I am)
    for some of the stimulation to the view defended here.

that Chomsky proposes that the items it concerns (words, sentences, phones, phonetic features) are not external to the agent. Just what the items *are* is not entirely clear. Chomsky (2000, 2003) suggests that they are simply "internal features" of the mind/brain. In Rey (2003), I have argued that this is implausible, and that the subject matter of at least computational/representational theories that linguists characteristically propose is more appropriately regarded as the *intentional content* of representations processed in the language faculty. An intuition, for example, that in (S3) 'he' cannot be 'John' is not an intuition about mind-independent "words," but simply an intuition with the intentional content (to a first approximation) [In 'He hopes John will win' he cannot be John].[19] Having the intuition about the sentence has roughly the same status as having an intuition that blue looks closer to green than to orange, or that the lines in the Müller-Lyer illusion look different lengths. Just as the latter presumably manifest facts about the intentional content of our perceptual system, so do linguistic intuitions manifest facts about the intentional content of our own I-language. They might, of course, be mistaken – but only if they aren't in fact the manifestations they appear to be.

To make this a little more precise, suppose, along the lines of my earlier supposition of a logic module, that a person is also endowed with a language faculty, whose nature is constituted by certain principles that (let us suppose) are explicitly represented in that faculty, and that a linguistic intuition is actually arrived at by being *deduced* from those principles.[20] If it were, and the principles were constitutive of the language faculty, then that would seem a conclusive reason to

---

19 The words, sentences, phonemes projected from this content don't themselves exist (and don't need to), either in the external world of the acoustic stream, or the internal world of the brain. I discuss this issue at length in my (forthcoming a and b).

20 Michael Devitt (forthcoming) has uncovered suggestions along these lines in the cognitive science literature, e.g., in Chomsky 1986, 270; Dwyer and Pietroski 1996, 342; Larson and Segal 1995, 10. I'm sympathetic to Devitt's (forthcoming) complaint that the empirical evidence as yet doesn't remotely establish the truth of such a model, but I doubt that its proponents actually think it does. I suspect they intend it, as do I, as a suggestion of simply one possible model of the production of intuitions.

regard the intuitions themselves as known *a priori*: after all, if some process is in fact a genuine derivation by absolutely reliable rules from principles that constitute the *domain* of the principles, then it couldn't *possibly* go wrong. Indeed, as we observed in the case of logic, the intuitions would be derived from principles that were the *truth-makers* of the domain: what *makes* it true that *he* can't be *John* in Section III is that that is just how the language faculty is structured. So insofar as someone's judgment manifests that structure, they know this fact independently of experience and, as in the case of logic, in a fashion that is absolutely reliable (relative, of course, to its having in fact been produced in this way).[21] Think of how one would answer the question, "So why do you think killings involve dyings?" It would surely be enough to say simply, "That's just what 'killing' and 'dying' mean for me (of course, I don't speak here for other speakers)." To be sure, one could be *wrong* about oneself – one might have overheard some mistaken linguistic pronouncements about oneself, or have become otherwise confused – but if the intuition had in fact been deduced by absolutely truth-preserving rules from domain-constituting principles, then necessarily it would be correct.

The analytic, then, would simply be a special case of this sort of knowledge of one's language. If the file for 'killing' were to involve a dying, and someone were to say "Killings involve dyings" as a result of deducing it from the content of that file, then they would be justified in believing it to be true in a way that is absolutely reliable, and in a way that does not depend upon experience.[22] Consequently, they would seem to have *a priori* knowledge of the analytic truth that killings involve dyings.

Again, I stress that I am not purporting to show that we do indeed have *a priori* knowledge of analytic truths; only that it is seriously *pos-*

---

21 I don't mean to suggest that the actual mechanisms by which we manifest, and in this way often come to know, our own attitudes is in the least obvious or well-understood. I'm relying only on the fact that it seems often to be reliable, and that if this reliability were due to the contents of a faculty that constitutes its own domain, then it would be a source of *a priori* knowledge.

22 Experience, of course, might have been necessary for the triggering of (the creation of a file for) the concept. The point is that, insofar as someone *has* the concept, intuitions manifesting its contents are not derived from experience.

sible that we do, along the lines of the model of a language faculty that I have sketched. Showing that human beings actually satisfy that model is, however, a formidable empirical question, not settled by either the analytic data or "rational intuitions" alone. I take it that it is simply not yet understood how lexical items have the constraints they seem to possess – just how, for example, the file for 'suicide' involves taking one's own life, or that for 'bachelor', being male. It would not be the first time that a simple and obvious fact proved difficult to explain. The data and intuitions provide us reason to *suspect* there are special faculties of logic and language that are absolutely reliable in the ways I have suggested, but they are hardly conclusive. Perhaps it will turn out that, at least for semantics, we are seamless Quinean machines after all. But, I submit, we have yet to be presented with an account of how such a Quinean machine would give rise to these analytic intuitions.

In any case, what is required is an epistemic "two-step": one step back to the meta-level at which we theorize empirically about our cognitive and linguistic abilities, and then, should that theorizing confirm the existence of such distinctive abilities along the above lines, one step forward to assert, then, that people have *a priori* knowledge both of logic and of analytic truths, after all.

V. Conclusion

Suppose linguistics *were* to succeed in delineating a class of analytic sentences that included many of the examples philosophers have discussed, perhaps even the claims of logic and (some of) mathematics. Would that provide the basis for *a priori* knowledge of claims in these areas that philosophers have sought?

Yes and no. It would certainly appear to provide us with an insight into the concepts we ordinarily deploy, at least when we are speaking a natural language. This may not be uninteresting, since many of the crucial questions that philosophers ask concern the proper understanding of ordinary notions such as *material object, event, person, action, freedom, coercion*, whose meaning may well be illuminated by a semantic theory of natural language. But some philosophers may want more. They'd like to know not merely about the concepts we deploy, which may or may not correspond to real phenomena in the world, but *about the real phenomena in the world themselves*. But it is just such a wonderful coincidence between our concepts and the actual phenomena of the world that a linguistic semantics alone is not likely to ensure. It is only if we can perform an epistemic two-step, and, stepping back, show on quite general grounds both

> (i) well established empirical theories about the structure of specific modularized (e.g., lexical) concepts,

and

> (ii) an independent reason to believe those concepts would apply to apply in all metaphysically possible worlds

that we could then step forward again and have reason to take their analytic entailments as providing us with *a priori* knowledge of the world. Present theories suggest (along the lines I mentioned) that we have such reasons only in the case of logic and maybe some parts of mathematics. If Kant were right, we could have some in the case of aspects of the structure of space, time, and causation. But, last time I looked, Kant didn't get it quite right. Perhaps someone else has, or will.

Consequently, appeals to the analytic cannot by themselves explain our knowledge of the truths of logical and mathematics in the direct way that the Positivists hoped and that Quine deplored. Quite as Bonjour (2001, 683–84) fears (see note 3), analytic truths by themselves provide us only knowledge of ourselves – specifically, our concepts – not knowledge of the world to which those concepts may turn out not to apply.

Nor can appeals to the analytic trump empirical research in the way that some philosophers seemed to have hoped. Scientific research can be regarded as involving a specific pragmatic use of language – and other non-natural symbolic systems – to describe and explain the world independently of our vacillating human concepts and concerns. As Kripke and Putnam have emphasized, we may use our ordinary concepts to fix the reference of what we're talking about, but not be confined to those concepts and their presumptions when we settle upon our ultimate account. Thus, much of our ordinary use of 'water', and perhaps the concept it expresses, may involve a liquid full of impurities, but it can be illuminating to find out that it is H_2O, if we want to know what the real stuff, *water*, is, independently of this ordinary use.[23] It might have been illuminating to find out that material objects are ideas. Or, to take a more pressing example, it has been suggested (e.g., by Wittgenstein 1953, §359–60, Ziff 1959), that it's analytic that a thinking thing must be alive. Suppose this claim were sustained by linguistic theory, showing that the ordinary notion expressed by 'thinking' is, indeed, correctly applied only to living things, and not to artifactual computers. Should this really satisfy the person worried about the possibility of artificial thought? It's hard to see why. The serious question that concerns people worried about whether artifacts could think concerns whether those artifacts could in fact share *the real, theoretically interesting, explanatory properties of being a thinking thing*. We may well have no reason to suppose that being alive actually figures among these – so much the worse for our ordinary, excessively chauvinistic conception of "thought."

There is a pragmatic heuristic employed by scientists that may obscure the issues here: perhaps in proposing some hypothesis, e.g., that machines could think, a scientist might use a word in a way that violates some feature of its lexical meaning. If his usage becomes sufficiently entrenched, the word might come to be used *without* that feature, and so, strictly speaking from the point of view of linguistics, the word would no longer mean what it used to mean. Why doesn't this bother the scientist – or even the layperson who may be wondering whether or not machines could think? I submit it's because the scientist and the layperson asking such scientific questions implicitly understand the pragmatic purpose at hand, and realize that there is no reason to tie our ways of talk to our linguistic faculty that we may use to fix reference. We can throw away the ladder, unsurprised that the world failed to conform to our ordinary conceptions of it.

Perhaps all this secures an analytic and the *a priori* that neither the Rationalist nor the Empiricist would think worth having. Fine. That would just show that not only were they rash in their assumptions

---

23 I leave as a delicate, as yet unsettled empirical issue to what extent our ordinary concept [water] itself countenances this possibility.

Georges Rey

about the availability of these categories, but also about what they hoped could be achieved with them.[24]

References

Bonjour, L. 1998. *In Defense of Pure Reason*. Cambridge: Cambridge University Press.

———. 2001. Replies. *Philosophy and Phenomenological Research* 63 (3): 673–98.

Burge, T. 1979. "Individualism and the Mental." In *Midwest Studies in Philosophy* IV, ed. P. French, T. Uehling and H. Wettstein. Minneapolis: University of Minnesota Press.

Chomsky, N. 1986. *Knowledge of Language: Its Nature, Origin, and Use*. New York: Praeger Publishers.

———. 2000. *New Horizons in the Study of Language*. Cambridge: Cambridge University Press.

———. 2003. "Reply to Rey." In *Chomsky and His Critics*, ed. L. Antony and N. Hornstein, 105–39. Oxford: Blackwell.

Dennett, D. 1991. *Consciousness Explained*. New York: Little Brown.

Devitt, M. 1996. *Coming to Our Senses: A Naturalistic Program for Semantic Localism*. Cambridge: Cambridge University Press.

———. 1997. "Replies." In *The Maribor Papers in Naturalized Semantics*, ed. D. Jutronic, 353–411. Maribor: Pedagoska Fakulteta Maribor.

———. forthcoming. *Ignorance of Language*.

Dwyer, S. and Pietroski, P. 1996. "Believing in Language." *Philosophy of Science* 63: 338–73.

Ewing, A. 1947. *The Definition of Good*. New York: Macmillan.

Fodor, J. 1983. *The Modularity of Mind*. Cambridge, MA: MIT Press.

———. 1987. *Psychosemantics*. Cambridge, MA: MIT Press.

———. 1990. *A Theory of Content and Other Essays*. Cambridge, MA: MIT Press.

---

24 Versions of this paper have been delivered at the department of philosophy at the Ohio State University in Columbus, the annual Canadian Philosophical Association meeting in Quebec City, Carleton University in Ottawa, l'Ecole Normale Supérieure in Paris, and at the concepts conference at the University of Bologna, Dec. 2001. I am indebted to those audiences, but especially to Paul Pietroski and Michael Devitt, for many stimulating discussions of the issues. Some passages have also appeared in my 1993, 2001a, and 2004.

———. 1998. *Concepts: Where Cognitive Science Went Wrong*. Oxford: Oxford University Press.

———. 2004. "Having Concepts: A Brief Refutation of the 20th Century." *Mind and Language* 19: 29–47.

Gettier, E. 1963. "Is Justified True Belief Knowledge?" *Analysis* 23: 121–23.

Grice, H.P. 1965. "The Causal Theory of Perception." In *Perceiving, Sensing and Knowing*, ed. R.J. Swartz. New York: Doubleday.

Heim, H. 1989. *The Semantics of Definite and Indefinite Noun Phrases in English*. New York: Garland.

Hornsby, J. 1997. *Simple Mindedness: In Defense of Naive Naturalism in Philosophy of Mind*. Cambridge: Harvard University Press.

Katz, J. 1972. *Semantic Theory*. New York: Harper & Row.

———. 1981. *Language and Other Abstract Objects*. Totowa, NJ: Rowman and Littlefield.

———. 1998. *A Realistic Rationalism*. Cambridge, MA: MIT Press.

Larson, R. and Segal, G. 1995. *Knowledge of Meaning*. Cambridge, MA: MIT Press.

Loewer, B. and Rey, G., eds. 1991. *Meaning in Mind*. Oxford: Blackwell.

McGinn, C. 1991. *The Problem of Consciousness*. Oxford: Blackwell.

Myers, D. 2004. *Intuition*. New Haven: Yale University Press.

Peacocke, C. 1992. *A Study of Concepts*. Cambridge, MA: MIT Press.

———. 1996. "Can Possession Conditions Individuate Concepts?" *Philosophy and Phenomenological Research* 56: 433–60.

———. 1998. "Implicit Conceptions, Understanding and Rationality." In *Concepts*, ed. E. Villanueva, 43–88. Atascadero: Ridgeview.

Putnam, H. 1962/75. "The Analytic and the Synthetic." In *Philosophical Papers* Vol. II, 33-69. Cambridge: Cambridge University Press.

———. 1975. *Mathematics, Matter and Method: Philosophical Papers*. Vol. I. Cambridge: Cambridge University Press.

Quine, W. 1953a. "On What There Is." In *From a Logical Point of View and Other Essays*, 1–19. New York: Harper and Row.

———. 1953b. "Two Dogmas of Empiricism". In *From a Logical Point of View and Other Essays*, 20–46. New York: Harper and Row.

———. 1960. *Word and Object*. Cambridge, MA: MIT Press.

———. 1970. *Philosophy of Logic*. Englewood Cliffs: Prentice-Hall.

———. 1986. "Reply to Henryk Skolimowski." In *The Philosophy of W.V. Quine*, ed. L. Hahn and P. Schilpp, 492–93. La Salle, IL: Open Court.

Quine, W. and Ullian, J. 1970/78. *The Web of Belief*. New York: Random House.

Recanati, F. 1993. *Direct Reference*. Oxford: Blackwell.

Rey, G. 1993. "The Unavailability of What We Mean: a Reply to Quine, Fodor and LePore." In *Grazer Philosophica* (Special Edition), ed. J. Fodor and E. LePore, 61–101.

———. 1994. "Dennett's Unrealistic Psychology." *Philosophical Topics* 22 (1–2): 259–89.

———. 1995. "Keeping Meaning More in Mind." *Intellectica* 2 (21) :65–80.

———. 1996. "Resisting Primitive Compulsions." Contribution to symposium on C. Peacocke, A Study of Concepts. *Philosophy and Phenomenological Research* LVI (2): 419–24. Reprinted in *Concepts: Core Readings*, ed. E. Margolis and S. Laurence. Cambridge, MA: MIT Press, 1999.

———. 1997. *Contemporary Philosophy of Mind: A Contentiously Classical Approach*. Oxford: Blackwell

———. 1998. "What Implicit Conceptions Are Unlikely To Do." Commentary on Chistopher Peacocke, "Implicit Conceptions, Understanding and Rationality." *Philosophical Issues 9: Concepts*, ed. E. Villanueva, 89–92. Atascadero: Ridgeview Press.

———. 2001a. "Digging Deeper for the A Priori." (Commentary on Laurence Bonjour, *In Defense of Pure Reason*.) *Philosophical and Phenomenological Research* 63: 649–56.

———. 2001b. "Physicalism and Psychology: A Plea for Substantive Philosophy of Mind." In *Physicalism and Its Discontents*, ed. Carl Gillet and Barry Loewer 99–128. Cambridge: Cambridge University Press.

———. 2003. "Intentional Content and a Chomskian Linguistics." In *Epistemology of Language*, ed. Alex Barber, 140–186. Oxford: Oxford University Press.

———. 2004. "The Analytic/Synthetic Distinction." *Stanford On-Line Encyclopedia of Philosophy*.

———. forthcoming-a. "The Intentional Inexistence of Language – But Not Cars." In Debates in Cognitive Science, ed. R. Stainton. Oxford: Blackwell.

———. forthcoming-b. *Representing Nothing: Intentional Inexistents in Cognitive Science*. Oxford: Oxford University Press.

Wittgenstein, L. 1953. *Philosophical Investigations*. Oxford: Blackwell.

Ziff, P. 1959. "The Feelings of Robots." *Analysis* 19: 64–68.

PART C

Mind

CANADIAN JOURNAL OF PHILOSOPHY
Supplementary Volume 30

Neural Materialism, Pain's Badness, and A Posteriori Identities

IRWIN GOLDSTEIN

Materialists say sensations and other kinds of mental states are physical events. Today, most materialists are neural materialists. They think mental states are neural events or material properties of neural events.

Orthodox neural materialists think mental states are neural events or orthodox material properties of neutral events. Orthodox material properties are defining properties of the physical. A *defining property* of the physical is a type of property that provides a necessary condition for something's being correctly termed 'physical' (a conjunction of all defining properties provides a sufficient condition.) Defining properties of the physical include *spatial* and *temporal* properties and *causal propensities* and *sensitivities*. A particle is an *electron*, for instance, by having a particular set of spatiotemporal properties and causal sensitivities and powers.

In this paper I give an argument against orthodox neural materialism. If successful, the argument would show at least some properties of some mental states are not orthodox material properties of neural events. The argument is not, however, a self-sufficient refutation of orthodox materialism. To support one of the argument's premises I appeal to views of pain, pleasure, and value I not defend here (though defend in detail elsewhere). My thesis in this paper is this: If these views are correct, we refute orthodox neural materialism with the argument presented here.

The contentions about pain, pleasure, and value are the following. First, ethical realism is true. 'Good' and 'bad' name properties.

An object is correctly called 'good' or 'bad' if it has the property the word names. Second, pain's intrinsic badness is an "objective" property of pain in that it does not hinge on our disliking and avoiding pain. Rather, being intrinsically bad, pain has an intrinsic character that grounds these reactions and so gives agents reason to dislike and avoid pain. (Good and bad are analyzable. Pleasure is good, approximately, by having a character that gives us reason to seek pleasure. Pain's badness is analyzable in a parallel way.) Third, intrinsic badness is a defining property of 'pain'. When 'pain' is used in the broad sense in which it encompasses all unpleasant experiences, and so both localized and non-localized pain, pain's badness is a property every pain has and a property by which localized pain sensations and non-localized emotional pain are, in qualitative character, a single kind of mental state. Finally, pleasure's link to intrinsic goodness parallels pain's link to intrinsic badness. Given this analysis, pain and pleasure are opposites through their intrinsic axiological character.[1]

Many people both (1) affirm causal role analyses of mind, and (2) claim token mental states are neural states in sentient beings on Earth. People who both affirm (1) and accept (2) commit to orthodox materialism. This conjunction of views is one target of my argument against orthodox materialism.

Causal theorists say a mental state's defining or essential properties lie in its causes and effects or "causal role." An event is pain, for instance, by having a particular set of causes and effects. While causal theorists say there could be sentient beings in which immaterial substances are the bearers of a mental state's causal role, theorists regularly say *neural states* are the bearers in sentient beings on Earth. Causal theorists who say (token) mental states are neural states in Earthlings commit to orthodox materialism for Earthlings. (If they reject orthodox materialism in their view of Earthlings, their thinking has internal inconsistencies.) For Earthlings, causal role theorists commit to an ontology of neural states and their causal roles, i.e., sets of their causes and effects. (Some causal theorists identify mental

---

1 The views of pleasure and pain, and the realist objectivist analysis of intrinsic value, I defend in various places. These include Goldstein 1980, 1989, 1994 (50—52), 2000 , 1980 and 2002.

states with the *causal roles*. Others identify (token) mental states, in Earthlings, with the *neural events* (they say) have these causal roles. Either way, their ontology is neural events and causal roles.) A neural event's causal role, its causes and effects, is an *orthodox material property*: It is a defining property of the physical – a kind of property that gives a necessary condition for being physical.[2]

What I call *orthodox materialism* is not what others call *reductive materialism*. (I do not use the reductive–anti-reductive distinction.) Many people insist causal theorists are *anti*-reductive. I call them orthodox materialists. My argument against orthodox materialism targets both what people consider reductive materialism (*viz.*, the identity theory) and views people consider anti-reductive.

Eliminativism is not a form of orthodox neural materialism, and so my argument does not oppose it. Orthodox neural materialists identify mental states with elements in the neural orthodox material. Eliminativists do not. They deny the existence of mental states.

I. The Argument

Here is my argument: 1. If orthodox neural materialism is true, the exhaust and dispense principle is true. 2. The exhaust and dispense principle is false. Therefore, 3. Orthodox neural materialism is false.

Both premises mention *the exhaust and dispense principle*. The principle has two components: the *exhaust* and *dispense* theses.

    i.   The *exhaust* thesis: It is possible, in principle, to identify every kind of mental state, and to specify every immediate property every mental state has, using the vocabulary of neuroscience and other physical sciences, i.e., with the kinds of words physical scientists use to identify neural

---

2 Some causal theorists mention a mental state's causal links to other mental states in their analyses. (They may mention 'desire' when defining 'pain'. They might partially define 'pain' by saying that what it names "causes a desire to flee.") Even so, causal theorists who "inter-define" psychological words so, do not intend to affirm non-causal, irreducibly psychical properties. Emphasizing causal roles and token mental-neural identities, they work from an ontology of neural states and causal roles.

events and specify their orthodox material properties. While declaring it is possible *in principle* to specify properties of mental states with a physical science vocabulary, proponents of the exhaust thesis need not suppose it is possible *in practice* for people to do so.

ii. The *dispense* thesis: People might dispense with psychological words. They would still be able, in principle, to identify every mental state and to specify every property every mental state has. They might do this with physical science words.

Premise 1 is true. We have words with which we can identify neural events and specify their spatiotemporal and other orthodox material properties. Were mental states neural events or their orthodox material properties, it would be possible in principle to identify mental states with the physical science words we might use to identify neural events and their orthodox material properties.[3] Thus, the exhaust thesis is true if orthodox materialism is true. Further, if the exhaust thesis is true, the dispense thesis also is. If we could identify mental states using physical science language, we could identify them without using psychological words. Thus, both the exhaust and dispense theses are true if neural materialism is true.

Some people will think the exhaust and dispense thesis is true, and hence that premise 2 is false. Part II contains my defense of premise 2.

II. Premise 2 Defended

Suppose we dispense with psychological words. We restrict ourselves to words we might use to specify neural events and their orthodox material properties. We use words for spatiotemporal properties and causal sensitivities and propensities. We use the vocabulary of neuro-

---

3 To say this is not directly to comment on the meanings of words. It is not directly to claim, for instance, that if pain were neural event *n* or physical property *p* of *n*, 'pain' would have the same meaning as a set of physical science words we might use to specify *n* or *p*.

science. When we are constrained so, there are some defining properties of 'pain' and 'pleasure' – pain's intrinsic badness and pleasure's intrinsic goodness – we cannot specify. By 'pain's intrinsic badness' I intend pain's second-order property of being intrinsically bad, not pain's qualitative character. (The qualitative character is the first-order property of pain that *has* the property of being intrinsically bad. Pain is intrinsically bad *because of* its qualitative character.) The property which makes both localized and emotional pain a single kind of mental state, which unites qualitatively diverse pleasures into a single kind of mental state, and which makes pleasure and pain opposites, we could not specify. The exhaust and dispense doctrine is false. Premise 2 is true.

People may reply as follows: "Premise 2 is false; the exhaust and dispense principle is true. Pain's intrinsic badness and pleasure's intrinsic goodness are specifiable in a physical language and without the use of psychological words. We can specify pain's intrinsic badness by referring to a property in pain – in both localized pain sensations and non-localized emotional pain – of disposing a person to avoid the occurrence intrinsically, as an end it itself. (Analyzed so, pain's badness does not hinge on our reactions to pain but causes these reactions.) Similarly, we can specify pleasure's intrinsic goodness by referring to pleasure's property of disposing a person to seek pleasure as an end."

With these proposals people do not succeed in upholding the exhaust and dispense doctrine. The proposals do not enable us to specify pain's badness and pleasure's goodness with physical science language and without psychological words. The proposals contain 'person', 'avoid', and 'seek'. 'Person' is not a physical science word. People have minds. In principle, mindless automata might have a person's physical properties. They fall short of being people through lacking minds and so mental properties. 'Avoid' here denotes a human action and so is partly psychological. In avoiding Sarah's dog, people *intentionally* move in ways they *think* will lead them not to face her dog. Intentional pain avoidance is an act and so an event with a cognitive component. Hence, when we try to analyze it by reference to pain "avoidance," we do not depict pain's badness in physical science terms. A parallel attempt to portray pleasure's goodness in physical science terms fails for a similar reason.

Pain's badness and pleasure's goodness are not specifiable in physical science language. They are not locations or other spatial properties, nor are they temporal properties or any other orthodox material properties of neural events. Orthodox neural materialism is false.

Were pain's badness an orthodox material property, the effects pain has through being bad would differ from what they are. A physical object's spatiotemporal properties produce their effects in non-teleological, brutely mechanistic ways. They have effects without anyone being aware of those properties or the objects that have them. Pain's badness does not have its effects in a brutely mechanistic way. It has its impact teleologically – through grounding or justifying the cognitively saturated responses it prompts.[4] In being bad, pain prompts our avoidance of pain by grounding or justifying that avoidance and so by giving us reason to avoid pain. For an object's badness to have effects we must be *aware* of what is bad. Thus pain's badness is not an orthodox material property.

Claiming pain's badness is an orthodox material property, materialists may argue as follows. "Some identities – between water and H_2O, for instance – are opaque and knowable only *a posteriori*." In the spirit of a new wave equation of goodness with some "natural" property, people might propose, "Pain's badness may be identical to some orthodox material property of a neural event. The identity may be knowable only *a posteriori*. Neuroscientists may discover it and thereby explain what pain's badness is." In Part III, I explain why no such discovery is possible.

III. There is No *A Posteriori* Identity between Pain's Badness and an Orthodox Material Property

How should we formulate the *a posteriori* identity materialists entertain? *Some normative properties are identical to some non-normative properties?* Expressed so and interpreted straightforwardly, this formulation of the identity is self-contradictory. We discover *o* both has and lacks a particular property (normativeness). We need not gaily anticipate a discovery of this form.

---

4 See Goldstein 2002.

Materialists might avoid self-contradiction in formulating the imagined discovery. For some *m* they might say, "Pain's intrinsic badness is identical to orthodox material property *m* of neural event *n*." For this proposal to be true: 1. It must represent an identity, and 2. There must be *a posteriori* identities – identities knowable only *a posteriori*. Neither condition is satisfied.

1. The standard proposals for mental-physical a posteriori identities are not viable candidates for identities.

Suppose pain's badness were identical to material property *m* of neural event *n*. If it were, we could not *explain* what pain's badness is, or analyze pain's badness, by reference to that material property. (We could no more do this than the reverse and explain what the material property is, or analyze it, by reference to pain's intrinsic badness.) Yet, people who propose *a posteriori* identifications of mental properties with neural properties regard the proposals as explanatory. They treat them as analyses. Materialists want to subsume pain's intrinsic badness and other intrinsic properties of mental states under the orthodox material. They expect thereby to explain what properties of mental states are by reference to the orthodox material. However, subsumption is not identity. In formulations of such alleged identities, proponents offer one-directional proposals, not reversible ones. (Neural materialists are *materialists*. They do not see themselves as claiming "Physical states are mental states." People who embrace the latter, reversed claim seem to endorse idealism, not materialism.) One-directional proposals are not identity statements.

2. There are no a posteriori identities.

Every object is identical to itself and only to itself. (No object is identical with an object having even one property it lacks.) This is knowable *a priori*. Thus, for any object it is knowable *a priori* what the object is identical with. In no case is what an object is identical with knowable only *a posteriori*. In no case is there a brute "explanatory gap" between something and what it is identical to.

If there are no *a posteriori* identities, there is no *a posteriori* identity between pain's badness and something. Hence, there is no *a posteriori* identity between pain's badness and some orthodox material property of a neural event. (Hence, in no ("token") pain is there an *a posteriori* identity between pain's badness and some orthodox material property.) In every pain, what pain's badness is identical with – *viz.*, itself – is knowable *a priori*.[5]

With this reasoning, aimed at proving there are no *a posteriori* identities, I speak *de re* not *de dicto*. I refer to objects and with what they are identical, and I speak of our ability to know with what something is identical. I do not directly refer to *sentences* said to report identities, or comment about the epistemic status of these sentences.

3. Some errors that facilitate belief in *a posteriori* identities.

One reason people believe in *a posteriori* identities is they conflate talk of 1. the epistemic status of identities with talk of 2. the epistemic status of *sentences* they assume represent identities. However, when I say this cat's self-identity is knowable *a priori*, I speak about the epistemological status of a particular fact – this cat's self-identity. I do not directly refer to some *sentence* about the cat or claim the truth of that sentence is knowable *a priori*.

To say every identity is knowable *a priori* is not to state or assume every statement that reports an identity is analytic. When rejecting *a posteriori* identities, I speak about objects and what they are identical to, and not about sentences about those objects.

In discussions of identity, people regularly assume identity concerns *two objects* identical to each other. (On these occasions people are not speaking *de dicto* and claiming, what is very different, that identity concerns two names for a single object.)[6] The assumption

---

5 People who identify mental properties with neural properties offer a posteriori identities. Suppose there are no a posteriori identities. Then no psychological property – not a sensation's intrinsic qualitative character or any other property of a sensation – has an a posteriori identity with a neural property.

6 "If two things, *x* and *y*, are identical, then they have exactly the same properties," David Armstrong writes (1999, 23).

"For any objects *x* and *y*, if *x* is *y*, then it is necessary that *x* is *y*," Saul Kripke writes (1971, 137). When using the plural 'objects' to classify "*x* and *y*," Kripke regards *x* as one object and *y* another. When people assign Leibnitz a belief in "the identity of indiscernibles," they use the plural term 'indiscernibles' to refer

facilitates a belief in *a posteriori* identities. Between *two* objects there are relations that are non-transparent and knowable only *a posteriori*. However, identity does not concern two objects. For every identity, there is *one* object identical to itself. That an object is identical to itself, and only to itself, is transparent and knowable *a priori*.

People believe in *a posteriori* identities primarily because they think they have examples of them. They assume certain kinds of *a posteriori* 'is'-sentences represent identities. Their analyses of these sentences and the discoveries people use the sentences to represent requires refinement. Here are four kinds of 'is'-sentences people present:

    i.   Cicero is Tully.

As people ordinarily intend the sentence, it is shorthand for 'The person named "Cicero" is also named "Tully".' (Somewhat similarly, in saying 'I am Irwin' I ordinarily announce my name and so say, in effect, 'My name is "Irwin".') The *a posteriori* knowledge I gain in learning the truth of 'Cicero is Tully' is linguistic – that the words 'Cicero' and 'Tully' name the same person. The linguistic knowledge I have in knowing that people use both 'Cicero' and 'Tully' to refer to a particular person is indeed attainable only *a posteriori*. (Indeed, the linguistic knowledge I have in knowing that people use only *one* name – 'Einstein' – to refer to my hamster also is attainable only *a posteriori*.) This *a posteriori* knowledge is distinguishable from the knowledge, attainable *a priori*, that a person is identical to himself and to no one else.

    ii.   The morning star is the evening star (Phosphorus is Hesperus).

What philosophers treat as a discovery of a single, simple fact (a fact they think they crisply identify with the single, short 'is'-sentence 'The morning star is the evening star') is analyzable into discoveries of distinguishable spatiotemporal and linguistic properties a particular

---

to the two objects. When people represent an identity as $a = b$, the presumption is that identity concerns two objects – that 'a' represents one object and 'b' a second. In this formula, 'a' and 'b' represent objects, not words for those objects.

heavenly body – Venus – has. Further knowledge of astronomical history might allow us to explain the advance in more detail.

When labelling a planet *the morning star*, the *Encyclopedia Americana* states, people deem it a "bright planet that becomes visible in the eastern sky shortly before sunrise." When calling a planet *the evening star*, this work states, people identify it as a "bright planet appearing in the western sky, near the horizon, shortly after sunset." There are five planets – Venus, Mercury, Mars, Jupiter, and Saturn – people label 'the morning star.' Each of the five, at times, satisfies the conditions for being labelled 'the morning star'. Each planet at times also meets the conditions for being designated 'the evening star'. For both morning and evening designations, Venus meets the conditions more often than do the other four planets. Venus is visible at the appropriate time and place more often than any of the other planets is.

With the words 'The morning star is the evening star' we do not crisply pick out a single fact. This 'is'-sentence is elliptical, and, expressed without qualification and detail, is misleading in various ways in contexts in which philosophers use the sentence. The sentence does not accurately capture the astronomical advance that underlies the philosophers' words. The following description of the advance is more accurate and informative. Scientists realized: "1. Any of five planets can be visible in the morning in the east, though Venus is visible at this time and place more often than the other four planets. 2. Though Venus is the planet most often visible in the evening in the west, any of five planets can be visible at that time and place. 3. More often than the other four planets, Venus has the (linguistic) properties of being labelled 'the morning star' and 'the evening star'. 4. When people assign the morning star's properties to one planet and the evening star's to a second, they err or think crudely. Rather, both sets of properties belong to a single planet – Venus (given the most common referent of 'the morning star' and 'the evening star')." Formulating the astronomical advance with more precision and detail than philosophers usually give, though still somewhat crudely, we might say, "Astronomers discovered that the spatial, temporal, and linguistic properties people assign what they call 'the morning star', and those that people assign what they call 'the evening star', belong to a single object – Venus." We might then say astronomers discovered these facts.

That a planet is identical to itself is knowable *a priori*. That certain planets have the properties of being visible from Earth at certain times of the day, and of not being visible at certain other times, and of appearing in various directions when visible, and of being identified with various names and expressions in human languages, is knowable only *a posteriori*.

People say astronomers discovered *Phosphorus* is identical to *Hesperus*. The example is akin to the 'The morning star is the evening star.' The *Phosphorus-Hesperus* discovery remains analyzable into spatiotemporal and linguistic components.

    iii.   Napoleon is the loser of Waterloo.

The *a posteriori* knowledge people have in knowing the truth of 'Napoleon is the loser of Waterloo' is that Napoleon has a particular property: having lost at Waterloo.

Suppose we convert the statement and say '*The loser of Waterloo is Napoleon*'. We say something different. We *identify* the loser of Waterloo, i.e., we state who lost at Waterloo.

    iv.   Water is H_2O.

This idiom, as philosophers ordinarily intend it, is a formula for water's composition. It does not represent an identity and so does not represent an *a posteriori* identity. (Philosophers habitually report the molecular analysis as 'Water is H_2O,' i.e., with a three-word set in which 'is' stands between 'water' and 'H_2O'. This habit reinforces the belief that scientists use this idiom to present an identity.) The statement is not reversible: 'H_2O is water' is not equivalent to 'Water is H_2O'. The latter does not parallel 'Cicero is Tully'. 'Water' names a substance, 'H_2O' (in this idiom) does not. To learn the truth of 'Water is H_2O' is to learn water's composition — that hydrogen-oxygen molecules make up water.[7]

---

7 'H_2O' has a secondary sense in which it is synonymous with 'water' and does not signify water's composition. ('H_2O' has this sense in talk of 'a bottle of H_2O'.) A person could intend 'H_2O' in this sense in 'Water is H_2O'. His sentence would then parallel 'The person called "Cicero" is also called "Tully".' Understood so, the sentence would be reversible. However, in this sense 'Water is H_2O' would not represent water's composition and so would not represent the scientific discovery philosophers intend with the expression 'Water is H_2O'.

Many other statements said to represent *a posteriori* identities – about gold, clouds, lightning, heat – resemble 'Water is H₂0' in being irreversible, composition statements. They represent analyses by reference to component physical parts.

I mentioned four kinds of alleged *a posteriori* identities. In each case the belief in the *a posteriori* identity is tied to *some* fact that is knowable only *a posteriori*. Each object referred to has *a posteriori* properties – properties it can be known to have only *a posteriori*. These include being named 'Tully', being visible in both the east in the morning and the west in the evening, having lost at Waterloo, having a particular molecular composition.

IV. Might Pain's Badness Have *A Posteriori* Properties?

Might pain's badness resemble water or lightning in having a particular atomic constitution that is knowable only *a posteriori*? Pain's badness differs from water and lightning in this respect. Pain's badness is not the sort of thing that has an atomic makeup. It is not a three-dimensional substance or a three-dimensional event that occupies some sector of space. Pain's being bad is similar to a pain's being rare, an argument's being valid, and a soup can's being to the left of the cat. None of these properties is a three-dimensional substance. None has a molecular composition scientists might discover.

People might think even if pain's badness is not itself an orthodox material property, it at least has an *a posteriori* property of *correlating* with such a property, and so of being intimately related in some way with one. Pain's badness might have the *a posteriori* property of supervening on an orthodox material property. These suggestions do not conflict with my thesis. In contending pain's badness is not an orthodox material property I do not claim, what is quite different, that it does not supervene on, or otherwise correlate with, such a property.

V. Conclusion

Were orthodox neural materialism true, the exhaust and dispense principle would be true. In principle, we could specify properties of mental states in physical science language. Suppose Sheena hoped to specify all intrinsic properties of her feelings. Would it be possible in principle for her to do so while dispensing with psychological words and solely by using physical science words to specify orthodox material properties of neural events in her brain? I think not. Many properties of mental states seem not to be specifiable in physical science language. In this paper, I have appealed only to one kind of property: the axiological. We cite this property in the analysis of pain and pleasure. Particular axiological properties of pain and pleasure, which I regard as defining properties, are not specifiable in physical science language. The exhaust and dispense principle is false. Orthodox neural materialism is false.

Might physical scientists expand their ontology and accept intrinsic goodness as a defining property of the physical? The development would not threaten my argument's conclusion. I conclude only that *orthodox* neural materialism is false, and hence that some properties of some mental states are not elements in the materialist's *current* ontology.[8]

References

Armstrong, D. 1999. *The Mind-Body Problem: An Opinionated Introduction,* Boulder: Westview Press.

Goldstein, I. 1980. "Why People Prefer Pleasure to Pain." *Philosophy* 55: 349–62.

———. 1989. "Pleasure and Pain: Unconditional, Intrinsic Values." *Philosophy and Phenomenological Research* 50: 255–276.

———. 1994. "Identifying Mental States: A Celebrated Hypothesis Refuted." *Australasian Journal of Philosophy* 72 (1): 46–62.

———. 2000. "Intersubjective Properties by Which We Specify Pleasure, Pain, and Other Kinds of Mental States." *Philosophy* 75: 89–104.

———. 2002. "The Good's Magnetism and Ethical Realism." *Philosophical Studies* 108 (1–2): 1–14.

Kripke, S. 1971. "Identity and Necessity." In *Identity and Individuation,* ed. Milton Munitz, 135–164. New York: New York University Press.

---

8 Thanks to David Barnett, Errol Bedford, Sheena Goldstein, John Heil, Dorothea Lotter, Al Mele, David Ohreen, Ulrich Meyer, David Papineau, J. J. C. Smart, Brendan O'Sullivan, Stuart Rachels, and Joan Weiner for valued feedback. This paper is dedicated to a cherished friend: Errol Bedford.

CANADIAN JOURNAL OF PHILOSOPHY
Supplementary Volume 30

Emotion and Rationality

MARK LANCE AND ALESSANDRA TANESINI

This paper is concerned with the roles played by emotions in rationality, a topic which has been generally, but unjustifiably, ignored by epistemologists. Silence on this matter is, we believe, indicative of the overly narrow view that epistemologists have had of their field. Whatever else we might accomplish by considering the rational role of emotions, we hope to motivate a number of questions and philosophical contexts not commonly considered by epistemologists.

Everyone knows that rationality depends on the doxastic state of the individual. Thus, whether an action, decision, inference, or belief is rational depends on what other things the individual believes, or is justified in believing in the given situation. This holds not just for rationality, but for epistemic norms in general. Many such normative statuses apply directly to beliefs, and all depend at least indirectly on the background doxastic status of the agent. In this paper, it is our purpose to argue that rationality, and epistemic norms more generally, depend as well on the *emotional* states of the agent. We argue that emotions play a crucial, particular, and essential role in rational thought, that the epistemic status of an agent's doxastic states depends on her background emotions and those she is epistemically entitled to, and that the only cognitive state an agent is justified in having, in many situations, is precisely an emotion. Generally we argue that one cannot characterize crucial features of the rational epistemic agent without recourse to the language of emotions.

In developing this view, we say little about what emotions are. That is, we offer nothing like a complete theory of the emotions and, in particular, do not claim that the epistemic role we attribute to them exhausts the identifying features of emotions. Given this, we cannot claim to have argued that any possible rational agent must have states with all the important characteristics of human emotions, but we do argue that there is a crucial epistemic job performed in us humans by emotions, and that any rational agent would have to have some state or other which did this job. Since the job is quite different from any for which standard propositional attitudes are suitable, any rational agent must have at least emotion-like states. Further, we offer some speculation regarding why various other features of human emotions coexist in a state performing this epistemic function.

I. Some Observations about Rational Thought

Case 1:   A scene from *Buffy The Vampire Slayer*:

> Buffy, Xander, Willow, and Cordelia have just gathered around a table to discuss how to deal with a ghost who is haunting their high school, possessing students, and influencing them to kill teachers.
> *Buffy*: Well, what do we know?
> *Xander*: We know that dog saliva is cleaner than human saliva.
> *Buffy*: Right. Besides that.

The point is that we all know *many things*. Intelligence is always in part, and often primarily, not a matter of what one knows, but of one's ability to organize that knowledge, and to determine which known propositions are salient or relevant to the issue at hand. The most rational person is quite typically not the one with the largest number of justified claims in her possession, nor the one capable of the most complex reasoning with the fewest inferential errors, but rather she who is best able to marshal those facts as fodder for reasoning which will be most useful in arriving at answers to the questions most salient in the current context. What was wanted in the scene from *Buffy* was not a list of things known, but candidates for information the inferential deployment of which would provide justification for a course of action *vis-à-vis* the haunting spirit.

The globally useful, but locally inconvenient breadth of human knowledge, and the consequent importance to rationality of selection among the range of facts known, applies equally well to inference. Any proposition entails infinitely many others, and stands as good reason to believe an infinite set of others that is far harder to generate. Inferring well is, thus, as much a matter of knowing which of the rationally acceptable inferences it will be intellectually fruitful to pursue in the current context as it is of knowing how to tell a rationally acceptable inference from an unacceptable one. Everyone who teaches logic has noted precisely this point, that it is far easier to see that a proof is valid than to see how to proceed in a proof in the first place, and the point is even more striking in such contexts as theoretical explanation. Any decent undergraduate science student can identify (at least in most cases) which purported explanations of phenomena are genuine, but to find the hypothesis which, through inferential manipulation, is likely to evolve into such an explanation is quite another matter.

We illustrate with an example from chess.

Case 2:   A typical scene in a chess lesson: The teacher and his student have reached an interesting position in playing through the student's recent tournament game.

Teacher: Now in this position, I'd be worried about my king's safety and the possibility of a sacrifice to break up my pawn position in front of my king.
Student: No, if he plays Rg8, I'll play....
Teacher: Slow down; I don't want to analyze yet. I'm *worried about, maybe even scared of,* a kingside attack.
Student: But I can attack the knight, and then win a pawn on b7.
Teacher: Look – in this position, you need *first* to be concerned about certain dangers, *then* to understand why they are threatening, *then* to calculate. You don't calculate how to win a knight pawn when you should be worrying about your king.

In a typical chess position, there are *many* things one could calculate (typically on the order of 10^{20} or 10^{30} distinct continuations). Successful brute force calculation of typical positions in chess is physically impossible, precluded by basic constraints involving the speed of light, the minimal distance between particles, and the time lapse of fundamental quantum transitions. The present point is that good players do not get worried about threats, or excited about opportunities, as a result of calculation, even in a partial and non-exhaustive manner. Rather, the worry, fear, excitement, etc. come first, and one chooses which moves to consider, and which lines to calculate, on the basis of this prior reaction to the "demands of the position." The best players, we are suggesting, are guided in what sorts of things to apply their calculative methods to in virtue of their well-honed emotional competence.

There is a stage in the investigation of many problems – whether intellectual or practical – in which the mark of a rational (competent, wise, experienced, knowledgeable) agent is simply that she knows what issues to investigate, that she is able to take the right – in the sense of reasonable – issues to be *salient*. The competent criminal investigator has a well developed sense of what leads to follow, what people to suspect, and what features of the crime scene to treat as potential clues. The competent mathematician is drawn to certain conjectures and potential strategies of proof. A good philosopher knows that certain ideas are worth investigating for several years and others not, and that certain ideas are likely to cohere and others not.[1] In each case this understanding – appreciation of salience, sense of where to look – is prior to the justification of beliefs, sometimes even to *having* beliefs, concerning the facts in question. In the case of chess, this point was summed up, in admittedly hyperbolic terms, by Jose Raul Capablanca, one of the top players in history, who was asked by a reporter how many moves ahead he looks in a game. Capablanca, annoyed by the cliché question, replied, "Just one, but it is a *very good* move."

---

1 In a recent presentation, one of us was claiming a certain virtue for an account of mind that involved connecting a Heideggerian notion of embodied tacit skill and a version of Sellarsian inferentialism. A questioner in the audience asked whether it wouldn't be possible to combine Brandom's account of language with a Cartesian dualism about mind, and whether there was an argument against such an approach. Though lacking any knock-down argument, we take it that being able to distinguish non-inferentially between the wisdom of pursuing the first connection and the foolishness of the second is a symptom of philosophical competence.

Now precisely the fact that this feature of intellectual competence occurs prior to the formation of beliefs, or even of explicit hypotheses to test, may suggest to some that it has little bearing on epistemology proper, since the latter is concerned not with rational behaviour within the context of discovery, but only with the context of justification. Apart from our general sense – i.e., our intellectual *suspicion* – that any program which pursues a radical separation between the justification of hypotheses and the rationality of investigators studying them is itself a prime example of a misguided orientation to the issues, the current separation cannot work.

Any epistemology which rejects the quest for Cartesian certainty will concede in one way or another that a belief can be justified even though one has failed to rule out certain logically possible alternative views. In some versions, this point shows up in a requirement that we rule out "relevant potential defeators," or that our belief forming mechanisms be reliable across the range of "relevant alternatives to the actual situation." Whether it is recognized explicitly or not, then, any non-Cartesian epistemology will have to recognize that one's normative relation to various alternative possibilities is a crucial determinant of one's justificatory status. Whether one is justified in believing p will depend on whether or not one was justified in ignoring possibility q which is incompatible with p.

For illustration, let us put the point in reliabilist terms. (Of course we don't for a minute wish to endorse reliabilism as a general theory of epistemology). Suppose that both S and S' have failed to investigate possibility q, and that in both cases they have done so because of some internal state, emotional or otherwise, of the sort discussed above, which led them to take seriously p, p', p'', but not q. In both cases, the agent then comes to believe p, and for the same reasons, but suppose that the mechanism which led S to ignore q was highly unreliable, a pre-doxastic sense which regularly leads her to ignore true and important hypotheses, and often leads her to pursue frivolous and false ones. S's pre-doxastic sense, on the other hand, is reliable in the same manner. We take it that in this case we would have reason to think S' justified in believing p and S unjustified, even though the narrowly justificatory mechanisms employed to support p – i.e., those other than the attention-focusing mechanisms in question, are the same. And we take it that similar points could be made from the perspective of any plausible epistemology. Whether one is justified in believing *p* on the basis of *r*, can depend upon whether one was rational in never bothering to look into the possibility of *q*. So if there is a sort of mechanism that determines whether or not one does look into *q*, justification will depend upon having such a mechanism in good, rational working order.

Thus, it is not merely the rationality of *actions* that can depend on the having of the appropriate pre-doxastic salience generators. Jones's *belief that* Nf6 is the best move in a given situation may well derive its justification, in part, from the fact that Jones has a reasonable, over-riding concern for the safety of her king in the given position and, hence, no lust for that pawn on the queenside. This concern does not flow from any beliefs about, or inferences involving, the merits of each course of action, but rather takes the form of a failure ever to form hypotheses about the pawn-grabbing strategy.[2]

When we move away from a precisely constrained and well defined, inferential environment like chess, to the sort of messy and unbounded context either of ordinary life or of scientific inquiry, the plausibility that we could do without any salience generator is even less. Can we so much as *imagine* a rational Buffy who addressed issues concerning the bacteriological content of canine saliva, *and every other such issue*, on the way to formulating a plan of what to do regarding the ghost? We have already noted that there are limits that make it physically impossible to consider every possible continuation even in a game of chess. Given that one possibility, and often the most rational one, in any inferential situation is to augment the language by the introduction of new conceptual resources, the impossibility in ordi-

---

2 Much has been made of the case of chess competence by Hubert and Stuart Dreyfus. They use this case to build an argument against a purely computational conception of understanding, in favour of a notion in terms of tacit skills. Much of what we have to say here draws on and develops this work. Dreyfus and Dreyfus also develop their criticisms of AI from an explicitly Heideggerian perspective, one developed in most detail in Dreyfus's 1991 *Being in the World*. Though we don't pursue the historical points here, the idea that such epistemic competence is deeply indebted to emotional states which serve to align our comportment toward various issues is, at least on the surface, quite along the lines of Heidegger's discussion.

nary situations of a non-directed strategy of inference checking seems logical.

The picture we are urging, then, is one according to which there is a sort of modular division of epistemic labour. Some kind of pre-doxastic sense – apparently one which typically makes use of emotions – leads us to investigate a certain range of hypotheses, issues, conjectures, etc. After having been so led to the right bushes, we beat around in them by marshaling various inferential competencies in an attempt to secure entitlement to the assertion or denial of claims we find there. Here too, crucially, our choice of strategies for justification, of what inferences to pursue, what hypotheses to test, is guided by similar salience generators.

The upshot of our overly brief discussion of the importance of ignoring most potential objections suggests that no strategy for justification of p, short of deductive proof from indubitable premises, will constitute a status of justification in itself. It must always be assessed *qua* justification by an agent who is already warranted in considering those claims in the vicinity of p and ignoring many others. It is argumentative strategies *in the context of salience attunements* which fall within the proper scope of justificatory norms.

This is not to say that epistemic entitlement to such pre-doxastic salience generators is categorically prior to justified belief, or that one could be justified in strategies of investigation without already being justified in lots of particular beliefs the consideration of which would result from the employment of such strategies. Quite the contrary. Though it may well be that in each case the directing of attention to some subset of the space of propositions precedes the believing or justifying of any propositions within it, one who did not count as justified in many beliefs could not count as entitled to any focus of attention.

Obviously, highly theoretical beliefs about, for example, the supervenience of thought on material facts about the world, make it rational to turn our investigatory focus away from certain sorts of paranormal explanations of various phenomena. But the fact that the epistemic status of salience generators depends upon the agent's having justified beliefs, and vice versa, does not generate a pernicious sort of circularity, for neither sort of dependence is specifically justificatory. It is not as if we need *first* supply as a premise that it is reasonable to consider p, and then start the justification of p, nor that we must offer up a justification of p as *prior grounds for* our inclination to pursue the truth value of q.

The inclination to consider certain claims is non-inferential, but as Sellars argues famously in "Empiricism and the Philosophy of Mind" (1956), non-inferential justification is both a normative and a contextual matter. To say that one is non-inferentially justified in believing or doing something is a species of saying that they are entitled to it, the species which says that they are entitled without deriving that entitlement inferentially from something else. But to say that the entitlement does not derive from a process of inference is not to deny other forms of dependence upon background beliefs. In particular, it is perfectly consistent to say that only an agent who also holds a range of justified beliefs may be so entitled.

Thus, the point is simply that only when one's cognitive state reaches a level of complexity such that one is entitled to many salience inclinations and to many beliefs is one entitled to either. There is a division of epistemic labour within the cognitive structure of the knowing subject, but only someone who is competent at both jobs can count as competent at either.

II. Some Elementary Facts about Emotions

Though we make no claim to offer a complete account of the emotions, we need to note certain facts about them if we are to make plausible our claims concerning their epistemic role. First, a minor and uncontroversial point: emotions are not (or at least not only) affective states. Even feelings are probably not identifiable with purely affective states, but in any event emotions clearly involve much more.

One reason for this conclusion is that there are far more emotions than there are affective states, and in many cases two quite distinct emotions typically involve exactly the same affective states. More importantly, however, emotions are typically conceptually structured. We are afraid *of the tiger*, worried *about the state of the economy*, or lustfully attracted *to that boy in A Death In Venice*. We hasten to emphasize that this is not to say that emotions have beliefs as parts, or are propositionally structured. Typical emotional states do not entail the having of any belief. One can be afraid without believing that the object of fear is dangerous, or be in love without believing any particular good fact about the individual. And we don't even know what candidate would be put forward as the belief entailed by titillation, disgust, or solicitude. Nonetheless, emotions are individuated conceptually, typically in terms of a nominative object. Of course there is a large literature arguing that emotions are, or entail, beliefs. Rather than dealing directly with these arguments, we focus on the role emotions play in rationality, and then argue that the intuitive fact that they don't necessarily involve beliefs is explained by the fact that no belief state could perform their function in rationality.

To say that emotions are not equivalent to beliefs is not to deny that they can play a role in justification. Clearly they have a role in practical inference: one can run out of the room because one is scared of the tiger, and not merely in the causal sense of 'because'. The emotion can be the justification for the action, and we have been building the case that they can play a role in theoretical inference.

The intentional object of an emotion can even be a proposition: one is afraid *that the grease will catch fire*. Indeed, the grammar of emotion language is such that one can meaningfully insert any nominalization into the scope of most emotion terms. Thus, tokens of particular emotional attitudes are potentially as conceptually rich as any cognitive attitude. But even in the case of those emotions that take a propositional object, they do not *consist in* a belief. To be afraid that the grease will catch fire is not necessarily to believe that it will, and emotions, though conceptual, are not propositional attitudes in the sense of requiring a propositional content.

Finally, a point which will be of significance at a later stage of our argument: to have a particular emotion often requires that one be involved in particular social practices. Cross-cultural and historical psychologists have argued that there are many examples of emotions which exist only within particular cultures, and which seem to require the particular practices of that culture in order to make sense. To pick one example almost at random, Rom Harre (1986) discusses the emotion of acedia, which is, he says, something like a particular sort of alienation from, and lack of enthusiasm for, the doing of routine labour to the glory of God. Such an explanation is rather misleading, however, for it suggests that it is an emotion we are familiar with – a combination of alienation and boredom – with an unusual object tacked on. In fact, though, it was experienced as a unified and *sui generis* emotion.

Acedia was not only common in medieval society, but much discussed by moral philosophers, theologians, and psychologists, who devoted long discourses to the evaluation, diagnosis, and treatment of those suffering from it. Our point is that without the existence of particular theological beliefs as well as the practice of assigning particular routine tasks to people, especially monks, as part of a ritualized routine of spiritual devotion through labour, the very cognitive space for this emotion evaporates.[3] The point here is not that one cannot have the idea of the emotion except in the context of the relevant practice. We can have the idea of the emotion from reading Harre's discussion. The claim is that the emotion itself is a particular kind of rational comportment towards the practice, an intellectual orientation within it. Thus, while we can have an idea of the emotion, we cannot have the emotion.

The dependency of emotions on social context is also illustrated by the fact that, in many cases, the distinction between various categories of emotions has to do with the kind of claim that is likely to be in the air in the presence of that emotion, or with the sort of context in which the emotion is appropriately attributed. Thus, the distinction between jealousy and envy has to do with the fact that jealousy typically involves some sort of allegation of moral violation of one's entitlements. This is not to say that to be jealous is, necessarily, to *believe* that one has been morally wronged – one can be jealous and yet recognize that there are no grounds – but it is to say that jealousy can only arise in contexts in which the jealous person is able to postulate standards of morally correct behaviour, especially *vis-à-vis* her rights over things or people.[4]

Our suggestion is that an emotion of jealousy is precisely an attunement toward claims involving moral wrong to oneself. Those with the emotion share an epistemic orientation which assigns importance to the settling of issues of moral entitlement, and as such must exist within a social context within which such issues make sense. But such emotions need not share any specific propositional commitments.

---

3 We take the account of the historical case on faith from Rom Harre 1988.

4 In this regard, Rom Harre (1988) reports an experiment in which people were asked to state whether people in a situation were jealous or envious.

III. Why Emotions?

Supposing that one is willing to grant that a competent sense of focus or attunement is essential to rationality, the question remains as to why the states which generate this focus should be emotions. So far, we have merely pointed to some typical examples, with an eye to suggesting that it typically is emotions that serve this purpose. It seems hard to deny that emotions can be rational or irrational, and that actions, inferences, and beliefs are themselves often rational as a result of their relations to justified emotional states. But we would like to understand whether it is mere chance that emotions serve as the rational salience generators in humans, or whether there is some more significant unity to the various features of these mental states.

We consider three features of emotions: their intentional focus, their social embedding, and their affective quality. As for intentional focus, it is already clear that this characteristic is of a piece with their rational utility. As for social embedding, this fits naturally with the role of emotions in rationality insofar as one conceives of theoretical and practical rationality as themselves essentially social. For us this is quite far indeed. In V, we address certain key social elements of rationality which seem deeply tied to and only explicable in terms of the emotions, and in a fuller treatment of rationality, we would emphasize many systematic ways in which it is essentially embedded in society.

Finally, there is the matter of the affective quality of emotions. Here, plausibly, is an aspect of emotion tied to the particulars of human embodiment, but to say this is not, on our view, to disparage its importance. Indeed, among the reorienting morals we would like epistemologists to draw from the investigation of emotions, the need to see rationality not purely in formal-computational abstractions, but as an embodied practice essentially dependent upon the mechanisms of the body and their rationally choreographed integration with environment and society, figures prominently.[5]

Insofar as affective states are involved with behaviour – and there is a great deal of psychological literature tying many of the affective states of emotions, moods, and feelings, to particular brain chemicals

---

5 And we have each done some work in this direction. See Tanesini 1998, and Lance 1999 and 2000.

which themselves stimulate or facilitate particular sorts of bodily reaction – and insofar as the rational upshot of emotional attunements and the consequent beliefs is a rational demand for action, we will have an explanation of the importance of associating an emotion with an affective feel. For example, if flight is a practical consequence of typical beliefs that would be rationally arrived at after a reaction of fear, and if we humans flee better in the presence of brain chemicals which also generate a given affective state, then we would understand the association of fear with that affect.

Is there anything more general and essential to say in this connection?[6] We are inclined to think there is, but to discuss this matter would take us rather far afield, and our thought thereon is far from settled. What difference would it make to the points we are arguing here? If there is nothing more essential, then we could not claim to have argued that the salience generating states essential to rational agency must necessarily have the sorts of affective quality of many human emotions. Thus, if one wanted to think of these affective states as essential to something's being an emotion, one would not think of emotions as necessary for rationality. We would be more inclined to say that this showed that affect is inessential to emotion, since the role in the regulation of rational attention seems so much more significant, but little hangs on this. In any event, there is a particular task of rationality performed not by belief-like states, but by another sort of which human emotions are a species.

Before leaving this section, we offer the following important case described by the neurobiologist Antonio Damasio, whose work we became acquainted with after writing most of this paper.

Case 3:   This case involves a patient "Elliot" who suffered from a tumor, specifically a meningioma, which "had begun

---

6   One idea is that the affective quality of emotions allows us to track, or to keep in order, what our bodies are doing. This idea figures in the neurobiological discussion of Antonio Damasio, which we discuss below. Damasio's discussion here is difficult to understand and evaluate, however, because he seems to treat emotions and feelings as far too similar, and to ignore the intentional, conceptual aspect of emotions altogether. Despite these problems, we feel this line of thought worth pursuing.

growing in the midline area, just above the nasal cavities, above the plane formed by the roof of the eye sockets. As the tumor grew bigger, it compressed both frontal lobes" (Damasio 1994, 35). Surgery was required resulting in significant frontal lobe damage, specifically to areas known to govern emotional response. The description of the resulting impairment is telling:

Not only was Elliot coherent and smart, but clearly he knew what was occurring in the world around him. Dates, names, details in the news were all at his fingertips. He discussed political affairs with the humour they often deserve and seemed to grasp the situation of the economy.... Elliot's smarts and his ability to move about and use language were unscathed. In many ways, however, Elliot was no longer Elliot.

Consider the beginning of his day: he needed prompting to get started in the morning and prepare to go to work. Once at work he was unable to manage his time properly; he could not be trusted with a schedule. When the job called for interrupting an activity and turning to another, he might persist nonetheless, seemingly losing sight of his main goal. Or he might interrupt the activity he had engaged, to turn to something he found more captivating at that particular moment. Imagine a task involving reading and classifying documents of a given client. Elliot would read and fully understand the significance of the material, and he certainly knew how to sort out the documents according to the similarity or disparity of their content. The problem was that he was likely, all of a sudden, to turn from the sorting task he had initiated to reading one of those papers, carefully and intelligently .... Or he might spend a whole afternoon deliberating on which principle of categorization should be applied.... One might say that Elliot had become irrational concerning the larger frame of behavior, which pertained to his main priority.... His knowledge base seemed to survive, and he could perform many separate actions as well as before. But he could not be counted on to perform the appropriate action when it was expected.

To date we have studied twelve patients with prefrontal damage of the type seen in Elliot, and in none have we failed to encounter a combination of decision-making defect and flat emotion and feeling. The powers of reason and the experience of emotion decline together, and their impairment stands out in a neuropsychological profile within which basic attention, memory, intelligence, and language appear so intact that they could never be invoked to explain the patients' failures in judgment. (Damasio 1994, 35-7)

It is nice when one's *a priori* arguments receive empirical verification, but it may be thought that though these results are welcome, they do not support our account of the essential role of emotions in rationality. On our account, patients without emotional faculties should be even more impaired, not merely at large scale focus, but small scale as well. They should not calculate, reason, even take tests well, because they should fail to focus on particular inferences as much as on particular topics.

We have a suggestion. Note that the standard methodology for determining a connection between a site in the brain and a cognitive ability is essentially correlational. We determine that people with damage to a given area, and not to others, lack particular functions. That suggests that any reason to make such an association depends upon a prior understanding of what is involved in the cognitive or mental function. Not surprisingly, given the received opinion, emotions are understood in the psychological literature in a way far more limited than the one we are urging. As we emphasize in the next section, the fundamental emotions turn out, on our account, to be things like interest in, attention to, etc. And these are precisely the intellectual emotions which are essential to all forms of cognitive competence.

They are also the emotions least likely to be recognized as such by psychologists and neuropsychologists. These scientists, following most of the Western intellectual tradition, consider only more specific and obviously affective emotions such as love, anger, fear, etc. Why this focus obtains is an interesting matter of historical speculation. We tend to think it is deeply tied into the history of patriarchy within which there have been regular attempts, at least as far back as Aristotle, to associate women with emotion and men with reason.

Now if obviously intellectual emotions like interest, curiosity, and theoretical focus were taken to be emotions, this dichotomy would have been absurd on its face. Thus there was a need to draw the line at a point which excluded these from the category.

Our unargued speculative suggestion, then, is that ideology pushed categorization, that categorization led correlational neuropsychology, and as a result, tests like those of Damasio actually concern people who have only lost certain specific emotional functions while maintaining more basic, generic ones. That even they are so severely cognitively impaired is strong support for our orientation to the issues.

IV. Why Emotions Are Not Beliefs

Emotion concepts, as we have noted, need not have a propositional object. In many cases, the object of an emotion is *pre*positional. One is envious *of* Lyle Lovitt, or excited *about* the upcoming Superbowl. But some emotion words allow for propositional objects as well, as when one is worried that capitalist commodification is not amenable to piecemeal reform. In any case, there are clearly (at least) three semantically significant elements of each emotion sentence: the agent, the particular emotion, and the object of the emotion.

We suggested above that the epistemic point of an emotion is to direct attention toward the object, in the sense of making salient issues regarding that object. If we are right that emotions play this epistemic role of directing the attention, this suggests that something like interest is the most generic emotion. That is, we want to claim that all emotions involve some specific sort of interest in the object of that emotion.

We mean interest in a thin way, as implying nothing but a direction of the attention. Thus, our claim should not be seen as incompatible with the fact that boredom is an emotion. Of course generalized and undirected boredom is not an emotion on our account, but merely a feeling, but boredom with government sex scandals is an emotion, and our point is that to be bored specifically with government sex scandals is a way of being interested in them as we are using the term 'interest'. It is, as Heidegger would say, a comportment toward them. As we put it earlier, it is a way of taking them to be salient in one's intellectual life, though in this case with the goal of making them go away, at least from one's consciousness.

Our present need, in order to argue for the centrality of emotions to rationality, is to clarify the way in which any state playing the salience-generating epistemic role of emotions differs from the beliefs and other propositional attitudes which are the usual concern of epistemology. The point is quite simple. To direct attention to, say the tiger in the way that fear does is to treat as equally salient both 'the tiger is dangerous' and 'the tiger is not dangerous'. Part of what it is for the tiger to have been thrust upon one as salient to possible danger is for the issue of whether it is actually dangerous to become central to one's investigative activity. One is concerned to see whether it is securely chained up, whether one can successfully run away, etc. But if the relation is to two incompatible propositions – and many others besides – then it is not a belief. An emotion is not, in itself, an undertaking of justificatory responsibility regarding a content, but is an attending to a range of possible contents one might, upon examination of the evidence, come to undertake a commitment to, a set that will not even purport to internal consistency.

If one were to try to assimilate this sort of salience-generating mental state to the category of belief, the best attempt would be as the belief that 'one ought to attend to sentences in class C', where C is some class of relevant propositions, or 'one ought to attend to topic T'. There are several problems. The first – also the deepest and the one we most obviously cannot pursue within the bounds of this paper – is that this suggestion presupposes that normative judgments are actually beliefs. This is a questionable presupposition, having to do both with the proper understanding of normative judgment and with how we ought to understand the category of belief.[7] For now, suffice it to say that one can think of normative assertions as a kind of speech act which has as much in common with an imperative as with a declarative, and that to assimilate its role in reason to that of a belief raises several subtle issues.

A second objection, though more shallow, is easier to pursue within the context of the present discussion. This has to do with the possibility of specifying the class of claims we have labeled as C above. If

---

7 One of us has written in some detail on each of these topics. On normative claims, see Lance 1998 (especially Chapter 3). On belief, see Lance 1999.

the only way to specify the class is as the class of sentences that the emotion makes salient, then the suggestion that we understand the role of the emotion in terms of the role of a belief will be circular. In fact, it isn't even clear to us that there is, in reality, a fixed and specific set of sentences toward which the emotion directs us. Our conception of rationality is that it is ultimately reliant on skill. What rational emotional attunement gives one is a skill at navigating the conceptual world of investigation. Just as one can know how to ride a bicycle, or to assess the significant dangers of a chess position, without being able to state a set of principles determinative of that skill, so our claim is that emotional attunements are ways of being directed toward a set of issues and concerns which operate on the level of skillful behaviour. To have such an attunement is to be able to attend to the right things, not to be able to state what these are, much less to capture theoretically how it is that one attends to them.

Nor does it help to say that the belief is that one ought to attend to the subject-matter of the belief, for part of the skill generated by the emotion is that it direct one to particular features of the subject matter, specific claims that call for investigation. When one is afraid of the tiger, not all aspects of tiger-studies become salient. One is not concerned with the tiger's blood type – unless one has a blood type–specific poison at the ready. Thus, again, the epistemic role of the emotion is not captured by any belief, for the emotion makes salient the subject matter in a specific way, one that directs our attention to certain sentences and not others.

So our first claim about the function of emotions is that in us humans they serve the role of salience generators. They direct our attention toward a loosely bounded class of sentences and recommend them as properly worthy of the sorts of epistemic attention we are used to considering: as worth gathering evidence for or against, as worth considering as sources of evidence for other claims, as worth acting upon. Not only do they perform this job, but the job is different from, and prior to, the sorts of jobs done by belief and inference.

Further, not only rationality, but justification and knowledge depend upon being well-attuned emotionally. Of course it can be reasonable to run away from the tiger, because it is reasonable to be afraid of it. It is also reasonable to think that someone will change the subject, because it is reasonable to be bored with the discussion. More importantly, one can be unjustified in believing in his friend's inno-cence because he should have been suspicious of her story, or ratio-nally inclined to doubt that an accepted theory is defensible because he is interested in an apparent anomaly. In short, what one is justified in believing depends upon what possibilities, what issues, one is justi-fied in ignoring. The choice to consider or to ignore a given issue is one that is based upon a tacit skill at navigating the space of possible issues. Thus, rational navigation of that space is a precondition for the holding of justified beliefs. Put another way, the significant difference between two people, one of whom is justified in believing *p* and the other of whom is not, can be that the former has, and the latter lacks, the relevant emotional attunement.

V. Dialogical Emotions and Rational Communities

We are particularly interested in certain interpersonal emotions which serve a crucial role in constituting rational discourse. We discussed earlier how social contexts are required for the existence of certain emotions, how those emotions only make sense and serve their par-ticular cognitive role against the background of particular social prac-tices. What the present examples will illustrate is the converse of this, that certain emotions serve to *constitute* practices.

This idea is not new. Indeed, it is a familiar view in ethics and polit-ical theory to suppose that various sorts of emotional engagement are constitutive of moral community. What we want to emphasize here is the way that they are constitutive of rational, dialogical social prac-tice.

To illustrate this is to take issue with a particular sort of Kantian ethicist, namely the sort who actually follows the views of Kant. This sort of Kantian denies that emotions are essential to moral life on the grounds that what it is to be a moral agent is merely to be a rational agent, and that morally correct behaviour is reducible to some sort of practical rationality accessible by any rational agent. The current discussion undercuts this move by attempting to show that rational agency itself requires emotional involvements of a particular sort.

V.i. Fallibilism

Fallibilism is generally thought to be an intellectual virtue. We take this not only to be true, but a basic fact of rationality. That is, rather than following by analogy a consequentialist account of virtue and saying that to be an intellectual virtue is to be the sort of state which leads to truth, we are inclined to say that rationality is inherently and fundamentally a matter of virtue, and that our grip on the likelihood of reaching truth is always dependent upon a prior assessment of intellectual virtue. But for now, this dispute need not detain us, since our goal is only to consider what the virtue is, not that in virtue of which it is a virtue.

Attempts to capture the intuitive virtue of fallibilism while producing an account that leaves it recognizably virtuous have always run into difficulty. Intuitively, fallibilism is the thesis that epistemic agents ought to exhibit an appropriate level of intellectual humility, ought to recognize that their epistemic practice is fallible, that in some sense they might be wrong.

The most natural readings of the claim that one might be wrong, however, clearly fail to capture the virtue in question. Certainly the ideal is not that we ought to take none of our beliefs to be necessary truths. We, to speak only for ourselves, have many beliefs about modal matters, and take many such claims to be necessarily true. But surely those of us who embrace the virtue of fallibilism think it a virtue even when we are discussing necessities.

Nor does the obvious epistemic reading seem to work. On this reading, fallibilism would come to the view that one's evidence was never sufficient to guarantee any claim, or that one's evidence never makes it rational to assign subjective probability of 1 to any claim. This is a principle which is somewhat more defensible than the *nothing is necessary* principle, but still seems to miss the point. We can think, quite reasonably, that we do have sufficient evidence, argument, or whatnot, to make a claim certain, without abandoning our epistemic humility in the relevant sense. Conversely, merely thinking that our claim is not certain is no mark of humility, as is evidenced by many actually existing Bayesians.

What we want to suggest is that we think of fallibilism – epistemic humility – as a kind of emotional state directed toward other agents in a dialogue, or toward positions incompatible with one's own. To be epistemically humble is not to believe that it is metaphysically or epistemically possible that one's view be false, but to be *open* in the right way to alternative views. It is to take as salient – specifically, as placing upon one a demand to listen attentively, attempt to understand, and assess fairly – views put forward as challenges to one's own.

We are all familiar with the phenomenon – sadly at least as common in philosophical circles as it is in the wider world – of a person who is perfectly rational in all those ways capturable as logical principles, a person who keeps their views consistent, gives reasons which relate in the right ways to their conclusions, marshals evidence, makes distinctions, etc., and to whom there is nonetheless simply no point whatsoever in talking. The familiarity of this phenomenon, the importance to the progress of rational dialogue of our *not* being this way and recognizing those who are, and the resistance of such dialogical irrationalities to principle-based cures, suggests that epistemology must take account of the distinction between those who *really listen* and attempt to understand another's position, and those who are unwilling to listen and dogmatic, yet able to be so with logical facility. This distinction is *constituted by* interpersonal emotions, emotions which thereby serve to constitute us collectively as an intellectual community.

V.ii. Other Interpersonal Emotions

Similar remarks apply to many other intellectual emotions. Since we cannot begin to discuss them all here, or any in sufficient detail, we confine ourselves to imploring epistemologists to take up the issue of the proper understanding and regulation of such crucial rational emotions as openness (to new ideas), suspicion (of certain explanations), critical distance (from one's own and one's teachers' views), interest (in specific topics and leads), sympathy for (unusual opinions), hostility to (foolish approaches to a problem), recognitions (of salience, as in, for example, certain medical results to questions in epistemology), curiosity (for new data, as in the Popperian imperative), discomfort (with theoretical tensions and anomalies), etc.

Our discussion of emotions, then, leads us to epistemic virtues, but not virtues understood in a derivative sense as that which reliably leads to truth, justification, or some other epistemic good. Rather, we seem to be heading towards a robust sense of epistemic virtue, toward a virtue epistemology which must grapple with such issues as the unity of the rational virtues, the nature of skills and embodiment, with particularism versus regulism, and with the nature of normativity. To so focus is to depart radically from an epistemological enterprise captivated by internalism and externalism, foundations, or the fourth condition on knowledge.

So much the better.[8]

References

Damasio, A.R. 1994. *Descartes' Error: Emotion, Reason,* and the Human Brain. New York: Avon Books.

Dreyfus, H.L. 1991. *Being in the World.* Cambridge, MA: MIT Press.

Elgin, C. Z. 1999. *Considered Judgment.* Princeton: Princeton University Press.

Harre, R. 1986. *The Social Construction of Emotions.* Oxford: Blackwell.

Lance, M. 1998. *The Grammar of Meaning.* Cambridge: Cambridge University Press.

———. 1999. "Some Reflections on the Sport of Language." In *Philosophical Perspectives 12: Language, Mind, and Ontology,* ed. J. Tomberlin, 219–40. Oxford: Blackwell.

———. 2000. "The Word Made Flesh: Toward a Neo-Sellarsian View of Concepts, Analysis, and Understanding." *Acta Analytica* 15 (25): 117–35.

Sellars, W. 1956. Empiricism and the Philosophy of Mind, eds. R. Brandom and R. Rorty,1997. Cambridge, MA: Harvard University Press.

Tanesini, A. 1998. *An Introduction to Feminist Epistemologies.* Oxford: Blackwell.

---

8 A number of people have been helpful to us in the development of the ideas in this paper. In particular, Rebecca Kukla, Richard Manning, and Maggie Little discussed these issues with us in depth after reading an earlier draft of the paper. Rob Stainton made many helpful comments on the penultimate version. We should also mention that the view here has some features in common with that of Catherine Z. Elgin, who also talks of emotions as salience-generators in Chapter 5 of Elgin 1999.

CANADIAN JOURNAL OF PHILOSOPHY
Supplementary Volume 30

Reading One's Own Mind: Self-Awareness and Developmental Psychology

SHAUN NICHOLS AND STEPHEN STICH

I Introduction

The idea that we have special access to our own mental states has a distinguished philosophical history. Philosophers as different as Descartes and Locke agreed that we know our own minds in a way that is quite different from the way in which we know other minds. In the latter half of the twentieth century, however, this idea came under serious attack, first from philosophy (Sellars 1956) and more recently from developmental psychology.[1] The attack from developmental psychology arises from the growing body of work on "mindreading," the process of attributing mental states to people (and other organisms). During the last fifteen years, the processes underlying mindreading have been a major focus of attention in cognitive and developmental psychology. Most of this work has been concerned with the processes underlying the attribution of mental states to *other people*. However, a number of psychologists and philosophers have also proposed accounts of the mechanisms underlying the attribution of mental states to *oneself*. This process of *reading one's own mind* or *becoming self-aware* will be our primary concern in this paper.

We'll start by examining what is probably the most widely held account of self-awareness in this literature, the "Theory Theory" (TT).

---

1 For more on Sellars' role in this challenge to the traditional view, see Stich and Ravenscroft 1994.

The basic idea of the TT of self-awareness is that one's access to one's own mind depends on the same cluster of cognitive mechanisms that plays a central role in attributing mental states to others. Those mechanisms include a body of information about psychology, a Theory of Mind (ToM). Though many authors have endorsed the Theory Theory of self-awareness (Gopnik 1993, Gopnik and Wellman 1994, Gopnik and Meltzoff 1994, Perner 1991, Wimmer and Hartl 1991, Carruthers 1996, C. Frith 1994, U. Frith and Happé 1999), it is our contention that advocates of this account of self-awareness have left their theory seriously under-described. In the next section, we'll suggest three different ways in which the TT account might be elaborated, all of which have significant shortcomings. In Section III, we'll present our own theory of self-awareness, the Monitoring Mechanism Theory, and compare its merits to those of the TT. Theory Theorists argue that the TT is supported by evidence about psychological development and psychopathologies; in Section IV we will review the developmental arguments and try to show that none of the evidence favours the TT over our Monitoring Mechanism Theory. Indeed, we'll maintain that a closer look at the evidence on development actually provides arguments *against* the TT.[2] Elsewhere, we consider the evidence from psychopathologies (Nichols and Stich 2003a, Nichols and Stich 2003b). Nichols and Stich 2003a is intended as a companion piece to this article. There, too, we argue that despite the advertisements, the evidence – in that paper our focus is on the evidence concerning psychopathologies – poses a problem for the Theory Theory.

We should note that there is considerable overlap between the present paper and Nichols and Stich 2003a. In both papers, we consider whether the evidence favours the Theory Theory or the Monitoring Mechanism Theory, and the theoretical background against which the arguments are developed is largely the same in both papers. So the

---

2 Although the Theory Theory is the most prominent account of self-awareness in this literature, there are two other widely discussed theories of self-awareness to be found in the recent literature: Alvin Goldman's (1993a, 1993b, 1997, 2000) phenomenological account and Robert Gordon's "ascent routine" account (Gordon 1995, 1996). We think that neither of these accounts can capture the basic facts about self-awareness, and we make our case against them in Nichols and Stich 2003a.

(cherished) reader familiar with that companion paper might skip to Section IV herein, where we take on the developmental arguments. We now turn to the task of setting out the background for the debate. Mindreading skills, in both the first person and the third person cases, can be divided into two categories which, for want of better labels, we'll call *detecting* and *reasoning*. *Detecting* is the capacity to *attribute* current mental states to someone. *Reasoning* is the capacity to *use* information about a person's mental states (typically along with other information) to make predictions about the person's past and future mental states, her behaviour, and her environment. So, for instance, one might *detect* that another person wants ice cream and that the person thinks the closest place to get ice cream is at the corner shop. Then one might *reason* from this information that, since the person wants ice cream and thinks that she can get it at the corner shop, she will go to the shop. The distinction between detecting and reasoning is an important one, because some of the theories we'll be considering offer integrated accounts on which detecting and reasoning are explained by the same cognitive mechanism. Other theories, including ours, maintain that in the first person case, these two aspects of mindreading are subserved by different mechanisms.

Like the other authors we'll be considering, we take it to be a requirement on theories of self-awareness that they offer an explanation for:

i. the obvious facts about self-attribution (e.g., that normal adults do it easily and often, that they are generally accurate, and that they have no clear idea of how they do it.)

ii. the often rather un-obvious facts about self-attribution that have been uncovered by cognitive and developmental psychologists (e.g., Gopnik and Slaughter 1991, Ericsson and Simon 1993, Nisbett and Wilson 1977).

However, we *do not* take it to be a requirement on theory building in this area that the theory address philosophical puzzles that have been raised about knowledge of one's own mental states.

In recent years, philosophers have had a great deal to say about the link between content externalism and the possibility that people can have privileged knowledge about their own propositional attitudes (e.g., McLaughlin and Tye 1998).[3] These issues are largely orthogonal to the sorts of questions about underlying mechanisms that we will be discussing in this paper, and we have nothing at all to contribute to the resolution of the philosophical puzzles posed by externalism. But in the unlikely event that philosophers who worry about such matters agree on solutions to these puzzles, we expect that the solutions will fit comfortably with our theory.

There is one last bit of background that needs to be made explicit before we begin. The theory we'll set out will help itself to two basic assumptions about the mind. We call the first of these *the basic architecture assumption*. What it claims is that a well-known commonsense account of the architecture of the cognitive mind is largely correct, though obviously incomplete. This account of cognitive architecture, which has been widely adopted both in cognitive science and in philosophy, maintains that in normal humans, and probably in other organisms as well, the mind contains two quite different kinds of representational states, beliefs and desires. These two kinds of states differ "functionally" because they are caused in different ways and have different patterns of interaction with other components of the mind. Some beliefs are caused fairly directly by perception; others are derived from pre-existing beliefs via processes of deductive and non-deductive inference. Some desires (like the desire to get something to drink or the desire to get something to eat) are caused by systems that monitor various bodily states. Other desires, sometimes called "instrumental desires" or "sub-goals," are generated by a process of practical reasoning that has access to beliefs and to pre-existing desires. In addition to generating sub-goals, the practical reasoning system must also determine which structure of goals and sub-goals is to be acted upon at any time. Once made, that decision is passed on

---

3 Content externalism is the view that the content of one's mental states (what the mental states are about) is determined at least in part by factors external to one's mind. In contemporary analytic philosophy, the view was motivated largely by Putnam's Twin Earth thought experiments (Putnam 1975) that seem to show that two molecule for molecule twins can have thoughts with different meanings, apparently because of their different external environments.

to various action controlling systems whose job it is to sequence and coordinate the behaviours necessary to carry out the decision. Figure 1 is a sketch of the basic architecture assumption.

Figure 1. The basic architecture of the cognitive mind.

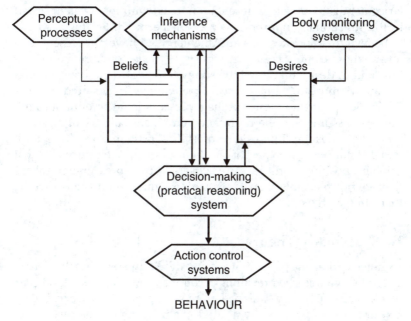

We find diagrams like this to be very helpful in comparing and clarifying theories about mental mechanisms, and we'll make frequent use of them in this paper. It is important, however, that the diagrams not be misinterpreted. Positing a "box" in which a certain category of mental states is located is simply a way of depicting the fact that those states share an important cluster of causal properties that are not shared by other types of states in the system. There is no suggestion that all the states in the box share a spatial location in the brain. Nor does it follow that there can't be significant and systematic differences among the states within a box. When it becomes important to emphasize such differences, we use boxes within boxes or other obvious notational devices. All of this applies as well to processing mechanisms, like the inference mechanism and the practical reasoning mechanism, which we distinguish by using hexagonal boxes.

Our second assumption, which we'll call *the representational account of cognition*, maintains that beliefs, desires and other propositional attitudes are relational states. To have a belief or a desire with a particular content is to have a representation token with that content stored in the functionally appropriate way in the mind. So, for example, to believe that Socrates was an Athenian is to have a representation token whose content is *Socrates was an Athenian* stored in one's Belief Box, and to desire that it will be sunny tomorrow is to have a representation whose content is *It will be sunny tomorrow* stored in one's Desire Box. Many advocates of the representational account of cognition also assume that the representation tokens subserving propositional attitudes are linguistic or quasi-linguistic in form. This additional assumption is no part of our theory, however. If it turns out that some propositional attitudes are subserved by representation tokens that are not plausibly viewed as having a quasi-linguistic structure, that's fine with us.

II. The Theory Theory

As noted earlier, the prevailing account of self-awareness is the Theory Theory. Of course, the prevailing account of how we understand *other minds* is also a Theory Theory. Before setting out the Theory Theory account of reading one's own mind, it's important to be clear about how the Theory Theory proposes to explain our capacity to read other minds.[4]

---

4 In previous publications on the debate between the Theory Theory and Simulation Theory, we have defended the Theory Theory of how we understand other minds (Stich and Nichols 1992, Stich and Nichols 1995, Nichols *et al.* 1995, Nichols *et al.* 1996). More recently, we've argued that the Simulation–Theory Theory debate has outlived its usefulness, and productive debate will require more detailed proposals and sharper distinctions (Stich and Nichols 1997; Nichols and Stich 1998). In this paper, we've tried to sidestep these issues by granting the Theory Theorist as much as possible. We maintain that even if *all* attribution and reasoning about other minds depends on theory, that still won't provide the Theory Theorist with the resources to accommodate the facts about self-awareness.

II.i. The Theory Theory Account of Reading Other People's Minds

According to the Theory Theory, the capacity to *detect* other people's mental states relies on a theory-mediated inference. The theory that is invoked is a Theory of Mind which some authors (e.g., Fodor 1992; Leslie 1994b) conceive of as a special purpose body of knowledge housed in a mental module, and others (e.g., Gopnik and Wellman 1994) conceive of as a body of knowledge that is entirely parallel to other theories, both commonsense and scientific. For some purposes, the distinction between the modular and the just-like-other-(scientific)-theories versions of the Theory Theory is of great importance. But for our purposes it is not. So in most of what follows we propose to ignore it (but see Stich and Nichols 1998). On all versions of the Theory Theory, when we detect another person's mental state, the theory-mediated inference can draw on perceptually available information about the behaviour of the target and about her environment. It can also draw on information stored in memory about the target and her environment. A sketch of the mental mechanisms invoked in this account is given in Figure 2.

Figure 2. Theory Theory of detecting others' mental states.

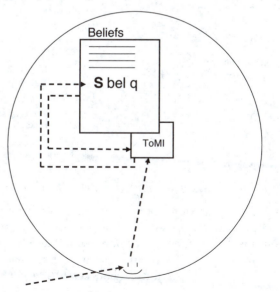

The theory that underlies the capacity to *detect* other people's mental states also underlies the capacity to *reason* about other people's mental states and thereby predict their behaviour. Reasoning about other people's mental states is thus a theory-mediated inference process, and the inferences draw on beliefs about (*inter alia*) the target's mental states. Of course, some of these beliefs will themselves have been produced by detection inferences. When detecting and reasoning are depicted together, we get Figure 3.

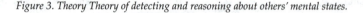

Figure 3. Theory Theory of detecting and reasoning about others' mental states.

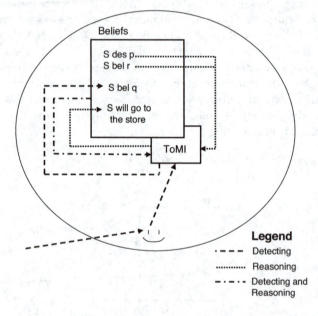

II.ii. Reading One's Own Mind: Three Versions of the TT Account

The Theory Theory account of how we read other minds can be extended to provide an account of how we read our own minds. Indeed, both the Theory Theory for understanding other minds and the Theory Theory for self-awareness seem to have been first proposed in the same article by Wilfrid Sellars (1956). The core idea of the

TT account of self-awareness is that the process of reading one's own mind is largely or entirely parallel to the process of reading someone else's mind. Advocates of the Theory Theory of self-awareness maintain that knowledge of one's own mind, like knowledge of other minds, comes from a theory-mediated inference, and the theory that mediates the inference is the same for self and other – it's the Theory of Mind. In recent years, many authors have endorsed this idea; here are two examples:

> Even though we seem to perceive our own mental states directly, this direct perception is an illusion. In fact, our knowledge of ourselves, like our knowledge of others, is the result of a theory, and depends as much on our experience of others as on our experience of ourselves. (Gopnik and Meltzoff 1994, 168)
> … if the mechanism which underlies the computation of mental states is dysfunctional, then self-knowledge is likely to be impaired just as is the knowledge of other minds. The logical extension of the ToM [Theory of Mind] deficit account of autism is that individuals with autism may know as little about their own minds as about the minds of other people. This is not to say that these individuals lack mental states, but that in an important sense they are unable to reflect on their mental states. Simply put, they lack the cognitive machinery to represent their thoughts and feelings as thoughts and feelings. (Frith and Happé 1999, 7)

As we noted earlier, advocates of the TT account of self-awareness are much less explicit than one would like, and unpacking the view in different ways leads to significantly different versions of the TT account. But all of them share the claim that the processes of reasoning about and detecting one's own mental states will parallel the processes of reasoning about and detecting others' mental states. Since the process of *detecting* one's own mental states will be our focus, it's especially important to be very explicit about the account of detection suggested by the Theory Theory of self-awareness. According to the TT:

> i. Detecting one's own mental states is a theory-mediated inferential process. The theory, here as in the third person

case, is ToM (either a modular version or a just-like-other-(scientific)-theories version, or something in between).

ii. As in the third person case, the capacity to detect one's own mental states relies on a theory-mediated inference which draws on perceptually available information about one's own behaviour and environment. The inference also draws on information stored in memory about oneself and one's environment.

At this point the TT account of self-awareness can be developed in at least three different ways. So far as we know, advocates of the TT have never taken explicit note of the distinctions. Thus it is difficult to determine which version a given theorist would endorse.

II.ii.i Theory Theory Version 1

Theory Theory version 1 (for which our code name is *the crazy version*) proposes to maintain the parallel between detecting one's own mental states and detecting another person's mental states quite strictly. The *only* information used as evidence for the inference involved in detecting one's own mental states is the information provided by perception (in this case, perception of oneself) and by one's background beliefs (in this case, background beliefs about one's own environment and previously acquired beliefs about one's own mental states). This version of TT is sketched in Figure 4.

Of course, we typically have much more information about our own minds than we do about other minds, so even on this version of the Theory Theory we may well have a *better* grasp of our own mind than we do of other minds (see, e.g., Gopnik 1993, 94). However, the mechanisms underlying self-awareness are supposed to be the same mechanisms that underlie awareness of the mental states of others. Thus, this version of the TT denies the widely held view that an individual has some kind of special or privileged access to his own mental states.

We are reluctant to claim that anyone actually advocates this version of the TT, since we think it is a view that is hard to take seriously. Indeed, the claim that *perception of one's own behaviour* is the prime source of information on which to base inferences about one's own mental states reminds us of the old joke about the two behaviourists who meet on the street. One says to the other, "You're fine. How am I?" The reason the joke works is that it seems patently absurd to think that perception of one's behaviour is the best way to find out how one is feeling. It seems obvious that people can sit quietly without exhibiting any relevant behaviour and report on their current thoughts. For instance, people can answer questions about current mental states like "What are you thinking about?" Similarly, after silently working a problem in their heads, people can answer subsequent questions like "How did you figure that out?" And we typically assume that people are correct when they tell us what they were thinking or how they just solved a problem. Of course, it's not just one's current and immediately past *thoughts* that one can report; one can also report one's own current desires, intentions, and imaginings. It seems that people can easily and reliably answer questions like, "What do you want to do?"; "What are you going to do?"; "What are you imagining?" People who aren't exhibiting much behaviour at all are often able to provide richly detailed answers to these questions. These more or less intuitive

Figure 4. Theory Theory of self-awareness, version 1.

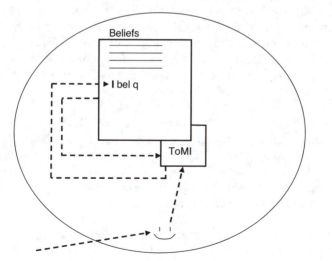

claims are backed by considerable empirical evidence from research programs in psychology (see, e.g., Ericsson and Simon 1993).

So, both commonsense and experimental studies confirm that people can sit quietly, exhibiting next to no overt behaviour, and give detailed, accurate self-reports about their mental states. In light of this, it strikes us as simply preposterous to suggest that the reports people make about their own mental states are being inferred from perceptions of their own behaviour and information stored in memory. For it's simply absurd to suppose that there is enough behavioural evidence or information stored in memory to serve as a basis for accurately answering questions like "What are you thinking about now?" or "How did you solve that math problem?" Our ability to answer questions like these indicates that Version 1 of the Theory Theory of self-awareness can't be correct, since it can't accommodate some central cases of self-awareness.

II.ii.ii. Theory Theory Version 2

Version 2 of the Theory Theory (for which our code name is *the underdescribed version*) allows that in using ToM to infer to conclusions about one's own mind, there is information available *in addition to* the information provided by perception and one's background beliefs. This additional information is available only in the first person case, not in the third person case. Unfortunately, advocates of the TT say very little about what this alternative source of information is. And what little they do say about it is unhelpful, to put it mildly. Here, for instance, is an example of the sort of thing that Gopnik has said about this additional source of information:

> One possible source of evidence for the child's theory may be first person psychological experiences that may themselves be the consequence of genuine psychological perceptions. For example, we may well be equipped to detect certain kinds of internal cognitive activity in a vague and unspecified way, what we might call "*the Cartesian buzz*." (Gopnik 1993, 11)

We have no serious idea what the "Cartesian buzz" is, or how one would detect it. Nor do we understand how detecting the Cartesian buzz will enable the ToM to infer to conclusions like: *I want to spend next Christmas in Paris* or *I believe that the Brooklyn Bridge is about eight blocks south of the Manhattan Bridge.* Figure 5 is our attempt to sketch Version 2 of the TT account.

Figure 5. Theory Theory of self-awareness, version 2.

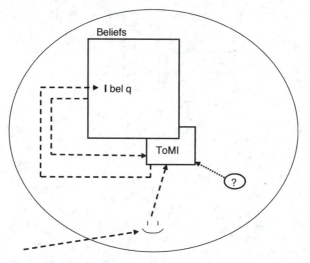

We won't bother to mount a critique against this version of the account, apart from observing that without some less mysterious statement of what the additional source(s) of information are, the theory is too incomplete to evaluate.

II.ii.iii. Theory Theory Version 3

There is, of course, one very natural way to spell out what's missing in Version 2. What is needed is some source of information that would help a person form beliefs (typically, true beliefs) about his own mental states. The obvious source of information would be the mental states themselves. So, on this version of the TT, the ToM has access to information provided by perception, information provided by background beliefs, *and information about the representations contained in the Belief Box, the Desire Box, etc.* This version of the TT is sketched in Figure 6.

Figure 6. Theory Theory of self-awareness, version 3.

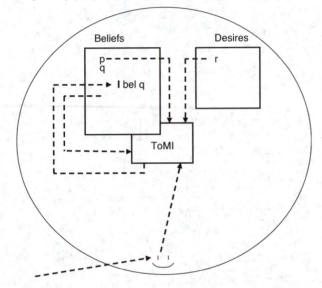

Now at this juncture, one might wonder why the ToM is *needed* in this story. If the mechanism subserving self-awareness has access to information about the representations in the various attitude boxes, then ToM has no serious work to do. So why suppose that it is involved at all? That's a good question, we think. And it's also a good launching pad for our theory, because on our account, Figure 6 has it wrong. In detecting one's own mental states, the flow of information is *not* routed through the ToM. Rather, the process is subserved by a separate, self-monitoring mechanism.

III. Reading One's Own Mind: The Monitoring Mechanism Theory

In constructing our theory about the process that subserves self-awareness we've tried to be, to borrow a phrase from Nelson Goodman

(1983, 60) "refreshingly non-cosmic." What we propose is that we need to add another component or cluster of components to the basic picture of cognitive architecture, a mechanism (or mechanisms) that serves (serve) the function of monitoring one's own mental states.

III.i. The Monitoring Mechanism and Propositional Attitudes

Recall what the theory of self-awareness needs to explain. The basic facts are that when normal adults believe that *p*, they can quickly and accurately form the belief *I believe that p*; when normal adults desire that *p*, they can quickly and accurately form the belief *I desire that p*; and so on for the rest of the propositional attitudes. In order to implement this ability, no sophisticated Theory of Mind is required. All that is required is that there be a Monitoring Mechanism (MM) (or perhaps a set of mechanisms) that, when activated, takes (take) the representation *p* in the Belief Box as input and produces (produce) the representation *I believe that p* as output. This mechanism would be trivial to implement. To produce representations of one's own beliefs, the Monitoring Mechanism merely has to copy representations from the Belief Box, embed the copies in a representation schema of the form *I believe that* ___, and then place the new representations back in the Belief Box. The proposed mechanism would work in much the same way to produce representations of one's own desires, intentions, and imaginings.[5] This account of the process of self-awareness is sketched in Figure 7.

Although we propose that the MM is a special mechanism for detecting one's own mental states, we maintain that there is no special mechanism for what we earlier called *reasoning about* one's own mental

---

5 Apart from the cognitive science trappings, the idea of an internal monitor goes back at least to David Armstrong (1968) and has been elaborated by William Lycan (1987), among others. However, much of this literature has become intertwined with the attempt to determine the proper account of consciousness, and that is not our concern at all. Rather, on our account, the monitor is just a rather simple information-processing mechanism that generates explicit representations about the representations in various components of the mind and places these new representations in the Belief Box.

states. Rather, reasoning about one's own mental states depends on the same Theory of Mind as reasoning about others' mental states. As a result, our theory (as well as the TT) predicts that, *ceteris paribus*, where the ToM is deficient or the relevant information is unavailable, subjects will make mistakes in reasoning about their own mental states as well as others'. This allows our theory to accommodate findings like those presented by Nisbett and Wilson (1977). They report a number of studies in which subjects make mistakes about their own mental states. However, the kinds of mistakes that are made in those experiments are typically not mistakes in *detecting* one's own mental states. Rather, the studies show that subjects make mistakes in *reasoning about* their own mental states.

The central findings are that subjects sometimes attribute their behaviour to inefficacious beliefs, and that subjects sometimes deny the efficacy of beliefs that are, in fact, efficacious. For instance, Nisbett

Figure 7. *Monitoring Mechanism Theory of self-awareness for beliefs.*

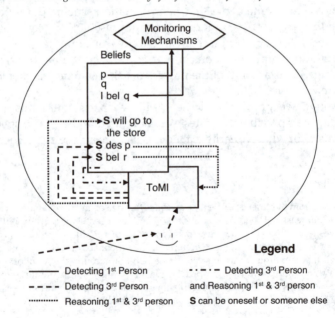

and Schacter (1966) found that subjects were willing to tolerate more intense shocks if the subjects were given a drug (actually a placebo) and told that the drug would produce heart palpitations, irregular breathing, and butterflies in the stomach. Although being told about the drug had a significant effect on the subjects' willingness to take shocks, most subjects denied this. Nisbett and Wilson's explanation of these findings is, plausibly enough, that subjects have an incomplete theory regarding the mind and that the subjects' mistakes reflect the inadequacies of their theory (Nisbett and Wilson 1977).

This explanation of the findings fits well with our account, too. For on our account, when trying to figure out the *causes* of one's own behaviour, one must reason about mental states, and this process is mediated by the ToM. As a result, if the ToM is not up to the task, then people will make mistakes in reasoning about their own mental states as well as others' mental states.

In this paper, we propose to remain agnostic about the extent to which ToM is innate. However, we do propose that the MM (or cluster of MMs) is (are) innate and comes (come) on line fairly early in development – significantly before ToM is fully in place. During the period when the Monitoring Mechanism is up and running but ToM is not, the representations that the MM produces can't do much. In particular, they can't serve as premises for reasoning about mental states, since reasoning about mental states is a process mediated by ToM. So, for example, ToM provides the additional premises (or the special purpose inferential strategies) that enable the mind to go from premises like *I want q* to conclusions like *If I believed that doing A was the best way to get q, then (probably) I would want to do A*. Thus our theory predicts that young children can't reason about their own beliefs in this way.

Although we want to leave open the extent to which ToM is innate, we maintain (along with many Theory Theorists) that ToM comes on line only gradually. As it comes on line, it enables a richer and richer set of inferences from the representations of the form *I believe (or desire) that p* that are produced by the MM.

Some might argue that early on in development, these representations of the form *I believe that p* don't really count as having the content *I believe that p*, since the concept (or "proto-concept") of belief is too inferentially impoverished. On this view, it is only after a rich set of inferences becomes available that the child's *I believe that p* representations really count as having the content *I believe that p*. To make a persuasive case for or against this view, one would need a well-motivated and carefully defended theory of content for concepts. And we don't happen to have one. (Indeed, at least one of us is inclined to suspect that much recent work aimed at constructing theories of content is deeply misguided [Stich 1992, 1996].) But, with this caveat, we don't have any objection to the claim that early *I believe that p* representations don't have the content *I believe that p*.

If that's what your favourite theory of content says, that's fine with us. Our proposal can be easily rendered consistent with such a view of content by simply replacing the embedded mental predicates (e.g., *'believe'*) with technical terms 'bel', 'des', 'pret', etc. We might then say that the MM produces the belief that *I bel that p* and the belief that *I des that q*; and that at some point further on in development, these beliefs acquire the content *I believe that p*, *I desire that q*, and so forth. That said, we propose to ignore this subtlety for the rest of the paper.

The core claim of our theory is that the MM is a distinct mechanism that is specialized for detecting one's own mental states.[6] However, it is important to note that on our account of mindreading, the MM is not the *only* mental mechanism that can generate representations with the content *I believe that p*; representations of this sort can also be generated by ToM. Thus it is possible that in some cases, the ToM and the MM will produce *conflicting* representation of the form *I believe that p*. For instance, if the Theory of Mind is deficient, then in some cases it might produce an inaccurate representation with the content *I believe that p* which conflicts with accurate representations generated by the MM. In these cases, our theory does not specify how the conflict will be resolved or which representation will guide verbal behaviour and other actions. On our view, it is an open, empirical question how

---

6 As we've presented our theory, the MM is a mechanism that is distinct from the ToM. But it might be claimed that the MM that we postulate is just a *part* of the ToM. Here the crucial question to ask is whether it is a "dissociable" part which could be selectively damaged or selectively spared. If the answer is no, then we think the evidence counts against this view (Nichols and Stich 2003a). If the answer is yes (MM is a dissociable part of ToM), then there is nothing of substance left to fight about: that theory is a notational variant of ours.

such conflicts will be resolved, and this feature of our view will be of some significance for our discussion of the developmental evidence in Section IV.

III.ii. The Monitoring Mechanism and Perceptual States

Of course, the MM Theory is not a complete account of self-awareness. One important limitation is that the MM is proposed as the mechanism underlying self-awareness of one's propositional attitudes, and it's quite likely that the account cannot explain awareness of one's own perceptual states. Perceptual states obviously have phenomenal character, and there is a vigorous debate over whether this phenomenal character is fully captured by a representational account (e.g., Tye 1995; Block forthcoming). If perceptual states can be captured by a representational or propositional account, then perhaps the MM can be extended to explain awareness of one's own perceptual states. For, as noted above, our proposed MM simply copies representations into representation schemas, e.g., it copies representations from the Belief Box into the schema 'I believe that ___.'

However, we're skeptical that perceptual states can be entirely captured by representational accounts, and as a result, we doubt that our MM Theory can adequately explain our awareness of our own perceptual states. Nonetheless, we think it is plausible that some kind of monitoring account (as opposed to a TT account) might apply to awareness of one's own perceptual states. Since it will be important to have a sketch of such a theory on the table, we will provide a brief outline of what the theory might look like.

In specifying the architecture underlying awareness of one's own perceptual states, the first move is to posit a "Percept Box." This device holds the percepts produced by the perceptual processing systems. We propose that the Percept Box feeds into the Belief Box in two ways. First, and most obviously, the contents of the Percept Box lead the subject to have beliefs about the world around her, by what we might call a Percept-to-Belief Mediator. For instance, if a normal adult looks into a quarry, her perceptual system will produce percepts that will, *ceteris paribus*, lead her to form the belief that *there are rocks down there*. Something at least roughly similar is presumably true in dogs, birds, and frogs. Hence, there is a mechanism (or set of mechanisms) that takes (take) percepts as input and produces (produce) beliefs as output. However, there is also, at least in normal adult humans, another way that the Percept Box feeds into the Belief Box: we form beliefs *about our percepts*. For example, when looking into a quarry, I might form the belief that *I see rocks*. We also form beliefs about the similarity between percepts – e.g., *this toy rock looks like that real rock*. To explain this range of capacities, we tentatively propose that there is a set of Percept-Monitoring Mechanisms that take input from the Percept Box and produce beliefs about the percepts.[7] We represent this account in Figure 8.

Figure 8. Percept-Monitoring Mechanism Theory.

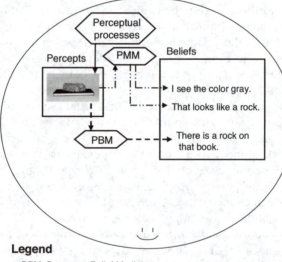

Legend
PBM: Percept to Belief Mediator
PMM: Percept Monitoring Mechanisms

---

7   How many PMMs are there? A thorough discussion of this is well beyond the scope of this paper, but evidence from neuropsychology indicates that there might be numerous PMMs, which can be selectively impaired by different kinds of brain damage. For instance, *achromatopsia* is a condition in which some subjects claim to see only in black and white, but can in fact make some colour

Note that the PMM will presumably be a far more complex mechanism than the MM, for the PMM must take perceptual experiences and produce representations about those perceptual experiences. We have no idea how to characterize this further in terms of cognitive mechanisms, and as a result, we are much less confident about this account than about the MM account.

IV. Developmental Evidence and the Theory Theory

The Theory Theory of self-awareness is widely endorsed among researchers working on mindreading, and there are two prominent clusters of arguments offered in support of this account. One of these clusters appeals to evidence on autism as support for a Theory Theory account of self-awareness (Baron-Cohen 1989, Carruthers 1996, Frith and Happé 1999); we consider and reject this cluster of arguments in a companion piece to this paper (Nichols and Stich 2003a). However, in this paper we restrict ourselves to the other cluster of arguments.

Perhaps the best known and most widely discussed arguments for the Theory Theory account of self-awareness come from developmental work charting the relation between performance on theory of mind

---

discriminations. "In cases of achromatopsia ... there is evidence that some aspects of colour processing mechanisms continue to function.... However ... there is no subjective experience of colour" (Young 1994, 179). Similarly, prosopagnosiacs claim not to recognize faces; however, many prosopagnosiacs exhibit covert recognition effects in their electrophysiological and behavioural responses (Young 1998, 283–87). Achromatopsia and prosopagnosia are, of course, independent conditions. Prosopagnosiacs typically have no trouble recognizing colours and patients with achromatopsia typically have no trouble recognizing faces. So, it's quite possible that prosopagnosia involves a deficit to a PMM that is not implicated in colour recognition, and that achromatopsia involves a deficit to a distinct PMM that is not implicated in face recognition. This issue is considerably complicated by the fact that some theorists (e.g., Dennett 1991) maintain that neuropsychological findings like these can be explained by appealing to the mechanisms that build up the multiple layers of the percept itself. We won't treat this complicated issue here. Our point is just that if achromatopsia and prosopagnosia do involve deficits to percept-monitoring mechanisms, it is plausible that they involve deficits to independent PMMs.

tasks for self and theory of mind tasks for others.[8] In this section, we propose to discuss the developmental arguments for and against the TT account of self-awareness.

It is our contention that the empirical evidence produced by developmental psychologists does not support the TT over our Monitoring Mechanism theory. Rather, we shall argue, in some cases both theories can explain the data about equally well, while in other cases the Monitoring Mechanism theory has a clear advantage over the Theory Theory. Before we present the arguments, it may be useful to provide a brief reminder of the problems we've raised for various versions of the TT account:

1. Version 1 looks to be hopelessly implausible; it cannot handle some of the most obvious facts about self-awareness.

2. Version 2 is a mystery theory; it maintains that there is special source of information exploited in reading one's own mind, but it leaves the source of this additional information unexplained.

3. Version 3 faces the embarrassment that if information about the representations in the Belief Box and Desire Box is available, then no theory is needed to explain self-awareness; ToM has nothing to do.

We think that these considerations provide an important *prima facie* case against the Theory Theory account of self-awareness, though we also think that, as in any scientific endeavor, solid empirical evidence might outweigh the prima facie considerations. So we now turn to the empirical arguments.

---

8 The label 'theory of mind tasks' is used to characterize a range of experiments that explore the ability to attribute mental states and to predict and explain behaviour. For example, as we will discuss later, one prominent theory of mind tasks is the 'false belief task'. In one version of this task, the subject is shown that a candy box has pencils in it, and the subject has to determine whether or not a target, who has not been shown what is in the box, will believe that the box has candy or pencils in it.

The Theory Theory predicts that subjects' performance on theory of mind tasks should be about equally good (or equally bad), whether the tasks are about one's own mental states or about the mental states of another person. In perhaps the most systematic and interesting argument for the TT, Gopnik and Meltzoff maintain that there are indeed clear and systematic correlations between performance on theory of mind tasks for self and for others (see Table 1, reproduced from Gopnik and Meltzoff 1994, Table 10.1). For instance, Gopnik and Meltzoff note that children succeed at perceptual tasks for themselves and others before the age of three. Between the ages of three and four, children begin to succeed at desire tasks for self and for other. And at around the age of four, children begin to succeed at the false belief task for self and for other. "The evidence," Gopnik and Meltzoff maintain,

> … suggests that there is an extensive parallelism between children's understanding of their own mental states and their understanding of the mental states of others…. In each of our studies, children's reports of their own immediately past psychological states are consistent with their accounts of the psychological states of others. When they can report and understand the psychological states of others, in the cases of pretense, perception, and imagination, they report having had those psychological states themselves. When they cannot report and understand the psychological states of others, in the case of false beliefs and source, they do not report that they had those states themselves. Moreover, and in some ways most strikingly, the intermediate case of desire is intermediate for self and other. (1994, 179–80)

This "extensive parallelism" is taken to show that "our knowledge of ourselves, like our knowledge of others, is the result of a theory" (Gopnik and Meltzoff 1994, 168). Thus the argument purports to establish a broad-based empirical case for the Theory Theory of self-awareness. However, on our view quite the opposite is the case. In the pages to follow, we will try to show that the data don't provide *any* support for the Theory Theory over the Monitoring Mechanism theory that we have proposed, and that some of the data that are comfortably compatible with MM cannot be easily explained by the TT. Defending this claim is rather a long project, but fortunately the data are intrinsically fascinating.

Table 1: From Gopnik and Meltzoff 1994, 180.

States	Other	Self
Easy		
Pretense	Before age 3 (Flavell, *et al.* 1987)	Before age 3 (Gopnik and Slaughter 1991)
Imagination	Before age 3 (Wellman and Estes 1986)	Before age 3 (Gopnik and Slaughter 1991)
Perception (Level 1)	Before age 3 (Flavell, *et al.* 1981)	Before age 3 (Gopnik and Slaughter 1991)
Intermediate		
Desire	Age 3–4 (Flavell, *et al.* 1990)	Age 3–4 (Gopnik and Slaughter 1991)
Difficult		
Sources of belief	After age 4 (O'Neill, *et al.* 1992)	After age 4 (Gopnik and Graf 1988)
False belief	After age 4 (Wimmer and Perner 1983)	After age 4 (Gopnik and Astington 1988)

IV.i. The Parallelism Prediction

Before we proceed to the data, it's important to be clear about the structure of Gopnik and Meltzoff's argument and of our counter-argument in favour of the Monitoring Mechanism theory. If Gopnik and Meltzoff are right that there is an "extensive parallelism," that would support the Theory Theory, since the Theory Theory *predicts* that there will be parallel performance on parallel theory of mind tasks for self and other. According to the Theory Theory, in order to determine one's own mental states, one must exploit the same Theory of Mind that one uses to determine another's mental states. So, if a child's Theory of Mind is not yet equipped to solve certain third person tasks, then the child should also be unable to solve the parallel first person task.

By contrast, for many of the tasks we'll consider our theory simply doesn't make a prediction about whether there will be parallel performance on self- and other-versions of the tasks. On our theory, the special purpose mechanisms for detecting one's own mental states (MM and PMM) are quite independent from the mechanism for reasoning about mental states and detecting the mental states of others (ToM). Hence, the ability to detect one's own mental states and the ability to detect another's mental states need not show similar developmental trajectories, though in some cases they might. What our theory does predict is that the capacity to detect one's own mental states, though not necessarily the capacity to reason about them, should emerge quite early, since the theory claims that the MM and the PMM are innate and on line quite early in development. Also, as noted in Section III, our theory allows for the possibility that the ToM *can* be used in attributing mental states to oneself. So it may well turn out that sometimes subjects produce inaccurate self-attributions because they are relying on the ToM. Since our theory provides no *a priori* reason to expect extensive parallel performance in detecting mental states in oneself and others, if there is extensive parallelism our theory would be faced with a major challenge: it would need to provide some additional and independently plausible explanation for the existence of the parallelism in each case where it is found. But if, as we shall argue, the parallelism is largely illusory, then it is the Theory Theory that faces a major challenge: it has to provide some plausible explanation for the fact that the parallelism it predicts does not exist.

IV.ii. Theory Theory Meets Data

Gopnik and Meltzoff argue for the TT by presenting a wide range of cases in which, they maintain, subjects show parallel performance on self- and other-versions of theory of mind tasks, and at first glance the range of parallels looks very impressive, indeed. However, we'll argue that on closer inspection, this impression is quite misleading. In some cases, there really is parallel performance, but these cases do not support the TT over our MM theory, since in these cases both theories do about equally well in explaining the facts; in some cases, the evidence for parallel performance is dubious; and in several other cases, there is evidence that performance is *not* parallel. These cases are of particular importance, since they are compatible with the MM account and *prima facie* incompatible with the Theory Theory. In the remainder of this section we will consider each of these three classes of cases.

IV.ii.i. Cases Where the Parallelism is Real

(i) The "easy" tasks

There are a range of tasks that Gopnik and Meltzoff classify as *easy for other and easy for self*. They claim that pretense, imagination, and perception (level 1 perspective taking) are understood for both self and other before age three. At least on some tasks, this claim of parallel performance seems to be quite right. Simple perceptual tasks provide perhaps the clearest example. Lempers and colleagues (Lempers *et al.* 1977) found that 2½-year-old children succeeded at level 1 perspective-taking tasks, in which the children had to determine whether another person could see an object or not. For instance, if a young child is shown that a piece of cardboard has a picture of a rabbit on one side and a picture of a turtle on the other, and if the child is then shown the turtle side, the child can correctly answer that the person on the other side of the cardboard sees the picture of the rabbit. Using similar tasks, Gopnik snd Slaughter (1991) found that three-year-old children could also successfully report their own past perceptions. As Gopnik and Meltzoff characterize it, this task is "easy" for other and "easy" for self, and Gopnik and Meltzoff put forward such cases as support for the TT.

As we see it, however, the fact that level 1 perspective-taking tasks are easy for other and for self does not count as evidence for the TT over our MM theory. To see why, let us consider first the *self* case and then the *other* case.

On our account, MM is the mechanism responsible for self-awareness of propositional attitudes and, we have tentatively suggested, another mechanism (or family of mechanisms), the Percept-Monitoring Mechanism, underlies (underlie) awareness of one's own perceptual states. The PMM, like the MM, is hypothesized to be innate and to come on line quite early in development. Thus, the PMM is up and running by the age of 2½, well before ToM is fully in place. So our theory predicts that quite young children should be able to give accurate reports about their own perceptual states.

Let's turn now to the *other* case. Both the Theory Theory and our theory maintain that the detection of mental states in others depends on the Theory of Mind and, like Theory Theorists, we think that evidence on visual perspective taking (e.g., Lempers *et al.* 1977) shows that part of the ToM is on line by the age of 2½. It is of some interest to determine why the part of ToM that subserves these tasks emerges as early as it does, though neither the TT nor our theory currently has any explanation to offer. For both theories, it is just a brute, empirical fact.

So here's the situation: Our theory predicts that awareness of one's own perceptions will emerge early, and has no explanation to offer for why the part of ToM that subserves the detection of perceptual states in others emerges early. By contrast, TT predicts that both self- and other-abilities will emerge at the same time, but has no explanation to offer for why they both emerge early. By our lights, this one is a wash. Neither theory has any clear explanatory advantage over the other.

Much the same reasoning shows that Gopnik and Meltzoff's cases of pretense and imagination don't lend any significant support to the Theory Theory over our theory. There is some evidence that by the age of three, children have some understanding of pretense and imagination in others (e.g., Wellman and Estes 1986), though as we'll see in Section IV.ii.iii, there is also some reason for skepticism. However, whatever the ontogeny is for detecting pretense and imagination in others, the TT account can hardly offer a better explanation than our account, since we simply *are* Theory Theorists about the detection of mental states in others, and neither we nor the Theory Theorists have any explanation to offer for the fact that the relevant part of ToM emerges when it does. As in the case of perception, our theory does have an explanation for the fact that the ability to detect one's own pretenses and imaginings emerges early, since on our view this process is subserved by the MM, which is up and running by the age of 2½, but we have no explanation for the fact (if indeed it is a fact) that the part of ToM that subserves the detection of pretenses and imaginings in others also emerges early. The TT, on the other hand, predicts that self- and other-abilities will both emerge at the same time, but does not explain why they both emerge early. So here, as before, neither theory has any obvious explanatory advantage over the other.

(ii) Sources of belief

A suite of studies by Gopnik, O'Neill and their colleagues (Gopnik and Graf 1988, O'Neill and Gopnik 1991, O'Neill *et al.* 1992) show that there is a parallel between performance on source-tasks for self and source-tasks for others. In the self-versions of these tasks, children came to find out which objects were in a drawer either by seeing the object, being told, or inferring from a simple cue. After establishing that the child knows what's in the drawer, the child is asked, "How do you know that there's an *x* in the drawer?" This question closely parallels the question used to explore children's understanding of the sources of another's belief (O'Neill *et al.* 1992). O'Neill and her colleagues found that while four-year-olds tended to succeed at the other person version of the task, three-year-olds tended to fail it; similarly, Gopnik and Graf (1988) found that four-year-olds tended to succeed at the self-version of the task, but three-year-olds tended to fail it. For instance, three-year-olds often said that their knowledge came from seeing the object when actually they had been told about the object, and three-year-olds made similar errors when judging the source of another person's knowledge.

These results are interesting and surprising, but they are orthogonal to the issue at hand. The Monitoring Mechanism posited in our theory is a mechanism for *detecting* mental states, not for reasoning about them. But questions about the sources of one's beliefs or knowledge cannot be answered merely by *detecting* one's own mental states. Rather, questions about how you gained knowledge fall into the domain of *reasoning* about mental states, and on our theory, that job is performed by the Theory of Mind. So, on our theory, questions about sources will implicate the ToM both for self and other. Hence, our theory, like the Theory Theory, predicts that there will be parallel performance on tasks like the source tasks.

IV.ii.ii. The Relevant but Dubious Data

In Gopnik and Meltzoff's table displaying extensive parallelism, there are two remaining cases that can't be dismissed as irrelevant. However, we will argue that the cases fall far short of clear support for the Theory Theory.

(i) False belief

The false belief task, probably the most famous theory of mind task, was first used by Wimmer and Perner (1983). In their version of the experiment, children watched a puppet show in which the puppet protagonist, Maxi, puts chocolate in a box and then goes out to play. While Maxi is out, his puppet mother moves the chocolate to the cupboard. When Maxi returns, the children are asked where Maxi will look for the chocolate. Numerous studies have now found that three-year-old children typically fail tasks like this, while four-year-olds typically succeed at them (e.g., Baron-Cohen *et al.* 1985, Perner *et al.* 1987). This robust result has been widely interpreted to show that the ToM (or some quite fundamental component of it) is not yet in place until about the age of four.

On closely matched tasks, Gopnik and Astington (1988) found a correlation between failing the false belief task for another and failing it for oneself. Gopnik and Astington (1988) presented children with a candy box and then let the children see that there were really pencils inside the box. Children were asked, "What will Nicky think is in the box?" and then "When you first saw the box, before we opened it, what did you think was inside it?" Children's ability to answer the question for self was significantly correlated with their ability to answer the question for other. Thus, here we have a surprising instance of parallel performance on tasks for self and other.[9] This is, of course, just the outcome that the Theory Theory would predict, for the Theory Theory maintains that ToM is crucial both in the detection of other people's beliefs and in the detection of one's own. Thus, if a child's ToM has not yet developed to the point where it can detect other people's beliefs in a given situation, it is to be expected that the child will also be unable to detect her own beliefs in that context. And this, it appears, is just what the experimental results show.

What about our theory? What explanation can it offer for these results? The first step in answering this question is to note that in the *self* version of the false belief task, the child is not actually being asked to report on her *current* belief, but rather to recall a belief she had in the recent past. Where might such memories come from? The most natural answer, for a theory like ours, is that when the child first sees the box, she believes that there is candy in it, and the MM produces

---

9 Similarly, Baron-Cohen (1991) found that in autism, there are correlations between failing the false belief task for other and failing the task for self.

a belief with the content *I believe that there is candy in the box*. As the experiment continues and time passes, that belief is converted into a past tense belief whose content is (roughly) *I believed that there was candy in the box*. But, of course, if that were the end of the story, it would be bad news for our theory, since when asked what she believed when she first saw the box the child reports that she believes *that there were pencils in the box*.

Fortunately, that is *not* the end of the story. For, as we noted in Section III, in our theory MM is not the only mechanism capable of generating beliefs with the content *I believe(d) that p*. ToM is also capable of producing such beliefs, and sometimes ToM may produce a belief of that form that will conflict with a belief produced by MM. That, we propose, is exactly what is happening in the Gopnik and Astington experiment when younger children fail to report their own earlier false belief. As the results in the other-version of the task indicate, the ToM in younger children has a strong tendency to attribute beliefs that the child actually believes to be true. So when asked what she believed at the beginning of the experiment, ToM mistaken concludes that *I believed that there were pencils in the box*.[10] Thus, on our account, there will be two competing and incompatible representations in the child's Belief Box. And to explain the fact that the child usually relies on the mistaken ToM generated belief, rather than on the correct MM generated belief, we must suppose that the memory trace is relatively weak, and that when the child's cognitive system has to decide which belief about her past belief to rely on, the MM generated memory trace typically loses.

At this point, we suspect, a critic might protest that this is a singularly unconvincing explanation. There is, the critic will insist, no reason to think that the MM generated memory will typically be weaker than the ToM generated belief; it is just an *ad hoc* assumption

---

10 Some theorists, most prominently Fodor (1992), have explained the results in the other-version of the task by claiming that young children do not use the ToM in these tasks. They arrive at their answer, Fodor argues, by using a separate, reality biased strategy. We need take no stand on this issue, since if Fodor is correct, then it is plausible to suppose that the same reality biased strategy generates a mistaken *I believed that there were pencils in the box* representation in the self-version of the task.

that is required to get our theory to square with the facts. And if this were the end of the story, the critic would be right.

Fortunately for us, however, this is not the end of the story. For there is evidence that provides independent support for our explanation and undercuts the TT account. Recent work by German and Leslie exploring performance on self- and other-versions of the false belief task indicates that *if memory enhancements are provided, young children's performance on self-versions improves, while their performance on other-versions stays about the same.*

German and Leslie devised a task in which a child would hide a biscuit and then search for it in the wrong place because it had been moved when the child was behind a screen. In one condition, the child was then shown a videotape of the entire sequence of events – hiding, moving and searching – and asked, at the appropriate point, "Why are you looking there?" and then, "When you were looking for the biscuit, where did you think the biscuit was?" In another condition, after the same hiding, moving, and searching sequence, the videotape was "accidentally" rewound too far, and the child watched another child in an identical situation. At the appropriate point, the child was asked "Why was she looking there?" and "When she was looking for the biscuit, where did she think the biscuit was?" German and Leslie found that children who were shown their own mistaken search were much more likely to offer a false belief explanation and to attribute a false belief than were children who were shown another's mistaken search (German and Leslie, forthcoming). This fits nicely with our proposed explanation for why young children fail the false belief task for the self. However, it's difficult to see how a Theory Theorist could explain these results, for according to the Theory Theory, if the child has a defective ToM, the child should make the same mistakes for himself that he does for another. If there is no MM to generate a correct belief that becomes a correct memory, then giving memory enhancements should not produce differential improvement.

(ii) Desire

Another source of data that might offer support to the TT comes from work on understanding desires. Gopnik and Meltzoff maintain that three-year-olds are just beginning to understand desire in others, and

Gopnik and Slaughter found that a significant percentage of children make mistakes about their own immediately past desires.

The Gopnik and Slaughter own-desire tasks were quite ingenious. In one of the tasks, they went to a daycare center just before snack time and asked the child whether he was hungry or not. The hungry child said "Yes" and proceeded to eat all the snacks he desired. Then the experimenter asked, "When I first asked you, before we had the snack, were you hungry then?" (Gopnik and Slaughter 1991, 102). Gopnik and Slaughter found that 30–40 percent of the three-year-olds mistakenly claimed that they were in their current desire-state all along.

This surprising result is claimed to parallel Flavell *et al.*'s 1990 finding that a significant percentage of three-year-olds make mistakes on desire tasks for others. In the Flavell tasks, the child observes Ellie make a disgusted look after tasting a cookie, and the child is asked, "Does Ellie think it is a yummy tasting cookie?" (Flavell *et al.* 1990, 918). Gopnik and Meltzoff remark that the "absolute levels of performance were strikingly similar" to the results reported by Flavell *et al.* (Gopnik and Meltzoff 1994, 179), and they cite this as support for the parallel performance hypothesis.

The central problem with this putative parallel is that it's not at all clear that the tasks are truly parallel tasks. In Gopnik and Slaughter's tasks, three-year-olds are asked about a desire that they don't currently have because it was recently satisfied. It would be of considerable interest to couple Gopnik and Slaughter's own-desire version of the hunger task with a closely matched other person version of the task. For instance, the experiment could have a satiated child watch another child beginning to eat at snack time and ask the satiated child, "Is he hungry?" If the findings on this task paralleled findings on the own-desire version, that would indeed be an important parallel.

Unfortunately, the putatively parallel task in Flavell *et al.* that Gopnik and Meltzoff cite is quite different from the Gopnik and Slaughter task. In the Flavell tasks, the child is asked whether or not the target thinks the cookie is "yummy tasting" (Flavell *et al.* 1990, 918). The task doesn't explicitly ask about desires at all. Flavell and his colleagues themselves characterize the task as exploring children's ability to attribute value *beliefs*. Further, unlike the Gopnik and Slaughter task, the Flavell *et al.* tasks depend on expressions of disgust. Indeed, there are so many differences between these tasks that we think it's impossible to draw any conclusions from the comparison.

In this section we have considered the best cases for the Theory Theory, and it is our contention that the data we've discussed don't provide much of an argument for the Theory Theory. For there are serious empirical problems with both cases, and even if we ignore these problems, the data certainly don't establish the "extensive parallelism" that is predicted by the Theory Theory. Moreover, there are results not discussed by Gopnik and Meltzoff which, we think, strongly suggest that the parallelism on which their argument depends simply does not exist.

IV.ii.iii. Evidence against the Self–Other Parallelism

In this section, we will review a range of data indicating that often there is *not* a parallel between performance on self- and other-versions of theory of mind tasks. We are inclined to think that these data completely uproot Gopnik and Meltzoff's parallelism argument, and constitute a major challenge to the Theory Theory of self-awareness itself.

(i) Knowledge *versus* ignorance

In knowledge-versus-ignorance experiments, Wimmer and colleagues found a significant difference between performance on closely matched tasks for self and other (Wimmer *et al.* 1988). After letting children in two conditions either look in a box or not look in a box, the researchers asked them, "Do you know what is in the box, or do you not know that?" The three-year-olds performed quite well on this task. For the other person version of the task, they observed another who either looked or didn't look into a box. They were then asked, "Does [name of child] know what is in the box or does she [he] not know that?" (1988, 383). Despite the almost verbatim similarity between this question and the self-version, the children did significantly worse on the other-version of this question (see also Nichols 1993). Hence, we have one case in which there is a significant *difference* between performance on a theory of mind task for self and performance on the task for other. And there's more to come.

(ii)Pretense and imagination

Gopnik and Meltzoff maintain that children under age three understand pretense for others and for self. Although there are tasks on which young children exhibit some understanding of pretense (e.g., Wellman and Estes 1986), the issue has turned out to be considerably more complicated. It's clear from the literature on pretend play that from a young age, children are capable of reporting their own pretenses. Indeed, Gopnik and Slaughter (1991) show that three-year-old children can easily answer questions about their past pretenses and imaginings. Despite this facility with their own pretenses, it doesn't seem that young children have an adequate theory of pretense (Lillard 1993; Nichols and Stich 2000). For instance, Lillard's (1993) results suggest that children as old as four years think that someone can pretend to be a rabbit without knowing anything about rabbits. More importantly for present purposes, although young children have no trouble detecting and reporting their own pretenses (e.g., Leslie 1994a), children seem to be significantly worse at recognizing pretense in others (Flavell et al. 1987, Rosen et al. 1997). Indeed, recent results from Rosen et al. (1997) indicate that young children have a great deal of difficulty characterizing the pretenses of others.

Rosen and his colleagues had subjects watch a television show in which the characters were sitting on a bench but pretending to be on an airplane. The researchers asked the children: "Now we're going to talk about what everyone on *Barney* is thinking about. Are they thinking about being on an airplane or about sitting on a bench outside their school?" (Rosen et al. 1997, 1135). They found that 90 percent of the three-year-olds answered incorrectly that everyone was thinking about sitting on a bench.

By contrast, in Gopnik and Slaughter's experiments, three-year-old children did quite well on questions about what they themselves were pretending or imagining. In one of their pretense tasks, the child was asked to pretend that an empty glass had orange juice in it; the glass was turned over, and the child was subsequently asked to pretend that it had hot chocolate in it. The child was then asked, "When I first asked you … what did you pretend was in the glass then?" (Gopnik and Slaughter 1991, 106). Children performed near ceiling on this task.

In Gopnik and Slaughter's imagination task, the children were told to close their eyes and think of a blue doggie, then they were told to close their eyes and think of a red balloon. The children were then asked, "When I first asked you ... what did you think of then? Did you think of a blue doggie or did you think of a red balloon?" (Gopnik and Slaughter 1991, 106). Over 80 percent of the three-year-olds answered this correctly.

Although the Gopnik and Slaughter pretense and imagination tasks aren't exact matches for the Rosen *et al.* task, the huge difference in the results suggests that children do much better on pretense and imagination tasks for self than they do on pretense and imagination tasks for another person. Hence, it seems likely that children can detect and report their own pretenses and imaginings before they have the theoretical resources to detect and characterize pretenses and imaginings in others.

(iii) Perspective-taking

As we noted earlier, children as young as 2½ years are able to succeed at "level 1" perspective taking tasks both for others and for themselves. However, there is a cluster of more difficult perspective taking tasks, "level 2" tasks, in which young children do significantly better in the self-version than in the other-version. These tasks require the child to figure our how an object looks from a perspective that is different from her own current perspective. In one task, for example, the child is shown a drawing of a turtle that looks to be lying on his back when viewed from one position and standing on his feet when viewed from another position. The child is asked whether the turtle is on its back or on its feet; then the child is asked how the person across the table sees the turtle, on its back or on its feet. Children typically don't succeed at these tasks until about the age of four.

However, contrary to the parallel performance hypothesis, Gopnik and Slaughter (1991) found that three-year-olds did well on a self-version of the task. They had the child look at the drawing of the turtle and then had the child change seats with the experimenter. The child was subsequently asked, "When I first asked you, before we traded seats, how did you see the turtle then, lying on his back or standing on his feet?" (1991, 106). Gopnik and Slaughter were surprised at how well the three-year-olds did on this task. They write, "Perhaps the most surprising finding was that performance on the level 2 perception task turned out to be quite good, and was not significantly different from performance on the pretend task. Seventy-five percent of the 3-year-olds succeeded at this task, a much higher level of performance than the 33% to 50% reported by Masangkay et al. (1974) in the other person version of this task" (Gopnik and Slaughter 1991, 107). Here, then, is another example of a theory of mind task in which the self-version of the task is significantly easier for subjects than the other-version of the task. So we have yet another case in which the Theory Theory's prediction of extensive parallelism is disconfirmed.[11]

IV.iii. What Conclusions Can We Draw From the Developmental Data?

We now want to step back from the details of the data to assess their implications for the debate between the Theory Theory and our Monitoring Mechanism Theory. To begin, let's recall what each theory predicts, and why. The TT maintains that the ToM is centrally involved in detecting and reasoning about both one's own mental states and other people's. But the TT makes no claims about when, in the course of development, various components of ToM are acquired or come on line. Thus TT makes no predictions about when specific mindreading skills will emerge, but it does predict that any given mindreading skill will appear at about the same time in self- and other-cases.

---

11 Gopnik and Meltzoff have also produced results that suggest a disparity between performance on self- and other-versions of a very simple perspective-taking task. They found that when 24-month-olds were asked to hide an object from the experimenter, they "consistently hid the object egocentrically, either placing it on the experimenter's side of the screen or holding it to themselves so that neither they nor the experimenter could see it" (reported in Gopnik and Meltzoff 1997, 116). Given that Gopnik and Meltzoff characterize the child's performance as "egocentric," it seems quite likely that the children would succeed at versions of this task that asked the child to hide the object from herself. Hence, one expects that children would perform significantly better on a self-version of the task than on the other-version of the task. If in fact the two-year-old child can't solve the hiding task for another person, but can solve it for self, then this looks like another case that counts against the extensive parallelism predicted by the Theory Theory.

MM, by contrast, maintains that ToM is involved in detecting and reasoning about other people's mental states and in reasoning about one's own mental states, but that a separate Monitoring Mechanism (or a cluster of such mechanisms) is (are) typically involved when we detect our own mental states. MM also claims that the Monitoring Mechanism(s) comes (come) on line quite early in development. Thus, MM predicts that children will be able to detect (but not necessarily reason about) their own mental states quite early in development. But it does not predict any particular pattern of correlation between the emergence of the capacity to detect one's own mental states and the emergence of the capacity to detect other people's mental states.

Which theory does better at handling the data we have reviewed? As we see it, the answer if clear: MM is compatible with all the data we have reviewed, while some of the data are seriously problematic for the TT.

To make the point as clearly as possible, let's assemble a list of the various mindreading phenomena we have reviewed:

(1) Level 1 perspective taking: This emerges early for both self and other. TT predicts the parallel emergence and is compatible with, but does not predict, the early emergence. MM predicts the early emergence in the self case and is compatible with but does not predict the early emergence in the other case. Neither theory has an advantage over the other.

(2) Pretense and imagination: It is clear that self-detection emerges early, as MM predicts. However, there is some recent evidence indicating that detection and understanding of pretense in others does not emerge until much later. If this is right, it is a problem for TT, though not for MM.

(3) Sources of belief: The ability to identify sources of belief emerges at about the age of four in both the self and the other case. Since this is a reasoning problem, not a detection problem, both theories make the same prediction.

(4) False belief: Recent evidence indicates that if memory enhancements are provided, young children do better on the self-version of false belief tasks than on the other-version. This is compatible with MM but quite problematic for TT.

(5)   Desire: The evidence available does not use well-matched tasks, so no conclusions can be drawn about either TT or MM.

(6)   Knowledge *versus* ignorance: three-year-olds do much better on the self-version than on the other-version. This is compatible with MM but problematic for TT.

(7)   Level 2 perspective taking: Here again, three-year-olds do better on the self-version than on the other-version, which is a problem of TT but not for MM.

Obviously, the extensive parallelism between self- and other-cases on which Gopnik and Meltzoff rest their case for the Theory Theory of self-awareness is not supported by the data. Conceivably a resourceful Theory Theorist could offer plausible explanations for each of the cases in which the parallel predicted by TT breaks down. But in the absence of a systematic attempt to provide such explanations, we think it is clear that the developmental evidence favours our theory of self-awareness over the Theory Theory.

V. Conclusion

The empirical work on mindreading provides an invaluable resource for characterizing the cognitive mechanisms underlying our capacity for self-awareness. However, we think that developmental psychologists have drawn the wrong conclusions from the data. Contrary to the claims of Theory Theorists, the developmental evidence indicates that the capacity for self-awareness does not depend on the Theory of Mind. It's much more plausible, we have argued, to suppose that self-awareness derives from a Monitoring Mechanism that is independent of the Theory of Mind. Hence, we think that at this juncture in cognitive science, the most plausible account of self-awareness is that the mind comes pre-packaged with a set of special-purpose mechanisms for reading one's own mind.[12]

------

12   We would like to thank Peter Carruthers, Catherine Driscoll, Luc Faucher, Trisha Folds-Bennett, Gary Gates, Rochel Gelman, Alison Gopnik, Alan Leslie, Brian Loar, Dominic Murphy, Brian Scholl, Eric Schwitzgebel, and Robert Woolfolk for

References

Armstrong, D. 1968. *A Materialist Theory of the Mind*. London: Routledge and Kegan Paul.

Baron-Cohen, S. 1989. "Are Autistic Children 'behaviorists'?". *Journal of Autism and Developmental Disorders* 19: 579–600.

———. 1991. "The Development of a Theory of Mind in Autism: Deviance and Delay?" *Psychiatric Clinics of North America* 14: 33–51.

Baron-Cohen, S., Leslie, A., and Frith, U. 1985. "Does the Autistic Child Have a 'Theory of Mind'?" *Cognition* 21: 37–46.

Block, N. forthcoming. *Mental Paint*.

Carruthers, P. 1996. "Autism as Mind-blindness: An Elaboration and Partial Defence." In *Theories of Theories of Mind*, ed. P. Carruthers and P. Smith, 257–273. Cambridge: Cambridge University Press.

Dennett, D. 1991. *Consciousness Explained*. Boston, MA: Little Brown.

Ericsson, K. and Simon, H.. 1993. *Protocol Analysis: Verbal Reports As Data*. Cambridge, MA: MIT Press.

Flavell, J., Everett, B., Croft, K., and Flavell, E.. 1981. "Young Children's Knowledge About Visual Perception." *Developmental Psychology* 17: 99–103.

Flavell, J., Flavell, E., and Green, F.. 1987 "Young Children's Knowledge About the Apparent-real and Pretend-real Distinctions." *Developmental Psychology* 23: 816–22.

Flavell, J., Flavell, E., Green, F., and Moses, L. 1990. "Young Children's Understanding of Fact Beliefs Versus Value Beliefs." *Child Development* 61: 915–28.

Fodor, J. 1992. "A Theory of the Child's Theory of Mind." *Cognition* 44: 283–96.

Frith, C. 1994. "Theory of Mind in Schizophrenia." In *The Neuropsychology of Schizophrenia*, ed. A. David and J. Cutting, 147–161. Hillsdale, NJ: LEA.

discussion and comments on earlier drafts of this paper. Earlier versions of this paper were presented at a conference sponsored by the Center for Philosophical Education in Santa Barbara, California, at the Rutgers University Center for Cognitive Science, and at the Institute for the Study of Child Development, Robert Wood Johnson Medical School. We are grateful for the constructive feedback offered by members of the audience on all of these occasions.

Frith, U. and Happé, F. 1999. "Theory of Mind and Self Consciousness: What Is It Like to Be Autistic?" *Mind & Language* 14: 1–22.

German, T. and Leslie, A. forthcoming. *Self–Other Differences in False Belief: Recall versus Reconstruction.*

Goldman, A. 1993a. *Philosophical Applications of Cognitive Science.* Boulder: Westview Press.

———— 1993b. "The Psychology of Folk Psychology". *Behavioral and Brain Sciences* 16: 15–28, 101–13.

————. 1997. "Science, Publicity, and Consciousness." *Philosophy of Science* 64: 525–46.

————. 2000. "The Mentalizing Folk." In *Metarepresentation*, ed. D. Sperber, 171–196. Oxford: Oxford University Press.

Goodman, N. 1983. *Fact, Fiction & Forecast.* Fourth edition. Cambridge, MA: Harvard University Press.

Gopnik, A. 1993. "How We Know Our Own Minds: The Illusion of First-person Knowledge of Intentionality." *Behavioral and Brain Sciences* 16: 1–14.

Gopnik, A. and Astington, J. 1988. "Children's Understanding of Representational Change and its Relation to the Understanding of False Belief and the Appearance–Reality Distinction." *Child Development* 59: 26–37.

Gopnik, A. and Graf, P. 1988. "Knowing How You Know: Young Children's Ability to Identify and Remember the Sources of Their Beliefs." *Child Development* 59: 1366–71.

Gopnik, A. and Meltzoff, A. 1994. "Minds, Bodies, and Persons: Young Children's Understanding of the Self and Others as Reflected in Imitation and Theory of Mind Research." In *Self-awareness in animals and humans,* ed. S. Parker, R. Mitchell, and M. Boccia, 166-186. New York: Cambridge University Press.

Gopnik, A. and Meltzoff, A. 1997. *Words, Thoughts and Theories.* Cambridge, MA: MIT Press.

Gopnik, A. and Slaughter, V.. 1991. "Young Children's Understanding of Changes in Their Mental States." *Child Development* 62: 98–110.

Gopnik, A. and Wellman, H. 1994. "The Theory Theory." In *Mapping the Mind,* ed. S. Gelman and L. Hirschfeld, 257–293. Cambridge: Cambridge University Press.

Gordon, R. 1995. "Simulation Without Introspection or Inference from Me to You" In *Mental Simulation: Evaluations and Applications,* ed. T. Stone and M. Davies, 53–67. Oxford: Blackwell.

———. 1996. "Radical Simulationism." In *Theories of Theories of Mind*, ed. P. Carruthers and P. Smith, 11–21. Cambridge: Cambridge University Press.

Lempers, J., Flavell, E., and Flavell, J. 1977. "The Development in Very Young Children of Tacit Knowledge Concerning Visual Perception." *Genetic Psychology Monographs* 95: 3–53.

Leslie, A. 1994a." Pretending and Believing: Issues in the Theory of ToMM." *Cognition* 50: 211–38.

———. 1994b. ToMM, ToBY and Agency: Core Architecture and Domain Specificity. In *Mapping the mind*, ed. L. Hirschfeld and S. Gelman, 119–48. Cambridge: Cambridge University Press.

Lillard, A. 1993. "Young Children's Conceptualization of Pretense: Action or Mental Representational State?" *Child Development* 64: 372–86.

Lycan, W. 1987. *Consciousness*. Cambridge, MA: MIT Press.

Masangkay, Z., McCluskey, K., McIntyre, C. Sims-Knight, J., Vaughan, B., and Flavell, J. 1974. "The Early Development of Inferences About the Visual Percepts of Others." *Child Development* 45: 357–66.

McLaughlin, B. and Tye, M. 1998. "Is Content Externalism Compatible With Privileged Access?" *Philosophical Review* 107: 349–80.

Nichols, S. 1993. "Developmental Evidence and Introspection." *Behavioral and Brain Sciences* 16 (1): 64–65.

Nichols, S. and Stich, S. 1998. "Rethinking Co-cognition." *Mind & Language* 13: 499–512.

Nichols, S. and Stich, S. 2000. "A Cognitive Theory of Pretense." *Cognition* 74: 115–47.

Nichols, S. and Stich. S. 2003a. How to Read Your Own Mind: A Cognitive Theory of Self-Consciousness. In *Consciousness: New Philosophical Essays*, ed. Q. Smith and P. Jokic, 157–200. Oxford: Oxford University Press.

Nichols, S. and Stich, S. 2003b. *Mindreading*. Oxford: Oxford University Press.

Nichols, S., Stich, S., and Leslie, A.. 1995. "Choice Effects and the Ineffectiveness of Simulation: Response to Kuhberger *et al.*" *Mind & Language* 10: 437–45.

Nichols, S., Stich, S., Leslie, A., and Klein, D. 1996. "Varieties of Off-line Simulation." In *Theories of Theories of Mind*, ed. P. Carruthers and P. Smith, 39–74. Cambridge: Cambridge University Press.

Nisbett, R. and Schacter, S.1966. Cognitive Manipulation of Pain. *Journal of Experimental Social Psychology* 21: 227–36.

Nisbett, R. and Wilson, T. 1977. "Telling More Than We Can Know." *Psychological Review* 84: 231–59.

O'Neill, D., Astington, J., and Flavell, J. 1992. "Young Children's Understanding of the Role that Sensory Experiences Play in Knowledge Acquisition." *Child Development* 63: 474–91.

O'Neill, D. and Gopnik, A.1991. "Young Children's Understanding of the Sources of their Beliefs." *Developmental Psychology* 27: 390–397.

Perner, J. 1991. *Understanding the Representational Mind.* Cambridge, MA: MIT Press.

Perner, J., Leekam, S., and Wimmer, H. 1987. "Three-year-olds' Difficulty with False Belief: The Case for a Conceptual Deficit." *British Journal of Experimental Child Psychology* 39: 437–71.

Putnam, H. 1975. "The Meaning of Meaning." In *Mind, Language and Reality: Philosophical Papers*, vol. 2. Cambridge: Cambridge University Press.

Rosen, C., Schwebel, D., and Singer, J. 1997. "Preschoolers' Attributions of Mental States in Pretense." *Child Development* 68: 1133–1142.

Sellars, W. 1956. Empiricism and the Philosophy of Mind. *Minnesota Studies in the Philosophy of Science*, vol. 1, 253–329. University of Minnesota Press. Reprinted in Sellars (1963), *Science, Perception and Reality*. London: Routledge & Kegan Paul.

Stich, S. 1992. "What Is a Theory of Mental Representation?" *Mind* 101: 243–61.

———. 1996. *Deconstructing the Mind.* New York: Oxford University Press.

Stich, S. and Nichols, S. 1992. Folk Psychology: Simulation or Tacit Theory. *Mind & Language* 7 (1): 35–71.

———. 1995. Second Thoughts on Simulation. In *Mental Simulation: Evaluations and Applications*, ed. A. Stone and M. Davies, 87–108. Oxford: Basil Blackwell.

———. 1997. "Cognitive Penetrability, Rationality, and Restricted Simulation." *Mind & Language* 12: 297–326.

———. 1998. "Theory Theory to the Max: A Critical notice of Gopnik & Meltzoff's *Words, Thoughts, and Theories*." *Mind & Language* 13: 421–49.

Stich, S. and Ravenscroft, I. 1994. "What *is* Folk Psychology?" *Cognition* 50: 1–3, 447–68.

Tye, M. 1995. *Ten Problems of Consciousness: A Representational Theory of the Phenomenal Mind.* Cambridge, MA: MIT Press.

Wellman, H. and Estes, D. 1986. "Early Understanding of Mental Entities: A Reexamination of Childhood Realism." *Child Development* 57: 910–23.

338

Wimmer, H. and Hartl, M. 1991. "The Cartesian View and the Theory View of Mind: Developmental Evidence from Understanding False Belief in Self and Other." *British Journal of Developmental Psychology* 9: 125–28.

Wimmer, H. and Perner, J.1983. "Beliefs About Beliefs: Representation and Constraining Function of Wrong Beliefs in Young Children's Understanding of Deception." *Cognition* 13: 103–128.

Wimmer, H., Hogrefe, G., and Perner, J. 1988. "Children's Understanding of Informational Access as a Source of Knowledge." *Child Development* 59: 386–96.

Young, A. 1994. "Neuropsychology of Awareness." In *Consciousness in Philosophy and Cognitive Neuroscience*, ed. A. Revonsuo and M. Kamppinen, 173–203. Hillsdale, NJ: LEA.

―――. 1998. *Face and Mind*. Oxford: Oxford University Press.

CANADIAN JOURNAL OF PHILOSOPHY
Supplementary Volume 30

The Argument from Diaphanousness

DANIEL STOLJAR

I. Introduction

In "The Refutation of Idealism," G.E. Moore observed that, "when we try to introspect the sensation of blue, all we can see is the blue: the other element is as if it were diaphanous" (1922, 25). Many philosophers, but Gilbert Harman (1990, 1996) in particular, have suggested that this observation forms the basis of an argument against qualia, usually called "the argument from diaphanousness or transparency".[1] But even its friends concede that it is none too clear what *the argument from diaphanousness* – as I will call it – is.[2] The purpose of this paper

---

1 Harman does not mention Moore by name, but as Shoemaker (1996, 101) notes, it is clear that he has Moore mainly in mind. Presentations and discussion of the argument can be found in Harman 1990 and 1996, Tye 1995 and 2000, Martin 1998 and 2002, Lycan 1996, and Jackson 2001. Criticisms of the argument can be found in Block 1990 and 2000, Lormand 1996, Robinson 1996, and Shoemaker 1994 and 1996). The diaphanousness of experience is well known in the history of philosophy of mind, receiving attention from such figures as Broad (1925, p. 308), Ryle (1949, 152) and Grice (1962, 144). It has also been widely discussed in the sense-datum literature, though I will not take up that issue in detail here; see Martin 2002 for discussion. A similar idea about the "diaphanousness of belief" is to be found in Evans 1982, but I will not discuss that issue here. For some recent discussion of the notion as it appears in Evans, see Peacocke 1998. Van Gulick (1993) presents an interesting discussion of diaphanousness, in which he traces the idea, or a similar idea, back to Kant.

2 Here is Tye: "I believe that experience is transparent. I also believe that its transparency is a very powerful motivation for the representationist view. I concede, however, that the appeal to transparency has not been well understood" (Tye 2000, 45).

is to formulate the argument, and to assess its merits. My conclusion will be that qualia realists have little to fear from the argument – provided both qualia and diaphanousness are properly understood.

II. Preliminaries

I begin by making a number of preliminary points about the contemporary background of the argument, its different versions, and the proper understanding of its target.

II.i. The Background Debate

Suppose I am looking at the gray filing cabinet in the corner of my office. This is an experience I am having – the experience of looking at a gray filing cabinet. And we can all agree that there is something it is like for me to have this experience – some *phenomenal character* of the experience, as it is usually put. Now, what makes it the case that my experience has this character? According to one group of philosophers – qualia realists – to explain phenomenal character one must postulate or assume particular qualities of the experience, qualia. These qualities are taken to be intrinsic to the experience, directly accessible to introspection, and, in some versions of the view, non-functional, non-intentional, and maybe even ineffable, primitive, and non-physical as well. On the other hand, according to another group of philosophers – intentionalists – what explains the phenomenal character of experience is simply the intentionality of experience, or perhaps the intentionality of experience combined with its distinctive functional role.[3]

What I have just said is one way of characterizing the contempo-

---

3 In speaking of the intentionality of experience, I mean that in having an experience one represents the world as being a certain way. There are a number of important philosophical issues concerning the nature of the intentionality of experience, but I will set these issues aside here. I mention the functional role of the experience simply to register the fact that many intentionalists (e.g., Lycan 1996) include this factor in the determination of phenomenal character. For some further discussion of this issue, see the discussion of the relational thesis, and the contrast between soft and hard intentionalism, in Section II.vi and Section VI below.

rary debate about qualia – at any rate *one* contemporary debate about qualia[4] – a debate which has attracted a lot of attention in recent philosophy of mind. It is this debate that forms the background of the recent discussion of the argument from diaphanousness. As usually presented, the argument is supposed to tell against qualia realism, and in favour of intentionalism.

II.ii. Remarks on Qualia

While it is simple enough on the surface, the contemporary debate about qualia is in fact rather complex. One source of complexity is the evident obscurity of the notion of qualia. As we have seen, all parties to the discussion agree that experiences have phenomenal character, and that we can sensibly talk about these characters without prejudicing their nature. So one might suggest that qualia simply *are* these phenomenal characters. But of course, in this neutral sense there is little doubt that there are such properties, and hence there is no hope that the argument from diaphanousness could tell us otherwise. In effect, then, the argument presupposes that we can articulate a more loaded sense of the notion. In this paper, therefore, we will use 'qualia' for this loaded notion, and use 'phenomenal character' for the less-loaded, or neutral, notion.

The problem is that it is not easy to see how to expound this loaded notion in a way which would command widespread assent. Certainly different traditions tend to use the word 'qualia' differently. In Australia, for example, it is common to hear that qualia are by definition non-physical. In the United States, it is common to deny this, and emphasize only that qualia are non-functional or non-intentional properties of experience. In addition, according to some views, qualia are thought of as theoretical features postulated to explain an agreed-on fact, the fact of phenomenal character. According to other views, qualia are thought of simply *as* phenomenal characters of a certain special sort.

---

4 Another debate is, of course, physicalism, but I think the physicalist debate can be profitably separated from the debate about qualia as we will discuss it here, and so I will set it aside.

In order to impose some order on this rather confusing situation, I will proceed here by stipulation. As I will use the term, qualia are mental or psychological properties of experiences which satisfy at least the following two conditions:

> *intrinsicness* – roughly, the condition that a property satisfies when it is intrinsic to experiences;

and

> *direct awareness* – roughly, the condition that a property satisfies when it is such that if one's experience has it, one *is* in a position to apprehend this directly by introspection.

In accordance with this stipulation, qualia realists are committed at least to the view that experiences have mental properties which satisfy both intrinsicness and direct awareness – qualia precisely are such properties. The argument from diaphanousness is, then, an argument which tells us that there are no such properties.

II.iii. Intentional Properties and the Scope of the Argument

The suggestion that qualia are properties which satisfy intrinsicness and direct awareness, and that the argument tells us that there are no such properties – or that such properties are not instantiated; I will ignore this complication in what follows – immediately raises an important issue about the scope of the argument. The issue may be brought out by noting that, even if qualia *do* satisfy these conditions, it is also true that *other* psychological properties satisfy them as well. Hence, if the argument militates against qualia, it would likewise militate against these other properties. And this means the argument is much wider in scope than it at first appears.

What might these other psychological properties be? Well, consider again the experience of looking at the gray filing cabinet. We noted earlier that this experience has both phenomenal character and intentionality, the property of representing the world as being in a certain way. Let us suppose in particular that it represents the world as containing the filing cabinet, and thus has the property *being as of a filing cabinet*. Offhand, *this* property of the experience – being as of a filing cabinet – satisfies intrinsicness and direct awareness just as much as any quale does. Hence, to the extent that the argument would show that my experience instantiates no qualia, it would likewise show that it is not as of a filing cabinet. But of course, this was not part of the bargain! As indicated earlier, the argument from diaphanousness is usually understood to weigh against qualia realism, and in favour of intentionalism. But, whatever else they think, intentionalists will certainly agree that my experience has the property of being as of a filing cabinet! So it appears that intentionalists *are* in the untenable position of wielding an argument against the qualia realist when that very argument would refute their own view.

As against this, a number of ideas might be floated: (i) one might say that the point is an ad hominem against the intentionalist, and does nothing to establish that the argument from diaphanousness is mistaken; (ii) one might say that the point *does* establish that the argument is mistaken, i.e., because it proves too much, but not where the mistake in it lies; (iii) one might say that the problem only shows that my interpretation of the argument and its target must be mistaken. In many discussions (e.g., Harman 1990), it is presupposed that qualia are non-intentional properties, and that the argument from diaphanousness attacks qualia so construed. As such, any interpretation which suggests that the argument would target intentional properties must be mistaken.

There is truth to some of this, but for the moment I want to make a different point, and in fact two points. First, I stand by the claim that the argument from diaphanousness would, if successful, refute any position which has it that there are psychological properties which satisfy intrinsicness and direct awareness. Hence, if *being as of a filing cabinet* satisfies these two conditions, the argument does indeed place that property squarely under attack. On the other hand – and here is my second point – this does not in itself refute intentionalism. For it is open to the intentionalist to respond that being as of a filing cabinet does *not* satisfy these conditions – either the property is not an intrinsic property of my experience, or it is not one of which I can become directly aware, or both. Contrast the qualia realist: it is simply not open to a qualia realist to say that qualia fail to satisfy these conditions. Subtract intrinsicness and direct awareness from qualia and you have nothing; perform the same operation on intentional properties and you have something.[5]

Of course, that it is possible that intentional properties fail to satisfy these conditions does not make it plausible. Indeed, my own view is that it is plausible to suppose that being as of a filing cabinet *does* satisfy – in the senses intended – both intrinsicness and direct awareness. So, from my perspective, a pleasing secondary effect of our discussion is that it becomes permissible to say of *both* qualia and intentional properties that they satisfy the conditions. But the point for now is only that, while the argument is certainly broad in its sweep, as stated it targets qualia realism in a way that it does not target intentionalism.

These remarks on the scope of the argument from diaphanousness prompt a more impressionistic comment on its philosophical significance. The idea that experiences have properties which satisfy intrinsicness and direct awareness is central to a broadly Cartesian approach to psychological properties. The philosophical interest of the argument is that it constitutes an attack on this tradition, and indeed does so on the basis of what one might think is the Cartesian's own materials and methodology, *viz.* phenomenology. If successful, therefore, the argument would reveal a major incoherence in Cartesianism. The qualia realist, *qua* contemporary representative of this tradition,

---

5   Sydney Shoemaker (1996) presents a version of qualia realism that, as I understand it, denies direct awareness. However, while Shoemaker's version of qualia realism is an important one which deserves extensive discussion, there are three reasons why I want to set it aside here. First, as Shoemaker himself emphasizes, his account of qualia is unorthodox in that by far the dominant conception in the literature is one which accepts direct awareness. Second, Shoemaker is explicitly responding to the argument from diaphanousness. According to him, the way in which a qualia realist should react to the argument is by revising the conception of qualia in such a way that one rejects direct awareness – but this provides further evidence that the conception of qualia that is targeted by the argument from diaphanousness is the one I have set out. Finally, it is worth emphasizing that, however one uses the word 'qualia', it remains a substantive issue whether or not there are properties of experience which are intrinsic and of which we are directly aware. It is this substantive issue which I take to be mainly at issue in the following discussion. It should be noted that Shoemaker's current view differs from the position presented in 1996. See Shoemaker 2002.

is in the foreground of our discussion, but in a sense it is the tradition, and not its contemporary representative, that matters. To put the point another way, in arguing that the diaphanousness of experience can be squared with intrinsicness and direct awareness, I am upholding this aspect of the Cartesian tradition.

II.iv. Two Versions of the Argument

One sort of complexity in the debate about qualia prompts a certain regimentation of the notion in the direction of direct awareness and intrinsicness. Another sort prompts us to distinguish two versions of the argument from diaphanousness (Martin 2002). In one version, the argument is a *negative* argument whose goal is to establish that qualia realism is mistaken. In another version, the argument is a *positive* argument whose goal is to establish that intentionalism is true.

Now, if the contrast between qualia realism and intentionalism were straightforward, this would of course be a distinction without a difference: any argument which would establish the falsity of qualia realism would *ipso facto* establish the truth of intentionalism. However, while I have written so far as if it is straightforward, this is unfortunately not the case. Qualia realism is in the first instance an ontological thesis to the effect that there *are* properties of experience which satisfy a certain job description. But intentionalism per se does not seem to take a stand on this ontological issue. All intentionalism says is that the intentionality of experience explains its phenomenal character. So there would appear to be room for versions of intentionalism that are compatible with, or even entail, qualia realism.

To illustrate the problem, consider projectivism about colour. According to projectivism, when I look at the gray filing cabinet, my experience represents the cabinet as having a particular quale G, and this very quale is also instantiated by my experience. So, on this view, the quale enters the picture twice: it qualifies the experience, and the experience represents *it* as qualifying something else, *viz.*, the filing cabinet. (According to projectivism, this quale *just is* grayness – but we can ignore that aspect of the position.) In addition, on at least some versions of projectivism, what makes it the case that my experience has the content it does is that it has the qualia it does. This version of projectivism is clearly a version of qualia realism, but it is also a version of intentionalism, for it is true on this view that the phenomenal character of my experience is explained by the intentionality of the experience. It is simply that the intentionality of the experience is explained by its qualia!

Perhaps the core idea of intentionalism – that the intentionality of experience explains its phenomenal character – can be developed or extended in such a way that the contrast between it and qualia realism will be made more precise. But whether that can be done or not, from the point of view of an examination of the argument from diaphanousness, it seems best to adopt the assumption that there are at least two versions of the argument. In consequence, I will concentrate here on the first version of the argument – the one that attacks qualia realism – and postpone discussion of the second version until Section VII.

II.v. A Puzzle about Moore

The suggestion that the argument from diaphanousness can or should be construed as an argument against qualia, however, raises a further puzzle which must be confronted before we proceed any further.[6] The puzzle starts from the observation that the Moore to whom the insight concerning diaphanousness is credited is the very same Moore who famously defended the sense-datum theory. But – one might say – the sense-datum theory is surely a version of qualia realism! So, barring the unlikely hypothesis that Moore was very confused indeed, it is difficult to see how the diaphanousness of experience is going to result in the denial of qualia.

There are a number of possible ways of responding to this puzzle: (i) one might say that the Moore of diaphanousness is not the Moore of the sense-data theory;[7] (ii) one might say that it is not clear that sense-data theorists are qualia realists – in view of the difficulty of

---

6 This puzzle is mentioned in different ways by a number of different authors, including Jackson (2001), Martin (2002) and Tye (2000).

7 As Alex Byrne pointed out to me, it is not clear that Moore held the sense-data theory at the time of "The Refutation of Idealism." However, it is equally not clear, to me at any rate, that when he did come to hold the sense-data theory, he gave up diaphanousness.

interpreting the central notions, there might be a legitimate interpretative approach according to which this assumption should or could be denied; (iii) one might say that a sense-data theorist as such *does* face a problem of diaphanousness after all. Martin (2002), for example, points out that, according to one way of spelling out the idea behind the diaphanousness argument, experience presents us with a series of mind-independent properties. He goes on to say that a sense-data theorist must deny this aspect of experience and to that extent presents a revisionist conception of experience.

It may be true that suggestions of this sort can be developed. However, rather than investigate further the notions of qualia, sense-data and mind-independence, I want here to finesse the puzzle about Moore rather than confront it directly. For it is possible to distinguish two sorts of qualia realist: a sort typified by Moore and the sense-datum theorist, and a sort typified by contemporary philosophers. For our purposes, it is reasonable to assume that only the second sort is being targeted by the argument.

The distinction between the two sorts of qualia realists emerges when we consider what I will call *the relational thesis*. According to the relational thesis, the phenomenal character of an experience is wholly determined by the objects that one is related to in having the experience. A wide variety of otherwise different approaches to experience might endorse the relational thesis. According to what is sometimes called "the naïve approach", for example, in having an experience such as the experience of looking at a filing cabinet, one is directly related to the filing cabinet itself.[8] Against the background of this naïve approach, the relational thesis tells us that the phenomenal character of the experience is determined by features of the filing cabinet. According to intentionalism, by contrast, to have an experience is in effect to stand in a relation to some intentional object – say a property or a proposition. Against the background of that approach, the relational thesis tells us that the phenomenal character of the experience is determined by features of the proposition or property that is the intentional object of the experience.

---

8 For some discussion of the naïve approach, see Martin 2002.

Now, one sort of qualia realist, the sort typified by the sense-datum theorist, holds the relational thesis. According to the sense-datum theorist, when I look at a gray filing cabinet, what I look at or am acquainted with in the first instance is a mental object which is both gray and filing-cabinet shaped. The properties of this object, according to sense-datum theorists, determine the phenomenal character of my experience. Indeed, on at least one well-established tradition, the qualities of this mental object are the paradigm examples of what qualia are supposed to be. It is clear, then, that so construed, the sense-datum theory endorses the relational thesis. But the sense-datum theory is also a version of qualia realism.[9]

On the other hand, another sort of qualia realist denies the relational thesis. One example of such a position emerges if we contrast the sense-datum theory with its traditional rival, adverbialism. Adverbialism denies the relational thesis, since it denies that in having an experience one is related to an object of any sort. According to adverbialism, the experience of looking at a gray object is just the experience of sensing gray-ly, but to sense gray-ly is not to be related to anything. On the other hand, an adverbialist is perfectly entitled to combine this position with qualia realism – the experience of sensing gray-ly might perfectly well have properties which satisfy intrinsicness and direct awareness. So in adverbialism we have a position which might combine qualia realism with the denial of the relational thesis.

Now adverbialism is not a position that many contemporary philosophers are attracted to.[10] But there is a version of qualia realism

---

9 The sense-datum theory is sometimes interpreted as a theory according to which the intentionality of the experience explains its phenomenal character (see Byrne 2001 for an interpretation like this, but see Jackson 2001 for a dissenting interpretation). So, from this point of view, we have here a second example of a position which combines qualia realism with intentionalism. As in the discussion of projectivism, I assume that intentionalism strictly so-called can be developed in such a way that it is not consistent with these versions of qualia realism. But I will not discuss the issue further here.

10 One reason that adverbialism fell out of favour is that it was often presented as an account of the logical syntax of perceptual vocabulary. On that interpretation, the thesis is subject to extremely serious objections; see Jackson 1977. But it is tempting to suppose also that another reason that adverbialism fell out of favour is that adverbialists offer no account of the intentionality of experience.

which agrees with adverbialism in rejecting the relational thesis. I have in mind the position held at one time by Sydney Shoemaker (1981), and most recently by Ned Block (1990), according to which we sharply distinguish the intentionality of an experience from the qualia it instantiates – the intentional from the phenomenal content of the experience, as it is sometime put.[11] On this sort of view – which we might call *the Shoemaker–Block view* – experiences generally have intentionality – that is what it means to say that experiences have intentional content. And in addition, experiences have qualia, properties which satisfy intrinsicness and direct access and which explain, or perhaps partially explain, the fact that the experience has the phenomenal character it does. However – and this is the crucial fact for our purposes – these properties are not themselves properties of the objects that one is related to in having the experience. So here we have a second position which denies the relational thesis, but still maintains that there are qualia. Indeed, I think it is fair to say that it is this sort of qualia realist, rather than the sort typified by either Moore or by adverbialism, which is the dominant sort in contemporary philosophy. So by 'qualia realist' I will henceforth mean proponents of the Shoemaker–Block view, unless the context suggests otherwise.[12]

Indeed, for adverbialists experiences lack intentionality altogether. For some development of this theme, particularly as it relates to the sense-datum theory, see Jackson 2001.

11 The Shoemaker–Block view is also closely allied to views such as that of Peacocke (1983). It is important to note, however, that Peacocke's position is often construed as a version of a sense-datum theory, but the Shoemaker–Block view is not. The Shoemaker–Block view is better interpreted as a compromise between intentionalism and adverbialism.

12 It is important to notice that the difference between kinds of qualia realists that I have just identified does not emerge when we consider only the form of words that is used to state the doctrines. Take the statement 'qualia are properties of experience that satisfy intrinsicness and direct access'. Both Moore and Block might well agree to this form of words, but they would understand it very differently. For Moore, the word 'experience' will mean, or might be taken to mean, the object that one is related to in having the experience, a sense datum. For Block, on the other hand, and for all qualia-realists who endorse the Shoemaker–Block view, the word 'experience' in this form of words will be taken to mean the psychological state of experiencing. Again, since I will operate with the Shoemaker–Block view here, I will follow them in this usage.

Daniel Stoljar

How does the distinction I have just drawn – between those qualia realists who endorse the relational thesis and those who don't – answer the puzzle about G.E. Moore? Well, as we will see presently, the argument from diaphanousness involves precisely the idea that while we are directly aware of objects that we are related to in having experiences, we are not directly aware of those experiences themselves, or of the intrinsic features of such experiences. Such a position certainly does threaten the Shoemaker–Block view, since according to that view there are properties of experience of which we *are* directly aware. But an argument of this sort does not threaten, or at least does not seem to threaten, the sense-datum theorist, since, according to that view, it is not at all obvious that there are properties of experience of which we are directly aware. Instead of convicting Moore of confusion, therefore, I will for the most part limit the following discussion to the opposition between the argument from diaphanousness and the Shoemaker–Block view.

II.vi. A Third Version of the Argument

Earlier, we distinguished two versions of the argument from diaphanousness, one against qualia realism and the other in favour of intentionalism. Having explicitly noted the relational thesis, however, it is natural to go further and suggest a *third* version of the argument. On this version, the argument is an argument for the relational thesis, or equivalently, an argument against the denial of that thesis.

The first thing to say is that construing the argument this way would certainly widen the scope of our discussion. For one thing, while it is true that there are qualia realists (e.g., Block) who deny the relational thesis, and qualia realists (e.g., Moore) who accept it, it is also true that there are qualia *non*-realists who *deny* the relational thesis. A qualia non-realist who rejects the relational thesis, for example, is Paul Churchland (1985). According to Churchland, one might envisage a future direction of science in which neuroscientific knowledge becomes such an everyday part of life that one might simply introspect directly the brain states with which various sensory states are to be identified. One might of course question Churchland's vision of future science, and also the extent to which science so envisioned would impact on our self-conception. However, for our purposes the important point is simply that Churchland is assuming that one might directly introspect intrinsic features of our mental states, and is also *not* assuming that those states have intentional objects of any sort. So, on at least this dimension, Churchland is to be grouped with Block and not with Harman when it comes to the relational thesis. And yet Churchland is a qualia non-realist.

Similarly, while it is true that there are both intentionalists and non-intentionalists who accept the relational thesis (e.g., Harman and Moore) it is also true that there are intentionalists who deny the relational thesis. An intentionalist who denies the relational thesis, for example, is Lycan (1996). Lycan holds a view which I will call *soft intentionalism* and which is to be contrasted with the more straightforward development of the position, which I will call *hard intentionalism*.[13]

The hard intentionalist holds the relational thesis since, according to that view, in having an experience one bears an attitude to a proposition, and the phenomenal character of the experience is wholly determined by the content of the proposition. Soft intentionalism, by contrast, supposes that the phenomenal character of an experience is determined, not solely by features of the proposition one is related to in having the experience, but in addition by features of the experience itself, including, in particular, functional features. The more a soft intentionalist emphasizes the functional role of the experience in the determination of phenomenal character, the less likely someone holding the position is to endorse the relational thesis. And yet soft intentionalism is recognizable as a version of intentionalism.[14]

So it seems that the relational thesis raises an issue that in a certain sense stands apart from the debate between intentionalism and qualia

---

13 Lycan's position is sometimes called "quasi-representationism" or "quasi-intentionalism". However, since I want to emphasize the fact that Lycan's position is a version of intentionalism, I will adopt a different phraseology here. Thanks to Philip Pettit for suggesting the phraseology.

14 It is important to stress that the difference between hard and soft intentionalism is mainly a matter of degree rather than kind. Most intentionalists *do* emphasize the functional role of experience to some extent; the crucial issue is to what extent they do so. See Block 2000, including in particular the discussion of whether Harman is a 'quasi-representationist' or not.

realism. Nevertheless, I think the suggestion that the argument from diaphanousness can be construed as an argument for the relational thesis is a good one. And this introduces a further complexity into our discussion. How should we deal with this complexity? As in the case of our distinction between the first two versions of the argument, I think an examination of the argument from diaphanousness has no choice but to consider this third version. Once again, however, to keep things manageable, my discussion here will remain focused on the question of whether the argument defeats qualia realism in the sense intended. I will return to this third version of the argument in Section VII.

III. The Argument

So far we have noted that there are three versions of the argument, and set the version we want mainly to discuss more sharply in focus. In this section I formulate the argument, and discuss which premise in it should properly be called "the thesis of diaphanousness".

III..i What it is

It is widely agreed that the argument from diaphanousness starts from the considerations presented both in the passage from Moore with which we began, and also in this famous passage from Gilbert Harman:

> When Eloise sees a tree before her, the colors she experiences are all experienced as features of the tree and its surroundings. None of them are experienced as intrinsic features of her experience. Nor does she experience any features of anything as intrinsic features of her experiences. And that is true of you too.... Look at a tree and try to turn your attention to intrinsic features of your visual experience. I predict that you will find that the only features there to turn your attention to will be features of the tree. (1990, 667)

Both passages are certainly suggestive, but what *exactly* is the argument they suggest?

My proposal is that the argument against qualia implicit in these passages and their supporting texts might be presented as proceeding in three stages. At the first stage, one makes a phenomenological point the formulation of which we can simply take over from Harman:

(1) Look at a tree and try to turn your attention to intrinsic[15] features of your visual experience. I predict you will find that the only features there to turn your attention to will be features of the presented tree.

Harman is here both giving instructions ("Look at a tree and try to turn your attention ...") and making a prediction about what we will find ourselves doing if and when we obey his instructions. Since both prediction and instruction are supposed to be presented as a neutral and non-committal description of the phenomena, we are so far only at the phenomenological stage of the argument.

At the next stage, one makes a theoretical point about introspection, which is intended to be grounded in the phenomenological point just presented, and perhaps is plausible also on its own terms. There are a number of ways to formulate this point, but I think a reasonable initial formulation is this:[16]

---

15 One should perhaps emphasize *psychological* or *mental* intrinsic features here – but I will largely leave that implicit in what follows.

16 My formulation of (2) has been greatly influenced by Martin 2002 and Tye 2000. Tye (51) says, for example, that "[w]hen we introspect our experiences and feelings, we become aware of what it is like for us to undergo them. But we are not directly aware of those experiences and feelings; nor are we directly aware of any of their qualities. The qualities to which we have direct access are the external ones, the qualities that, if they are qualities of anything, are qualities of external things. By being aware of these qualities, we are aware of phenomenal character." It is important to note that (2) embodies a certain conception of experience which is friendly to an intentionalist, since it speaks of objects and properties represented by the experience. As we will note in Section VI, there are more general ways to state the thesis, but I will ignore this aspect of the issue until then.

(2)   In introspection, one is, or becomes, aware of the intrinsic
features of one's experience *by* attending to the objects and
properties represented by that experience.[17]

Notice that (2) does not by itself prejudice the issue of whether or not
there are qualia in the sense we have intended, that is, whether or not
there are properties of experience which satisfy the job-description
of qualia. It simply says that one apprehends the intrinsic features of
one's experience by doing something else.

In the final stage of the argument, one draws the moral from this
theoretical point for the debate about qualia. Once again, there might
be different ways to state this moral, but a reasonable formulation is
this:

(3)   In introspection, one is not *directly* aware of the intrinsic
features of one's experience.

The force of (3) is of course that qualia realism in the sense at issue is
mistaken. If qualia realism is true, there must be intrinsic features of
experiences of which we are directly aware in introspection. But, by
(3), there are no such features.

In summary, the argument from diaphanousness takes us from (1)
to (2) to (3), and (3) is something the qualia realist is committed to
denying.

III.ii. What is "The Diaphanousness of Experience"?

The formulation of the argument from diaphanousness that I have
just offered raises the question about *which* claim here should be identified with the thesis of *the diaphanousness of experience*.

On the one hand, one might think that this thesis should be identified with (1) or something like it. After all, the diaphanousness of
experience is often thought to be grounded in, or perhaps just to be,

---

17   One may speak not only of the objects and properties represented *by* the
experience but also of the object and properties presented *in* the experience. I
will sometimes adopt this latter expression as a stylistic alternative.

a piece of phenomenology. On the other hand, one might think that the thesis should be identified with the 'by'-claim summarized in (2), where (2) is, as we have noted, a theoretical claim about introspection and about what is involved in being, or becoming, aware of the intrinsic features of one's experiences. Perhaps this choice is in some respects terminological, but in any event, so far as I can see the most natural interpretation is to treat (2) as the thesis of the diaphanousness of experience, and I will talk for the most part in those terms.

Even if one can afford to be somewhat sanguine about which of (1) or (2) should be treated as the thesis of diaphanousness, it is important to note that one should not be sanguine, or at least should not be so sanguine, about whether (3) should be treated as the thesis of diaphanousness. For suppose that (3) *were* thought of as the thesis of diaphanousness. Then there would be no interesting question about how there could be an argument *from* diaphanousness *to* the denial of qualia realism. For (3) obviously impacts on qualia realism. On the other hand, as will emerge in due course, the crucial question I want to focus on is precisely whether or not there is a decent argument *from* the thesis of diaphanousness – that is, (2) – to the denial of qualia realism. On the assumption that (3) were the thesis of diaphanousness, therefore, the central question of our inquiry could not be raised.

Of course one might say that this is all to the good from the point of view of the argument. And perhaps there is some temptation in the literature to identify (3) with the thesis of diaphanousness. But this maneuver simply conceals the issue rather than solving it. For the fact is that in most presentations of the argument people begin by making remarks like (1) or (2). The question which will concern us is how it is that these remarks bear on the issue of qualia realism, a question we have formulated in terms of an argument from the thesis of diaphanousness. Dubbing (3) the thesis of diaphanousness makes our question more difficult to express, but it does not make it disappear.

III.iii. An Alternative Formulation

The importance of not treating (3) as the thesis of diaphanousness emerges in more detail when we contrast the formulation of the argument that I have offered with an alternative formulation. According to this alternative, the argument should be understood as proceeding, not from (2) to (3), but rather from (2) to (3*):

(3*)   In introspection, one is *only* directly aware of the objects and properties represented by one's experience.

(3*) is logically distinct from (3). (3*) presupposes, while (3) does not, that there *are* objects and properties represented by experience and that we are directly aware of them: it simply says that this is all we are aware of. In addition, (3) presupposes, while (3*) does not, that there *are* intrinsic features of experience: it simply says that we are not aware of them. So it seems that we do here have a genuinely different formulation of the argument: one proceeds from (2) to (3), and the other proceeds from (2) to (3*).

I think it should be agreed that this is an alternative, but it is a formulation I want to set aside in what follows. While (3) and (3*) are certainly not logically equivalent, it is reasonable to assume that, in the context of our discussion, they amount to largely the same thing, or at least that one can relatively easily move back and forth between them. On the one hand, it seems reasonable to infer (3) from (3*) given the assumption that projectivism is false: if it is true that one is only directly aware of presented features, and presented features are not also intrinsic features, then one is not directly aware of intrinsic features. On the other hand, it seems reasonable to infer (3*) from (3) given the assumption that one is directly aware of something in having an experience: if one is not directly aware of intrinsic features, and is directly aware of something, then presumably what one is directly aware of are presented features. But if that is true, then it seems reasonable to conclude that the distance between (3) and (3*) is not something over which we can make much hay. For this reason I will continue to focus on (3).[18]

---

18 In his commentary on this paper at the conference in Melbourne, Frank Jackson suggested that one might think about the structure of the argument in a slightly different way. According to Jackson, from the premise that one is only directly aware of the objects and properties presented in experience one may conclude that there are no qualia – the reason being that the properties that one is aware of

Even if (3*) is set aside, however, it is important to notice that, as in the case of (3), one must resist the temptation to identify (3*) with the thesis of diaphanousness. Our focus is on the question of how observations such as Harman's about Eloise and the tree support (3*). And we have articulated that question by asking how the thesis of diaphanousness has an impact on qualia realism. On the assumption that (3*) *were* the thesis of diaphanousness, we would be obliged to reformulate our question, even if, as we have already noted, the question would certainly not disappear entirely.

IV. Block's Critique

In recent literature, the philosopher who has done most to criticize the argument from diaphanousness is Ned Block. In this section I set out his criticisms and explain why I think they fail. I will start by pointing out two claims which a proponent of it is *not* committed to. I will then argue that Block's criticisms largely rely on mistakenly attributing these claims to a proponent of the argument.

IV.i. Intrinsicness

First, a proponent of the argument is *not* committed to the denial of intrinsicness, the idea that there are psychological properties of experience which are intrinsic to the experience. The argument we just considered certainly involves the suggestion that there are no intrinsic properties which meet direct awareness, but intrinsicness itself is left untouched.

---

are intentional rather than real, and thus need not be instantiated in experiences. Surely, however, qualia are properties which are instantiated in experiences. This interpretation of the argument is interesting and is different from the version that I consider in the text. Nevertheless, I think we can set aside this suggestion here. Given our distinction between (3) and (3*), what Jackson is doing is providing novel grounds to move from (3*) to (3). As noted in the text, however, my focus here is not on the move from (3*) to (3), but rather on the move from (2) to (3), or – something I take to be largely equivalent in the context – the move from (2) to (3*). So far as I can see, Jackson's point does not affect what I have so say about that transition.

IV.i.i.

The suggestion that the argument does not involve denying intrinsicness might seem initially strange. Proponents of the argument certainly say things which on the surface suggest the opposite. Concerning Eloise, for example, Harman says that she does not "experience any features of anything as *intrinsic* features of her experiences" (1990, 667, emphasis added). The idea here, I think, is that when we spell out the ways in which Eloise takes the world to be in perception, one might say that she takes the world to contain a tree, with a certain shape and colour, which occupies a position at such and such a distance from her, and so on. But nowhere does one need to say that Eloise takes the world to contain objects which instantiate intrinsic properties which are *also* intrinsic properties of her experiences. In short, Eloise takes the world to be a certain way in perception, but in spelling out that way one does not need to mention intrinsic features of her experiences.

However, the difficulty here is in moving from a claim of this form – which certainly has a good deal of plausibility to it[19] – to any claim which seems to threaten qualia. One might say that the qualia realist is committed to the idea that qualia exist *only if* we are directly aware of them in perception as intrinsic features of objects, but put so baldly, it is not at all clear why anyone would make such a claim. Similarly, one might say – Harman *does* say – that qualia realists are guilty of confounding intrinsic properties of objects represented by experience with intrinsic properties of experience. But even if this charge of confusion is true, it would only be an explanation of why people might believe that qualia exist, assuming that belief to be false. It does not at all encourage the suggestion that belief in qualia is false to begin with. Finally, one might say that what these claims suggest is that one is directly aware only of intrinsic features of objects and that one is aware of the intrinsic features of one's experiences by being aware

---

19 As Josh Parsons pointed out to me, there is one sort of intrinsic property of an experience which one might say is both a property of the tree and of Eloise's experience: the property of being such that there is an experience. But it is not clear that one needs to appeal to this property in spelling out how Eloise takes the world to be in visual experience.

of the intrinsic features of objects represented in experiences. But to say this is simply to embrace a version of the argument already presented.

VI.i.ii.

There is also a second reason why it might seem initially strange that the argument from diaphanousness does not target intrinsicness. Proponents of the argument usually write from a functionalist or intentionalist perspective, and one might think that from that perspective, it is just *obvious* that there are no intrinsic psychological features of experience.

The short answer to this is that there is a difference between what a proponent of the argument is committed to *qua* intentionalist or functionalist, and what a proponent of the argument is committed to *qua* proponent of the argument. My point is only that the argument does not strictly speaking attack intrinsicness, not that people who propound the argument do not attack it as a matter of fact.

The longer answer is that there is in fact no reason at all why an intentionalist or functionalist must deny intrinsicness. The plausibility of the claim that there are psychological properties which are intrinsic to experience depends largely on what one thinks an experience *is*. On the one hand, one might identify an experience with what Shoemaker (1996) calls its "core realizer". This is the particular or local neural state which, as Shoemaker says, comes and goes as the state comes and goes. Now, on this view, the intrinsicness condition is quite an implausible claim, and, moreover, it is so regardless of whether functionalism or intentionalism is true or not. For, on this conception of experience, to say that some psychological property of an experience is intrinsic to the experience is to say that this property is wholly determined by matters that are internal to its core realizer. But this *is* highly implausible. At any rate, to assert boldly of any psychological property of an experience that it is determined by matters internal to its core realizer is a wild empirical speculation, something that goes far beyond what anyone could reasonably claim at the moment.

Now, one response to this is to say that psychological properties are not intrinsic to experiences, i.e., to deny the intrinsicness condition. But a better response is to deny that experiences ought to be identified with their core realizers, and to look for an alternative.[20] For there *is* an alternative available. The alternative is to identify an experience with what Shoemaker calls its "total realizer".[21] This is the total state of the brain or nervous system that one is in when one has a certain experience. On this view, to say that a property is intrinsic to an experience is to say that this feature of the experience is wholly determined by goings-on internal to the total realizer. But this claim is not at all implausible *even if* one is a functionalist or intentionalist. For this claim amounts to nothing more than the claim that someone who is in that same total or overall brain state will also have the experience – if you like, on this view, the idea that phenomenal character is intrinsic to experience is tantamount to the claim that phenomenal character is intrinsic to the subjects of that experience, rather than simply the experience. This is a claim that has certainly been denied in contemporary philosophy, but it is not one which off-hand is particularly implausible, nor one that is in conflict with intentionalism or functionalism.

The moral is that once intrinsicness is to be understood in a way that makes it plausible – that is, when the background conception of experience identifies experiences with total realizers, rather than core realizers – it is not at all clear that functionalists or intentionalists must deny it. But that means – to return to our main line of argument – that there is no reason why a functionalist or intentionalist who endorses the argument from diaphanousness must deny intrinsicness.[22]

---

20 To what extent is the idea that experiences are to be identified with their core-realizers influencing those who deny intrinsicness? This interpretative question is difficult to resolve. However, it is important to note that both Harman (1990) and Block (1990) are operating with a 'language of thought' conception according to which an experience is to be identified with a linguistic vehicle of some sort. I take it that this conception of experience is at least close to *a* version which identifies an experience with its core realizer.

21 Another alternative would be to deny the identity between experiences and their core-realizers and adopt some variety of constitution thesis. Thanks to Martin Davies for pointing out this option to me.

22 Two further points concerning intrinsicness should be noted: (1) Philosophers who support internalism in the philosophy of mind, or at least do so in certain specific cases, argue that intentional properties are (or at least are in some cases)

IV.ii. Direct Awareness, not Awareness Tout Court

Proponents of the argument from diaphanousness are not only not committed to denying intrinsicness, they are also not committed to denying that we are aware of the intrinsic features of our experience. The conclusion of the argument is that one is not *directly* aware of those features. But if 'direct' is doing any work at all, here, we cannot conclude from this that one is not aware of those features. To say that one is not directly aware of something leaves open the possibility that one is aware of it, but to say that one is not aware *at all* closes off that possibility.

The point that a proponent of the argument is not committed to the denial of awareness of intrinsic features is important when we consider the overall credibility of the argument. After all, if the argument *did* involve the suggestion that one is not aware in introspection of one's experience, then it would be fair to say that it should be treated as presenting a paradox rather than as something to which one might look to decide between competing positions in philosophy of mind. For surely it is a datum, something on which everybody can agree, that one can be aware of one's experience in introspection!

One might respond that this underestimates the radicalness of the proponent of the argument from diaphanousness. A proponent of that argument, one might think, is certainly committed to the claim that one is directly aware of the objects and properties presented in one's experience. But this should not be interpreted in such a way that it is consistent with the claim that one is also *indirectly* aware of one's experiences. Rather it should be interpreted in such a way that it entails or suggests that one is not aware of one's experiences *at all*. Moreover, one might suggest, the "datum" that one is aware of one's experiences derives only from a confusion between the properties presented in one's experience and the experiences themselves.

However, someone who adopts this radical course is, in my view, faced with rather serious difficulties. For contrast visual perception

---

intrinsic in the second sense. For a recent general defense of internalism, see Segal 2000, and for discussion of how the externalism/internalism issue figures in the debate about qualia and intentionalism, see Block 2000 and Jackson 2001. (2) The notion of intrinsicness is in any case extremely puzzling. For a recent discussion, see Langton and Lewis 1998 and the references therein.

with visual imagination.[23] If I were sufficiently adept at visual imagination, I might be able to conjure up in imagination a situation that is identical to the visual experience I am having right now. In other words, it seems quite possible to contrast the situation in which I am visually under the impression that *p* with a counterpart situation in which I only visually imagine that *p*. If it were really true that in introspection I am not aware, or could not become aware, of my experiences themselves, it would seem to follow that introspection alone could not allow me to discern these two situations one from the other. But surely I *can* tell the imagination case from the impression case on the basis of introspection alone. In the impression case, I am going to feel inclined to believe that *p*. In the imagination case, on the other hand, I am *not* going to feel inclined to believe that *p*. The explanation for this, of course, is that perception and imagination have very different functional roles in the mental life of a person: to imagine something is an act of will in the way that to be visually aware of something is not. But since the respective contents of perception and imagination are in this instance presumed to be the same, it follows that I must be aware, not simply of the intentional objects my experiences, but also of the experiences themselves.

We will return to the contrast between imagination and perception at a later stage. For the moment the important point is simply that it *is* a datum that we are, or can become, aware of intrinsic aspects of our experience. And so the argument from diaphanousness could not possibly tell us otherwise.

IV.iii. Block's Objections

We are now in a position to demonstrate that Block's three objections to the argument from diaphanousness misfire.

IV.iii.i

Block's first objection is that the argument represents "an error in philosophical method." He goes on: "Looking at a blue wall is an easy thing to do, but it is not easy (perhaps not possible) to answer on the

---

23 See Martin 2002 for an extended discussion of this contrast.

basis of introspection alone the highly theoretical question of whether in so doing I am aware of intrinsic properties of my experience" (1990, 689). As I understand this objection, Block is suggesting that, whatever the argument from diaphanousness is exactly, its premise is based on phenomenology or introspection, and its conclusion is that one is not aware of intrinsic properties. His suggestion is that it is an error to infer from premises to conclusions of this sort.

Block may or may not be right that inferences like this are mistaken, but even so his objection does not touch the argument from diaphanousness. For, at least as I have set it out here, that argument does *not* conclude with the claim that one is not aware of the intrinsic properties of experience. For consider: we have seen that it is consistent with advancing the argument that one thinks that experiences have intrinsic properties. And we have also just seen that the argument does not attack the idea that we are aware of those properties if they exist and are instantiated. Putting these two points together, we derive the result that the argument does not involve, contrary to Block's objection, the suggestion that one is not aware of intrinsic properties.

One might respond that the distinction between direct awareness and awareness *tout court* does not touch the basis of Block's objection, because that objection can simply be reformulated to accommodate it. On this interpretation, Block's objection is that we cannot decide, on the basis of introspection alone, the question of whether we are *directly* aware of the intrinsic properties of our experiences or not. However, the response to this version of the objection is that the argument does not ask us to decide this question "on the basis of introspection alone." The only thing that is to be decided on the basis of introspection alone is the phenomenological point (1). But (1) is supposed to provide *evidence* for (2), which is not something that one can decide on the basis of introspection alone, but is rather a theoretical claim about introspection. On the other hand, you need (2) to get you to (3), the denial of direct awareness. The argument that Block is attacking effectively cuts out the middle man; that is, it is an argument that moves directly from (1) to (3). But that is evidently not the argument from diaphanousness as we have been discussing it here.[24]

---

24 There is a further point here that might also be mentioned. Block is contrasting a theoretical question and a question that might be answered on the basis of

IV.iii.ii.

A similar criticism – that the position attacked is not the position defended – is also appropriate when we turn to a second objection mounted by Block against the argument:

> Harman relies on the diaphanousness of perception (Moore 1922), which may be defined as the claim that the effect of concentrating on experience is simply to attend to and be aware of what the experience is of. As a point about attention in one familiar circumstance – e.g., looking at a red tomato, this is certainly right. The more one concentrates on the experience, the more one attends to the redness of the tomato itself. But attention and awareness are distinct, and as a point about awareness, the diaphanousness claim is both straightforwardly wrong and misleading. One can be aware of what one is not attending to. For example, one might be involved in intense conversation while a jackhammer outside causes one to raise one's voice without ever noticing or attending to the noise until someone comments on it – at which time one realizes that one was aware of it all along. Or consider the familiar experience of noticing that the refrigerator compressor has gone off and that one was aware of it for some time, even though one didn't attend to it until it stopped. (Block 2000, 7)

---

introspection alone. But is not clear that there is any genuine contrast here. Certainly if one lacks a certain concept, one cannot answer on the basis of introspection alone the question of whether the concept applies – but the issue of concept-possession does not seem to be relevant to the case Block has in mind. On the other hand, if one *possesses* the relevant concept, one might well be able to decide the question of whether it applies on the basis of introspection alone. The issue turns on whether the concept is the sort of concept for which introspection provides a proprietary evidential basis. If so, there is no reason to suppose that introspection alone should not furnish sufficient information for one to be able to decide that the concept applies. The problem for Block is that it is not at all clear that the concepts in question are not of this sort.

Block is certainly correct that there is a distinction between attention and awareness – indeed, we will come back to this distinction later on. Nevertheless, the objection which I take him to be making in this passage derives again from a mistake about what someone is committed to in advancing the argument from diaphanousness. Block is assuming, I think, that a proponent of the argument is committed to the claim that one is not aware of the intrinsic features of my experience. The point about awareness and attention certainly *would* defeat that position: from the fact that one does not attend (in the strict sense) to one's experience, it does not follow that one is not aware of it. But as we have seen, a proponent of the argument need not, or should not, adopt the position that one is not aware of the intrinsic features of one's experiences. What is at issue is direct awareness, not awareness *tout court*.

IV.iii.iii.

Block's third objection is that the step from (1) to (2) is fallacious. (1) might be true and also conform to (2), but there are plenty of examples of experiences which do not:

> [c]lose your eyes in daylight and you may find that it is easy to attend to aspects of your experience. If all experiences that have visual phenomenology were of the sort one gets with one's eyes closed while awake in daylight, I doubt that the thesis that one cannot attend to or be aware of one's experience would be so popular. (Block 2000, 8)

The crucial fact about an example such as this – elsewhere Block also mentions orgasms and phosphenes – is that here we seem to have an experience which lacks (or might lack) intentionality. In these cases, Block says, experience is not diaphanous, that is, it is not the case that one is, or becomes, aware of the features of an experience by attending to the object and properties represented by the experience – for in this case there are no such objects and properties! It would thus seem that the step from (1) to (2) is fallacious. Of course, *some* experiences are such that claims like (1) are true of them. Nevertheless, (2) is a massive overgeneralization from these isolated examples.

One thing to say about this objection is that it does not suffer from the sort of problem I identified with the previous two. Unlike the previous two objections, this objection really *would* attack the argument as I have formulated it. Nevertheless, there are two reasons why I want to set it aside.

First, even if Block is right about closing one's eyes in daylight, orgasms, and so on, Harman *still* seems to be right about experiences which uncontroversially have intentionality, such as experiences of colour. But surely the qualia realist does not want to be maneuvered into the position of saying that colour experiences lack qualia. It would be an odd sort of position indeed which postulates qualia but then adds that qualia are only instantiated in cases in which you face the Sun with closed eyes, or else are in states of sexual climax!

Second, the question of whether experiences of the kind mentioned by Block lack intentionality or not is a controversial issue (see, e.g., Tye 2000). Part of the general issue raised by the debate about qualia with which we began is precisely the question of whether there are sensations which have phenomenal character but lack intentionality – whether there is a distinction between sensation and perception, as it is often put. Of course there is a tradition in which it is obvious that there is such a distinction, and arguably ordinary thought recognizes a distinction along these lines. But on the other hand, there have been persistent efforts in philosophy to undermine this distinction. There is first of all the Galilean tradition in which one treats perception as a species of sensation, a tradition partially revived and defended by the adverbialists of the twentieth century. Then there is the sense-datum tradition, which reduces both sensation and perception to something else: a mental act in which one is acquainted with a sense-datum. Finally, there are contemporary intentionalists who try to show that both sensations and perceptions are species of propositional attitude.

In Block's third objection we are in effect being asked to accept (a version of) the sensation–perception distinction and so reject the argument from diaphanousness. However, whatever is the ultimate truth about that distinction, this is unlikely to be a persuasive response to someone who advances the argument from diaphanousness. For such a person is very likely to reject the sensation–perception distinction in the first place. So I think we need to leave Block's third objection aside, and look elsewhere.

V. The Step from (2) to (3)

I have been concerned so far only to set out the argument from diaphanousness, to point out what one is not committed to in advancing it, and to defend it from some criticisms made by Block. I now turn to my own suggestion about what is wrong with the argument. My focus is the step from:

> (2)　In introspection, one is, or becomes, aware of the intrinsic features of one's experience *by* attending to the objects and properties represented by that experience

to:

> (3)　In introspection, one is not *directly* aware of the intrinsic features of one's experience.

I will argue that this step is fallacious. Even if it is true that I apprehend the features of my experience by attending to the objects presented in that experience, it does not follow that I am not *directly* aware of those features. In fact, there are two ways of developing this objection. The first proceeds via a closer examination of the direct awareness condition; the second via a closer examination of the notion of attention.

V.i. The First way to Develop the Objection

In thinking about the direct-awareness condition, we need to focus on two questions. The *directness question* asks: what does it mean to say that one is *directly* aware of intrinsic features of experience? In other words, the directness question brackets the issue of what it is to be aware of the intrinsic properties of experience, and asks instead what it is to be directly aware. The *awareness question* asks: what does it mean to say that one is directly *aware* of the intrinsic features of experience? In other words, the awareness question brackets the issue of directness, and asks instead what it is to be *aware* of experience in the first place.

Now, as regards the directness question, I think it is plausible to operate with a rather schematic account of what it is to be directly aware of something, an account which may be extracted from classic discussions by William Alston on epistemic immediacy and Frank

Jackson on perceptual immediacy (see Alston 1971; Jackson 1977).[25] According to this account, one first defines what it is to be indirectly aware of something, as follows: S is indirectly aware of x just in case one is aware of x by being aware of y, where y is distinct from x. One then defines what it is to be directly aware of something as follows: S is directly aware of x just in case (a) S is aware of x; and (b) S is not (merely) indirectly aware of x.[26] So to say that one is directly aware of experience is to say that one is aware of it but one is not aware of it by being aware of anything else.

As regards the awareness question, the crucial distinction to draw initially is one drawn by Fred Dretske between f-awareness, o-awareness and p-awareness (Dretske 1999). Dretske introduces the distinction with the example of looking at a moving object. In such a case, one might be aware of the object itself – this is object or o-awareness. Or else one might be aware of the movement of the object – this is property or p-awareness. And finally one might be aware *that* the object is moving – this is fact or f-awareness. Similarly, in the case of experiences and their intrinsic properties, one might be aware of the experience itself – this is o-awareness. Or else one might be aware of the intrinsic properties of the experience – this is p-awareness. And finally one might be aware that the experience has those intrinsic properties – this is f-awareness. Dretske argues persuasively that these notions are logically independent: one might, for example, be f-aware that one's experience e has property C, and be neither o-aware of e nor p-aware of C.

In the light of Dretske's distinction among species of awareness, as well as the schematic account of directness, the bad news is that it now appears that there are no fewer than *nine* ways to interpret the direct-awareness condition:

    (4a)   S is o-aware of experience e but not by being o-aware of anything else.

---

25 For further discussion of the notion of immediacy, see Armstrong 1980.

26 The 'merely' is required here to rule out the case in which one is both directly and indirectly aware of something.

(4b)   *S* is *o*-aware of experience *e* but not by being *p*-aware of anything else.

(4c)   *S* is *o*-aware of experience *e* but not by being *f*-aware of anything else.

(4d)   *S* is *p*-aware of the character *C* of experience *e* but not by being *o*-aware of anything else.

(4e)   *S* is *p*-aware of the character *C* of experience *e* but not by being *p*-aware of anything else.

(4f)   *S* is *p*-aware of the character *C* of experience *e* but not by being *f*-aware of anything else.

(4g)   *S* is *f*-aware that experience *e* has character *C* but not by being *o*-aware of anything else.

(4h)   *S* is *f*-aware that experience *e* has character *C* but not by being *p*-aware of anything else.

(4i)   *S* is *f*-aware that experience *e* has character *C* but not by being *f*-aware of anything else.

On the other hand, the good news is that there is a decent case for supposing that it is interpretation (4i) which is the correct one for our purposes.

In the first place, as Dretske points out, the usual way of explicating *o*-awareness or *p*-awareness is by assimilating them to certain perceptual relations. One is *o*-aware of the moving object just when one sees it, and one is *p*-aware of the movement of the object just when one sees its movement. But that suggests that the idea that we are *o*-aware of experiences or *p*-aware of properties of experience is simply the idea that a perceptual model of introspection is true, and moreover is true in a rather extreme form. On the other hand, if one wants to avoid the perceptual model, as most contemporary philosophers do, it would seem that the only option is to operate with *f*-awareness and to adopt (4g–4i).[27] In the second place, of these three interpretations, it is really only (4i) that articulates a reasonable notion of direct awareness.

---

27   The assertion that most modern philosophers are not attracted to the perceptual model might seem strange in light of the fact that some, like Armstrong (1968) and Lycan (1996), express their allegiance to it. But this strangeness is avoided when we notice that for Armstrong and Lycan the perceptual model at issue is what Shoemaker (1996) calls a "broad perceptual model", that is, on this model

To see this, consider the case in which I am aware of the fact that the filing cabinet is in my office by seeing either it or its shape. This is not the sort of case that is normally classified as a case of indirect awareness. Indeed, in the epistemological literature, cases such as this are the paradigmatic cases in which one has direct awareness of something. And yet both (4g) and (4h) represent cases in which I am, or become, aware of some fact but not by being *o*- or *p*-aware of something else. So it seems natural to set (4g–4h) aside and operate only with (4i).

Now, however, it should be perfectly clear that the step from (2) to (3) is illegitimate. On our preferred interpretation, what (3) is telling us is that one is aware of the fact that one's experience has certain intrinsic features by being aware of some *other* fact. But (2) provides no grounds at all for that claim. What (2) tells us is that one is, or becomes, *f*-aware of the intrinsic features of one's experience by attending to properties and objects represented in that experience. But to say this is not to say that there is some *other* fact which is such that when one becomes *f*-aware of it, one becomes *f*-aware of those features. On the contrary, it is not to mention any other fact at all.

To illustrate, suppose I come to know, or be, *f*-aware of the fact that the filing cabinet is in my office by seeing or attending to the cabinet. As we have just seen, intuitively this is not the sort of case that one would describe as a case of indirect knowledge. On the contrary, this is usually thought of as a paradigm case of *direct* perceptual knowledge. And indeed, the schematic account of directness delivers this result. For in this case, it is not the case that I am aware of one fact – the fact that the filing cabinet is in my office – by being aware of another. Nevertheless, this paradigm of direct knowledge is certainly one in which I know something by seeing or attending to something else – that is, I know something about the cabinet by attending to it. So it seems that the idea that I am directly *f*-aware of something is perfectly compatible with the idea that I am *f*-aware of it by perceiving or attending to something else. By analogy, therefore, it is hard to see how the mere fact – assuming it to be a fact – that I am, or become, *f*-aware of the intrinsic features of my experience by attending to some-

---

one's awareness that one has an experience of a certain sort is *f*-awareness. In short, the perceptual model rejected by Dretske is *not* the theory defended under that name by Armstrong.

thing else entails that here we are in the presence of anything other than direct *f*-awareness.

Admittedly, there are points of disanalogy between the two cases. In the cabinet case, I am aware of the fact of the form *a is F* by being, seeing, or attending to *a* – in other words, one is aware of a fact by attending to something which is (in an intuitive sense) a constituent of that very fact. I am aware *that* the cabinet is in the office by being aware *of* the cabinet. In the experience case, however, I am not aware of a fact of the form *a is F* by attending to something which is a constituent of that fact. Rather, I am aware that my experience has some intrinsic features by being aware of something which is neither my experience nor a feature of that experience.

However, at least given the account of directness I have introduced so far, it is hard to see why this disanalogy matters. For directness in the sense at issue involves a *negative* claim, and this negative claim is something that both cases share. What is important for directness is the question of whether or not I come to know a certain fact by coming to know some *other* fact. If this is not the case, my awareness or knowledge counts as direct. But in neither the experience case nor the filing-cabinet case has it been established that I come to know a certain fact by knowing some other fact. Thus it has not been established that (3) is true.[28]

---

28 When I gave a version of this paper at MIT, Alex Byrne objected that that the position in the text takes over from Dretske a questionable assumption, namely that perception does not involve *f*-awareness. But consider (Byrne said) the difference between the experience of seeing a red triangle and a blue square, on the one hand, and the experience of seeing a blue triangle and a red square on the other. Since the properties in question here – red, blue, square, triangle – are the same, it would seem that *p*-awareness won't distinguish these two experiences. But then *f*-awareness must distinguish them, and perception involves *f*-awareness. The argument is ingenious but falters in the step from the (correct) negative point about *p*-awareness to the positive point about *f*-awareness. That *p*-awareness does not distinguish the two experience does not show that *f*-awareness must. It only shows that Dretske's taxonomy of awareness leaves something out, which I will call "state-of-affairs awareness", or "*s*-awareness", for short. The distinction is this: If I am *f*-aware that *p*, it follows that *p* is true, but if I am *s*-aware of *p* (i.e., aware of state of affairs in which *p*), it does not follow that *p* is true. Byrne's example shows that one needs a category of *s*-awareness, but it does not show that I am aware of facts in perception. Thanks to Ralph Wedgwood and Susannah Siegel for discussion on this point.

V.ii. The Second Way to Develop the Objection

The suggestion I have just made – that because of considerations of awareness the step from (2) to (3) is illegitimate – faces a number of different responses. Before considering them, however, I want to consider a different reason for supposing that the crucial inference is illegitimate. This reason brings out a further source of complexity in our discussion which I have so far been ignoring.

It is important to distinguish two meanings, or uses, of 'attention'.[29] In one sense, 'attention' just means to think about – let us call this *cognitive* attention. This is the notion of attention that is at issue when, for example, one says "Let us now attend to the second flaw of the argument," or "The program made us attend even more than we had before to the effects of salination on the nation's rivers." In another sense, however, 'attention' means, in the first instance, to focus on various items in one's field of vision, and perhaps also in other sensory fields – let us call this *perceptual* attention. This is the notion at issue when one says, "John didn't notice the pedestrian crossing because he was attending to the spider on the windscreen," or "The spaceship only appears when you focus your attention *through* the painting, rather than *at* the painting."

Now, so far in our discussion, we have been assuming that the notion of attention in play is the perceptual notion. However, it is important also to notice that in the initial phenomenological premise of the diaphanousness argument, the word 'attention' appears twice. Here is the premise again, with emphasis added:

(1) Look at a tree and try to turn your *attention* to intrinsic features of your visual experience. I predict you will find that the only features there to turn your *attention* to will be features of the presented tree.

Now, I think it is clear that Harman intends the notion of attention to be univocal, here. But that assumption creates a problem for the argument. Suppose that, in its first occurrence, 'attention' means percep-

---

29 For some excellent discussion of this see Martin 1997. See also Shoemaker 1996 and Martin 1998.

tual attention. Then Harman's instructions could only be carried out if one *could* perceptually attend to the intrinsic features of one's visual experience. In turn, however, if one is in a position to perceptually attend to the intrinsic features of one's visual experiences, it would seem that some version of the perceptual model of introspection is true, for to perceptually attend to something is at least to perceive it. This suggests that, unless the perceptual model of introspection is going to be assumed from the start, in its first occurrence, 'attention' ought to be interpreted as cognitive attention.

What then of the second occurrence of the word? If we continue with the assumption of univocality, we have no choice but to conclude that the second occurrence is likewise supposed to mean cognitive attention. But this doesn't seem to be right. The most natural interpretation is that when Harman is making predictions about what will happen when we try to attend, he is telling us that we will find ourselves *perceptually* attending to the tree. So Harman's prediction is most naturally interpreted as involving perceptual, and not cognitive, attention.

So far, then, we have failed to find a univocal interpretation of the initial premise of the argument. Should we then impose a non-univocal reading on the premise? Of course there is the textual inconvenience that Harman seems to want a univocal interpretation. But perhaps we should ignore this and say that what Harman *should* have said is summarized in (1a)

(1a)   Look at a tree and try to turn your *cognitive* attention to the intrinsic features of your visual experience. I predict you will find that the only features there to turn your *perceptual* attention to will be features of the presented tree.

On this interpretation, Harman is instructing us to think about or consider the intrinsic features of our visual experience. And he is predicting that when we try to do this, we will find ourselves attending – that is, perceptually attending – to features of the presented tree.

I think this is in fact the most plausible interpretation of the initial premise of the argument. However, there is problem lurking here, and this is that once we allow this interpretation to filter through to the rest of the argument, it is plain once again that the inference from (2) to (3) is mistaken. For consider: if (1) is properly interpreted as (1a), likewise (2) is properly interpreted as (2a):

> (2a)   In introspection, one cognitively attends to (i.e., thinks about) the intrinsic features of one's experience *by* (perceptually) attending to the objects and properties represented by that experience.

But it is quite clear that (2a) will not result in (3):

> (3)   In introspection, one is not *directly* aware of the intrinsic features of one's experience.

After all, what (2a) says – that is, what (2) says when you interpret it in the way indicated – is that in introspection one thinks about the phenomenal character by perceptually attending to something. But even if this is true, the inference to (3) now looks to be a *non sequitur*.

The point may again be illustrated by my experience of seeing the filing cabinet. Suppose that I know that I am having this experience, and that I know this directly. In other words, suppose I am directly aware that I am having an experience of seeing the filing cabinet. As we have noted, to be aware of something is not yet to attend to it, and thus to suppose that I am aware of my experience is not yet to say that I attend to it. But suppose now that I begin to think about my experience – to cognitively attend to it. In doing so, I may well focus on the filing cabinet, just as the thesis of diaphanousness predicts. My experience is thus *diaphanous* to introspection: when I think about my experience of the cabinet, I find myself attending to the cabinet. But none of this provides one with any temptation at all to *take back* the claim that my knowledge that I am having the experience is in any sense not direct. More generally, (2a) gives us no grounds at all for (3). (2a) tells me something about how I think about what I know. But (3) tells me something about how I know what I know in the first place.

Earlier, we saw that Block's appeal to the distinction between attention and awareness misfired because he was attacking the argument from diaphanousness in the wrong form. What we have just seen, however, is that there is something importantly right in the suggestion that the argument trades on a conflation between attention and awareness, and thus Block is at least partially vindicated. On our revised interpretation, Moore's point about diaphanousness – *viz.*, (2) – should be interpreted as (2a). But (2a) is a thesis about attention: it tells us what happens when we try to attend to the intrinsic features of our experience. On the other hand, (3) is a thesis about awareness or knowledge: it tells us that we are, or become, aware of the intrinsic features by being, or becoming, aware of something else. However, since attention is one thing and awareness is another, the step from (2) to (3) is illegitimate.

VI. Replies and Rejoinders

How might a proponent of the argument from diaphanousness reply to the objection that, when one articulates the direct awareness condition in the right way, and when one distinguishes the two notions of attention, it is clear that (2) does not entail (3)?

VI.i A Perceptual Model of Introspection?

The first reply I want to consider rejects the assumption – which we took over from Dretske – that awareness of experience is *f*-awareness. It is important to notice that this assumption has been critical to the argument. On the assumption that the notion of awareness in play is *f*-awareness, it becomes rather difficult to establish that my awareness of the intrinsic features of my experience is indirect. For the only way to establish that would be to produce some *other* fact on the basis of which I become aware that my experience has such and such an intrinsic feature. In effect, what I have been suggesting so far is that considerations of diaphanousness fail to make it plausible that there is some other fact, and thus fail to refute qualia realism.

But what if the notion of awareness in play is not *f*-awareness, but *p*-awareness? On that assumption, it seems easier to establish that my awareness of intrinsic features of experiences is indirect. For, on that assumption, to show that my awareness of intrinsic properties is indirect one needs to produce, not another fact, but only another property, and then to make it plausible that I am *p*-aware of the intrinsic features by being aware of this other property. But the considerations of diaphanousness precisely *do* seem to make this plausible! After all, those considerations make it plausible that I am *p*-aware of features of my experience by being *p*-aware of features of objects in my environment. So if it can be made out that I am *p*-aware of the intrinsic features, it would seem that the argument can be resuscitated.

Now, earlier, our reason for operating with *f*-awareness rather than *p*-awareness was that to operate with *p*-awareness was to commit one-self to the perceptual model of introspection, and that there is ample reason to want to avoid that model. However, in light of what has just been said about *p*-awareness, one might respond that it is really not clear that the perceptual model is as a bad as its reputation. At any rate, one might respond that I have certainly not shown that it is.

Now is not the time for a full-scale discussion of the perceptual model, but perhaps it will suffice to note that, whether or not the perceptual model is true, a proponent of the argument from diaphanousness is in a particularly weak position to say that it is. For consider again the passage from Moore with which we began. One implication of what Moore is saying here is that my relation to my sensation, whatever that is, is not at all the relation I bear to the blue. However, since I *see* the blue, we may conclude that I do not literally see the sensation. And, on the assumption that I *am* aware of my sensation, that is just to say that the perceptual model is false. So it will clearly do no good to appeal to the perceptual model as a potential method of patching up the argument from diaphanousness.

One might reply that the thesis of diaphanousness and the perceptual model of introspection are only in tension if one assumes that one is aware of one's sensations. But couldn't one deny this? As we have noted, proponents of the argument are sometimes interpreted as holding that one is not aware of experiences. And perhaps one might read that into the passage from Moore.[30] After all, the word 'diaphanous' at least suggests that experience is not perceived at all. And if introspection just is perception, it follows from this interpretation of the diaphanousness point that I am not introspectively aware of my own experience.

---

30 I think this would be a misreading, since Moore is careful to say that the sensation is *as if* it were diaphanous. But the interpretative issues are difficult and I will not attempt to address them here.

But at this point we are in the position of using a Moorean fact against Moore himself, or at any rate against Moore as we are currently interpreting him. As we in effect noted previously, surely it is a Moorean fact that we are aware of our sensations. Surely we are more sure that we are aware of our sensations than we are of the perceptual model of introspection. To put the point differently, the package of views that Moore on this interpretation is committed to – the perceptual model of introspection *plus* the diaphanousness of experience – has the result that one is not aware of one's own sensations. But since we evidently *are* aware of our own sensations, one or both members of this package has to give. Hence, a proponent of the argument is in no position to dispense with diaphanousness, and it is obvious that what should be dispensed with is the perceptual model.[31]

Alternatively, and more generally, one might suggest that this point misconstrues the role of the perceptual model in the debate about diaphanousness and qualia. Perhaps the point is not that the perceptual model is true, but rather that a qualia realist is committed to the perceptual model, i.e., that the very notion of direct access is somehow bound up with the perceptual approach to introspection. If so, the argument from diaphanousness would indeed seem to be on a collision course with qualia realism.

But of course, the problem with this suggestion is that it is completely unobvious that any qualia realist need, or should, endorse the perceptual model. As we have seen already, the idea of direct awareness can certainly be spelled out in terms of the idea that one is aware of the fact that one's experience has its phenomenal character not in virtue of being aware of anything else. But that does not involve commitment to the perceptual model. It is true, of course, that there is a

---

31 One might attempt to defend the package from this criticism by introducing a distinction between direct and indirect introspection on the model of direct and indirect perception. In Berkeley's famous example, I directly hear the clip-clop of the horse's hooves, but I only indirectly hear the carriage. By analogy, one might say that while I only directly see the blue in introspection, I indirectly see the sensation. However, the problem with this suggestion is that the claim that I indirectly see the sensation is only marginally less implausible than the claim that I directly see it. To say that I hear the carriage indirectly is to say that I hear it. It is not to say that it is inaudible. But to say that experience is diaphanous would seem to imply that I do not see it at all.

tradition according to which commitment to qualia and commitment to the perceptual model go hand in hand, *viz.*, the sense-data tradition. But as we have noted, the version of qualia realism that we are concerned with is not a version of the sense-datum theory.

VI.ii. A Non-perceptual Model?

Our discussion of the perceptual model was motivated by the thought that perhaps one could drop the assumption that awareness of experience was *f*-awareness and operate with *p*-awareness. And the problem we have run into is that the perceptual model is implausible, or else it is not something which a proponent of the argument can appeal to.

However, one might point out that two things have been run together here: the idea of *p*-awareness and the idea of the perceptual model. Surely not all *p*-awareness or *o*-awareness is perceptual. After all, it seems quite possible that one can be aware of, for instance, the virtues of Gandhi without supposing that one *sees* the virtues of Gandhi. But if that is so, might one not introduce an account of introspection according to which one is *p*-aware of phenomenal character? In that case, we seem to have the indirectness claim back again. Moreover, we seem to have it back in a form that does not involve us in a discussion of the perceptual model of introspection.

The suggestion that one might be *p*-aware of something and yet not be perceptually aware of it raises the general topic of non-propositional intentional states. This is an enormous and interesting topic in its own right. Still, I think we can see what is wrong with this method of defending the argument from diaphanousness without discussing that issue in depth.

Suppose it is true that there is a notion of introspective awareness that is distinct from perceptual awareness. And suppose also that the awareness at issue is *p*-awareness rather than *f*-awareness. Would that help the proponent of the argument respond to our objection? The answer to this question is no, for the fact is that once one draws a distinction between perceptual and introspective awareness, we need to confront a further dimension of difference in the argument from diaphanousness that we have so far been suppressing.

On the schematic account of directness that we adopted from Alston and Jackson, one is indirectly aware of something just in case one is aware of it, but not by being aware of anything else. Now, the suggestion that there are different ways of spelling out the notion of awareness forces us to consider whether, in any putative case of indirect awareness, the awareness in both cases is the same.

One dimension of difference that is relevant here concerns whether the notion of awareness that is in play is *o*-awareness, *p*-awareness, or *f*-awareness – this is the dimension that we have so far been discussing. However, a quite different dimension comes into focus when one distinguishes between perceptual and introspective awareness. When we focus on that dimension of difference, it seems reasonable to think that the only case in which a case of awareness will count as indirect is when the awareness in both cases is of the same sort. So a case of introspective awareness will count as indirect if it is based on another case of *introspective* awareness. Similarly, a case of *perceptual* awareness will count as indirect only if it is based on another case of perceptual awareness. On the other hand, in thinking about this sort of issue, we arrive at yet further reason for supposing that (2) does not yield (3).

The issue might be presented compactly if we look back, once again, at (2):

(2)   In introspection, one is, or becomes, aware of the intrinsic features of one's experience *by* attending to the objects and properties represented by that experience.

Setting aside for the moment the distinctions between attention and awareness, and between *f*- and *p*-awareness, one might think that (2) admits of a simple variation, as follows:

(2b)   In introspection, one is, or becomes, aware of the intrinsic features of one's experience *by being, or becoming, aware of* the objects and properties represented by that experience.

But (2b) can be interpreted in two quite different ways. On the one hand, we might take the phrase 'in introspection' to govern the entire construction. In that case, (2b) means something like:

(2ba)   In introspection, one is, or becomes, aware of the intrinsic features of one's experience by being, or becoming, *intro-*

spectively aware of the objects and properties represented by that experience.

On the other hand, we might take 'in introspection' to govern only the sentence that comes before 'by.' In that case, (2b) means something like:

> (2bb)   In introspection, one is, or becomes, aware of the intrinsic features of one's experience by being, or becoming, *perceptually* aware of the objects and properties represented by that experience.

But now the problem is transparent. On the interpretation of direct awareness with which we are working, to derive (3) the proponent of the argument from diaphanousness needs to establish (2ba). For only then will it be true that one introspects the phenomenal character of one's experience by introspecting something else. One other hand, all (1) seems to support is (2bb), and (2bb) does not yield (3).

Indeed, it is worth pointing out that, on the interpretation we have introduced, the argument is flawed in two quite separate ways. One way is that (2ba) seems not to be supported by (1). But another is that (2ba) looks to be nonsense. Surely it is not merely false, but nonsensical, to say that I can introspect objects in the external world; that would be like saying that one can remember future events. The point is important because proponents of the argument from diaphanousness sometimes talk as if one could "introspect" properties of external objects – something which in my view should raise alarm bells about the cogency of the argument.[32]

VI.iii. A Different Notion of Directness?

The two replies we have considered so far both respond to our assumption that awareness of phenomenal character is *f*-awareness.

---

32 At one point, for example, Tye says that "[v]ia introspection, you are directly aware of a range of qualities that you experience as being qualities of surfaces at varying distances away and orientations" (2000, 47).

However, the final reply I want to consider criticizes the objections I have made at altogether a different juncture. My assumption so far has been that direct awareness it to be explicated on the model offered by Alston and Jackson. But – one might point out – there are at least two other accounts of direct awareness available, and these must be disposed of before our objection to the argument from diaphanousness can be assumed to be successful. The first of these articulates direct awareness in terms of the notion of inference. On this interpretation, the idea behind denying direct awareness might be brought out as follows. I know what my experience is like because I first know what the objects and properties represented in my experience are like, and I infer what my experience is like on the basis of this. On this account, my access to phenomenal character will be direct just in case I know what it is like, but I do not know what it is like on the basis of an inference from any other knowledge.

However, there are three responses to this idea. The first is the (*ad hominem*) point that proponents of the argument from diaphanousness tell us that what is involved here is not an inference (Tye 2000, 47). The second is that it is in any case implausible to say that I infer facts about my experience from facts about my environment. It *is* plausible to say, for example, that one might infer the phenomenal character of the experience of others on the basis of their behaviour, but given that my own access to the phenomenal character of my mental states is supposed to be very different, inference does not seem to be the appropriate notion, here. The third is that in any case, (2) does not entail (3) even on this account of direct awareness. What (2) tells us is that I apprehend in introspection the phenomenal character of my experience by attending in perception to something. But it does not say that I apprehend the phenomenal character by knowing anything.

The second way of interpreting the notion of directness takes up and develops a suggestion of Dretske's. At one point, Dretske (1999, 164) says that one is directly *f*-aware of some fact *F* just in case *F* is constituted by *o* and *P* and one is directly *o*-aware of *o* and directly *p*-aware of *P*. On this understanding, if one is *f*-aware of the fact that one's experience *e* has phenomenal character *C*, one can only be directly aware of this if one is *o*-aware of *e* and *p*-aware of *C*. It follows from this that the diaphanousness of experience will easily establish that one is only indirectly aware that one's experience has any phenomenal character because diaphanousness does suggest that one is not *o*-aware of *e* or *p*-aware of *C*.

Now, there is no point doubting that, on this account of directness, my awareness of the intrinsic features of my experience is indirect. However, it does not follow from this that we have a version of the argument that is successful, for it should not be at all surprising that one might be able to articulate notions of directness according to which my awareness will count as indirect. The point is whether or not the qualia realist can appeal to a workable notion of directness according to which they *are* direct. As we have seen, the schematic account of awareness that we have introduced *does* seem to capture such a workable notion. To put the point differently, one can agree that there are senses of directness according to which any particular case of awareness is indirect. But the crucial point is whether or not the argument from diaphanousness can disprove the idea of direct awareness as that idea is developed by the qualia realist.

VII. Conclusion

The argument from diaphanousness, as I have been considering it, aims to show that there are no psychological properties of experience which satisfy both intrinsicness and direct awareness, and, in particular, that there are no psychological properties which satisfy direct awareness. My suggestion has been that the argument is unsound because there is no way to defend the inference from the claim that I apprehend the intrinsic features of my experience by apprehending objects and properties represented in experience to the claim that I only indirectly apprehend those features. As we have seen, there are various ways of understanding what direct awareness and attention might amount to, but on none of these does the 'by'-claim summarized in (2) support the denial of direct awareness summarized in (3).

I want now to close the paper by returning to the two versions of the argument noted but set aside in Section II and by summarizing the main points.[33]

---

33   Attentive readers will note that I have switched the order of discussion here.

VII.i The Argument Construed as an Argument for the Relational Thesis

In discussing the puzzle about Moore in Section II.iii, we took note of the relational thesis, the thesis that the phenomenal character of an experience is determined by the properties of the objects that one is related to in having the experience. We saw that the relational thesis crosscuts the debate between intentionalists and qualia realists: hard intentionalists and sense-data theorists endorse it; soft intentionalists and qualia realists such as Block deny it. Nevertheless – as we also noted – it is plausible to suppose that the relational thesis is in the background of the contemporary debate about the argument from diaphanousness. So in this section, I want to ask whether there is a version of the argument that provides any support for the thesis.

This issue is in fact a rather large one, and so I will limit myself here to two points. The first point is that if the thesis of the diaphanousness of experience is going to be a premise in an argument for the relational thesis, then it would need to be adjusted slightly. The reason is that the thesis as we have been considering it presupposes that there are intrinsic properties of experience. But the relational thesis would seem to deny this, or at any rate, would seem to deny it as far as phenomenal character is concerned. For suppose that the phenomenal character of an experience is determined by the objects that one is related to in having the experience. Then it is hard to see how the phenomenal character of the experience might count as an intrinsic, or, at any rate, as a non-relational, property of that experience. However, it is not hard to see how one might adjust the thesis to accommodate this complication. Instead of (2) or the variants that we have introduced, the thesis should now be rendered as (2c):

(2c)   In introspection, one is, or becomes, aware of the phenomenal character of one's experience *by* attending to the objects that one is related to in having the experience.

This thesis differs from our original thesis in two respects. First, we are now talking about the phenomenal character of experience, rather than specifying that the phenomenal character is intrinsic. Second, the thesis now explicitly includes the picture of experience with which the relational thesis operates, *viz.*, the picture according to which in

Daniel Stoljar

having an experience one is related to a range of objects. As we noted in Section II.iii, there are a wide variety of otherwise quite different approaches to experience which conform to the experience thesis; hence, there is a wide variety of otherwise different approaches to experience which can agree with (2c).

The second, and more straightforward, point is that there is in any case a good reason for supposing that there is no (convincing) argument from (2c) to the relational thesis. For the fact is that, while (2c) might be true – at any rate, nothing I have said militates against it – the relational thesis is false. To illustrate this, reconsider the contrast noted in Section IV.ii between the situation in which I am under the visual impression that p and the situation in which I visually imagine that p. The relational thesis implies that the phenomenal characters of these two experiences are then identical. For according to that thesis, the phenomenal character of an experience is determined by the features of the object that one is related to in having the experience. But in this case, there is surely a strong sense in which the phenomenal characters here are *not* identical. As we noted, in the visual-impression case I am going to feel inclined to be believe that p. In the imagination case, on the other hand, I am not going to feel inclined to believe that p. However, since these inclinations are surely part of the phenomenal character of imagination and perception, it is natural to suppose that what explains the phenomenal character of an experience cannot simply be properties of the objects that one is related to in having the experience – the nature of the experience itself must be included also. But if that is right, then the relational thesis is false, and thus there can be no persuasive argument from diaphanousness to the relational thesis.

VII.ii. The Argument Construed as an Argument for Intentionalism

The final issue I want to consider concerns the point noted in Section II.ii that, while the argument from diaphanousness is often formulated as a negative argument whose conclusion is that there are no qualia, it is often also formulated as a positive argument whose conclusion is that intentionalism is true. And we also saw that, because the contrast between qualia realism and intentionalism was not straightforward, it was necessary to treat the two versions of the argument separately.

386

In this final section, therefore, I will consider this version of the argument. We can start with the observation that, given the distinction between hard and soft intentionalism, the only issue that requires discussion is whether or not the diaphanousness of experience supports soft intentionalism. For the difference between hard and soft intentionalism can be expressed in terms of the relational thesis: hard intentionalism endorses the relational thesis, soft intentionalism denies it, and we have already seen that the relational thesis is false. In consequence, hard intentionalism is false also. Hence there can be no (convincing) argument from the diaphanousness of experience to hard intentionalism. Hence the only issue to be considered is whether or not the thesis of the diaphanousness of experience provides any support for soft intentionalism. Put differently, the issue is whether or not the 'by'-claim summarized in (2) tells us that soft intentionalism is true.

The first thing to say is that this step is certainly not one of entailment. To see this, consider the step from (4) to (5):

(4)   One apprehends the feelings of others by attending to their (actual and potential) behaviour.

(5)   The feelings of others are completely explained by their actual and potential behaviour.

It should be clear the step from (4) to (5) is invalid. It is perfectly true that one apprehends the feelings of others by attending to their behaviour. But behaviourism – for (5) is nothing else but a formulation of behaviourism – is as false as any philosophical doctrine could be. Since (4) is true, and (5) is false, the inference from (4) to (5) is not valid. But – and here is our objection – the inference from (2) to intentionalism is of the same form as that from (4) to (5).

One might of course agree that the step from (2) to intentionalism is invalid, while at the same time insisting that intentionalism nevertheless provides the best explanation of (2). Here too, however, the analogy with behaviourism is instructive. Suppose the behaviourist says that (5) provides the best explanation of (4), and that is why we should believe it. Our response, I think, would be to grant that behaviourism provides *a* potential explanation of (4), but to point out that there are others. The other account is roughly that the feelings of others find causal expression in their behaviour. Once we have another account of why (4) is true, likewise we may look to another account of why (2) is true. (2) is true – one might say – because if we were in a situation in which our experiences were veridical, the world that we would then find ourselves in would cause us to have certain experiences. In other words, while it might very well be true that (2) represents a striking fact which cries out for explanation, it does not at all follow that intentionalism is the best, or only, way to explain it.

Of course none of this shows that soft intentionalism is false, nor does it show that soft intentionalism might not draw a certain limited level of support from considerations of diaphanousness. As I have noted previously, the relation of intentionalism to qualia realism, and therefore also the truth of intentionalism, is in fact a highly complex issue. The important point for our purposes, however, is only that the argument from diaphanousness does not provide the short, sharp argument for intentionalism that it is sometimes presented as doing in the literature.

VII.iii Summary

Let me summarize the main points I have tried to make. I began by noting that the argument from diaphanousness comes in three versions: (a) a version which attacks the sort of qualia realism which is prevalent in modern philosophy, typified by the Shoemaker–Block view; (b) a version which supports the relational thesis; and (c) a version which supports intentionalism, the idea that the phenomenal character of an experience is explained by its intentionality. I then argued that there is no version of the argument which is successful, though the failure in the case of (a) and (b) is more stark than in the case of (c). [34]

---

34 I presented previous versions of this paper to audiences at the Australian National University, Canberra, Australia; the Language, Mind and World Conference, Tlaxcala, Mexico; the Australian Association for the History; Philosophy and Social Studies of Science Conference, Melbourne; and at MIT. I am very much indebted to all who took part on those occasions, and to the very many others with whom I have discussed this material. Comments and advice from

References

Alston, W. 1971. "Varieties of Privileged Access." *American Philosophical Quarterly* 8 (3): 223–41.

Armstrong, D. 1968. *A Materialist Theory of the Mind*. London: Routledge.

———. 1980. "Immediate Perception." In *The Nature of Mind and Other Essays*, 119-131. St. Lucia, Queensland: University of Queensland Press.

Block, N. 1990. "Inverted Earth." In *Philosophical Perspectives 4*, ed. J. Tomberlin, 52–79. Reprinted in Block *et al.*, eds. 1997. *The Nature of Consciousness: Philosophical Debate*, 677-693. Cambridge, MA: MIT Press.

———. 2000. "Mental Paint." In *Essays in Honor of Tyler Burge*, ed. M. Hahn and B. Ramberg. Cambridge, MA: MIT Press. (References are to the PDF version.)

Broad, C.D. 1925. *The Mind and Its Place in Nature*. London: Routledge.

Byrne, A. 2001. Intentionalism Defended. *Philosophical Review* 110: 199-240..

Churchland, P. 1985. "Reduction, Qualia, and the Direct Introspection of Brain States." *Journal of Philosophy* 82: 8–28.

Dretske, F. 1999. "The Mind's Awareness of Itself." In *Perception, Belief and Knowledge*, 158-177. Cambridge: Cambridge University Press.

Evans, G. 1982. *Varieties of Reference*. Oxford: Oxford University Press.

Grice, P. 1962. "Some Remarks about the Senses." In *Analytical Philosophy*, ed. R.J. Butler, 133-153. New York: Barnes and Noble.

Harman, G. 1990. "The Intrinsic Quality of Experience." In *Philosophical Perspectives 4: Action Theory and Philosophy of Mind*, ed. J. Tomberlin, 31–52. Atascadero, CA: Ridgeview.

———. 1996. "Explaining Objective Color in Terms of Subjective Reactions." In *Philosophical Issues 7*, ed. E. Villanueva, 1-17. Atascadero, CA: Ridgeview.

Jackson, F. 1977. *Perception*. Cambridge: Cambridge University Press.

———. 2001. Experience and Representation. MS.

Langton, R and Lewis, D. 1998. "Defining 'Intrinsic'." *Philosophy and Phenomenological Research* 58: 333–45.

---

the following have had a particular impact on the paper: Frank Jackson (my commentator at the Melbourne conference), Judith Jarvis Thomson, Sylvain Bromberger, Alex Byrne, Jim Pryor, Susannah Siegel, Philippe Chuard and Dan Lopez.

Lormand, E. 1996. *Inner Sense Until Proven Guilty.* MS. Available at: http://www-personal.umich.edu/~lormand/phil/cons/inner_sense.htm

Lycan, W. 1996. *Consciousness and Experience.* Cambridge, MA: MIT Press.

Martin, M.G.F. 1997. "Sense, Reference and Selective Attention: The Shallows of the Mind." *Proceedings of the Aristotelian Society* 71: 75–98.

———. 1998. "Setting Things Before the Mind." In *Current Issues in Philosophy of Mind*, ed. A. O'Hear, 157-179. Cambridge: Cambridge University Press.

———. 2002. "The Transparency of Experience." *Mind and Language* 17 (4): 376–425.

Moore, G.E. 1922. "The Refutation of Idealism." In *Philosophical Studies*, G.E. Moore, 1-30. London: Routledge. (Original Publication: 1903.)

Peacocke, C. 1983. *Sense and Content.* Oxford: Oxford University Press.

———. 1998. "Consciousness, Attention and Self-Knowledge." In *Knowing Our Own Minds*, ed. C. Wright, B. Smith C. and C. Macdonald, 63-98. Oxford: Oxford University Press.

Robinson, W. 1996. "Intrinsic Qualities of Experience: Surviving Harman's Critique." *Erkenntnis* 47: 285–309.

Ryle, G. 1949. *The Concept of Mind.* London: Routledge.

Tye, M. 1995. *Ten Problems of Consciousness.* Cambridge, MA: MIT Press.

———. 2000. *Color, Content and Consciousness.* Cambridge, MA: MIT Press.

Segal, G. 2000. *A Slim Book on Narrow Content.* Cambridge, MA: MIT Press.

Shoemaker, S. 1981. "The Inverted Spectrum." *Journal of Philosophy* 79 (7): 357–81.

———. 1994. "Phenomenal Character." *Noûs* 28: 21–38.

———. 1996. *The First Person Perspective and Other Essays.* Cambridge: Cambridge University Press.

———. 2002. "Introspection and Phenomenal Character." In *Philosophy of Mind: Classical and Contemporary Readings*, ed. D. Chalmers, 457-472. Oxford: Oxford University Press.

Van Gulick, R. 1993. "Understanding the Phenomenal Mind: Are We All Just Armadillos?" In *Consciousness: Psychological and Philosophical Essays*, ed. M. Davies. and G.M. Humphreys, 137-154. Oxford: Blackwell.

CANADIAN JOURNAL OF PHILOSOPHY
Supplementary Volume 30

What is Doubt and When is it Reasonable?

PAUL THAGARD

I. Introduction

Descartes contended that "I am obliged in the end to admit that none of my former ideas are beyond legitimate doubt" (1964, 64). Accordingly, he adopted a method of doubting everything: "Since my present aim was to give myself up to the pursuit of truth alone, I thought I must do the very opposite, and reject as if absolutely false anything as to which I could imagine the least doubt, in order to see if I should not be left at the end believing something that was absolutely indubitable" (1964, 31). Similarly, other philosophers have raised doubts about the justifiability of beliefs concerning the external world, the existence of other minds, and moral principles; philosophical skepticism has a long history (Popkin 1979).

The concept of doubt is not only of philosophical interest, for it plays a central role in the legal system when jurors are instructed not to convict an accused person unless they are convinced of guilt beyond a reasonable doubt. Surprisingly, however, there is little consensus in the theory and practice of law concerning what differentiates reasonable from unreasonable doubt. Faust (2000a, 229) reports a "firestorm of controversy" concerning the proper legal meaning of the term "reasonable doubt," and furnishes an extensive annotated bibliography.

My aim in this paper is to propose (1) a descriptive theory of doubt as a cognitive/emotional mental state, and (2) a normative theory of the conditions under which doubt can be viewed as reasonable. After describing previous philosophical accounts of doubt, I develop an account of doubt as emotional incoherence that provides a framework for a general account of when doubt is reasonable or unreasonable in philosophical, legal, and scientific contexts.

II. Cold and Hot Doubt

Social psychologists distinguish between cold cognition and hot cognition, where the latter involves emotions tied in with personal goals and motivations (Kunda 1999). Similarly, I shall distinguish between cold doubt and hot doubt, where the latter involves an attitude toward a proposition that is emotional as well as cognitive. Most philosophers and legal theorists have discussed cold doubt, but I shall follow Charles Peirce in treating doubt as hot, that is, as involving an attitude toward a proposition that has a central emotional component. First, let us consider accounts of cold doubt.

Nathan Salmon (1995) proposes the following definition for the word 'doubt':

> A doubts $p =_{def}$ (A disbelieves p) or (A suspends judgment concerning p)
> A disbelieves $p =_{def} A$ believes not-p
> A suspends judgment concerning $p =_{def}$ not-(A believes p) and not-(A disbelieves p)

Salmon acknowledges that this definition constitutes a departure from standard usage in that it does not require that a believer has a grasp of a proposition and has attempted consciously to choose between the proposition and its negation. It follows from his definitions that for any proposition p, either A believes p or A doubts p. This is a very odd result: it implies that a person who has never even considered a proposition, for example, that there are more than a million trees in Newfoundland, either believes it or doubts it. Salmon's definition of doubt also does not take into account the contention of Bertrand Russell (1984, 142) that doubt "suggests a vacillation, an alternate belief and disbelief." For both Salmon and Russell, doubt is an entirely cognitive rather than emotional phenomenon, a matter of belief and disbelief.

Similarly, Jennifer Faust's (2000b) discussion of reasonable doubt in the law assumes that it is a purely cognitive matter. She distinguishes two senses of doubt that generate two senses of reasonable doubt:

> S doubts$_1$ that $p =_{def} S$ believes that not-P.

S doubts$_2$ that $p =_{def} S$ does not believe that P.
S reasonably doubts$_1$ that $p =_{def} S$ has sufficient reason to believe that not-p.
S reasonably doubts$_2$ that $p =_{def} S$ does not have sufficient reason to believe that p. (Faust, 2000b, 1)

Faust makes a convincing case that some prevalent legal instructions concerning reasonable doubt mistakenly confuse the first and second senses, so that jurors are told that acquitting an accused person requires having sufficient reason to believe that the accused was not guilty (sense 1 of 'doubt' and 'reasonable doubt'). The more appropriate instruction is that acquitting an accused person requires only not having sufficient reason to believe that the accused was guilty (sense 2). As for Salmon and Russell, Faust's doubt is a matter of cold cognition.

An alternative hot conception of doubt was developed by Charles Peirce in the 1860s and 1870s. He attacked Descartes' method of doubt by arguing that complete doubt is a mere self-deception: "Let us not pretend to doubt in philosophy what we do not doubt in our hearts" (Peirce 1958, 40). According to Peirce, beliefs are habits of mind that guide our desires and shape our actions. Doubt is not merely a matter or belief or disbelief, but is an *irritation* that causes inquiry, which is a struggle to attain a state of belief (1958, 99). The Cartesian exercise of questioning a proposition does not stimulate the mind to struggle after belief, which requires a "real and living doubt" (1958, 100). According to Peirce, "the action of thought is excited by the irritation of doubt, and ceases when belief is attained" (1958, 118). Doubt is not the result of an internal exercise: "Genuine doubt always has an external origin, usually from surprise" (1958, 207). For Peirce, doubt is intimately tied up with goals and motivations to increase knowledge, as well as with emotional states involving irritation, excitement, and surprise. Doubt is a matter of hot cognition.

III. Doubt as Emotional Incoherence

I think that Peirce's account of doubt captures much more of the nature of real doubt than Salmon's cold account, but Peirce does not offer a general theory of what doubt is. First, it is useful to have some concrete examples of what Peirce called "real and living" doubt to make it clear what needs to be explained. I am not proposing a definition of the concept of doubt, since such analyses are rarely successful or fruitful. Rather, my aim is to develop a theory about the nature and causal origins of the mental state of doubting.

Here are some real philosophical, scientific, and legal examples of doubt:

> *Philosophy*: Many students taking their first course in philosophy of mind are surprised to learn that most work in the field adopts some form of materialism, in contrast to their religious views that assume there is a non-material soul that survives death. The students doubt that mind is just the brain, and feel considerable anxiety at the possible challenge to their religious beliefs.

> *Science*: In 1983, medical researchers heard a young Australian, Barry Marshall, propose that most peptic ulcers are caused by infection by a newly discovered bacterium, now known as *Helicobacter pylori*. The researchers strongly doubted that Marshall could be right about the causes of ulcers, and were very annoyed that a beginner would propose such a preposterous theory. (Thagard 1999)

> *Law*: In 1995, the jury in the O.J. Simpson trial learned that some of the evidence was sloppily handled and that one of the detectives in the case had a long history of racism. For these and other reasons, they doubted that Simpson murdered his ex-wife, and quickly and enthusiastically voted to acquit him. (Thagard 2003)

In each of these cases, people encountered a proposition or set of propositions that did not fit with what they already believed, and they reacted emotionally as well as cognitively.

These cases fit the following prototype of the mental and social situation in which doubt arises. Note that this prototype is not proposed as a definition of the word 'doubt', but as a description of the typical nature and origins of doubt. Typically, people doubt a proposition when:

1. Someone makes a claim about the proposition.
2. People notice that the proposition is incoherent with their beliefs.
3. The people care about the proposition because it is relevant to their goals.
4. The people feel emotions related to the proposition.
5. The emotions are caused by a combination of the claim, the incoherence, and the relevance of the proposition.

Let us examine each of these facets of doubt in more detail.

In all three of the cases I described, doubt arises by virtue of claims made by others: mind is material, ulcers are caused by bacteria, O.J. is guilty. But doubt does not have to arise by virtue of a claim made by someone else. Occasional cases of real doubt are internally engendered: I think that my gloves are in my coat pocket, but then it occurs to me that I might have forgotten to put them there. Hence Peirce exaggerated when he stated that genuine doubt always has an external cause, but he was for the most part right in understanding doubt as externally inspired, in contrast to an internal Cartesian exercise. External causes of doubt are most often the claims of others, as in my prototype above, but can also be interactions with the world, as when scientists collect data that cause them to doubt prevailing theories. In the gloves example, my doubt that my gloves are in my coat pocket may be caused by seeing something that reminds me that I put my gloves elsewhere. The typical external origins of doubt are important for the kinds of emotional states involved in doubt, such as surprise when the world does not turn out to be as it was expected to be, or annoyance that someone is making a claim incoherent with one's own beliefs.

Doubt always involves the incoherence of a proposition with the rest of what one believes. Incoherence is best understood in terms of a theory of coherence as constraint satisfaction that I have developed at length elsewhere (Thagard 2000). On this theory, inference is a matter of accepting and rejecting representations on the basis of their coherence with other representations. Coherence is determined by the constraints between representations, with different kinds of constraint and different kinds of representation for six kinds of coherence: explanatory, conceptual, perceptual, deductive, analogical, and deliberative. For example, in explanatory coherence, the representations are propositions and the constraints include positive ones that arise between two propositions when one explains another, and negative ones that arise between propositions that are contradictory or in explanatory competition. Competing theories in science, law, and ordinary life can be evaluated by accepting or rejecting propositions based on the extent to which doing so maximizes satisfaction of multiple, conflicting constraints. Various algorithms for maximizing coherence are available.

A proposition is incoherent with a person's belief system when the process of coherence-maximization does not lead to its acceptance into that belief system. The most obvious source of incoherence is contradiction, when a claim is made that contradicts what one already believes. But incoherence can be looser, when a claim has weaker kinds of negative constraints than contradiction. For example, in the ulcer case, the claim that bacteria cause ulcers did not logically contradict the claim that excess acidity causes ulcers, yet medical researchers saw them as competing hypotheses. Doubt can even arise analogically, when a hypothesis is recognized as analogous to one such as cold fusion that has previously been recognized as dubious. So the incoherence that a doubted claim has with a belief system need not be based on contradiction. In all cases of doubt, a claim is not accepted because doing so would diminish coherence.

Just as Salmon distinguishes between disbelief and suspension of judgment, we can distinguish between *strong incoherence*, in which a proposition is rejected, and *weak incoherence*, in which a proposition is neither accepted nor rejected. This can happen with the connectionist (artificial neural network) algorithm for maximizing coherence, in which the activation of an artificial neuron representing a proposition can vary between 1 (acceptance) and –1 (rejection), with activation close to 0 signifying a state of neither acceptance nor rejection. Doubt requires non-acceptance, but it does not require rejection, for it can involve either strong or weak incoherence.

Doubt does not require the conscious recognition of incoherence: we can feel unease about a proposition without being at all aware of the source of the discomfort. Coherence calculations, like most inferences, are performed by the brain unconsciously, with only some of the results being conveyed to consciousness. Hence noticing that a proposition is incoherent with one's belief system (facet 2 in the prototype above) need not involve the conscious thought "I can't believe that because it does not fit with my other beliefs" but merely a negative emotional reaction to the claim.

Facet 3 in my doubt prototype posits that people only doubt propositions that they care about, where care is a matter of relevance to their goals, both epistemic and practical. The two main epistemic goals are truth and understanding, where the latter is achieved by unifying explanations. If your goals include the achievement of truth and understanding, then you will be provoked by someone who makes a claim that you are convinced is false. Gastroenterologists were in part annoyed by Barry Marshall because his claims about ulcers seemed to them false and inimical to understanding. But personal, practical goals can also contribute to doubt: if a claim is a potential threat to your well-being or self-esteem, then you may be motivated to look at it more critically. For example, the beginning philosophy students may doubt materialist philosophy more intensely because of its potential threat to the solace and social connections that they derive from their religious beliefs, producing a kind of motivated inference (Kunda 1999). Practical goals need not involve only personal interests, but could also be concerned with the general welfare of people, or with questions of fairness. As I will discuss further below in connection with reasonable doubt, inferences in science and law are not merely aimed at acquiring truths. Science also often has a practical goal of increasing human welfare through useful technology – for example, using antibiotics to cure ulcers. And the law is concerned not only to find out the truth, but also to ensure that the accused gets a fair trial and is presumed to be innocent until proven otherwise. Epistemic and practical goals must be relevant to a claim, for there is no point in wasting your time doubting (or even entertaining) a claim that you do not care about.

There are a wide variety of emotions involved with the feeling of doubt, most of them negative. The mildest negative emotions associated with doubt include Peirce's irritation and the unease and discomfort that I mentioned. These emotions can be sufficiently vague and ill-defined that it is not even obvious what their objects are – for example, whether you are irritated by the claim that aroused doubt or by its proponent. If a claim is not strongly incoherent with your belief system, so that rejection is not obviously called for, the tension between accepting and rejecting the proposition may cause anxiety, especially if the proposition is highly relevant to your personal goals.

Intense negative emotions can also be associated with doubt. If someone makes a claim that is both strongly incoherent with your belief system and highly relevant to your epistemic and practical goals, then doubting the claim can involve emotions such as annoyance, outrage, and even anger. Believing that the proposed claim is to be rejected is tied in not only with disliking the claim, but also with disliking the proponent of the claim. For example, the medical researchers who challenged Barry Marshall called him "crazy" and "irresponsible", and were angry that he kept defending claims that they thought were absurd. According to the seventeenth-century philosopher John Wilkins (1969), doubt is a kind of fear. This claim is not generally true, but there are cases where fear may be part of doubt, as when a scientist fears that new data may show a favoured theory to be false.

There are also unusual cases in which doubt is associated with positive emotions. Suppose you are told by a doctor that you need open-heart surgery, but you read on the Internet that your condition might be treated less invasively by a new drug. Then you doubt that you should have the surgery, and are happy at the prospect of avoiding a risky procedure. In this case, you are happy to doubt that you need surgery. However, if you are unsure of which treatment to pursue, you may feel strong negative emotions, such as anxiety, because you have doubts about not getting surgery as well as about getting surgery.

The five facets of my doubt prototype do not deductively imply that Cartesian and Humean doubts are not real, since the facets are typical features rather than necessary conditions. But it is clear that skeptical questions about the external world, other minds, and induction fail to fit the prototype. These claims have not been made seriously by anyone who believes them, they are too fanciful to be relevant to anyone's goals, and concern with them is an intellectual exercise rather than an emotional reaction.

We now have the ingredients of the causal network that produces the emotions associated with doubt. Because someone makes a claim that is incoherent with what you believe and that is relevant to your goals, you respond emotionally to the claim and sometimes also to the claimant. Prototypically, doubt is emotional incoherence.

IV. Reasonable Doubt

If doubt is a cognitive/emotional state caused by the incoherence of a claim relevant to a person's goals, then what is reasonable doubt? This question is of philosophical, legal, and scientific importance. In philosophy, we can ask whether the doubts raised by Descartes, Hume, and other skeptics, in ethics as well as epistemology, are reasonable. Is it reasonable to doubt whether there is an external world, whether the future will be like the past, and whether there is an objective difference between right and wrong?

In the law, the issue of what constitutes reasonable doubt has been vexing, for practical as well as theoretical reasons. For example, the Supreme Court of Canada recently overturned a number of convictions on the grounds that the judges in the original trials had given an incorrect instruction to the jury concerning the nature of reasonable doubt. Psychological experiments have found that whether mock jurors decide to convict an accused can be influenced by what they are told about the nature of reasonable doubt (Koch and Devine 1999).

In science, there are not only epistemic issues about whether scientists are reasonable in doubting a newly proposed theory, but also practical issues about when it is reasonable to doubt the desirability of technological applications of science. For example, were gastroenterologists in 1983 reasonable in doubting the truth of the bacteria theory of ulcers and the efficacy of treatment of ulcers by antibiotics? I will propose a general account of reasonable doubt as *legitimate* emotional incoherence, and then discuss its application to philosophy, law, and science and technology.

On my view, the reasonableness of doubt is both an epistemic and a practical matter, involving epistemic standards concerning truth and understanding, and also practical standards concerning welfare and fairness. In keeping with the prototype of doubt that I advanced in the last section, I will specify that doubt in a proposition is *reasonable* when:

1. A claim about the proposition has been made.
2. The noticed incoherence of the proposition with other beliefs is based on a legitimate assessment of coherence.

First, the aptness of doubt requires that a claim about a proposition has been made, normally by someone other than the person who doubts it. This rules out the fanciful, imaginary cases of doubt that Peirce rightly derided. The second condition is much more demanding, requiring that, when people come to doubt something because it is incoherent with their beliefs, they have performed a legitimate calculation of coherence.

Legitimacy depends on the kind of coherence involved. For explanatory coherence, which is the kind most relevant to factual claims in metaphysics, law, and science, the requirements of legitimacy include:

1. The available relevant evidence has all been taken into account.
2. The available alternative hypotheses have all been taken into account.
3. The available explanatory relations have all been used to establish constraints among the hypotheses and evidence.
4. Constraint maximization has been performed, consciously or unconsciously, producing a coherence judgment about which propositions to accept or reject.

Doubt can fail to be reasonable according to these legitimacy conditions when people make their judgments of incoherence without taking into account all the available relevant information.

It is tempting to say that a *set* of propositions can be reasonably doubted if there is reasonable doubt about one of the members of the set. But from a coherence perspective, it is better not to aggregate propositions by mere conjunction. In real legal and scientific cases, groups of propositions can form wholes through interconnections by explanation relations, as when one hypothesis explains another, or two hypotheses together provide an explanation. We should therefore maintain that it is reasonable to doubt a group of propositions when a claim about the group has been made and when the noticed incoherence of the group with other beliefs is based on a legitimate assessment of coherence.

This discussion has been rather abstract, so let me now relate it to philosophical, legal and scientific cases of reasonable and unreasonable doubt. The philosophy students' initial doubts about materialist theories of mind strike me as reasonable, at least initially. They encounter the claim that there is no soul in lectures or reading, and the claim is indeed incoherent with their religious and metaphysical beliefs. Because they care, for both theoretical and personal reasons, whether there is a soul, they feel negative emotions such as discomfort arising from the materialist claim. Of course, the doubt will remain reasonable only if, as they learn more about the evidence for materialism and against mind–body dualism, they continue to perform a legitimate coherence calculation. My own view is that, once all the available evidence and explanations are taken into account, materialism has more explanatory coherence than dualism (Thagard 2000). But students initially do not have all this information available to them, so their doubt is reasonable. In contrast, Cartesian doubt about whether one exists is not reasonable: no one claims non-existence, and the hypothesis is not incoherent with other beliefs. The same is true for Humean doubt about whether the future will be like the past. There are no negative emotions involved in these philosophical exercises; if there were any people seriously worried about whether they exist, we would judge them to be mentally ill.

In legal trials, the reasonableness of doubt depends on the kind of legal investigation. It is of crucial importance that the standard of "beyond reasonable doubt" that applies in criminal trials is not used in civil trials, where jurors' conclusions need only be based on a preponderance of evidence. A crucial aspect of criminal trials in the English tradition is that there is a presumption of innocence. This is clearly not related to the epistemic goal of truth: there no reason to believe that the prior probability of innocence is greater than that of guilt, and in fact the conditional probability of guilt given arrest is usually much higher than the conditional probability of innocence given arrest. Rather, the presumption of innocence is maintained in order to ensure that trials are fair, not just in the sense that the accused and the prosecution are treated equally, as the plaintiff and defendant are supposed to be in civil trials, but in the stronger sense that we place a high moral value on not convicting the innocent. Because fairness is a goal of criminal trials in addition to truth, negative emotions concerning claims about the guilt of the accused can arise that are more intense than would be inspired by explanatory coherence alone. Convicting the innocent is a moral as well as an epistemic mistake, and appropriately provokes outrage.

Finally, consider the reasonableness of doubt in scientific and technological contexts. It might be assumed that scientific doubt is a purely epistemic matter, but Richard Rudner has convincingly argued otherwise:

> Since no scientific hypothesis is ever completely verified, in accepting a hypothesis on the basis of evidence, the scientist must make the decision that the evidence is sufficiently strong or that the probability is sufficiently high to warrant the acceptance of the hypothesis. Obviously, our decision with regard to the evidence and how strong is "strong enough" is going to be a function of the importance, in the typically ethical sense, of making a mistake in accepting or rejecting the hypothesis. Thus, to take a crude but easily manageable example, if the hypothesis under consideration stated that a toxic ingredient of a drug was not present in lethal quantity, then we would require a relatively high degree of confirmation or confidence before accepting the hypothesis – for the consequences of making a mistake here are exceedingly grave by our moral standards. In contrast, if our hypothesis stated that, on the basis of some sample, a certain lot of machine-stamped belt buckles was not defective, the degree of confidence we would require would be relatively lower. How sure we must be before we accept a hypothesis depends on how serious a mistake would be. (1961, 32–33)

Thus doubt in science is in part a function of our practical goal of avoiding harm that might result from premature acceptance of a hypothesis. In theoretical astrophysics, the risk of harm is trivial, so doubt can be based largely on epistemic goals, but doubts can have a partially practical basis in areas like medicine (relevant to treating the sick) and nuclear physics (relevant to the construction of power plants and bombs). Just as the concern to acquit the innocent can intensify doubts in legal contexts, so the concern to avoid technological harm can intensify doubts in scientific contexts.

Medical doubts can be reasonable for both epistemic and practical reasons. When gastroenterologists first encountered the bacterial theory of ulcers, they had strong negative emotional reactions in part because it was incoherent with their beliefs about the causes of ulcers and the absence of bacteria in the stomach, but also because of their concern about people being treated inappropriately. Their doubts about Barry Marshall's views were reasonable in 1983, because there was little evidence then that bacteria cause ulcers, and none that killing the bacteria could cure ulcers. By 1994, however, the situation had changed dramatically as the result of carefully designed studies that showed that many people's ulcers had been cured by the right combination of antibiotics. At this point, coherence with the relevant medical information required acceptance of the bacterial theory of ulcers, so doubt was unreasonable.

Many epistemologists think that rational belief-fixation is a probabilistic rather than a coherence-based process, so that reasonable doubt depends on the probability of a claim. For example, Davidson and Pargetter (1987) give three requirements for a guilty verdict:

1. the probability of guilt given the evidence is very high,
2. the evidence on which the probability is based is very reliable, and
3. the probability of guilt is highly resilient relative to any possible evidence.

But there are powerful reasons why probability theory is not the appropriate tool for understanding reasonable doubt.

First, the interpretation of probability is problematic in legal, scientific, and philosophical contexts. It is obvious that the probability of guilt given the evidence is not the objective, statistical sense of probability as a frequency in a population: we have no data that allow us to say in a particular trial that the accused would be guilty in a specifiable proportion of such trials. So probability must be some kind of logical relation that has never been clearly defined, or a subjective degree of belief.

Second, there is considerable psychological evidence that people's degrees of belief do not obey the rules of the probability calculus (Kahneman, Slovic, and Tversky 1982; Tversky and Koehler 1994). Many psychological experiments have shown that the degrees of confidence that people place in propositions are often not in keeping with the rules of probability theory. Probability theory is a relatively recent invention, having been developed only in the seventeenth century (Hacking 1975). Yet people have been making judgments of uncertainty for thousands of years, without the aid of probability theory. Coherence provides a much more plausible descriptive and normative account of non-statistical human inference than does probability theory.

Third, probability theory is often orthogonal to the aims and practice of law. Cohen and Bersten (1990) argue that high probability is not even a necessary condition of finding someone guilty, which requires satisfying a number of legal rules that must be followed in order to ensure that the accused is given the benefit of the presumption of innocence. Allen (1991, 1994) has described numerous ways in which deliberation in legal trials much better fits a coherence account than a probabilistic one.

Fourth, there are technical reasons why probabilities are difficult to compute in real-life cases in law and other areas. A full probability-calculation is impossible in cases involving more than the handful of propositions, because the size of a full joint-distribution increases exponentially with the number of propositions. Powerful computational tools have been developed for calculation of probabilities in Bayesian networks, but they require more conditional probabilities than are usually available, and strong assumptions of independence that are rarely satisfiable. Computing probabilities in legal and similar cases is much more difficult than coherence computations based on maximization of constraint satisfaction (Thagard 2004). Hence, incoherence is a more plausible basis for reasonable doubt than low probability.

Finally, probability does not provide the basis for understanding reasonable doubt because it is not directly tied in with emotion. I have argued that doubt is a mental state that usually involves negative emotions such as discomfort and fear, whereas probability judgments are purely cognitive. In contrast, coherence judgments routinely give rise to positive emotions such as feelings of satisfaction and even beauty, whereas incoherence judgments give rise to negative emotions such as anxiety (self-reference omitted). If doubt is emotional incoherence, then there must be more to reasonable doubt than just a probability calculation.

V. Conclusion

This paper has advanced and defended several novel claims about the nature of doubt and reasonable doubt. First, doubt is not just a cold, cognitive matter of belief and disbelief, but also involves a hot, emotional reaction to a claim that has been made. Second, doubt is not based on the low probability of a claim, but on its incoherence with a thinker's beliefs and goals, where coherence can be computed in a psychologically realistic manner by parallel satisfaction of multiple constraints. Third, what makes a doubt reasonable is not a probability calculation, but a coherence computation that takes into account constraints based on the full, available range of evidence, hypotheses, and explanatory and other relations. Reasonable doubt is legitimate emotional incoherence.[1]

References

Allen, R.J. 1991. "The Nature of Juridical Proof". *Cardozo Law Review* 373: 373–422.

———. 1994. "Factual Ambiguity and a Theory of Evidence." *Northwestern University Law Review* 88: 604–60.

Cohen, S. and Bersten, S. 1990. "Probability Out of Court: Notes on 'Guilt Beyond Reasonable Doubt.'" *Australasian Journal of Philosophy* 68: 229–40.

Davidson, B. and Pargetter, B. 1987. "Guilt Beyond Reasonable Doubt." *Australasian Journal of Philosophy* 65: 182–87.

Descartes, R. 1964. *Philosophical Writings*. Trans. and ed. E. Anscombe and P.T. Geach. London: Nelson.

Faust, J. 2000a. "Proof Beyond a Reasonable Doubt: An Annotated Bibliography." *The APA Newsletters (American Philosophical Association)* 99 (2): 229–35.

———. 2000b. "Reasonable Doubt Jury Instructions." *The APA Newsletters (American Philosophical Association)* 99 (2): 226–29.

---

1 I am grateful to Christine Freeman-Roth for research assistance, and to her, Jing Zhu, Marcia Sokolowski, Tim Kenyon, and Rob Stainton for helpful suggestions. This research was supported by the Natural Sciences and Engineering Research Council of Canada.

Hacking, I. 1975. *The Emergence of Probability*. Cambridge: Cambridge University Press.

Kahneman, D., Slovic, P., and Tversky, A. 1982. *Judgment Under Uncertainty: Heuristics and Biases*. New York: Cambridge University Press.

Koch, C.M. and Devine, D.J. 1999. "Effects of Reasonable Doubt Definition and Inclusion of a Lesser Charge on Jury Verdicts." *Law and Human Behavior* 23: 653–74.

Kunda, Z. 1999. *Social Cognition*. Cambridge, MA: MIT Press.

Peirce, C.S. 1958. *Charles S. Peirce: Selected Writings*. New York: Dover.

Popkin, R.H. 1979. *The History of Scepticism from Erasmus to Spinoza*. Berkeley: University of California Press.

Rudner, R. 1961. "Value Judgments in the Acceptance of Theories." In *The Validation of Scientific Theories*, ed. P. G. Frank, 31-35. New York: Collier Books.

Russell, B. 1984. *Theory of Knowledge (Collected Papers, vol. 7)*. London: George Allen & Unwin.

Salmon, N. 1995. "Being of Two Minds: Belief with Doubt." *Noûs* 29: 1–20.

Thagard, P. 1999. *How Scientists Explain Disease*. Princeton: Princeton University Press.

———. 2000. *Coherence in Thought and Action*. Cambridge, MA: MIT Press.

———. 2003. "Why Wasn't O.J. Convicted: Emotional Coherence in Legal Inference." *Cognition and Emotion* 17: 361–83.

———. 2004. "Causal Inference in Legal Decision Making: Explanatory Coherence vs. Bayesian Networks." *Applied Artificial Intelligence*, 18: 231-249.

Tversky, A. and Koehler, D.J. 1994. "Support Theory: A Nonextensional Representation of Subjective Probability." *Psychological Review* 101: 547–67.

Wilkins, J. 1969. *Of the Principles and Duties of Natural Religion*. New York: Johnson Reprint Corp.

CANADIAN JOURNAL OF PHILOSOPHY
Supplementary Volume 30

What Computations (Still, Still) Can't Do: Jerry Fodor on Computation and Modularity

ROBERT A. WILSON

I. Introduction

Jerry Fodor's *The Mind Doesn't Work That Way* (2000; hereafter *Mind*) purports to do a number of things. To name three: First, it aims to show what is problematic about recent evolutionary psychology, especially as popularized in Steven Pinker's *How the Mind Works* (1997). Fodor's particular target here is the rose-coloured view of evolutionary psychology as offering a "new synthesis" in integrating computational psychology with evolutionary theory. Second, Fodor's book poses a series of related, in-principle problems for any cognitive theory that revolve around the putative tension between the *local* nature of computational processing and the *global* nature of at least some cognitive processing. And third, it reiterates Fodor's earlier argument, in *The Modularity of Mind*, for the hopelessness of trying to extend the notion of modularity from "input systems" to "central systems."

The third of these themes is developed via the second, which in turn provides the basis for the first. I shall concentrate here on the more fundamental parts to this overall argument, namely, the second and third claims listed above. Even though the chief aim of *Mind* is to deflate the current enthusiasm for evolutionary psychology in the cognitive-science community, what I find most interesting about Fodor's argument is the way in which it draws on familiar and widely accepted views – about the nature of computation and cognition – in doing so. So I shall not really discuss Fodor's critique of evolutionary psychology here (see Okasha 2003), but will examine views that underlie that critique.

Part of my interest here stems from my view that such views are in fact mistaken. It is no part of my aim to defend evolutionary psychology, here or elsewhere. Instead, I take reflection on Fodor's critique of evolutionary psychology to provide an opportunity to tackle several views that have become dogmata in the cognitive sciences.

II. Some Cognitive Dissonance for an Aficionado of Fodoriana

Let me begin confessionally: I am puzzled. And although I'm prepared to adjust my set, I am sort of hoping that the fault is in reality. Here is the puzzle. For someone like me, raised on Fodor's earlier writings and the debates they gave shape to – from *The Language of Thought* (1975) to the essays in *Representations* (1981) to *The Modularity of Mind* (1983) – Fodor has been the leading figure in the naturalistic turn in the philosophy of mind that started in the 1960s. Fodor taught many of us, by example, to take psychology and the cognitive sciences seriously in our philosophical thinking about the mind. But when we look to Fodor's work since that time (from *Psychosemantics* (1987) to *A Theory of Content and Other Essays* (1990) to *The Elm and the Expert* (1994) to *Concepts: Where Cognitive Science Went Wrong* (1998b) to *In Critical Condition* (1998a) to *Mind*), the naturalistic turn seems to have become ... well, the crotchety turn. "Taking psychology seriously," for Fodor, for the last twenty years, has amounted chiefly to showing that major theoretical departures within the cognitive sciences from the views that Fodor first articulated and defended prior to that time – the connectionist modeling of the 1980s, the techniques of cognitive neuroscience and the neural turn of the 1990s, and now the extension of modularity theory within evolutionary psychology – are all fundamentally mistaken. One might expect that the basis for rejecting these views has been the resounding empirical success of their competitors, or there own empirical shortfalls, but for the most part this hasn't been Fodor's argumentative tack. Rather, it has been strangely *a priori*. The puzzle, in short, is that Fodor's work since *Modularity* hasn't practiced what the earlier work both practiced and preached. What has happened?

Something radical, to be sure. But we can sneak up on this, and lessen the shock to the system, by taking the puzzle in the small at first. What has happened to Fodor's views of modularity and computation in the last twenty years?

In *Modularity*, Fodor proposed a bold, two-part thesis about the structure of the mind: that part of it was *modular* – roughly speaking, what he called the "input systems" – and part of it was *non-modular* – what he called "central systems." Fodor argued that we have a real chance of understanding only the modular part of the mind using the resources of computational psychology. Moreover, the reason why we'd never understand the non-modular part of cognition was that it involved processes that were sensitive, in several ways, to properties of the entire cognitive system, "global properties." Hence Fodor's First Law for the Non-Existence of Cognitive Science: the more global a psychological process, the less chance anyone has of understanding it.

Fodor's two-part thesis, particularly the first part, spurred a whole range of research into modular cognitive systems, some of which was already underway, particularly in linguistics and in vision research. In fact, we might more accurately represent the State of Things at that time in this way: Fodor's book drew some general morals about the nature and future of cognitive science from several of the research programs in cognitive science that he had been immersed in over the preceding dozen years or so, but these general morals themselves became instrumental in directing research in a variety of areas. Included here are developmental psychology – from the idea of a naïve physics, to folk biology, to the theory-of-mind module; cognitive neuroscience – involving the search for the neural underpinnings of Fodorean (what we might call *cognitive*) modularity theory as well as the development of a more fine-grained, smaller-scale notion of modularity; and evolutionary psychology.

The specific form of cognitive dissonance for the aficionado of Fodoriana is this: Fodor's argument in *Mind* does little more than spell out in more explicit detail the general argument underlying the second part of his two-fold modularity thesis, and as such, is directed not only at evolutionary psychology but at other extensions of the notion of modularity beyond what Fodor views as their proper reach. The book could, then, simply be read as a slap on the wrist for those who had not taken Fodor's First Law seriously enough. But what I find puzzling is that there is essentially *no* reference in *Mind* to *anything* that Fodor finds remotely plausible in cognitive science over the past twenty years, either in support of his First Law, or in response to objections to it. And this is puzzling because it is simply hard to believe that *nothing* in the literature in twenty years could speak in favour of, or against, an adventuresome, speculative proposal about the nature of cognition and its study (see Jackendoff 2002). What's been going on? I think two distinct things.

First, Fodor's initial arguments, like his more recent ones regarding modularity, proceed largely *a priori*, i.e., they don't turn on empirical details. In *Mind*, there's the putative incompatibility between local computations and global effects of cognition (Chapter 2), and what Fodor calls *the input problem* (71 ff.), neither of which turns on any empirical details. In *Modularity*, there was the charge that central processes were *Quinean* and *isotropic*, based largely on an analogy to claims about the nature of scientific confirmation, rather than on an analysis of empirical work on any such processes, such as reasoning, problem-solving, or decision-making.

Second, large areas of developmental and cognitive psychology are now quite far down paths that follow one of the wrong turns that Fodor thinks that cognitive science has taken – the extension of modularity theory beyond its proper domains. As also intimated above, Fodor also doesn't care much for the neuroscientific turn of the '90s (remember the Decade of the Brain?), nor for many of the other shifts in the climate of cognitive science, including dynamic approaches to cognitive phenomena and the recent work on the embodiment of cognition (e.g., Clark 1997, 2001; Port and van Gelder 1995). Since Fodor also thinks little of other West Coast enthusiasms, such as cognitive linguistics, and has savaged philosophers, psychologists, and linguists for their attempts to understand concept-acquisition and conceptual structure (Fodor 1998b), there's not much left for him to draw on from the recent cognitive sciences.

As an aside, Fodor has my partial sympathy vis-à-vis neuroscience, insofar as it is typically *very* difficult to read off conclusions about large-scale cognitive structure from relatively small-scale findings in the neurosciences (despite the rabid enthusiasm for doing so within cognitive neuroscience). Even with the recent advancements in imaging technologies, particularly fMRI and PET, there is hardly ever a direct path linking larger-scale findings in cognitive neuroscience to claims about cognitive architecture. There has been a flurry of experimental results using such technology that purport to find the neural basis for a given cognitive ability, skill, or process. But as Dan Lloyd (2000) has recently pointed out, without a cross-study analysis of what sorts of abilities, skills, and processes tend to be associated with activity in which brain regions, and vice-versa, individual studies here show little, except perhaps the researcher's localistic biases in their research methodology (see also Uttal 2001).

I shall aim to do two things in the body of the paper before coming back to grapple with the larger question of "What happened?" The first will be to make some brief points about Fodor's two chief arguments for the skeptical part of his modularity thesis (Sections III and IV). Following that, I shall identify some work in cognitive science that does seem relevant for assessing the conclusion of those arguments (Section V).

III. Argument 1: Local Computation, Global Cognition

To assess the claim that there is an inherent tension between the local nature of computational processes and the (occasional) global effects of cognition, we should begin with two questions:

> Is computation local?
> Are there global effects of cognition?

Is computation local? Fodor has returned, over the years, to the idea that computation is local, and in *Mind* he approaches this via the idea that the syntactic properties of representations are local,

> which is to say that they [syntactic properties] are constituted entirely by what parts a representation has and how these parts are arranged. You don't have to look 'outside' a sentence to see what its syntactic structure is, any more than you have to look outside a word to see how it is spelled (2000, 20).

To say that computations are local is to say that the representations they operate over are "constituted entirely" by their parts and the arrangements of those parts. To deny this is to claim that there are some factors beyond a given representation, R, that in part "constitute" it.

There is a trivial reading of this claim about computation that should be put to one side, one that takes 'constitution' to refer to or be treated as *physical* constitution. On this reading, claiming that computations are local would be only to claim that their representations have parts related in certain ways, and that those parts and those relations together physically constitute the representation. This claim has no modal dimension, and while it may be too flippant to characterize this as a completely trivial claim, it is one that few would get excited about. There is something stronger that I think Fodor means to imply in claiming that computation is local.

That something stronger – needed in fact to generate a *prima facie* conflict between computation and abduction – can be expressed in the dual language of determination and supervenience: it is that the "here and now" properties of representations provide a determining, subvenient base for the computational operations performed on them, at least *qua* computational processes. This is a substantial thesis, in that it implies that the only relational properties relevant to computations involving R are those that are, or are determined by, the parts of R and their relations to one another. So construed, computation is *individualistic*.

This view of computation, popular as it is, is mistaken. I originally argued this, in effect, in developing a *wide computational* alternative to mainstream computationalism, which makes this assumption that computation is local, and hence individualistic (Wilson 1994; 1995, Chapter 3). There, I had conceived of wide computationalism as a simple extension of the local view of computation to computational systems that extend beyond the boundary of the individual cognizer, but I now think that wide computationalism has some more radical implications for how we think about computation, and whether or not it is "local."

Wide computationalism is the view that at least some of the computations that individual cognizers perform extend beyond the boundary of those cognizers. Motivating wide computationalism is a conjunction of two ideas: first, that the notion of a computational *system* is basic, with particular computational relations and processes characterized in terms of it; and second, that (cognitive) computational systems and individual agents can stand in either a part–whole *or* a whole–part relation, just which depending on the details of the particular cognitive system being considered. In terms I have used elsewhere (Wilson 2001), computational systems can be realized either as *entity-bounded* or as *wide* systems, i.e., in systems that physically extend beyond the boundary of the individual cognizer.

Since I have discussed the second of these two motivating ideas in detail elsewhere, here I want to attend to the first idea – that of the primacy of the notion of a computational *system* – in the context of a discussion of some broader metaphysical questions. I don't think that the "local" view of computation falls out of Turing's work on computation (despite Fodor's own comments, e.g., *Mind*, Chapter 1), but owes much of its force instead to broader metaphysical views. And I think that we need to move beneath the glosses on "local" as syntactic, non-semantic, formal, mechanical, physical, etc. that Fodor has provided over the years. Going all metaphysical at this point seems to me necessary to assess the idea that computation is local.

The idea that computational properties, as a type of mechanical or causally efficacious property, are, or are determined by, the intrinsic properties of individual representational tokens, together with the relations between such tokens, is a species of a view that I have dubbed *smallism* (Wilson 1999, 2004): discrimination in favour of the small, and so against the not-so-small. Smallism is a sort of global metaphysics that has played an influential role in contemporary physicalism in the philosophy of mind and in general philosophy of science. Or, rather, it is a general attitude that lies in the background of a number of such global metaphysical views, such as theses of microstructural and Humean supervenience. David Lewis eloquently expresses the latter doctrine in the Preface to Volume II of his collected papers:

> [a]ll there is to the world is a vast mosaic of local matters of particular fact, just one little thing and then another ... we have local qualities: perfectly natural intrinsic properties which need nothing bigger than a point at which to be instantiated. For short: we have an arrangement of qualities. And that is all (1986, ix).

The question to be asked of all such views is what account they provide of relational properties. As Lewis's talk of an "arrangement of qualities" suggests, smallist views typically appeal to the relations that hold between very small things with intrinsic properties, and claim that all properties and relations are determined by these. But there is a systematic problem such views face. Suppose that A and B are related via R to form C. Then *perhaps* it is true that all of C's intrinsic properties are determined by the intrinsic properties of A, B, and R. However, C's *relational* properties won't be so determined, but will be determined in part by things extrinsic to C. Smallist views are typically *aggregative* in this respect, and the problem with this sort of aggregative determination is that if there are relational properties of the aggregation, they can't be accounted for solely in terms of the constitution of the aggregation.

The same holds true of the view that computation is local, and is one of the things that drives the systemic view of the nature of computation. Whether any given physical property of a representational token is a computational property depends on facts about the broader computational system in which it functions, including the nature of the code it uses and what are usually thought of as implementational details (e.g., compilation, configuration). Fodor has, over a long period of time, referred to "shape" as a paradigm of a computational property of mental representations. But particular computational systems are sensitive only to particular shapes, and so whether a *given* shape (i.e., an instantiated, determinate shape) functions computationally or not can vary from system to system, and so, *qua* computational property, is *not* an intrinsic property of the tokens that have it. This is true of computational systems at both the "highest" levels (e.g., word-processing systems) and the "lowest" levels (e.g., binary). True, something shaped as an 'A', together with something shaped as '$A{\rightarrow}B$' will lead, computationally, to something shaped as 'B', but only in a computational system that includes *modus ponens* (or some such rule).

There is some affinity between the systemic view of computation and some rather extreme departures from standard views of computation, but we should be clear on both the affinities and the differences here. John Searle (1992) has claimed that syntax is an ascriber-relative property in deepening his argument against the computational theory of mind. Likewise, Steven Horst (1996) has defended a semiotic analysis of 'symbol' in arguing that the ascription of computational status presupposes semiotic conventions. What these views share with the systemic view of computation is the denial that small, particulate bits of the physical world are themselves symbolic, syntactic, formal, or computational. Where the views of Searle and Horst differ from the systemic view is in seeing this as the basis for rejecting computationalism altogether, rather than modifying it to reflect the fact that larger bits of the physical world, structured so as to contain parts that correspond to the parts of formal systems, such as symbols and rules linking them, *are* computational in and of themselves. There really are things that compute, but those things are systems of entities, with the computational status of those entities being derivative from that of the systems in which they operate.

Are there global effects of cognition? In *Modularity*, Fodor argued that "central processes" were Quinean and isotropic – i.e., sensitive in degree and kind to global properties of cognitive systems – via an analogy to scientific confirmation. In *Mind*, Fodor makes much the same claim without relying as explicitly on the analogy to confirmation. The common problem shared by both versions of Fodor's claim here is that it remains extremely unclear just what a "global effect" of cognition, or a "global property" of a cognitive system, is. Fodor says that "[S]implicity is, I think, a convincing example of a context-dependent property of mental representations to which cognitive processes are responsive" (*Mind*, 25), and goes on (33–37) to discuss *conservatism* (i.e., not changing your beliefs without reason) as another example.

In both cases, Fodor begins by pointing to the *normative* roles that each of these notions plays in accounts of rationality, appealing to simplicity and conservativism as "part of rationality" and "constitutive of rationality," respectively. He then moves on to the claim that as cognizers, we can and do make judgments of simplicity, and in fact are conservative in belief change, and asks how this is possible, given the computational nature of thought. Let us take these points one at a time.

First, the normative point seems simply irrelevant to the question of whether there are global effects of cognition or not. That there are norms governing rationality that appeal to "global properties" of cognitive processes, such as simplicity or conservativism, tells us nothing about whether cognition abides by those norms. Notoriously, standard accounts of rationality are cast in terms of norms, such as various forms of optimization or maximization that cognizers like us, with limited resources, can at best approximate. So the burden of Fodor's argument falls on his claim that we are actually sensitive to properties such as simplicity and conservativism in adjusting our cognitive sets.

But this point about what properties of propositions and claims we are actually sensitive to is, I think, more difficult to connect to the claim that there are "global effects" of cognition than Fodor supposes. We make judgments about all sorts of things, and use a variety of criteria to adjust the contents of our minds. It is extremely unclear how these facts amount to cognition being "global."

Consider simplicity, a property we attribute to certain propositions, theories, or claims. The question of *how* we do that – a question to which the computational theory of mind is a general answer – is quite distinct from this fact about the attribution of simplicity. Likewise, conservativism is a tendency that (suppose) our cognition exhibits. That is a property of our cognitive set as a whole, or significant chunks of it. That it is, in some sense, global implies nothing about how that tendency is manifested, or how conservative change takes place. In short, Fodor's "global effects of cognition" are *products* of cognitive processes, not features of cognitive processes themselves. Moreover, unless one supposes that processes that generate an effect must share the properties that those effects have – in this case, being global – there seems no basis for making claims about the processes based on claims about features of the products of those processes.

IV. Argument 2: The Input Problem

Fodor poses the input problem as a problem for a proponent of the view that the entire mind is modular in nature, arguing that "[M]echanisms that operate as modules *presuppose* mechanisms that don't" (71). Although the argument is run as a dilemma by Fodor on the question of whether inputs to modules are determined to have the properties relevant to their status as inputs by one or two distinct mechanisms, it can be expressed succinctly as follows. There must be some process that determines whether a given representation has the properties sufficient for it to be an input to any given modular process, M. But that input-determining process must be less modular than M, for it is a mechanism, in effect, for selecting or creating input representations for M from representations more generally. Supposing that there are distinct such input-determining mechanisms for each module only defers the problem, since the same is true of whichever mechanism provides *its* inputs. Either way, there must be parts of the mind that are less modular than any given module in order for there to be identifiable inputs to that module. Hence, not all of the mind can be modular.

This argument in fact entails only that not all of the mind can be *equally* modular; it is compatible with all of the mind being modular, and differing by degree in the level of modularity that its various parts have. Yet there is something strange about the argument, so modified, since what it strictly implies is that each cognitive process, however modular it is, must be "fed" by a less modular process, and so the least modular processes are those that process the most basic inputs, i.e., perceptual input systems (or even transducers, in Fodor's (1983) terms). But these are our (and Fodor's) paradigmatic modular systems, so the conclusion that they are less modular than "downstream" modules is *prima facie* surprising.

The problem, I think, lies in a dual failure on Fodor's part: his exclusive focus on inputs to the exclusion of outputs, and the linear, more-to-less (or general-to-specific) construal of the temporal dimension of cognitive processing. Fodor focuses on the nature of a mechanism's inputs since that is directly related to its *domain-specificity*: the narrower the range of inputs to which it responds, the more domain-specific, and hence modular, it is. But a highly modular mechanism can still be complicated in terms of the range of outputs it generates, and this means that just a few domain-specific mechanisms can feed a large number of modules. Thus, the chain of processing is not necessarily from domain-general to domain-specific, with a pattern of reticulation corresponding to the temporal sequence of cognitive operations; rather, this chain might form a mosaic of branching and reticulating trees, where those that branch can be as domain-specific, and hence as modular, as those that reticulate.

V. How Full is the Glass?: Some Empirical Considerations

So are we likely to have a computational, modular theory of intuitively "central processes," such as decision-making or reasoning, or does Fodor's First Law really hold? It is not just the specific arguments that Fodor offers that I have criticized in Sections III and IV that do not settle this issue, but *a priori* arguments more generally. It is a broadly empirical issue. So what sorts of empirical considerations do I think are most relevant to settling it? In this section, I mention three.

These considerations are not meant to respond to Fodor's arguments for a measure of skepticism about "massive modularity," since I have already indicated that those arguments are not empirical in nature, and in any case, are not very good arguments (see Sperber 1994, 2001). Rather, I want to point to work on cognition whose consideration should play a role in determining whether to share Fodor's skepticism about any sort of generalized modularity thesis, whether it be the "massive modularity thesis" of evolutionary psychology or the "core domains" view within developmental psychology (Hirschfield and Gelman 1994; Sperber, Premack, and Premack 1995). That is, once we get beyond *a priori* arguments for or against the modularity of "central processes," these are areas of cognitive science whose details surely are relevant to assessing claims about whether a modular approach to understanding all of the mind is hopelessly confused or not.

(i) Developmental Neuroscience

For the most part, developmental neuroscience has been ignored by both Fodor and by evolutionary psychologists. I think this is for two reasons. First, both have leaned heavily on the thesis that psychology is autonomous from neuroscience, and on the corresponding distinction between higher-level laws and lower-level mechanisms. Second, both have conceptualized modules as innate, hard-wired mechanisms of the mind. In so doing they have assumed that any developmental detail would simply inform us about the triggering conditions for the activation of innately structured modules, or lay out how modules unfold over time.

Neither of these assumptions remains tenable in light of the complexities of brain development revealed within developmental neuroscience. In general terms, the human brain quadruples its size after birth, with this increase being distributed unevenly throughout the brain. The neocortex, that part of the cortex supposedly shared by all mammals, increases most dramatically, and in fact is dispropor-tionately larger in humans than in non-human mammals. In terms of the specific developmental trajectories that the cortex undergoes, it manifests both patterns of equipotentiality and more, special-pur-pose, dedicated neural pathways. For example, the visual cortex can process auditory input projected to the thalamus, but there is already widespread differentiation in the cortex before there is innervation from extracortical structures, suggesting a built-in specialization of cortical areas from the start (Levitt, Barbe, and Eagleson 1997; Finlay and Niederer 1999).

Such facts give pause to the sort of linkage made by Fodor, and by the evolutionary psychologists he criticizes, between modularity and nativism. Since the structure of the brain itself emerges over time in a variety of experiential-dependent, and experiential-neutral ways (see also Buller and Hardcastle 2000, Quartz 2003), attention to the actual patterns of neural development and neural plasticity would seem critical for assessing any particular claims about the modular structure of cognition. Were the post-natal development of the human brain minor, or the effects of experience on its development relatively uniform, then both assumptions could be defended as methodologi-cal simplifications. Our minds might have been like the software pro-grams installed on many desktop computers that simply need a few parameters to be set before they spring into action. Instead, however, it is as if whatever programming is already built in not only alters the very kind of computer we end up with, but that the program itself is significantly adjusted in light of user-interaction, and this varies greatly across different parts of the computer. If that is more like our situation, as developmental neuroscience itself suggests, then the developmental details simply cannot be bracketed in considering questions of modularity.

(ii) Kludgy Cognitive Modeling

Fodor himself sees the frame problem as central to cognitive science, and as a beacon for any murky claims about the reasoning, prob-lem-solving, or inferential capacities of cognitive models, especially those within classical artificial intelligence. Yet the frame problem is a problem equally for (a) human beings, and (b) actual computational systems that in fact work pretty well. The fact that both of these manage to avoid the frame problem, or to solve it, should make us question the status that Fodor ascribes to that problem. There is an analogy here to the problem of induction: it is not that there is no real problem with induction, but it would be a mistake to conclude from that problem that people (or machines, for that matter) can't perform inductions. Clearly, they do. In both cases, we can construe the problem as setting some sort of normative ideal, the path to which seems inherently problematic.

But rather than keep either problem exclusively in that light, one might attend instead to how actual systems manage to kludge well enough to solve the corresponding problem well enough, enough of the time. Although the notion of a kludge was introduced in artificial intelligence with more than a hint of being something to avoid, in fact kludges are simply the natural product of heuristically driven, pragmatic solutions to cognitive (or other) problems. In problem-solving and decision-making, Herbert Simon's (1969) ideas of bounded rationality and satisficing, and the theories they have generated, are widely accepted, and they were introduced in opposition to theories of cognitive performance, such as rational-choice theory, tied to unachievable normative goals (see also Gigerenzer and Selten 2001). Optimality does not drop out of such views here, but is reconceptualized in terms of sets of constraints and bounds on cognition. This is no different from how optimization is reconceptualized within current adaptationist paradigms in evolutionary biology (Orzack and Sober 2001).

So perhaps the mind is primarily kludgy, and areas within cognitive science to explore more fully in evaluating Fodor's First Law, and the pessimism it expresses, are those that take kludges more seriously. Included here would be work on embodied cognition, drawing on constraints derived from the fact that minds operate in or via bodies (Clark 1997, Grush 2003), work within cognitive neuroscience that builds on constraints derived from neural processing (Glimcher 2003), and work in computational intelligence on induction and learning, especially that building on computational learning theory (Valiant 1984, Dietterich 1990).

(iii) Induction, Analogy, and Inference

Those outside cognitive science encountering Fodor's claim that there is an inherent tension between computation and abduction may be surprised to know that there is in fact a considerable body of empirical and theoretical work on induction, analogy, and inference conducted within a computational framework. It *may* be that Fodor's pessimism about the history of artificial intelligence is justified, but without discussion of any real examples of modeling and engineering work, this is difficult to see. Turning to some examples of work in general areas that I think has made some progress and provided some insight into "central" cognitive processes, particularly inductive or abductive processing, consider two.

First, there is Paul Thagard's work (e.g., 2000) on *coherence* as constraint satisfaction, and its application to a range of problems that human beings solve most likely non-deductively. Thagard acknowledges the "in principle" limits that exist to the computational solution of NP-hard problems, i.e., problems that are intrinsically difficult for a non-deterministic Turing machine to solve in polynomial time. But, more importantly, he also indicates a range of approximative techniques, such as harmony maximization in connectionist networks (e.g., in ECHO) and greedy local search in classic cognitive architectures, that allow actual systems to produce viable and plausible solutions to such problems. Of course, such strategies are not optimal in the sense that they are not guaranteed to find the best possible solution; but there is also no evidence that I know of that *we* do so, and much evidence to suggest that we don't.

Second, some of the most interesting work currently being done on inference occurs at the intersection of classical and connectionist approaches, particularly work on Bayesian networks and machine learning (see Jordan and Russell 1999, Pearl 2000). The general idea is to integrate causal and probabilistic considerations into existing frameworks to produce computational systems that are more flexible and context-sensitive. For all that, they are no less mechanistic in how they operate, and solve, in specific contexts, abductive, "global" problems through standard computational means.

VI. Relieving Some Cognitive Dissonance: Jerry Fodor as ...

So what has happened to the Jerry Fodor who put the Quinean view of philosophy as continuous with the natural sciences into practice in thinking about the mind? It's a platitude of folk psychology that people change, and one we might adopt here to relieve a little cognitive dissonance. Fodor has changed. (I feel better already.) But into whom?

Jerry Fodor as Colin McGinn? Fiona Cowie (1999) has argued that there is a mysterian strand to Fodor's views of nativism about concepts: there's something that no theory of concepts can tell us – how concepts are acquired – and this limitation is principled, in much the way that there's just something about consciousness that we'll never manage to get our minds around (McGinn 1991). Maybe one way to understand Fodor is to view him as holding that much of the mind is like that.

Jerry Fodor as Hubert Dreyfus? Although Dreyfus's *What Computers Can't Do* (1972) might be thought of as an indictment of the computationalism that forms the core of Fodor's views of the mind, through-a-glass-darkly its basic message is not that different from that of *Mind*. Computational approaches to understanding the mind are quite limited. True, Dreyfus is up to his armpits in *Dasein* – something that Fodor doesn't even like dipping his big toe into – and turns out to be something of a connectionist groupie. But just as Dreyfus reinforced his basic views of the limitations of a computer-oriented view of cognition twenty years later, in *What Computers Still Can't Do* (1992), Fodor has done the same with his view of the limitations of computational psychology in *Mind*.

Jerry Fodor as Granny? Fodor has always been fond of his Granny. Granny, the defender of folk wisdom about the mind, has rocked in her chair these last forty years, and Fodor has dedicated no inconsiderable amount of his considerable energy to showing that his views of the mind give Granny only reason to smile. But, as Janet Leigh found out at the Bates Motel, sometimes filial fondness comes with its own price. Has Fodor *become* Granny, defender of the status quo and content to rock and say, "I told you so"? (see Dennett 1991).

I close with what we might see as Fodor's own diagnosis (1991, 280), offered in reply to Dennett:

My view about the psychology of central processes is not that it's impossible in principle, and of course it's not that 'scientists should be [prohibited] from attempting empirical explorations....' My view is this: there are some problems you can't solve because key ideas are missing. Blustering doesn't help, throwing money at the problems doesn't help, arguments of the form 'some theory must work, this is some theory, therefore this theory must work' don't help (although that's often quite a good form of argument); nothing helps until somebody gets some key ideas.

So, wanted: a few good ideas. The only question is where we might find these.

References

Buller, D., and Hardcastle, V.G. 2000. "Evolutionary Psychology, Meet the Developing Brain: Combating Promiscuous Modularity." *Brain and Mind* 1: 307–25.

Clark, A. 1997. *Being There: Putting Brain, Body, and World Together Again.* Cambridge, MA: MIT Press.

———. 2001. "Reasons, Robots and the Extended Mind." *Mind and Language* 16: 121–45.

Cowie, F.1999. *What's Within? Nativism Reconsidered.* New York: Oxford University Press.

Dennett, D.C. 1991. "Granny's Campaign for Safe Science." In *Meaning in Mind: Fodor and his Critics*, ed. B. Loewer and G. Rey, 87–94.. Cambridge, MA: Blackwell.

Dietterich, T.G. 1990. "Machine Learning." *Annual Review of Computer Science* 4: 255–306.

Dreyfus, H.L.1972. *What Computers Can't Do: A Critique of Artificial Reason.* New York: Harper and Row.

———. 1992. *What Computers Still Can't Do: A Critique of Artificial Reason.* Cambridge, MA: MIT Press.

Finlay, B., and Niederer, J.K. 1999. "Neural Development." In *The MIT Encyclopedia of the Cognitive Sciences*, ed. R.A. Wilson and F.C. Keil, 594–96. Cambridge, MA: MIT Press.

Fodor, J.A. 1975. *The Language of Thought*. Cambridge, MA: Harvard University Press.

———. 1981. *Representations*. Sussex, England: Harvester Press.

———. 1983. *The Modularity of Mind*. Cambridge, MA: MIT Press.

———. 1987. *Psychosemantics*. Cambridge, MA: MIT Press.

———. 1990. *A Theory of Content and Other Essays*. Cambridge, MA: MIT Press.

———. 1991. "Replies." In *Meaning in Mind: Fodor and his Critics*, ed. B. Loewer and G. Rey, 255–319. Cambridge, MA: Blackwell.

———. 1994. *The Elm and the Expert*. Cambridge, MA: MIT Press.

———. 1998a. *In Critical Condition: Polemical Essays on Cognitive Science and the Philosophy of Mind*. Cambridge, MA: MIT Press.

———. 1998b. *Concepts: Where Cognitive Science Went Wrong*. New York: Oxford University Press.

———. 2000. *The Mind Doesn't Work That Way*. Cambridge, MA: MIT Press.

Gigerenzer, G. and Selten, R., eds. 2001. *Bounded Rationality: The Adaptive Toolbox*. Cambridge, MA: MIT Press.

Glimcher, P.W. 2003. *Decisions, Uncertainty, and the Brain: The Science of Neuroeconomics*. Cambridge, MA: MIT Press.

Grush, R. 2003. "In Defense of Some 'Cartesian' Assumptions Concerning the Brain and its Operation." *Biology and Philosophy* 18: 53–93.

Hirschfeld, L., and Gelman, S., eds. 1994. *Mapping the Mind: Domain Specificity in Cognition and Culture*. New York: Cambridge University Press.

Horst, S. 1996. *Symbols, Computation, and Intentionality: A Critique of the Computational Theory of Mind*. Berkeley: University of California Press.

Jackendoff, R. 2002. Review of *The Mind Doesn't Work That Way*. *Language* 78: 164–70.

Jordan, M., and Russell, S. 1999. "Computational Intelligence." In *The MIT Encyclopedia of the Cognitive Sciences*, ed. R. A. Wilson and F.C. Keil, lxxiii–xc. Cambridge, MA: MIT Press.

Levitt, P.M., Barbe, F., and Eagleson, K.L. 1997. "Patterning and Specification of the Cerebral Cortex." *Annual Review of Neuroscience* 17: 109–32.

Lewis, D.K. 1986. *Philosophical Papers, Volume 2*. Oxford: Oxford University Press.

Lloyd, D., 2000, "Terra Cognita: From Functional Neuroimaging to the Map of the Mind", *Brain and Mind* 1: 93–116.

McGinn, C. 1991. *The Problem of Consciousness*. Oxford: Blackwell.

Okasha, S. 2003. "Fodor on Cognition, Modularity, and Adaptationism." *Philosophy of Science* 70: 68–88.

Orzack, S., and Sober, E., eds. 2001. *Adaptationism and Optimality*. New York: Cambridge University Press.

Pearl, J. 2000. *Causality: Models, Reasoning, and Inference*. New York: Cambridge University Press.

Pinker, S., 1997, *How the Mind Works*. New York: Norton.

Port, R., and van Gelder, T., eds. 1995. *Mind as Motion*. Cambridge, MA: MIT Press.

Quartz, S. 2003. "Innateness and the Brain." *Biology and Philosophy* 18: 13–40.

Searle, J.R. 1992. *Rediscovery of the Mind*. Cambridge, MA: MIT Press.

Simon, H.A. 1969. *The Sciences of the Artificial*. Cambridge, MA: MIT Press.

Sperber, D. 1994. "The Modularity of Thought and the Epidemiology of Representations." In *Mapping the Mind: Domain Specificity in Cognition and Culture*, ed. L.A. Hirschfeld and S.A. Gelman, 39–67. New York: Cambridge University Press.

———. 2001. "In Defense of Massive Modularity." In *Language, Brain, and Cognitive Development: Essays in Honor of Jacques Mehler*, ed. E. Dupoux, 47–57. Cambridge, MA: MIT Press.

Sperber, D., Premack, D., and Premack, A., eds. 1995. *Causal Cognition: A Multidisciplinary Debate*. New York: Oxford University Press.

Thagard, P. 2000. *Coherence in Thought and Action*. Cambridge, MA: MIT Press.

Uttal, W.R. 2001. *The New Phrenology: The Limits of Localizing Cognitive Processes in the Brain*. Cambridge, MA: MIT Press.

Valiant, L. 1984. "A Theory of the Learnable." *Communications of the ACM* 27: 1134–1142.

Wilson, R.A. 1994. "Wide Computationalism." *Mind* 103: 351–72.

———. 1995. *Cartesian Psychology and Physical Minds: Individualism and the Sciences of the Mind*. New York: Cambridge University Press.

———. 1999. "The Individual in Biology and Psychology." In *Where Biology Meets Psychology: Philosophical Essays*, ed. V.G. Hardcastle, 357–74. Cambridge, MA: MIT Press.

———. 2001. "Two Views of Realization." *Philosophical Studies* 104: 1–30.

———. 2004. *Boundaries of the Mind: The Individual in the Fragile Science: Cognition*. New York: Cambridge University Press.

Notes on Contributors

Dorit Bar-On is Professor of Philosophy at the University of North Carolina at Chapel Hill. Her research interests lie in philosophy of mind, philosophy of language, and epistemology. She is the author of *Speaking My Mind: Expression and Self-Knowledge*. She has published papers on indeterminacy of translation and of semantic theory, truth conditional theories of meaning, deflationism, scepticism, externalism, self-knowledge, and avowals, amongst other topics.

Herman Cappelen is Associate Professor at the University of Oslo, and works primarily in the philosophy of language. He has recently co-authored, with Ernest Lepore, the book *Insensitive Semantics: A Defense of Semantic Minimalism and Speech Act Pluralism*. His publications include articles on quantifiers, quotation and indirect speech reports, semantic theory, the role of context, and pragmatics.

Joshua Dever is Assistant Professor at the University of Texas at Austin. He has teaching and research interests in philosophy of language, metaphysics, epistemology, and logic. He has published papers on the slingshot argument (with Stephen Neale), compositionality, and demonstratives.

Maite Ezcurdia is Research Fellow at the Instituto de Investigaciones Filosóficas of the Universidad Nacional Autónoma de México. She has research interests in philosophy of language, philosophy of mind, and epistemology. She is editor-in-chief of *Crítica: Revista Hispanoamericana de Filosofía*, editor of *Orayen: De la Forma Lógica al Significado*, and co-editor, with Olbeth Hansberg, of *La Naturaleza de la Experiencia: Vol. 1 Sensaciones* and Vol. 2 *Percepción*. Her publications include articles on indexicals, descriptions, names, propositional attitude reports, the semantics/pragmatics distinction, linguistic understanding, knowledge of language, and indexical thoughts.

427

Irwin Goldstein is Professor of Philosophy at Davidson College and works primarily in philosophy of mind, ethics, and philosophy of language. He has published articles on the mind-body relation, functionalism, pain, pleasure, emotion, Wittgenstein's private language discussion, and the purported relations between language and scepticism.

Guillermo Hurtado is Research Fellow and Director of the Instituto de Investigaciones Filosóficas of the Universidad Nacional Autónoma de México. His main research interests lie in ontology and epistemology. He is author of *Proposiciones Russellianas* and is editor of *Subjetividad, Representación y Realidad, Filosofía Analítica y Filosofía Tomista*, amongst others. He has published papers on realism, personal identity, fallibilism, the nature of doubt, propositions, properties, and relations.

Jeffrey C. King is Professor of Philosophy at the University of Southern California, and his areas of specialization include philosophy of language, formal semantics, and philosophical logic. He is the author of *Complex Demonstratives: A Quantificational Account* and has written numerous papers on anaphora, descriptions, propositions, quantifiers, tense, and the semantics/pragmatics distinction.

Mark Lance is Associate Professor at Georgetown University. He works mostly in the areas of philosophy of language, epistemology, philosophy of logic, metaphysics, and political philosophy, and is the author of *The Grammar of Meaning* (with John O'Leary Hawthorne). He has published many papers on topics such as relevance logic, normativity, meaning, Bayesianism, entailment, quantification, and sexual identity.

Ernest Lepore is Professor of Philosophy at Rutgers University. His research interests are in the philosophy of language, semantics, philosophical logic, metaphysics, and philosophy of mind. He has authored the following books: *Meaning and Argument: An Introduction to Logic through Language, Insensitive Semantics: A Defense of Semantic Minimalism and Speech Act Pluralism* (with Herman Cappelen), *Holism: A Shopper's Guide* and *The Compositionality Papers* (with Jerry Fodor), and *What Every Student Should Know* (with Sarah-Jane Leslie). He has edited several books, including *The Philosophy of Donald Davidson: Perspectives on Inquires into Truth and Interpretation*, *The Philosophy of Donald Davidson: Perspectives on Action and Events* (with Brian McLaughlin), *What is Cognitive Science?* (with Zenon Pylyshyn). He is author of numerous articles on topics such as truth conditional semantics, quotation, demonstratives, the role of context in semantics, tense, pragmatics, compositionality, concepts, meaning, quantifiers, and mental causation, amongst others.

Josep Macià is Associate Professor at the Universitat de Barcelona, and he is mostly interested in philosophy of language, philosophy of logic, and formal semantics. He is co-editor of *Two Dimensional Semantics* (with Manuel García-Carpintero) and has published articles on the relation between formal languages and natural language, anaphora, proper names, pragmatics, two dimensionalism, and presupposition.

Shaun Nichols is Professor at the University of Utah. His research interests are in the philosophy of mind, cognitive science, and moral psychology. He is the author of *Sentimental Rules: On the Natural Foundations of Moral Judgment*, co-author of *Mindreading: An Integrated Account of Pretense, Self-awareness and Understanding Other Minds* (with Stephen Stich), and editor of *The Architecture of the Imagination: New Essays on Pretense, Possibility, and Fiction*. He has written numerous articles on imagination, introspection, mindreading, folk psychology, free will, and moral judgments, amongst other topics.

Diana I. Pérez is Associate Professor at the Universidad de Buenos Aires. Her research interests lie primarily in philosophy of mind and the philosophy of psychology. She is the author of *La Mente Como Eslabón Causal* and the editor of *Los Caminos del Naturalismo*, and of the journal *Análisis Filosófico*. She has published papers on naturalism, supervenience, qualia, folk psychology, and mental causation.

Georges Rey is Professor of Philosophy at the University of Maryland. His work is mainly in the philosophy of mind, cognitive science, moral psychology, and philosophy of language. He is the author of *Contemporary Philosophy of Mind: A Contentiously Classical Approach* and has co-edited, with Barry Loewer, *Meaning in Mind: Jerry Fodor* *and His Critics*. He has written numerous articles on functionalism, qualia and consciousness, akrasia and self-deception, folk psychology, eliminativism, intentionality, and the a priori.

Robert Stainton is Associate Professor of Philosophy at the University of Western Ontario and an editor of the *Canadian Journal of Philosophy*. His research interests lie in the philosophy of language, formal semantics, philosophy of mind, cognitive science, epistemology, and pragmatics. He is the author of *Philosophical Perspectives on Language* and *Knowledge and Mind* (with J.A. Brook). He is editor of the following volumes (amongst others): *Perspectives in the Philosophy of Language: A Concise Anthology, Ellipsis and Non-Sentential Speech* (with Reinaldo Elugardo), *Papers in Honour of Michael Gregory* and *Proposals for a Communication Linguistics* (both with J. DeVilliers), and *Philosophy and Linguistics* (with K. Murasugi). His many published papers deal with issues concerning Chomskian linguistics, meaning, reference, quantifier phrases, definite descriptions, quotation, relevance theory, interrogatives, assertion, and ellipsis, to name some.

Stephen Stich is Professor of Philosophy at Rutgers University, and he is a member of Rutgers Center for Cognitive Science. His areas of research are philosophy of mind, cognitive science, epistemology, and philosophy of language. He is the author of the following books: *From Folk Psychology to Cognitive Science: The Case Against Belief, The Fragmentation of Reason: Preface to a Pragmatic Theory of Cognitive Evaluation, Deconstructing the Mind*, and *Mindreading* (with Shaun Nichols). He is the editor of *The Blackwell Guide to Philosophy of Mind* and *Mental Representation* (both with Ted A. Warfield), *The Cognitive Basis of Science* (with Peter Carruthers and Michael Siegal), *Benacerraf and His Critics* (with Adam Morton), *Philosophy and Connectionist Theory* (with William Ramsey and David E. Rumelhart) and *The Recombinant DNA Debate* (with David A. Jackson), amongst others. His numerous published articles have covered topics on folk psychology, knowledge of language, innateness, subdoxastic states, belief, mental representation, connectionism, intentionality, and rationality.

Daniel Stoljar is Senior Fellow in the Philosophy Program of the Research School of Social Sciences at the Australian National University.

His research interests are in philosophy of mind, metaphysics, philosophy of language, and metaethics. He has a forthcoming book *Mind and Ignorance: On the Epistemic Origin of the Problem of Consciousness,* and he has published various articles on qualia and consciousness, intentionality, reference, physicalism, response-dependence, and on issues regarding neuroscience and explanations of the mind.

Alessandra Tanesini is Senior Lecturer in Philosophy at Cardiff University. Her research and teaching interests are in epistemology, philosophy of feminism, and philosophy of language. She is the author of *An Introduction to Feminist Epistemologies* and *Wittgenstein and Feminism.* She is co-editor, with Joanna Hodge, of *Feminism and Philosophy of Language: A Special Issue of Women's Philosophy Review.* Her various published articles include topics on emotions, rationality, feminism and the philosophy of language, knowledge, justification, and normativity.

Paul Thagard is Professor of Philosophy, with cross appointment to Psychology and Computer Science, and Director of the Cognitive Science Program, at the University of Waterloo. His interests are in philosophy of science, cognitive science, and philosophy of mind. He is the author of *Coherence in Thought and Action, How Scientists Explain Disease, Mind: Introduction to Cognitive Science, Conceptual Revolutions* and *Computational Philosophy of Science.* He has also co-authored two books: *Mental Leaps. Analogy in Creative Thought* (with Keith J. Holyoak) and *Induction: Processes of Inference, Learning and Discovery* (with John H. Holland, Keith J. Holyoak, and Richard E. Nisbett). His various articles cover on topics such as analogy, coherence, decision-making, conceptual change, explanatory reasoning, discovery and innovation, emotions and consciousness, and theories and explanations in bio-medicine.

Christopher Viger is Assistant Professor at the University of Western Ontario. His research interests are in philosophy of mind, philosophy of language, philosophy of psychology, and cognitive science. He has written and published on the language of thought, innateness, associationism, Dennett's stances, the Ontological Argument, and experience.

Robert A. Wilson is Professor of Philosophy at the University of Alberta. His main areas of interest are philosophy of psychology, cognitive science, philosophy of science, and philosophy of biology. He is the author of both *Genes and the Agents of Life: The Individual in the Fragile Sciences: Biology* and *Boundaries of the Mind: The Individual in the Fragile Sciences: Cognition*. He is editor of *Species: New Interdisciplinary Essays* and of *Explanation and Cognition* (with Frank Keil). His published papers include work on individualism, computationalism, cognitive development, metarepresentation, psychological explanation, realization, essentialism in biology, the nature of species, levels and units of natural selection, group-level cognition, organisms, natural kinds, pluralism, and the levels of selection in evolutionary theory.

Index